Forensic Psychology

DATE DUE

NOV 1 8 2004	

BRODART   Cat. No. 23-221

Forensic Psychology
Concepts, debates and practice

Edited by

Joanna R. Adler

WILLAN
PUBLISHING

Published by

Willan Publishing
Culmcott House
Mill Street, Uffculme
Cullompton, Devon
EX15 3AT, UK
Tel: +44(0)1884 840337
Fax: +44(0)1884 840251
e-mail: info@willanpublishing.co.uk
website: www.willanpublishing.co.uk

Published simultaneously in the USA and Canada by

Willan Publishing
c/o ISBS, 920 NE 58th Ave, Suite 300
Portland, Oregon 97213-3786, USA
Tel: +001(0)503 287 3093
Fax: +001(0)503 280 8832
website: www.isbs.com

First published 2004

ISBN 1-84392-009-3 (paperback)
ISBN 1-84392-010-7 (hardback)

British Library Cataloguing-in-Publication Data
A catalogue record for this book is available from the British Library

Project management by Deer Park Productions
Typeset by GCS, Leighton Buzzard, Beds
Printed and bound by T.J. International, Padstow, Cornwall

Contents

Notes on contributors

Joanna R. Adler is a Chartered Forensic Psychologist and Principal Lecturer in Psychology at Middlesex University. She is the Postgraduate Programme Leader for the MSc in Forensic Psychology and member of the Applied Psychology Research Group. Her previous research has included investigations into fear in prisons; bullying, violence and victimisation; cross-gender supervision in prisons; efficacy of offending behaviour programmes – particularly when provided by non-governmental agencies/organisations and the psychological ramifications of fear of crime.

Ian P. Albery is a registered Chartered Health Psychologist, and Senior Lecturer in Psychology at London South Bank University. His research interests lie in the area of social psychology and cognitive processes, and he has a special concern with health beliefs and health behaviour. He has published a number of recent articles on substance misuse and addiction.

Laurence Alison is Academic Director of the National Centre for the Study of Critical Incident Decision Making and Senior Lecturer in Forensic Psychology at the Centre for Forensic and Family Psychology, University of Birmingham. His research interests broadly concern developing the potential for psychological contributions to criminal investigations, specifically focusing upon police decision-making, the investigation of sexual offences and the processes associated with the collection of evidence.

Emma Barrett is carrying out research on the development of investigator expertise, in conjunction with several UK police forces, as part of an ESRC-funded PhD at the National Centre for the Study of Critical Incident Decision Making, University of Birmingham. Her research interests also include the novel application of psychological research to investigative problems, interview strategies for suspects and informants, and the moral values of 'gangland' figures. Before returning to academia, Emma spent several years working with UK law enforcement agencies and government departments.

Graham Davies is Head of School and Professor of Psychology at Leicester University. His main research interests lie in the area of witness identification and testimony in children and adults. He has co-authored or co-edited some six books including *Children's Testimony: a handbook of psychological research and forensic practice* and *Recovered Memories: seeking the middle ground* and over 100 papers in scientific and professional journals. He also serves as a Magistrate on the Melton, Belvoir and Rutland Bench.

Vincent Egan is Director of the postgraduate forensic psychology courses at Glasgow Caledonian University. He is a Chartered Forensic Clinical Psychologist. His professional approach is informed by an unambiguously Eysenckian (and neo-Eysenckian) 'London School' approach to individual differences. His current interests are personality traits and personality disorders, sexual offenders, soft and hard pathognomic signs and ways of inferring neuropsychological impairment in HIV-positive drug misusers. He has nearly 50 publications, and is a member of both the British Psychological Society and the International Society for the Study of Individual Differences.

David P. Farrington is Professor of Psychological Criminology at Cambridge University. He has been President of the American Society of Criminology, the British Society of Criminology, and the European Association of Psychology and Law. He has received the Sellin-Glueck and Sutherland awards of the American Society of Criminology and the prize for distinguished scholarship of the American Sociological Association Criminology Section. He has published 24 books and over 300 articles on criminological and psychological topics.

Fiona Gabbert is a research fellow at Aberdeen University. Her interests are in co-witness collaboration, age differences in eyewitness performance, and social influences on eyewitness memory. Her work has been published in international journals, and is currently being funded by a grant from the Leverhulme Trust.

Elizabeth L. Gilchrist is a Principal Lecturer and the Research Lead in Psychology at Coventry University, having previously worked at the University of Birmingham. She is a Chartered Forensic Psychologist with a background in criminological and criminal justice research. Dr. Gilchrist has researched in criminal justice decision-making and fear of crime and is currently focusing on domestic violence. She has led a number of projects on domestic violence, exploring the issue both from the perpetrator and the victim/survivor perspective.

Anthony R. Goodman is a Principal Lecturer at Middlesex University. He has extensive experience of probation teaching and practice, which was the subject of his doctorate. He has recently evaluated four parenting programmes and is currently researching Children's Fund and Youth Inclusion Support Programmes.

Andrew Guppy is Professor of Applied Psychology at Middlesex University. His teaching and research interests cover the occupational, health and forensic areas of psychology. Andrew's research and consultancy has focused on health and safety, particularly alcohol and drug misuse, accident analysis and prevention, risk assessment and occupational stress. Recent research programmes have been funded by the Ministry of Defence, the Home Office and the Health and Safety Executive.

Lorraine Hope is a research fellow at Aberdeen University. Her research interests are in eyewitness testimony, memory, judgement and decision making in industrial and forensic contexts. Her work has been published in international journals.

Mike Hough is Director of the Institute for Criminal Policy Research at the School of Law, King's College London. He has extensive experience in quantitative research methods, especially large-scale sample surveys such as the British Crime Survey and the Policing for London survey. He has published widely on topics including crime prevention and community safety, policing, sentencing, probation and drugs.

Paul Johnson (BSc, MSc) is a serving officer with North Yorkshire Police. He has had responsibility for co-ordinating drug-related activities within the force for many years. He has contributed significantly to the development and operation of Drug Arrest Referral Schemes and has held Home Office grants for research into drug misuse.

Mark Kebbell works at James Cook University in New Zealand, and completed his PhD at the University of Liverpool on the subject of eyewitness evidence. His expertise and research is in the area of witness evidence particularly concerning competency, presentation of evidence in court, vulnerable witnesses (e.g. people with intellectual disabilities, rape victims). He also researches eyewitness interviewing, suspect interviewing, and sexual offending. He wrote the guidelines for police officers in England and Wales (with Dr. Wagstaff, University of Liverpool, UK) for the assessment of eyewitness evidence.

Nancy Loucks is an independent criminologist who specialises in prison policy research. Recent work includes a comparison of prison rules in England and Wales with European standards, and perceptions of justice and fairness amongst prisoners and staff in England, Sweden and France. She has conducted extensive research into women in prison, young offenders, prison violence, and the maintenance of prisoners' family ties.

Tim McSweeney is a Research Fellow at the Institute for Criminal Policy Research, School of Law, King's College London. He is currently involved in an EU-funded study in partnership with eight organizations from six countries, examining the processes and effectiveness of court-ordered treatment for drug-dependent offenders across Europe. He has also been involved in evaluating a number of community and treatment based criminal justice initiatives aimed at reducing drug use and drug-related crime.

Amina Memon is a Professor in Forensic Psychology at Aberdeen University. Her interests are in cognitive and social influences on eye-witness memory, child witnesses and jury decision-making.

Terrie E. Moffitt researches the interplay between nature and nurture in the origins of problem behaviours. Her particular interest is in antisocial behaviours. She directs the Environmental-Risk Longitudinal Twin Study ('E-risk'), which follows 1,116 British families with 2,232 twins from childhood to test how family adversity, peer influence, and neighbourhood effects interact with genetic influences on children's antisocial behaviour problems, and is also Associate Director of the Dunedin Multidisciplinary Health and Development Study in New

Zealand, which conducts a 32-year longitudinal study of a birth cohort of 1,000 individuals. She is now Professor of Social Behaviour and Development at the Institute of Psychiatry at King's College London, and Professor of Psychology at the University of Wisconsin, Madison.

Alex R. Piquero is Associate Professor of Criminology at the University of Florida, a member of the National Consortium on Violence Research, and Associate with the MacArthur Foundation's Research Network on Adolescent Development and Juvenile Justice. His research interests include criminal careers, criminological theory, and quantitative research methods.

Lorraine Sheridan is a lecturer in psychology at the University of Leicester. She wrote her PhD dissertation on psychological aspects of stalking and harassment, and has published numerous articles, book chapters and an edited book (with Dr Julian Boon) on this topic. Dr. Sheridan's other research interests include understanding racist and Islamophobic behaviour, and the psychological correlates of violent crime.

Graham Towl is Head of Psychological Services for HM Prison Service and the National Probation Service. Previously he has worked in prisons and the National Health Service, and had visiting academic posts at the Universities of Cambridge, Kent, Birmingham and Portsmouth. His recent publications include *Psychology in Prisons* (2003) and *Applying Psychology to Forensic Practice* (2004). He is co-editor of the *British Journal of Forensic Practice*. This year he was the recipient of the British Psychology Society's award for Distinguished Contribution to Professional Psychology.

G. Tendayi Viki is a lecturer in forensic psychology at the University of Kent. His PhD (from the University of Kent) was awarded the most outstanding thesis in social psychology (2003) by the British Psychological Society's Social Psychology Section. His research interests include attitudes to crime and punishment, perceptions of sexual violence and proclivity to commit gender violence.

Mark Wallace-Bell is a Chartered Health Psychologist and is based at the National Addiction Centre, Christchurch, New Zealand where he is a Senior Lecturer in Addiction. While much of his work has focused on smoking cessation, Mark has also completed recent research evaluating the impact of short-term rehabilitation interventions for drug misusers.

Brandon C. Welsh, PhD, is an Assistant Professor in the Department of Criminology at the University of Massachusetts Lowell. He is the author or editor of five books, including *Evidence-Based Crime Prevention* (Routledge, 2002, with Lawrence Sherman, David Farrington and Doris MacKenzie), and was an editor of a special issue of the *Annals of the American Academy of Political and Social Science*, entitled *What Works in Preventing Crime: systematic reviews* of *experimental and quasi-experimental research* (2001). He received his PhD in Criminology from Cambridge University.

Tom Williamson retired from the police service in 2001 from the post of Deputy Chief Constable of the Nottinghamshire Police. He is also a criminologist and chartered forensic psychologist. He is a founder member of the Institute of Criminal Justice Studies, University of Portsmouth where he is a Senior Research Fellow. His research interests include investigative interviewing, miscarriages of justice, crime reduction and police performance management.

Jane Wood is a Chartered Psychologist working as a Lecturer in Forensic Psychology in the Department of Psychology at the University of Kent. Her research interests include attitudes to crime and punishment, group formation and behaviour amongst incarcerated offenders, domestic violence and the effectiveness of treatment programmes in prison. Recent publications have been on the role of personality and blame attribution in prisoners' experience of anger and staff perceptions of prisoners' gang activity in prison.

Preface

Forensic Psychology: concepts, debates and practice will be of interest to practitioners as well as students who want and need to go beyond introductory texts. It seeks to raise questions for research and to pose problems for practice. It provides evidence of success and examples of where forensic psychology can clarify the criminal justice maelstrom. As such, we aim this book at academics, students and practitioners. This text is rich in content and style. It challenges perspectives on practice and theoretical developments, giving a flavour of the diversity and depth of forensic psychology.

Over recent years, the world-wide field of forensic psychology has grown rapidly. Unsurprisingly, there are now a number of forensic psychology text books on the market. Some are more legal in focus, others concentrate on treatment and therapeutic jurisprudence, whilst still others look at such matters as the aetiology and prevention of offending. With expansion of the field and growth of sub-disciplines, it is becoming rare to see a text book that is both accessible and successfully manages to tackle the whole arena. This book does not pretend to draw definitive conclusions about the essence of forensic psychological practice. It does not claim to provide the reader with a complete over-view to the field of criminological psychology and it does not promise any students that this one stop will fulfil all their requirements for legal psychology. We aim rather to promote discussion and raise some of the key issues that characterise theoretical and policy debates.

Given those aspirations, it should not surprise the reader to see that this text is not about introductory concepts. We have provided a contextual setting and explanation where necessary, but this is largely a book that assumes knowledge of at least some basic ideas in either the practice or theory of forensic psychology. The authors in this collection were asked to produce chapters that would help to portray a picture of the state of the discipline and provide pointers for evolution and change.

This book is proffered in an attempt to make a significant addition to a burgeoning field, and forms part of Willan Publishing's expanding range of forensic psychology titles. As editor, I am thrilled about the diversity of contributors to this text. They are drawn from a wide variety of settings: from eminent theoreticians and chairs of psychological and criminological associations, to one of the major employers of forensic psychologists in this country; from the United States of America to Europe and Australia; from people who have been practising for more than 30 years, to those who are at the outset of their careers. The resultant book is a cornucopia of analysis and evaluation, written by people with real expertise, great potential and an abundance of talent.

Joanna R. Adler

Section I

Forensic Psychology in Context

The first two chapters of this book aim to orientate the reader. In Chapter 1, the editor gives us a flavour of some of the historical and current debates in the practice and theoretical development of forensic psychology, in Europe and beyond. The chapter considers some of the key areas of current and future work in forensic psychology within the context of the somewhat parochial nature of definitional problems within the discipline.

In Chapter 2, Jane Wood and Tendayi Viki provide us with a detailed assessment of public attitudes towards crime and punishment. We have a duty of care to the public on whom and for whom we weave our professional practices. In order to protect them properly, we need first to understand them. Of course, we also sometimes seek to change them and their attitudes. Public attitudes and fears about crime and punishment are central to the political debate in this country. They can be played upon by the cynical, can be alleviated where appropriate and at the very least, warrant further exploration and understanding.

Chapter 1

Forensic psychology: concepts, debate and practice

Joanna R. Adler, Middlesex University

In many parts of the world today, it is possible to find psychology being practised with a forensic twist. Forensic psychologists evaluate offender behaviour programmes, design risk assessments, aid investigative processes, support victims, provide treatment and generally try to facilitate justice. Psychological testimony is now fairly commonplace in the courts themselves. It may be given in cases ranging from the prosecution of war crimes to an adoption hearing. Most people would concur that forensic psychology is a discipline concerned with providing psychological information to people, agencies and systems, involved directly and sometimes indirectly, in the implementation of justice (Dushkind 1984). There are some who define forensic psychology more narrowly, as work provided solely for use by the courts (Gudjonsson and Haward 1998). This definition is based on a literal reading of the word 'forensic' but is not that which has been adopted in practice in this country.

Whether the broader or more circumscribed definition is followed, there are no particular skill sets that definitively separate a forensic psychologist from any other type of psychologist. Rather, it is the context within which we practise and apply our knowledge that makes it forensic (Blackburn 1996). For those practising as forensic psychologists, licensing or statutory registration are relatively recent innovations. The American Psychological Association and the British Psychological Society each have divisions concerned with forensic psychology, that were only fully established within the last 30 years. In England and Wales, Statutory registration for all chartered psychologists, irrespective of type, is still in the legislative process of becoming a reality. At the moment, protection of the British public is largely self regulatory.

Within the British Psychological Society, the Division of Forensic Psychology is also currently engaged in protracted debate as to how people should best acquire and demonstrate necessary knowledge and skills for full membership. In part, the debate reflects individuals' very different understandings of what makes a forensic psychologist. In part, it is a debate as how best to interpret competency based criteria that were painstakingly drawn up over years of consultation. As the borders come down across the European Union and its membership expands, professions are expected to make welcome their compatriots from elsewhere in the confederation of states. Differences in training, practice and professional expectations have the potential to cause border disputes along the parameters of a discipline and to endanger the public through mismatches in expectations and needs.

Potential problems are clear but the solutions are far from simple. This may be demonstrated by a brief exploration of our transatlantic cousins' certification procedures. In the USA, board certification is controlled by State not Federal regulations. Firstly, there has arisen something of a divide between 'legal psychologists' and 'forensic psychologists', with the latter being cast more as practitioners, often with a clinical expertise and the former as consultants/academics. This is an oversimplification but the labels do matter. Not least, they matter because without appropriate certification from the State concerned, psychologists cannot testify directly to the courts. Thus, an expert from one State with many years' knowledge and experience, both in research and evidentiary matters, is not necessarily able to give advice to the courts, or be called by interested parties in another State.

Even when evidence can be given to the courts, by the best available people, we do not always agree as to what to say. Nor do we agree about the relative merits of the research studies on which much of the evidence is based. Like other social scientists, forensic psychologists have argued long and hard regarding generalisability and ecological validity of approaches to research and how robust the findings may be, when applied to the 'real world'. There is lively discussion about when and where laboratory based research is appropriate and how such findings should be interpreted within the contexts of police practice, court decision making, and the implementation of justice. It is easy to see why, for example, one may want to impose rigorous experimental control into designs trying to assess exactly how cognitive processes might be operating. It is equally easy to see why one might seek to investigate the possibility of improving policy or practice in more realistic settings than the eponymous research cubicle. Without rigorously controlled research designs, alternative explanations for findings will abound, requiring us to equivocate our advice. Yet, if we wish to pass commentary on criminal justice systems, then we need to ensure that our work is going to be as meaningful and contextually appropriate as any other piece of applied psychology.

The potential problems with evidence and the reliability of eyewitness testimony is a good case in point. What is common to all factions of the eyewitness reliability disagreements is that they are concerned with producing justice from the criminal courts. To concatenate it somewhat, the people involved differ in terms of their research frame of reference and their preferred means of analyses of data. Whilst a different methodology may sound inconsequential, the net effect can, and has resulted, in polar opposite conclusions and very public differences of opinion as to the best advice to give the courts (Egeth 1993; Loftus 1983a; Loftus 1983b; Loftus 1993; McCloskey and Egeth 1983; McCloskey, Egeth and McKenna 1986). The first round of the debate was conducted largely in 1983, the second in 1993. At the time of writing, this author, for one, is looking forward to seeing if 20 year reappraisals are to be published.

With this emphasis on recent debates and the problems of self definition, it would be understandable to think of forensic psychology as a social scientific neophyte. Yet, for as long as psychology has been dealt with as a separate area of endeavour, the enterprise has encompassed the forensic realm. For well over 100 years, psychological practice and research have been directed at ways of improving the implementation of justice, explaining and minimising criminal behaviour and the ramifications of crime (Gudjonsson 1991). The courts' uses of evidence that we might now classify as psychological, and/or criminological, goes back somewhat further than the turn of the last century. Beccaria and Lombroso had been working on explanations for crime and criminal behaviour for several years before the end of the nineteenth century. Similarly, insanity rules have been a feature of various jurisdictions for generations. A broad reaching excuse to culpability was introduced to France in 1810. In England, the later, more narrow rules based on the case of Daniel M'Naghten, have been largely unchanged for 150 years, although they have been supplemented.

The first person generally acknowledged to have written specifically about the use of expert evidence in court is Münsterberg, whose book has become a classic text (Münsterberg 1908). As such, he should be credited with much of the establishment and popularising of the use of psychology in courts. Even at the start of the twentieth century though, the use of psychological evidence was not without controversy, and had its detractors (Wigmore 1909). We can also see that, from the start, psychological tools were being utilised to bring about justice way beyond the confines of the courtroom. By 1916, Terman had revised Binet's and Simon's intelligence test (Binet and Simon 1905) and was advocating its use in the selection of police (and fire) officers. He also gathered together studies on potential relationships between criminal behaviour and intelligence, thereby applying psychology to criminal behaviour itself.

Terman wrote at a time when there were related publications and statistics coming from elsewhere in North America and the rest of the world. For example, in Britain, Charles Goring was making similar arguments (Goring 1913). Like Goring, Terman took issue with Lombroso's conclusions about the physical differences between offenders and the law abiding, which was itself derived from Lavater in 1789 and Lauvergne in 1848 (Walsh 2003). Drawing on a series of studies conducted in reformatories, Terman concluded that intelligence tests:

> have demonstrated, beyond any possibility of doubt, that the most important trait of at least 25 per cent of our criminals is mental weakness. The physical abnormalities which have been found so common among prisoners are not the stigmata of criminality, but the physical accompaniments of feeble-mindedness. They have no diagnostic significance except in so far as they are indications of mental deficiency. Without exception, every study which has been made of the intelligence level of delinquents has furnished convincing testimony as to the close relation existing between mental weakness and moral abnormality. (Terman 1916)

That statement neatly encapsulated one side of an argument regarding criminality, intelligence, moral development and the associated issues of both culpability and treatment that continues to this day.

Like the debate regarding eyewitness evidence, differences in opinion regarding intelligence run deep. When taken in conjunction with the difficulties in defining our profession as a distinct group, they help to demonstrate that the forensic field is replete with complex theoretical and practical dimensions. We have, however, managed to make some significant collaborative inroads with other disciplines and in tackling specific problems thrown up by the practices of justice systems and agencies. In much of Europe, the relationship between criminology and psychology has become strengthened in recent years with the growth of 'effective practice' initiatives. Applied psychology has generally expanded and given greater credence to sociological theories. Likewise, applied sociological disciplines have been able to consider contributions made by psychology. This can be seen in the foreword to the third edition of the *Oxford Handbook of Criminology* where there is an acknowledgement that 'in recent years, psychological approaches to crime have become increasingly prominent in both academic criminology and public policy' (Maguire, Morgan and Reiner 2002). However, this is not to claim that all is rosy in our collaborative gardens. If within disciplines there is debate as to what constitutes a proper approach and who is the most qualified to conduct work, so it is that outwith the disciplines we still sometimes strive to show that we have a right to be present at the table. At the American Society of Criminology annual meetings, it is not uncommon for presenters drawing on forensic psychological theory to predicate their work with explanations of and justifications for the very discipline itself, even in symposia clearly marked as being psychological in orientation.

One area in which forensic psychologists have been active alongside people working in related disciplines is in the 'what works?' debate. We have been involved in designing and evaluating programmes targeted at reducing recidivism, often in violent, sexual and or mentally disordered offenders. Alongside that work, much effort has been expended on risk assessments, both in their design and conduct (Bonta, Law, and Hanson 1998; Harris, Rice and Quinsey 1993; Quinsey, Rice and Harris 1995; Sreenivasan, Kirkish, Garrick, Weinberger and Phenix 2000). In England and Wales, as elsewhere, the merits of different sorts of risk assessment are not only a source of contention, but a good example of how psychological tools may be used by legislative authorities. As mentioned above, there is a long history of psycho-legal involvement in dealing with or 'disposing of' the mentally or personality disordered offender. At the time of writing, there are long overdue plans to revise the Mental Health Act of 1983. Pre-empting the stalled Mental Health Bill, the Home Office, Prison Service and Department of Health have jointly introduced pilot schemes to manage those the government has deemed to be 'Dangerous and Severely Personality Disordered' (DSPD).

DSPD is not a clinical diagnosis. It is a policy inspired label that describes the few mentally disordered people 'who suffer from a severe personality disorder and because of their disorder, also pose a significant risk of serious harm to others' (Bell *et al.* 2003). The DSPD policies are partially a replacement for the uses of the psychopathic label although the two are by no means the same. Aside from the various clinical means of identifying it, psychopathy is also a legal concept, defined within the Mental Health Act of 1983. Within that legislative description is included the notion of persistent and untreatable behaviour. Yet when applied by the criminal justice system, psychopathy could result in an

7

indeterminate stay in a Special Hospital, or high security facility for offenders with serious psychiatric and psychological problems. There is a deeply felt and much argued debate as to whether psychopathic offenders are able to benefit from a stay in such a hospital. Some would say that as they are untreatable, by definition, they should be incarcerated in prison, on the basis of their offending behaviour alone. Others argue that the effects of their personality disorder may be ameliorated under certain sorts of regime and that the therapeutic milieu is helpful in and of itself, particularly if the personality disorder co-presents with other, treatable disorders. It is a debate that touches on fundamentals of psychiatry, psychology and treatment (e.g. Prins 1991 and Szasz 1963). There are also human rights implications as a stay in a Special Hospital is usually indeterminate, often resulting in a longer period of confinement than the normal corresponding period of incarceration in prison. Over recent years, psychopathic offenders have been held in prisons and the Special Hospitals alike. High profile cases, such as the Russell family killings by Michael Stone, highlighted holes in the psychiatric protective net and are strongly associated with the development of the term and policies pertaining to DSPD.

In practice, 'DSPD might be seen as an attempt to quantify a distinction between the general category of mentally disordered offenders and a more extreme subgroup whose disorder is manifested in the kinds of extreme violence and sexual aggression that have caused most public concern' (Perkins and Bishopp 2003). To be in this group, an individual must demonstrate a high level of personality disorder, be more likely than not to offend seriously (cause serious physical or psychological harm with significant effects on the victim(s)) and, crucially, there must be a functional link between those two (Bell *et al.* 2003). Although these policies are already being implemented, there are still major issues of definition and practice to be resolved and legislation that has yet to be brought before the Houses of Parliament. Not only are there questions about how to measure the entry criteria and define someone as DSPD in the first place, but what would be the criteria for successful treatment and release or progression to less secure environments? Perkins and Bishopp (2003) have raised this alongside a useful consideration of the very nature of dangerousness and conceptualisation of both personality and personality disorder. In the same volume, Logan points us to the glaring lack of research pertaining to violent women in general, and potential DSPD women in particular. She concludes that:

… the treatment of women in the same way as men in services for so-called DSPD individuals would seem premature and likely to lead to the involvement of more women in such services than may subsequently be seen to have been necessary … There can be little justification – empirical or ethical – for proceeding ahead of the completion of the research necessary to underpin the legal and therapeutic provisions to come. (Logan 2003)

We have been here before. Modern prisons policies in North America and much of Europe have been characterised by swings from re-habilitative to punitive and back again. Regimes for women, young offenders, and members of religious or ethnic minorities have made few concessions that they are in any ways different to the majority white, adult, male offending population. The experiential and evaluative commentary from ex-prisoners, sociologists, criminologists, philosophers and even a few psychologists, posed questions that were never fully answered. Essentially, what is the prime purpose of imprisonment, how can we assess whether its espoused aims have been met and does it disproportionately affect some more than others? In reality, such basic questions can only be answered in a dynamic way and never definitively. Policy and therapeutic aims shift with time, resources, public opinion and political will. This time though, it seems that forensic psychologists are at the forefront of the debate.

As Stephenson has pointed out, forensic psychologists have some-times seemed to publish in something of a social vacuum (Stephenson 1992). We described phenomena, labelled behaviours and people without always acknowledging the contextual realities of their lives or the social infrastructures around them. This book is partly designed to show that we can look at context, using it to inform our theories and using our theories to influence that context in turn. The contributors to this text have been selected to reflect a wide diversity of approaches and the topics chosen because they reflect issues of concern. Not every one of the authors would call him or herself a forensic psychologist. Every one of the chapters does, however, concern the aetiology or ramifications of crime, offending and the implementation of justice and every one of them utilises well established psychological techniques in their con-sideration of the problems posed. There is something of a deliberate bias towards analysis of real offenders, patients, victims and witnesses. The chapters are here because they deal with areas of research and policy that relate to the practice of forensic psychology, to the running of criminal justice and to the ways of tackling and preventing offending behaviour within society today.

This book is not presented as a compendium of all things forensic psychological. Such a tome would be a veritable doorstopper. We have compiled instead a series of selected snapshots of current debates. Many of those debates have been with us since Münsterberg, others are more recent responses to policy. We have tried to set the work within an appropriate historical frame. However, there is insufficient space in a volume such as this to devote anything other than a fleeting glance at the history of forensic psychology. Fortunately, there are several other good sources of information, for example Bartol and Bartol 1999; Gudjonsson 1996; Ogloff and Finkelman 1999. This text concentrates on forensic psychology as related to crime. We are aware, of course, that forensic psychologists also have a distinguished commitment to civil justice. Unfortunately, it was not possible for us to include any materials on the coroners' or civil courts, in general.

Material in the rest of this chapter is presented to give the reader a flavour for the selection of forensic psychological areas considered more fully in the following pages. The book has been organised into broad sections that are further broken down into topic or issue based chapters. Following on from this chapter is the second one putting forensic psychology into context. Within it, Jane Wood and Tendayi Viki continue the work they recently completed for the Esmee Fairburn Charitable Trust, exploring public attitudes to crime. Crime control is seen as a vote winner and politicians engage in increasingly vitriolic public debates about criminals without always seeking to educate themselves or the populace as to the causes of crime or the most effective preventative strategies. Wood and Viki reiterate points about public ambivalence towards crime and set this within an empirical environment.

In the second section of this book, we turn to matters of investigation and prosecution. Chapter 3 is a comparative evaluation of responses to miscarriages of justice in the United Kingdom and in the United States of America. Tom Williamson draws on his years of practice as both police officer and psychologist to evaluate research, policy and outcomes of police interviews and court procedures in the context of life sentences and the continued use of capital punishment. In Chapter 4, Laurence Alison and Emma Barrett evaluate offender profiling. Their thorough consideration of the field, as it has evolved and is evolving, gives the reader pause for thought. There are questions about how we should provide evidence to outside practitioners, how the public receives our expertise and how psychological explanations for criminal actions may be both offered and perceived.

Many an undergraduate psychology student examination has included questions about whether eyewitness evidence can be trusted. The parameters of the debate have expanded and this book aims to present information pertinent to the facilitation of accurate and helpful evidence. The third section explores how evidence is elicited and testimony is given: in Chapter 5, Mark Kebbell and Elizabeth Gilchrist present us with an introduction to how evidence is used in courts. They go on to assess the impact that cross examination has on the nature and quality of that testimony. Following that, in Chapter 6, Amina Memon, Fiona Gabbert and Lorraine Hope have summarised much of their innovative research into the implications of ageing as regards eyewitness evidence. Their starting point is the predictable finding that, overall, older witnesses display more errors in memory than do younger witnesses. From there, they move on to explore more fully the nature of the related memory errors. By considering the underlying mechanisms of such errors and assessing their practical implications, they give us a chapter that has direct relevance in our ever ageing communities.

From uses of evidence in the court room, we move to our fourth section, in which we turn to an assessment of some correlates of criminality. Prediction of anti-social behaviour is core to the implementation of justice and much of the practice of psychology. In Chapter 7, Vincent Egan examines how one cluster of interests and behaviours has been used to indicate the risk of serious, violent offending. His recent research is cited to help build up a picture of how sensational interests may be useful to predict risk. By going beyond the basics of actuarial assessment, he gives us a model for further development and contributes to the ongoing debate as to uses of clinical judgements and measures in risk assessments. In Chapter 8, Ian Albery, Tim McSweeney and Mike Hough provide the reader with a contemporary assessment of the relationship between drugs and crime. They evaluate whether drugs use may be seen as a predictive risk factor for offending behaviour and provide a deeper level of analysis than is normally presented. They question pat assumptions about potential causal links between drugs and acquisitive crime, within an informative discussion about the correlational links that have been found. Following on from that chapter, Andrew Guppy, Paul Johnson and Mark Wallace-Bell present an evaluation of a drugs arrest referral scheme. People targeted for such schemes are offenders arrested for a plethora of crimes who also misuse drugs. Such referral schemes have different approaches but normally aim to intervene at early stages. Chapter 9 gives us practical exemplars and case studies to show that there are effective alternatives to the traditional punitive approaches taken towards such offenders.

This brings us to the fifth section of the book and it deals with persistent offending. In Chapter 10, Alex Piquero and Terrie Moffitt present a comprehensive analysis of an aspect of Moffitt's ground breaking work on the aetiology of offending and its potential persistence over the life span. Drawing on their own and others' empirical work, they explore the utility and predictive power of her developmental taxonomy. They address criticisms levelled at the model and point to directions for future research. We follow such a broad chapter with a focus on one specific cluster of behaviours that seem to persist. In Chapter 11, Lorraine Sheridan and Graham Davies consider stalking. Although specific legislation regarding stalking and harassment is a relatively new phenomenon, the behaviours are not. Stalking is persistent, intrusive, protracted and repetitive in nature. For the victim, its effects can be psychologically traumatic and physically dangerous. Yet, it is difficult to predict in advance. Sheridan and Davies elucidate both who is likely to stalk another person and who it is that they are likely to victimise. They set the chapter within the context of legislation, both current and proposed, and include some practical approaches to this distressing, potentially life threatening crime.

From persistence, we turn to intervention and prevention and the sixth section consists of three chapters. Chapter 12 picks up on one of the issues raised by Sheridan and Davies. In their assessment of interventions to prevent intra-familial violence, Elizabeth Gilchrist and Mark Kebbell address a number of the common misconceptions about the nature and reality of domestic violence held by people working within criminal justice agencies. They provide a systematic exploration of evidence, assess the current interventions targeted at perpetrators and set the support needs of the victims within a multi-modal context. Brandon Welsh and David Farrington also highlight the importance of multi-component approaches to intervention and prevention in Chapter 13. They present a review of some of the programmes aimed at preventing offending that have demonstrated their efficacy both within deterrence and fiscal terms. There are a number of studies that can demonstrate benefits in significant excess to the costs and it is these that are the central focus. Welsh and Farrington move on from this to make some far-sighted suggestions for practice in this country. Their chapter shows how effective policy decisions could be based on thoroughly evaluated, well researched social scientific principles. The subsequent chapter has a narrower focus: Anthony Goodman and Joanna Adler seek to give a deeper flavour of people's experiences when targeted by interventions such as those mentioned by Welsh and Farrington. Chapter 14 again draws on the benefits of context specific, multi-faceted programmes, and sets them within the frame of other youth justice and parenting initiatives in England and Wales.

In our last section, we take two looks at aspects of imprisonment and correction. In Chapter 15 Nancy Loucks assesses the literature and possible ways forward for the imprisonment of women whilst in Chapter 16 Graham Towl reassesses the opportunities for forensic psychology within Her Majesty's Prison and Probation Services. Chapter 15 draws on a range of literature and Loucks' own work in Europe, Scandinavia and the United States of America. World-wide, the numbers of imprisoned women are much lower than men, and as elsewhere within criminal justice, their needs are often marginalised. This chapter presents a picture of a largely disenfranchised, disempowered population. Many female prisoners have needs that would be dealt with far better outside the prison than within its walls. Finally, Chapter 16 is written by Graham Towl. As the person in charge of psychological services for both the Prison and Probation services, he is in an excellent position to consider the role of psychology in corrections and future directions. Chapter 16 closes the book with a return to some of the issues mentioned in this opening chapter, what does make a forensic psychologist and how can we work with others, within forensic settings?

References

Bartol, C.R. and Bartol, A.M. (1999) 'History of forensic psychology', in A.K. Hess and I.B. Weiner (eds) *Handbook of Forensic Psychology* (2nd edn). London: John Wiley and Sons.

Bell, J., Campbell, S., Erikson, M., Hogue, T., McLean, Z., Rust, S. and Taylor, R. (2003) 'An overview: DSPD programme concepts and progress', in A. Lord and L. Rayment (eds) *Dangerous and Severe Personality Disorder* (Issues in Forensic Psychology 4). Leicester: British Psychological Society, Division of Forensic Psychology.

Binet, A. and Simon, T. (1905) 'Upon the necessity of establishing a scientific diagnosis of inferior states of intelligence', in W. Dennis (ed.) *Readings in the History of Psychology*. New York: Appleton Century Crofts.

Blackburn, R. (1996) 'What is forensic psychology?', *Legal and Criminological Psychology*. Feb 1996; Vol 1 (Part 1) 3–16.

Bonta, J., Law, M. and Hanson, R.K. (1998) 'The prediction of criminal and violent recidivism among mentally disordered offenders', *Psychological Bulletin*, 123: 123–42.

Dushkind, D.S. (1984) 'Forensic psychology – a proposed definition', *American Journal of Forensic Psychology*, 2 (4): 171–72.

Egeth, H.E. (1993) 'What do we not know about eyewitness identification?', *American Psychologist*, 48 (5): 577–80.

Goring, C. (1913) *The English Convict: A statistical study*. London: His Majesty's Stationary Office.

Gudjonsson, G. (1991) 'Forensic psychology – the first century', *Journal of Forensic Psychiatry*, 2 (2): 129.

Gudjonsson, G.H. (1996) 'Forensic psychology in England – one practitioner's experience and viewpoint', *Legal and Criminological Psychology*. Vol 1 (Part 1) 131–42.

Gudjonsson, G.H. and Haward, L.R.C. (1998) *Forensic psychology: A guide to practice*. London: Routledge.

Harris, G.T., Rice, M.E. and Quinsey, V.L. (1993) 'Violent recidivism of mentally disordered offenders: The development of a statistical prediction instrument', *Criminal Justice and Behavior*, 20: 315–35.

Loftus, E.F. (1993) 'Psychologists in the eyewitness world', *American Psychologist*, 48 (5): 550–52.

Loftus, E.F. (1983a) 'Silence is not golden', *American Psychologist*, 38: 564–76.

Loftus, E.F. (1983b) 'Whose shadow is crooked?', *American Psychologist*, 38: 576–77.

Logan, C. (2003) 'Women and dangerous and severe personality disorder: Assessing, treating and managing women at risk', in A. Lord and L. Rayment (eds), *Dangerous and Severe Personality Disorder* (Issues in Forensic Psychology 4). Leicester: British Psychological Society, Division of Forensic Psychology.

Maguire, M., Morgan, R. and Reiner, R. (eds) (2002) *The Oxford Handbook of Criminology* (3rd edn). Oxford: Oxford University Press.

McCloskey, M. and Egeth, H. (1983) 'Eyewitness identification: What can a psychologist tell a jury?', *American Psychologist*, 38: 550–63.

McCloskey, M., Egeth, H. and McKenna, J. (1986) 'The experimental psychologist in court – The ethics of expert testimony', *Law and Human Behavior*, 10: 1–13.

Münsterberg, H. (1908) *On the Witness Stand – Essays on psychology and crime*. New York: Doubleday Page.

Ogloff, J.R.P. and Finkelman, D. (1999) 'Psychology and law: An overview', in R. Roesch *et al.* (eds) *Psychology and Law the State of the Discipline*. New York: Kluwer Academic Press.

Perkins, D. and Bishopp, D. (2003) 'Dangerous and severe personality disorder and its relationship to sexual offending', in A. Lord and L. Rayment (eds) *Dangerous and Severe Personality Disorder* (Issues in Forensic Psychology 4). Leicester: British Psychological Society, Division of Forensic Psychology.

Prins, H. (1991) 'Is psychopathic disorder a useful clinical concept? A perspective from England and Wales', *International Journal of Offender Therapy and Comparative Criminology*, 35 (2), 119–25.

Quinsey, V. L., Rice, M. and Harris, G. (1995) 'Actuarial prediction of sexual recidivism', *Journal of Interpersonal Violence*, 10: 85–105.

R v M'Naghten (1843–1860) All ER 229.

Sreenivasan, S., Kirkish, P., Garrick, T., Weinberger, L.E. and Phenix, A. (2000) 'Actuarial risk assessment models: A review of critical issues related to violence and sex-offender recidivism assessments', *The Journal of the American Academy of Psychiatry and the Law*, 28: 438–48.

Stephenson, G.M. (1992) *The Psychology of Criminal Justice*. Oxford: Blackwell.

Szasz, T. (1963) *Law, Liberty and Psychiatry*. New York: MacMillan.

Terman, L.M. (1916) *The Uses of Intelligence Tests* (Classics in the History of Psychology, Internet Resource http://psychclassics.yorku.ca/index.htm ed.). Boston: Houghton Mifflin.

Walsh, A. (2003) 'The Holy Trinity and the legacy of the Italian school of criminal anthropology: Review of 'Born to Crime: Cesare Lombroso and the Origins of Biological Criminology' by Mary Gibson, 2002 Praeger Press. *Human Nature Review*, 3 (15 January): 1–11.

Wigmore, J.H. (1909) 'Professor Münsterberg and the Psychology of Testimony – Being a report of the case of Cokestone v. Münsterberg', *Illinois Law Review*, 3: 399–445.

Chapter 2

Public perceptions of crime and punishment

Jane Wood and G. Tendayi Viki,
University of Kent

The rhetoric of the media and political speeches may give the impression that the public in Britain favour punitive sanctions for criminal behaviour (Hough and Moxon 1985; Hough and Roberts 1998). Politicians in Britain and the USA, intent on appeasing voters, often cite findings from opinion polls suggesting the public wants tougher policies on crime (Applegate, Cullen and Fisher 1997; Cullen, Wright and Chamlin 1999). It would seem that people are more concerned with punishing convicted criminals through the use of tougher prison sentences than they are with rehabilitating offenders. Yet this seemingly straight-forward public demand, may not be quite so clearcut. There seems to be some disparity between media opinion polls, scientifically conducted research and the political spin placed on findings. This chapter explores a number of reasons why examinations of people's attitudes to crime and punishment often produce conflicting results. We focus on some of the factors that may have bearing on the opinions people express. We argue that without taking these factors into account, a clear and accurate picture of people's beliefs concerning crime and punishment is unlikely to be captured.

Public perceptions of offenders

Historically, public representations of the 'criminal' seem to reflect a certain ambivalence towards perpetrators of criminal activity. Melossi (2000) observes how public attitudes towards offenders may fluctuate with social and economic conditions. During certain societal periods, some criminals have been considered more as innovators and heroes than villains and rates of imprisonment decline accordingly. Melossi (2000) argues that at other times, largely due to social construction by agents of a normative order, the criminal becomes the villain, a 'public enemy', and becomes morally repugnant to authority and public alike. Not surprisingly, at such times the use of imprisonment rises. The defining feature of these intermittent social conditions seems to be financial prosperity. As the economy flourishes, the use of imprisonment falls and as economic conditions deteriorate, so the use of imprisonment rises (Chiricos and DeLone 1992; Melossi 2000).

Sparks (2000) adds to the above economic paradigm by explaining how people's attitudes to punishment may be shaped by the 'doctrine of less eligibility'. This is essentially the notion that prison conditions must be worse than the living conditions of the working poor in that society. Sparks (2000) argues that during times of high unemployment, members of the public expect prison conditions to be more austere than the conditions endured by the poorest members of society. Consistent with this argument, Kury and Ferdinand (1999) observed that members of the public in Eastern European countries became more punitive in their attitudes to offenders during the social uncertainties brought about by the demise of communism. As such, from a sociological perspective, it seems reasonable to assume that public attitudes to crime and justice may reflect the socio-economic dynamics of a given culture. Consequently, attempts to assess attitudes may not always yield a consistently accurate measure of public beliefs.

When politicians indicate that public opinion favours more punitive sanctioning of offenders, this may not always be the case. Hough and Mayhew (1985) reviewed findings from the British Crime Survey (BCS) and noted the possibility that the public may not actually be as punitive as politicians seemed to believe. Building on this, Hough and Roberts (1998) reviewed the 1996 BCS and reported that there was less support for prison sentences than expected. Similarly, Mattinson and Mirrlees-Black (2000) examined the 1998 BCS and observed a public preference for community based sentences rather than the use of imprisonment. Such evidence is not unique to the UK. Researchers in the USA and Canada also report that public attitudes to crime and punishment are less punitive than political rhetoric would suggest (e.g. Cullen, Skovron, Scott and Burton 1990; Applegate, Cullen and Fisher 1997; Sprott and Doob 1997; Sundt, Cullen, Applegate and Turner 1998).

Apparently, there is a discrepancy between public attitudes and politicians' assumptions about those public attitudes. Kury and Ferdinand (1999) argue that this inconsistency results from politicians' over-reliance on data obtained from poorly interpreted opinion polls. It is a matter for concern that, inevitably, inaccuracies in the methodology of opinion polls will have an impact on the findings, which in turn may thread into subsequent policies. For example, Kury and Ferdinand (1999) note that the majority of opinion polls which, report the public as punitive, employ broad measures of attitude such as, 'In your view are sentences too harsh, about right, or not harsh enough?' (p. 375). Roberts (1992) maintains that this kind of question will inevitably generate the finding that the majority of the public want harsher penalties since there is no opportunity for individuals to express views on alternative types of sentence, for example, community sanctions or imprisonment. This ambiguous approach has led some social scientists to call for more precise items evaluating specific aspects of the criminal justice system if there is to be any hope of accurately capturing attitudes to crime and punishment (e.g. Thomson and Ragona 1987; Roberts 1992; Cullen *et al.* 1999).

Clearly a breakdown of public views, according to more explicit aspects of crime and punishment, is likely to yield a more accurate, if less accessible, assessment of public opinion than a broad based approach. The whole issue involves so many factors and is so varied that any single assessment attempting to encapsulate this diversity under one method-ological roof is likely to be distorted to the point where it becomes meaningless. The discrepancy between public attitudes and politicians' assumptions is understandable, if political assertions are founded on broad-based polls. Consequently, it is necessary to look at certain factors that are specific to members of the public or specific to aspects of crime and punishment.

Socio-demographics and attitudes to crime and punishment

Research has acknowledged that people's attitudes towards crime and punishment may differ according to the individual's membership of a particular socio-demographic category such as social class or gender and may well be linked to their explanations for the causes of crime (e.g. Langworthy and Whitehead 1986; Sanders and Hamilton 1987; Hough and Roberts 1998). For example, in Britain, Hough and Moxon (1985) observed that some of the variance in public attitudes to sentencing could be explained by generation and class differences. The authors found that older participants held more punitive attitudes than did younger respondents. These findings were echoed in the USA by Cullen, Clark, Cullen and Mathers (1985) who found that older respondents were more punishment oriented than were younger participants. Hough and Moxon (1985) also noted how manual workers and their families favoured custodial penalties, whereas non-manual workers did not. Similarly, findings from the 1996 British Crime Survey suggest that respondents with low educational attainment and respondents from manual worker households were more likely to view sentencing as lenient (Hough and Roberts 1998; Mattinson and Mirrlees-Black 2000).

Researchers have also examined the role of gender in attitudes to crime and punishment. Some work has revealed no differences between the genders in terms of support for community-based interventions, such as increasing employment opportunities (McGarell and Flanagan 1985). Similarly, Sanders and Hamilton (1987) found no gender differences in punishment norms and Hough and Moxon (1985) reported only marginal gender differences, except for items concerning rape and soliciting. Perhaps somewhat surprisingly, men were more likely to favour custodial sentences for rape than were women and women were more likely to favour custodial sentences for soliciting. In contrast, findings from the 1996 British Crime Survey suggest that women are more concerned about the lenient sentences handed down for rape convictions than are men. However, women were also more likely to underestimate the length of sentence those convicted of rape received (Hough and Roberts 1998). Mattinson and Mirrlees-Black (2000) note that the 1998 BCS reveals some gender differences in attitudes. Men were more likely than women to consider sentencing as 'too soft,' favour the use of imprisonment and regard magistrates and judges as out of touch.

Consequently, the research into the role of gender in attitudes to crime and punishment offers conflicting results that provide no basis for generalisation. Some studies indicate a gender difference in attitudes (e.g. Mattinson and Mirrlees-Black 2000) whilst other studies imply no gender difference (e.g. Sanders and Hamilton 1987). Of the work suggesting gender differences in attitudes to crime and punishment, the inference seems to be that men favour more punitive sanctions than do women. This notion does, however, stand out against the finding that women report the sentencing of rapists as too lenient (Hough and Roberts 1998). There are a number of possible reasons why women may feel that sentences are lenient, although Hough and Roberts (1998) point to false impressions that were held about actual sentencing practice. Even if there were no contradictory results in these gender studies, it would still be difficult to reach any comprehensive conclusions about the role of gender in attitudes to punishment. If men and women have different understandings of sentencing practices and possibly different experiences and understanding of court room processes in general, not to mention different responses to specific classes of offence, then comparisons between the two groups on attitudes to appropriate sentencing are unlikely to reveal results from which noteworthy inferences may be drawn.

Similarly, the small amount of research examining racial differences in attitudes to punishment also fails to show consistent effects (Langworthy and Whitehead 1986). In the United States, although African-Americans seem to hold negative attitudes towards the criminal justice system (e.g. Decker 1981; Flanagan and Vaughn 1996; Weitzer and Tuch 1999), race does not appear to have any influence on people's basic values in terms of crime and punishment (Langworthy and Whitehead 1986). For example, whilst some studies reveal Blacks are less tolerant to deviance and favour longer sentences than do Whites (e.g. Dunwoody and Frank 1994), other research fails to produce similar effects (e.g. McGarell and Flanagan 1985). Despite the indications from America that some race differences may exist, the somewhat limited research conducted in Britain reveals no differences in attitudes to crime and punishment according to race of respondent (Hough and Roberts 1998; Mattinson and Mirrlees-Black 2000). As a result, based on the limited and conflicting results of research into race and attitudes to crime and punishment, it is no more possible to draw definitive conclusions than it was with gender.

The above examples indicate that the relationships between demographic variables and attitudes to crime and punishment are far from clear. As such, it is not possible to conclude which sections of society are most likely to hold which attitudes. The inconsistencies in the research may result from methodological differences, but they may also be a function of underlying dimensions such as psychosocial mechanisms.

For example, Langworthy and Whitehead (1986) examined data obtained from a national poll conducted by ABC News in America. They concluded that it would be misleading to describe demographic differences in attitudes to punishment without reference to differences in levels of fear of crime. The authors argue that older people tend to agree with more punitive sanctions than younger people but this is not a direct effect of difference in age. Their findings strongly suggest that elderly individuals are more punitive than young people because older people experience greater fear of criminal victimisation than do younger individuals (see Hale 1996). Thus, differences in attitudes to crime attributed to age may, in reality, be more a function of differences in the experience of fear of crime and people's self perceived vulnerabilities.

Similarly, in an interesting series of studies, Gault and Sabini (2000) attempted to explain why there might be differences between male and female attitudes to the disposal of offenders. The authors argue that, due to socialisation processes, men and women have different emotional orientations. So, when encountering the same stimulus (e.g. an offender), they may respond differently. Emotions are capable of strongly influencing people's responses by focusing attention and motivating actions (Schwarz and Clore 1983). For instance, when an offence occurs, one person might focus on the perpetrator(s), become angry and develop a desire to punish them, whereas another individual might focus on the victim, become sympathetic and feel a desire to comfort them (Gault and Sabini 2000). Gault and Sabini's results revealed that women were consistently less punitive than were men and that these differences were mediated by gender differences in empathy. Although this research provides useful information as to potential explanations for gender differences in attitudes, it does not account for the lack of difference found in other studies. Also, since the participants in all four of Gault and Sabini's (2000) studies were American students, it is uncertain that a similar pattern of results would emerge from the general population in the UK or even in the USA.

In a similar vein, the examination of race and attitudes to crime and punishment seems to make more sense when considered in terms of racial prejudice (e.g. Dovidio, Smith, Donella and Gaertner 1997). In this respect, it is not only the race of the observer that is important, the race of the offender and the victim must also be taken in to consideration. Dovidio et al. (1997) observed that White participants who scored highly on racial prejudice scales were more likely to recommend the death penalty for Black defendants than White defendants. Low scoring participants recommended the death penalty for Black defendants only when it was also advocated by a Black juror. Hurwitz and Peffley (1997) note how negative stereotypes associated with racial minorities in America may have some impact on attitudes to crime and punishment. Using computer assisted telephone interviewing, Hurwitz and Peffley (1997) found that White Americans who agreed that 'most criminals come from ethnic minorities' were more likely to support punitive criminal justice policies. Thus, it seems that as well as noting a person's racial group, direct examination of potential prejudiced beliefs needs also to be made when trying to get a clear idea of who holds which attitudes to crime and punishment.

Clearly, although it is tempting to categorise people's attitudes to crime and punishment according to demographic factors, the evidence so far suggests that this would offer only a part of the picture and an un-clear one at that. The above discussion strongly indicates that, although socio-demographic categories may *seem* to influence attitudes to crime and punishment, these effects are not direct. Rather, the influence of demographic factors appears to be mediated by psychosocial issues such as emotional orientation, prejudice and fear of crime. Consequently, it is useful to examine more closely the research that has focused specifically on some of these psychosocial factors as predictors of punitive attitudes.

Fear of crime and attitudes to crime and punishment

Fear of crime is a critical issue in contemporary criminal justice policy because of its potential to create social misunderstanding concerning the reality and nature of crime (Ito 1993). Although some awareness and concern about crime could be considered to be healthy or even adaptive, taken to its extremes, fear of crime can impede individuals' behaviour and negatively affect their quality of life (Hale 1996). Fear of crime can destroy a sense of community by transforming certain parts of the neighbourhood into no-go areas and making residents fearful of their neighbours (Wilson 1975; Hale 1996). People who experience fear of crime may change their behaviour, preferring to remain at home and avoiding activities such as travelling on public transport due to the potential danger they present (Garafalo 1981; Patterson 1985; Hale 1996). There is also evidence suggesting that people may fear specific crimes. For instance, some women avoid going out alone at night or going to certain places in their neighbourhoods due to fear of sexual assault (Warr 1985; Gordon and Riger 1989; Mirrlees-Black and Allen 1998). Elderly people are reported to have become so afraid that they are virtually prisoners in their own homes (Wallace 1990; Joseph 1997). Such withdrawal from the community can contribute to the further breakdown of social attachments and result in the fragmentation of neighbourhood life (Hale 1996).

Besides the above effects, researchers have also examined the potential for fear of crime to influence attitudes to crime and punishment. It has been argued that fear of crime can lead to an increase in punitiveness of public attitudes and concomitant reduction in the appeal of liberal criminal justice policies (Hale 1996). However, the results obtained from research in this area remain equivocal. For example, Ouimet and Coyle (1991) examined the relationship between fear of crime and attitudes to sentencing in the general public in Canada. Results revealed no relationship between fear of crime and attitudes favouring severe sentencing. Other researchers have also found no relationship between fear of crime and attitudes to crime and punishment (e.g. Fagan 1981; Flanagan, McGarell and Brown 1985; Langworthy and Whitehead 1986). These findings have led researchers such as Brillon (1988) to conclude that there is no relationship between fear of crime and punitive attitudes.

In contrast, other researchers note that there does appear to be a relationship between fear of crime and punitive attitudes. For instance, research has revealed that people who believed their neighbourhood to be unsafe were more likely to perceive the courts as too lenient (Myers 1996). Rossi, Simpson and Miller (1985) presented participants with vignettes describing different types of crime and found that individuals who were more worried about crime were also more likely to recommend harsher sentences. In the UK Hough and Moxon (1985) found that those more fearful of crime were also more likely to advocate tougher sentences. Adding to this, Hough, Lewis and Walker (1988) report that fear of crime was one of the factors significantly associated with attitudes favouring punitive sentencing in England and Wales.

A more recent study, conducted in Canada, attempted to deal with the discrepancies regarding the role of fear of crime in attitudes to crime and punishment (Sprott and Doob 1997). The authors noted that most of the inconsistency in the research may result from differences in the methodologies used by previous researchers. For instance, where some researchers focused on sentencing severity for specific cases, others employed more global measures. Furthermore, Sprott and Doob (1997) argue that asking respondents to 'sentence' offenders is not the only or even the best indicator of people's attitudes to crime and punishment. The authors assessed the relationship between fear of crime and attitudes to the courts and the police. They found that the higher an individual's level of fear, the more likely they were to rate sentences as too lenient and to view the courts and the police negatively. These effects were still apparent when other demographic variables such as age and gender were controlled.

The above results show how the majority of recent studies (e.g. Myers 1996; Sprott and Doob 1997) suggest that fear of crime is associated with attitudes favouring a more punitive form of sanctioning. If people fear crime, regardless of their demographic backgrounds, then they are more likely to want harsher sanctions, in the hope that offending behaviour and, consequently, their levels of fear may be reduced. Again, the evidence outlined above is not clear-cut regarding a possible relationship between this psychosocial factor and attitudes to crime and punishment. It seems possible that attitudes to crime and punishment may have foundations in more personal experiences of crime and justice.

Victimisation and attitudes to crime and punishment

Although it may seem reasonable to suggest that a personal experience of victimisation might facilitate punitive attitudes to crime and punishment, researchers have generally failed to produce evidence to support this. In fact, researchers have failed to show a conclusive link between the experience of victimisation and fear of crime (Sheley 1985; Langworthy and Whitehead 1986; Hale 1996). Dull and Wint (1997) conducted a longitudinal study using American college students. The study assessed how attitudes towards the criminal justice system might change over a four-year period as a result of victimisation. Participants' attitudes were initially measured in the freshman (first) year, then again in the senior (final) year of their studies. The researchers found that individuals who had been victimised during the period of the study were more likely to express negative attitudes towards the police and beliefs that the courts were not effective in dealing with crime. Sprott and Doob (1997) also noted a complex relationship between victimisation and attitudes to crime and punishment. They found that victims of more serious crimes such as crimes of violence did not hold more punitive views on sentencing practices. Interestingly, the authors found that victims of robbery and burglary expressed somewhat more punitive views than did victims of sexual or physical assault. Of similar interest and echoing Hough and Roberts' (1998) results, was the finding that women were somewhat more likely to indicate sentences as too lenient than were men. However, the authors in this instance did not take measures of the accuracy of people's knowledge of sentencing practices. As a result it is impossible to know if the women in Sprott and Doob's (1997) research also held inaccurate views of actual sentencing practices like the women noted within the Hough and Roberts (1998) work, nor did they explore the detail of people's experiences of the criminal justice system processes they encountered post-victimisation.

Nevertheless, such findings are rare in the research literature. The majority of studies show no relationship between victimisation and punitive attitudes. This is especially the case in studies conducted in the UK. Hough and Moxon (1985) report that in the 1984 British Crime Survey, '... victims of crime were no more punitive than others' (p. 171). Findings from the 1996 British Crime Survey also show no indication that victimisation fuels a desire for harsher penalties (Hough and Roberts 1998). Mattinson and Mirrlees-Black (2000) add to this body of evidence by reporting that the 1998 BCS fails to support the idea that being a victim of crime relates to more punitive attitudes. Studies conducted in the USA and Canada have also found that neither direct nor vicarious victimisation has an influence on attitudes to the criminal justice system (e.g. Garafalo 1981; Langworthy and Whitehead 1986). Consequently, with a few exceptions, research seems to suggest that victimisation does not relate to more punitive attitudes. It therefore seems possible that people's attitudes to crime and punishment may relate more to other attitudes or beliefs they hold, than to personal experience in terms of criminal behaviour.

Individual principles and attitudes to crime and punishment

People's ideological beliefs have a pervasive impact on how they respond to a variety of social stimuli (*c.f.* Finamore and Carlson 1987). For example, Rubin and Peplau (1975) demonstrated a link between a belief in a just world[1] and support for government institutions. In a similar fashion, a number of researchers have been interested in the link between ideological beliefs and attitudes towards crime and punishment. For instance, Finamore and Carlson (1987) conducted a study in which they examined the relationship between beliefs in a just world, religiosity and crime control attitudes in American college students. Results revealed that both religiosity and just world beliefs predicted punitive attitudes and that neither variable moderated the other's effects. Highly religious participants and people with a strong belief in a 'just world' were found to hold the most punitive attitudes towards offenders. In a similar series of studies, Grasmick and colleagues (e.g. Grasmick, Bursik and Kimpel 1991; Grasmick, Morgan and Kennedy 1992; Grasmick and McGill 1994) found that Christian fundamentalism strongly predicted individual support for the use of corporal punishment and punitive criminal justice policies. This led the authors to conclude that people who are highly religious seem to hold people more accountable for their actions, thereby deserving punishments (Grasmick and McGill 1994).

Research has also explored conservatism[2] as a potential reason why people may hold punitive attitudes (Taylor, Scheppele and Stinchcombe 1979; Stinchcombe, Adams, Heimer, Schepple, Smith and Taylor 1980; Scheingold 1984; Cullen, Clark, Cullen and Mathers 1985). In Canada, Baron and Hartnagel (1996) conducted a telephone survey to assess the relationship between conservatism and punitive attitudes toward juvenile offenders. Results indicated that respondents holding conservative social values were consistently more punitive in their attitudes towards juvenile offenders than were liberal respondents. These effects have also been replicated by a number of independent studies conducted in the USA and Canada (e.g. Taylor, Scheppele and Stinchcombe 1979; Stinchcombe et al. 1980; Scheingold 1984; Cullen, Clark, Cullen and Mathers 1985). For example, Taylor et al. (1979) found that conservative people, regardless of their levels of fear of crime, were more punitive. Similarly, Stinchcombe et al. (1980) reported that liberal political views were consistent with more lenient criminal justice attitudes. In an attempt to explain the link between conservatism, religiosity and punitive attitudes, Langworthy and Whitehead (1986) argue that highly religious and conservative people are more punitive because they believe that criminals choose to offend. Conversely, liberals tend to hold more positivistic attitudes about criminal behaviour and consider environmental factors as important determinants of any social behaviour, criminal or otherwise. Research does indicate that individuals who hold people accountable for their behaviour, are more likely to endorse punitive criminal justice policies (e.g. Cullen et al. 1985).

In the USA, Tygart (1992) examined the relationship between traditional or orthodox religious beliefs, political conservatism and the philosophical belief in free will, and attitudes towards the use of insanity or mental illness as a defence in court. Results revealed that individuals who were highly religious, politically conservative or held philosophical beliefs in 'free-will' were less inclined to accept an insanity plea as a defence. Homant, Kennedy, Kelly and Williams (1986) also found that ideological beliefs were a significant determinant of an individual's attitudes to the insanity plea as a defence. Individuals who felt that people should be held accountable for their behaviour were less likely to accept insanity or mental illness pleas.

It would seem, therefore, that there is some link between a philosophical belief in 'free will' and punitive attitudes. As early as 1959, Nettler reported an American study, which showed that individuals who believed people are free to choose how to behave were more likely to endorse punitive sanctions. However, Viney, Waldman and Barchilon (1982) failed to replicate this relationship and instead found that determinists[3] were more likely to be punitive towards offenders. Stroessner and Green (1990) suggest that the relationship between belief in free will and attitudes towards punishment may not be a simple one, since there could be a difference between psychosocial and religious-philosophical determinism. The authors point out that psychosocial determinists believe that environmental factors determine behaviour; while religious-philosophical determinists believe that deities or fate act to control behaviour.

Using American college students, Stroessner and Green (1990) measured and statistically differentiated between these two constructs.

However, contrary to their predictions, they found that individuals who scored high on psychosocial determinism were more punitive than religious-philosophical determinists and respondents who endorsed free will. The authors explain this finding by arguing that those who scored high on the psychosocial determinism scale may be those who believe that behaviour is influenced by psychological and sociological forces primarily at an early age. These individuals, Stroessner and Green (1990) point out, may advocate punitive measures, even the death penalty, rather than rehabilitative measures, because they believe little or nothing can be done to modify criminal behaviour in adulthood.

Clearly the research offers differential conclusions. Religious and conservative beliefs seem to go hand in hand with more punitive attitudes and some claim this is the case because conservative and religious individuals assume offenders choose to offend (e.g. Langworthy and Whitehead 1986). On the other hand, research also reveals that those who consider offending behaviour as a matter of determinism, i.e. shaped by external forces rather than a matter of choice, also endorse punitive sanctions (e.g. Stroessner and Green 1990). Threading its way through the research, is a notion of responsibility. Thus, accountability and different ideologies seem to dictate the extent to which individuals endorse levels of punishment. As Stroessner and Green (1990) contend, it may be that the relationship between free will and determinism, and attitudes to crime and punishment results from a complexity of belief systems that make the relationship difficult to understand. It certainly appears to be the case that the issue of attitudes to punishment may be complicated due to people having diverse concepts of the aims of punishment. Stroessner and Green (1990) acknowledge this and maintain that some people may consider punishment as an appropriate rehabilitative tool. This raises the concern that attitudes to crime and punishment may be shaped in part by what people expect from a punishment system. Some may see punishment as a tool useful for changing behaviour whereas others may consider it primarily as a form of retribution.

Type of offence and punitiveness

In light of the above, it seems plausible to consider that people's views on punishment may also function according to the levels of perceived harm caused by the type of offence. For example, some researchers have found that the severity of punishment favoured by members of the public was determined by the perceived harm done and consequently varied according to the seriousness of the crime (Hamilton and Rytina 1980). Adding to this, Jacoby and Cullen (1998) observed that members of the public did not consistently recommend prison for all types of offence. Instead, incarceration was favoured for violent perpetrators and sex-offenders rather than for crimes such as larceny involving small amounts of money. In the same vein, research examining attitudes relating to the early release of prisoners found that people were more likely to favour leniency for non-violent offenders (Cumberland and Zamble 1992). In Britain, the indications are that people believe sentences to be too lenient but only for those who commit burglary (Hough and Moxon 1985) and those who commit rape (Hough and Roberts 1998).

It also seems that the type of offender has a part to play in the construction of public attitudes to crime and punishment. One series of studies reported that the American public did not strongly support the death penalty in cases involving juvenile offenders (Sandys and McGarell 1995; McGarell and Sandys 1996). Recidivist offenders, however, elicit little sympathy from members of the public (Roberts 1996). In one study, American participants were asked to 'sentence' offenders with different levels of repeat offending (Finkel, Maloney, Valbuena and Groscup 1996). Results indicated that if the offender's previous convictions were revealed, then participants favoured more punitive sentencing. If the offender's previous convictions were not made known, then participants favoured more lenient forms of punishment. Similar results have been observed in Britain: participants were found to favour more punitive sanctions for recidivist offenders, regardless of the offence type (Mattinson and Mirrlees-Black 2000). It seems to be the case that if offenders fail to change their ways following a conviction, the public adopts more punitive attitudes towards them when they re-offend. Mattinson and Mirrlees-Black (2000) concluded that when the word 'persistent' was applied to offenders, it seemed to trigger more punitive attitudes.

Consequently, it would be a mistake to assume that people hold uniformly punitive attitudes towards all types of offenders. The age of the offender may influence the punitive sanctions people consider appropriate. Perhaps it is the case that people see younger offenders as more likely to reform or, perhaps, the public finds the idea of executing juvenile offenders as inappropriate or even abhorrent. However, public inclination towards punishment largesse does not extend as far as recidivist offenders. The research suggests that the more offending behaviour the individual has been involved in, the more punitive the public becomes towards them. What is not clear is exactly what the public believes harsher penalties for recidivist offenders will achieve. For instance, it could be that people believe harsher sanctions may once and for all deter an offender's inclination to offend. It is equally possible that people believe tougher penalties will function primarily to remove the most persistent offenders from society for longer periods of time, resulting in a welcome respite from their offending behaviour. Again, this raises the issue of what it is people expect punishment to achieve. If people have differential expectations of punishment, then perhaps those expectations should be considered when assessing public attitudes to crime and punishment.

Expectations of punishment and attitudes

Even the more straightforward structures within the criminal justice system seem to reflect the disparate aims of punishment. For instance, prisons may have more than one function, striving to incapacitate, deliver retribution, deter reoffending and rehabilitate (see Duff and Garland 1994). Given that these are distinct roles, each with different aims and potential outcomes, it could be argued that people's attitudes need to be examined separately, in light of potentially differential expectations to each component. Chung and Bagozzi (1997) investigated whether retribution, deterrence and rehabilitation are distinct components of attitudes to punishment. The authors developed three verbal measures of each component and assessed attitudes accordingly. Statistical analyses indicated that attitudes did consist of three components demonstrating that global assessments cannot hope to offer a complete analysis of people's attitudes to crime and punishment.

In addition, Applegate, Cullen and Fisher (1997) conducted a study in which they specifically focused on people's attitudes to rehabilitation as a prison goal. The authors maintained people's attitudes were not adequately tapped by previous work, which had focused exclusively on the retributive aims of the criminal justice system. The study assessed the views of more than 500 residents of Ohio on what they thought the main function of imprisonment should be; to punish, to protect society or to rehabilitate offenders. Results showed that, contrary to previous research, there was strong support for the rehabilitative function of imprisonment. The authors concluded that previous researchers might have over-estimated the punitive attitudes of the American public due to biased global measures of attitudes. Although Applegate *et al.*'s (1997) research, based on one sample from one area in the USA, cannot be considered as conclusive evidence that public attitudes favour rehabilitation *rather* than retribution, it does cast some doubt on the assumption that people are singularly punitive in their attitudes to crime and punishment.

Along the same lines, research conducted in Canada examined demographic differences in more than 10,000 people's attitudes to specific aspects of the criminal justice process (Kaukinen and Colavecchia 1997). The study focused on public perceptions of the ability of courts to fulfil the dual role of protecting victims whilst also maintaining the rights of the accused. Data analysis revealed an interesting pattern of results. Respondents from higher socio-economic groups most often expressed dissatisfaction with the ability of the courts to protect victims. In contrast, respondents from lower socio-economic categories were more dissatisfied with the ability of courts to protect the rights of the accused. The authors explain these findings in terms of class threat, arguing that upper class dissatisfaction with the courts' ability to protect the interests of victims reflects upper class fears of becoming victims.

In contrast, lower socio-economic groups may have more experience, direct or indirect, of the unfair treatment of individuals accused of criminal activity. In addition, given the abundance of literature citing the influence of extra-legal factors such as race and social class, it is not surprising that members of social groups most likely to be accused of crime are aware that their group membership may influence how they are treated by the justice system (Kaukinen and Colavecchia 1999). These findings clearly indicate the difficulties inherent in any attempt to make generalisations in terms of attitudes to the criminal justice system. The contextual nature of individual perceptions noted above clearly acts as an impediment to the possibility that global assessments of public opinion offer anything other than a muddied view of attitudes to crime and punishment.

Furthermore, research has also revealed that many respondents underestimated the severity of sentencing practices. For instance, Mattinson and Mirrlees-Black (2000) noted how 56 per cent of respondents in the BCS (1998) believed that less than 60 per cent of adult males convicted of rape were sentenced to immediate custody, when the actual number is 99 per cent. Of course, in rape cases, their misperceptions could be related to the exceptionally low conviction rates rather than sentencing practice in isolation. The incorrect, but widespread, beliefs in the leniency of sentences may be related to a general air of dissatisfaction, or lack of confidence in the system as an entity in and of itself. Nevertheless, what is expressed, and what our policy makers hear, are concerns about the leniency of sentences.

If public attitudes to crime and punishment feed on the mis-apprehension that sentencing is more lenient than it actually is, it is hardly surprising that some people consider sentences to be 'too soft'. Similarly, if people judge sentences as 'too soft', it is only to be expected that they will also have a jaundiced view of those handing down the sentences. In their study Hough and Roberts (1998) found that more than three-quarters of people considered judges to be out of touch with the public. Magistrates, although faring somewhat better than judges, were also viewed as out of touch by nearly two-thirds of the sample.

Although it is possible that even if people were educated in terms of sentencing practices they might still express punitive attitudes, research suggests this is not the case. Work in Canada examining attitudes to parole revealed that individuals who were more familiar with the mechanisms of the criminal justice system tended to favour parole whereas individuals who had little knowledge of the justice system did not (Samra-Grewal and Roesch 2000). The indications here are that in the absence of sound knowledge of the justice system, people may form attitudes based on punitive sanctions they *believe* to be in place rather than the informed judgements a number of researchers and politicians take them to be. As a result, it is impossible to draw definitive conclusions about public opinion if the accuracy of public knowledge of sentencing practices is assumed rather than assessed by those who gather the evidence.

Conclusions

This chapter has provided an overview of some of the many empirical studies that have attempted to assess public attitudes to crime and punishment. By examining the diverse nature and areas of study that have attempted to glean an accurate picture of people's views, it is clear that we cannot expect the probability or generalisability that are the hallmarks of psychological research. The inconsistency of research evidence, even when examining specific areas, is probably testament to the ambiguous nature of people's feelings in terms of offenders and offending behaviour. In other words, people's attitudes to crime and punishment are contextual. The evidence presented in this chapter suggests people's attitudes are at the mercy of the social/economic climate, the kind of offence and offender, the expectations of what punishment should achieve and even the underlying influence of other belief systems. In addition, there is the possibility of dubious methodological approaches forcing respondents' choices and the misconceptions that people may have of actual sentencing practices. Consequently, it is not surprising that so much incongruity exists in the research, especially in work aiming to achieve global assessments of public attitudes to crime and punishment. What is clear is that political rhetoric asserting public desire for tougher sentencing is more likely to be based on a blurred snapshot of public opinion, rather than the accurate assessment that empirical rigour demands.

Notes

1 This is the belief that good things happen to good people and bad things will happen to bad people, it was further expanded by Lerner (1980).
2 Conservatism is usually measured by examining people's levels of agreement with statements that endorse traditional social values (e.g. marriage, family, etc.).
3 People who believe that factors outside individuals' control (e.g. genetic, social or environmental) are more important in accounting for human behaviour.

References

Applegate, B.K., Cullen, F.T. and Fisher, B.S. (1997) 'Public support for correctional treatment: The continuing appeal of the rehabilitative ideal', *The Prison Journal*, 77: 237–58.

Baron, S.W. and Hartnagel, T.F. (1996) 'Lock 'em up: Attitudes toward punishing juvenile offenders', *Canadian Journal of Criminology*, 38: 191–212.

Brillon, Y. (1988) 'Punitiveness, status and ideology in three Canadian provinces', in N. Walker and M. Hough (eds) *Public Attitudes to Sentencing: Surveys from five countries*. Aldershot: Gower.

Chiricos, T.G. and DeLone, M.A. (1992) 'Labor surplus and punishment: A review and assessment of theory and evidence', *Social Problems*, 39: 421–46

Chung, W. and Bagozzi, R. (1997) 'The construct validity of measures of the tripartite conceptualization of punishment attitudes', *Journal of Social Service Research*, 22: 1–25.

Cullen, F.T., Clark, G.A., Cullen, J.B. and Mathers, R.A. (1985) 'Attribution, salience and attitudes toward criminal sanctioning', *Criminal Justice and Behaviour*, 12: 305–31.

Cullen, F.T., Skovron, S.E., Scott, J.E. and Burton, V.S., Jr. (1990) 'Public support for correctional treatment: The tenacity of rehabilitative ideology', *Criminal Justice and Behaviour*, 17: 6–18.

Cullen, F.T., Wright, J.P., and Chamlin, M.B. (1999) 'Social support and social reform: A progressive crime control agenda', *Crime and Delinquency*, 45: 188–208.

Cumberland, J. and Zamble, E. (1992) 'General and specific measures of attitudes toward early release of criminal offenders', *Canadian Journal of Behavioural Science*, 24: 442–55.

Decker, S. (1981) 'Citizen attitudes toward the police: A review of past findings and suggestions for future policy', *Journal of Police Science and Administration*, 9: 80–7.

Dovidio, J.F., Smith, J.K., Donella, A.G. and Gaertner, S.L. (1997) 'Racial attitudes and the death penalty', *Journal of Applied Social Psychology*, 27: 1468–487.

Duff, A. and Garland, D. (1994) *A Reader on Punishment*. Oxford: Oxford University Press.

Dull, R.T. and Wint, A.V.N. (1997) 'Criminal victimization and its effects on fear of crime and justice attitudes', *Journal of Interpersonal Violence*, 12: 748–59.

Dunwoody, P.T. and Frank, M.L. (1994) 'Effects of ethnicity on prison sentencing', *Psychological Reports*, 74: 200.

Fagan, R.W. (1981) 'Public support for the courts: An examination of alternative explanations', *Journal of Criminal Justice*, 9: 403–18.

Finamore, F. and Carlson, J.M. (1987) 'Religiosity, belief in a just world and crime control attitudes', *Psychological Reports*, 61: 135–38.

Finkel, N.J., Maloney, S.T., Valbuena, M.Z. and Groscup, J. (1996) 'Recidivism, proportionalism and individualised punishment', *American Behavioural Scientist*, 39: 476–89.

Flanagan, T.J., McGarell, E.F. and Brown, (1985) 'Public perceptions of the criminal courts: The role of demographic and related attitudinal variables', *Journal of Research in Crime and Delinquency*, 22: 66–82.

Flanagan, T.J. and Vaughn, M.S. (1996) 'Public opinion about police abuse of force', in W. Geller and H. Toch (eds) *Police Violence*. New Haven, CT: Yale University Press.

Garafalo, J. (1981) 'The fear of crime: Causes and consequences', *Journal of Criminal Law and Criminology*, 82: 839–57.

Gault, B.A. and Sabini, J. (2000) 'The role of empathy, anger, and gender in predicting attitudes toward punitive, reparative and preventative public policies', *Cognition and Emotion*, 14: 495–520.

Gordon, M.T. and Riger, S. (1989) *The Female Fear*. New York: Free Press.

Grasmick, H.G., Bursik, R. Jr. and Kimpel, M.L. (1991) 'Protestant fundamentalism and attitudes toward corporal punishment of children', *Violence and Victims*, 6: 283–93.

Grasmick, H.G. and McGill, A.L. (1994) 'Religion, attribution style and punitiveness toward juvenile offenders', *Criminology*, 32: 23–46.

Grasmick, H.G., Morgan, C.S. and Kennedy, M.B. (1992) 'Support for corporal punishment in the school: A comparison of the effects of socio-economic status and religion', *Social Science Quarterly*, 73: 177–87.

Hale, C. (1996) 'Fear of crime: A review of the literature', *International Review of Victimology*, 4: 79–150.

Hamilton, L. and Rytina, S. (1980) 'Social consensus on norms of justice: Should the punishment fit the crime?', *American Journal of Sociology*, 85: 1117–125.

Homant, R.J., Kennedy, D.B., Kelly, T.M. and Williams, M.O. (1986) 'Ideology as a determinant of views on the insanity defense', *Journal of Criminal Justice*, 14: 37–46.

Hough, M., Lewis, H. and Walker, N. (1988) 'Factors associated with punitiveness in England and Wales', in N. Walker and M. Hough (eds) *Public Attitudes to Sentencing: Surveys from five countries*. Aldershot: Gower.

Hough, M. and Mayhew, P. (1985) *Taking Account of Crime: Key findings from the second British Crime Survey*. London: HMSO.

Hough, M. and Moxon, D. (1985) 'Dealing with offenders: Popular opinion and the views of victims. Findings from the British Crime Survey', *The Howard Journal*, 24: 160–75.

Hough, M. and Roberts, J. (1998) *Attitudes to Crime and Punishment: Findings from the British Crime Survey*. London: HMSO.

Hurwitz, J. and Peffley, M. (1997) 'Public perception of race and crime: The role of racial stereotypes', *American Journal of Political Science*, 41: 375–402.

Ito, K. (1993) 'Research on the fear of crime: Perceptions and realities of crime in Japan', *Crime and Delinquency*, 39: 385–93.

Jacoby, J.E. and Cullen, F.T. (1998) 'The structure of punishment norms: Applying the Rossi-Berk model', *Journal of Criminal Law and Criminology*, 89: 245–305.

Joseph, J. (1997) 'Fear of crime among the black elderly', *Journal of Black Studies*, 27: 698–718.

Kaukinen, C. and Colavecchia, S. (1999) 'Public perceptions of the courts: An examination of attitudes toward the treatment of victims and accused', *Canadian Journal of Criminology*, 41: 365–85.

Kury, H. and Ferdinand, T. (1999) 'Public opinion and punitivity', *International Journal of Law and Psychiatry*, 22: 373–92.

Langworthy, R.H. and Whitehead, J.T. (1986) 'Liberalism and fear as explanation of punitiveness', *Criminology*, 24: 575–91.

Lerner, M.J. (1980) *The Belief in a Just World*. New York: Plenum.

Mattinson, J. and Mirrlees-Black, C. (2000) *Attitudes to Crime and Criminal Justice: Findings from the 1998 British Crime Survey*. London. HMSO.

McGarell, E.F. and Flanagan, T.J. (eds) (1985) *Sourcebook of Criminal Justice Statistics – 1984*. Washington, DC: Government Printing Office.

McGarell, E.F. and Sandys, M. (1996) 'The misperception of public opinion toward capital punishment: Examining the spuriousness explanation of death penalty support', *American Behavioural Scientist*, 39: 500–14.

Melossi, D. (2000) 'Changing representations of the criminal', *British Journal of Criminology*, 40: 296–320.

Mirrlees-Black, C. and Allen, J. (1998) *Concern About Crime: Findings from the 1998 British Crime Survey*. London. HMSO.

Myers, L. (1996) 'Bringing the offender to heal: Views of the criminal courts', in T.J. Flanagan and D.R. Longmire (eds) *Americans View Crime and Justice: A national public opinion survey*. Thousand Oaks, CA. Sage.

Ouimet, M. and Coyle, E. (1991) 'Fear of crime and sentencing punitiveness: Comparing the general public and court practitioners', *Canadian Journal of Criminology*, 33: 149–62.

Patterson, A.H. (1985) 'Fear of crime and other barriers to the use of public transportation by the elderly', *Journal of Architectural and Planning Research*, 2: 277–88.

Roberts, J.V. (1992) 'Public opinion, crime and criminal justice', in M. Tonry (ed.) *Crime and Justice: A review of research*. Chicago: University of Chicago Press.

Roberts, J.V. (1996) 'Public opinion, criminal record and the sentencing process', *American Behavioural Scientist*, 39: 488–90.

Rossi, P.H., Simpson, J.E. and Miller, J.L. (1985) 'Beyond crime seriousness: Fitting the punishment to the crime', *Journal of Quantitative Criminology*, 1: 59–90.

Rubin, Z. and Peplau, L.A. (1975) 'Who believes in a just world', *Journal of Social Issues*, 31: 64–89.

Samra-Grewal, J. and Roesch, R. (2000) 'The Parole Attitudes Scale (PAS): Development of a 15-item scale to assess attitudes toward conditional release', *Canadian Journal of Criminology*, 42: 157–70.

Sanders, J. and Hamilton, L. (1987) 'Is there a "common law" of responsibility?', *Law and Human Behaviour*, 11: 277–98.

Sandys, M. and McGarell, E.E. (1995) 'Attitudes toward capital punishment: Preference for the penalty or mere acceptance?', *Journal of Research in Crime and Delinquency*, 32: 191–213.

Scheingold, S.A. (1984) *The Politics of Law and Order: Street crime and public policy*. New York: Longman.

Schwarz, N. and Clore, G.L. (1983) 'Mood, misattribution and judgement of well being: Informative and directive functions of affective states', *Journal of Personality and Social Psychology*, 45: 513–23.

Sheley, J.F. (1985) *America's Crime Problem: An Introduction to Criminology*. Belmont, CA: Wadsworth Publishing.

Sparks, R. (2000) 'Penal "austerity": The doctrine of less eligibility reborn?', in R. Matthews and P. Francis, Prison 2000: *An International Perspective on the Current State and Future of Imprisonment*. London: Macmillan.

Sprott, J.B. and Doob, A.N. (1997) 'Fear, victimization, and attitudes to sentencing, the courts and the police', *Canadian Journal of Criminology*, 39: 275–91.

Stinchcombe, A.L., Adams, R., Heimer, C.A., Schepple, K.L., Smith, T.W. and Taylor, D.G. (1980) *Crime and Punishment: Changing attitudes in America*. San Francisco: Josey-Bass.

Stroessner, S.J. and Green, C.W. (1990) 'Effect of belief in free will or determinism on attitudes toward punishment and locus of control', *Journal of Social Psychology*, 130: 789–90.

Sundt, J.L., Cullen, F.T., Applegate, B.K. and Turner, M.G. (1998) 'The tenacity of the rehabilitative ideal revisited: Have attitudes toward offender treatment changed?', *Criminal Justice and Behaviour*, 25: 426–42.

Taylor, D.G., Scheppele, K. and Stinchcombe, A. (1979) 'Salience of crime and support for harsher criminal sanctions', *Social Problems*, 26: 413–24.

Thomson, D.R. and Ragona, A.J. (1987) 'Popular moderation versus governmental authoritarianism: An interactionist view of public sentiments toward criminal sanctions', *Crime and Delinquency*, 33: 337–57.

Tygart, C.E. (1992) 'Public acceptance/rejection of the insanity defence for defendants in criminal homicide case', *Journal of Psychiatry and Law*, 20: 375–89.

Viney, W., Waldman, D.A. and Barchilon (1982) 'Attitudes toward punishment in relation to beliefs in free will and determinism', *Human Relations*, 35: 939–50.

Wallace, S. (1990) 'Race versus class in health care of African-American elderly', *Social Problems*, 37: 517–33.

Warr, M. (1985) 'Fear of rape among urban women', *Social Problems*, 32: 238–50.

Weitzer, R. and Tuch, S.A. (1999) 'Race, class and perceptions of discrimination by the police', *Crime and Delinquency*, 45: 494–507.

Wilson, J.Q. (1975) *Thinking About Crime*. New York. Basic Books.

Section 2

Investigation and Prosecution

In trying to maximise the efficiency of justice, there are a number of arenas in which forensic psychologists have been very visible. One in particular, is in the revision of police interview procedures of both witnesses and suspects. Another, is in providing tools to aid the investigative process.

In this section and the one to follow, we deal with the reliability and validity of evidence, and the related field of how systems produce and process testimony. There has been much general and academic interest in these areas and they are directly related to conviction and sentencing decisions. It is not surprising that so much effort has been expended on these topics, particularly in states where capital punishment is still used. They are, quite literally, matters of life and death.

The success of forensic psychological work has been mixed. On the one hand, sections of constitutional law have been rewritten; most of Europe has laws regarding the proper ways in which the police may gather and use evidence, something along the lines of the Police and Criminal Evidence Act; and the cognitive interview has become a policing norm in many jurisdictions. On the other hand, a look across the Atlantic reminds us that different States have different laws, different guidance and differential risks of false confessions, falsified evidence and miscarriages of justice.

In Chapter 3, Tom Williamson draws on a diverse body of psychological evidence and real cases. His chapter makes disturbing reading as it is clear that wrongful convictions are neither rare, nor are they always unavoidable. Far too many are entirely predictable and the net results are obvious, wrong people are imprisoned and some are executed.

Further, the actual perpetrators are not brought to justice, victims are not best served and society at large is left to question both the efficacy and reliability of the system that is supposed to serve and protect it from harm. The chapter concludes with useful suggestions that, if implemented, would help to lessen the frequency of wrongful convictions and better serve the interests of justice.

One tool that has been offered for investigation is the offender profile. It is popular with both the public and police. However, there has been some disquiet about the different types of profile that can be constructed and on what they are based. Some profilers use their intuitive, clinical judgement whereas others prefer a more systematic approach, developing instruments and programs that can sort and present data based on well established, empirical principles. In Chapter 4, Laurence Alison and Emma Barrett set offender profiles in a critical context. They show us how they have been used, and misused and suggest ways of taking them forward.

Chapter 3

USA and UK responses to miscarriages of justice

Tom Williamson, University of Portsmouth

Miscarriages of justice invariably draw attention to police incompetence and sometimes to police corruption (MacPherson 1999). Psychologists have made significant contributions to identifying what the investigatory processes are, drawing attention to their weaknesses and making recommendations for their improvement that can minimise the risk of wrongful conviction. There are however no grounds for complacency and plenty for continued vigilance. Stephenson reviewed the psychology of criminal justice and concluded that,

> at each stage of criminal processing, findings have been accumulated that seriously challenge conventional views and assumptions about the propriety of the system. This knowledge should be used to fuel critical evaluation of the law's activities. (Stephenson 1992: 243)

This chapter will consider miscarriages of justice primarily in the United Kingdom and the response by its government and criminal justice agencies. Although the criminal justice systems in the UK and the United States of America share many similarities, the response to growing numbers of well-documented miscarriages of justice in the US has been very different to that in the UK. The reasons for this will be considered. We will examine:

- concerns about police competence in criminal investigations
- the over-reliance on confession evidence in adversarial systems of justice

- UK legislation regulating custodial questioning
- factors contributing to miscarriages of justice in the USA
- USA/UK responses to miscarriages of justice
- opportunities for greater involvement of forensic psychologists in the future in ways that can minimise miscarriages of justice.

Concerns about police competence in criminal investigations

The role of the police in criminal investigations

Concerns about police competence and corruption are recurring themes in criminological research. The Royal Commission on Criminal Procedure (1981) was appointed amid growing concern about the police role in the investigation of offences. An excellent example of a police agency making use of surveys in order to document public concern is the Police and People in London series which discovered that seven types of serious misconduct by the police were believed to occur:

- threats in questioning suspects
- false records of interviews
- excessive force on arrest
- unreasonable violence at police stations
- fabrication of evidence
- accepting bribes
- accepting favours.

The Policy Studies Institute Report found:

> The use of threats and unfair pressure in questioning is the kind of misconduct that is thought to be most widespread. About half of informants think it happens at least occasionally, but perhaps more important, one-quarter think that it often happens – that it is a usual pattern of behaviour by police officers. The other kinds of misconduct are thought to happen at least occasionally by a substantial proportion of Londoners, while about one in ten Londoners think police officers fabricate evidence, and use violence unjustifiably on people held at police stations. These findings suggest that there is a complete lack of confidence in the police among at least one in ten Londoners, and that about half of Londoners have serious doubts about the standards of police conduct, though in most cases they do not think there is a pattern of frequent or usual misconduct. (Smith 1983: 325)

One third of young white people thought the police often used threats or unreasonable pressure during custodial questioning whereas 62 per cent of young West Indians believed they did so which led Smith to conclude that 'the lack of confidence in the police amongst young West Indians can only be regarded as disastrous' (*op cit.*: 254).

The Islington Crime Survey found that the public were more critical of the police where

- they have a high degree of contact with the police
- they are subject to a high level of victimization.
  (Jones, MacLean and Young 1986)

This kind of research provides a rich picture of the nature and quality of the relationship between the citizen and the police. It provides evidence of the areas of dissatisfaction with policing practice and performance that forms the basis for a relationship of reciprocity between citizens and State in a democratic country (Wright 2002).

What psychologists found about the pre-PACE primacy of interrogation in detecting offences

The Royal Commission on Criminal Procedure (1981) commissioned a series of research studies including one that examined the police role in the investigation of offences (Steer 1981). In a study of detectives in the Thames Valley Police, Steer found that the majority of offenders were detected in circumstances that did not involve the exercise of detective skills. Only 40 per cent of offenders were detected following an investigation and, of those, 17 per cent were one of a small group of people who could have committed the offence, 11 per cent were detected as a result of intelligence or forensic evidence such as a fingerprint, and an accomplice implicated 12 per cent during an interrogation. This points to the importance of interrogation in detecting offences. Mawby (1979) found that 40 per cent of detections were as a result of interviews with suspects arrested for a different offence. Bottomley and Coleman (1980) found that only 10 per cent of cases were detected as a result of intelligence or forensic evidence. The interrogation of suspects was clearly the most important means of detecting offences. In 1977 approximately 25 per cent of all detections were offences 'taken into consideration' by the courts for sentencing purposes that resulted from the questioning of someone arrested for other offences.[1]

In an observational study for the Royal Commission of how police interrogations were conducted in four police stations, Softley and his colleagues found that about 60 per cent of suspects made a full confession or a damaging admission (Softley 1981). In a similar study, Irving (1981) found that obtaining a confession was the main purpose of a police interrogation. In an examination of cases heard in the Crown Court, Baldwin and McConville found that 13 per cent would have failed to reach a *prima facie* level without confession evidence and another four per cent would probably have been acquitted. Where suspects had made statements to the police, half of them amounted to a full confession.

At this point in the history of criminal investigation in the United Kingdom, it would appear that the police role in detecting offences was primarily one of interrogation and less that of enquiry. To understand why a confession was so important it is necessary to consider the way in which various systems of justice operate.

A search for the truth or getting a conviction?

The adversarial system is not a search for the truth (Zander 1994a). Zander argues that

> the common law system has never made the search for the truth, as such, its highest aim. It is not that there is any objection to the truth emerging. But, centuries ago it was appreciated that the truth is many-sided, complex, and difficult to ascertain. Even when all the relevant evidence is admissible, we commonly do not know for sure whether the defendant was, or, was not, innocent or guilty. The common law system does not ask whether the defendant is guilty or innocent but rather the more manageable question – can it be proved beyond a reasonable doubt that he is guilty?

The Royal Commission on Criminal Procedure, 1993 addressed this issue. In an adversarial system, the judge is considered to be a neutral umpire who leaves the presentation of the case to the prosecution and defence who prepare their case, call, examine and cross examine witnesses.

The 'inquisitorial' system purports to be a search for the truth. Here, the judge is not neutral but will play a major part in the presentation of the evidence at the trial. It is the judge who calls and examines the defendant and the witnesses while the lawyers for the prosecution and defence can only ask supplementary questions.

The Royal Commission argued that, 'It is important not to overstate the differences between the two systems: all adversarial systems contain inquisitorial elements, and vice versa' (para.12). Over the last 100 years within adversarial systems of justice, it is the police who have developed the responsibility for discharging this inquisitorial function. The manner in which the product of the investigation is then dealt with in court led the Royal Commission to acknowledge,

> But, we do recognise the force of the criticisms which can turn a search for the truth into a contest played between opposing lawyers according to a set of rules which the jury does not necessarily accept or even understand (*op cit*).

The Commission was against the fusion of the functions of investigation and prosecution found in inquisitorial systems. It regarded as fundamental the principle that the prosecution in an adversarial system had to establish the guilt of the defendant beyond all reasonable doubt. The burden of proof lay with the prosecution. The court was not interested in the truth *per se*, it simply had to decide whether guilt had been established beyond all reasonable doubt. Given this context, it is not surprising that confession evidence assumed primacy and was relied upon too much.

Analysis of the police role indicates that it was aimed at successful prosecution of a suspect rather than an impartial investigation or a search for the truth. Getting a conviction largely depended on getting a suspect to confess. As the Police and Londoners Survey (*op cit*) had found, many Londoners believed that the police used force to obtain a confession or they fabricated it.

An independent prosecution service was created in 1986 as a result of the Prosecution of Offences Act 1985 so separating the role of investigation from that of prosecution.

Manipulating the paper reality

The way in which a prosecution case was prepared was examined by McConville *et al.* (1991) who argued that the investigation was not a search for the truth. The investigative process turned on the central role of interrogation. Custodial detention placed, and still places, the suspect in a hostile environment where custodial questioning takes place on police terms. Rarely would the suspect have the benefit of legal representation. Irving (1981), in his study of interrogations at Brighton police station, showed how the police could easily manipulate the decision making of suspects.

The US Supreme Court in the case of Miranda *v.* Arizona addressed the vulnerability of suspects facing custodial questioning. The Supreme Court considered custodial questioning to be inherently coercive and ensured that no statement made during police questioning and no evidence discovered as a result of that statement can be admitted in evidence at trial unless suspects are first warned of, among other things, their right to consult with and to have counsel present during questioning. If unable to afford a lawyer, one will be provided at public expense. Any waiver to the right has to be made explicitly by the suspect. The members of the Royal Commission on Criminal Procedure (1981) were clearly influenced by the Miranda rules and this was reflected in the proposals that they made for regulating custodial interviews in England and Wales. Their recommendations were included in the Police and Criminal Evidence Act 1984 and the Codes of Practice issued under Section 66.

Miscarriages of justice as a driver for change

Miscarriage of justice cases played a role in bringing about the Royal Commission on Criminal Procedure 1981. The government of the United Kingdom had been taken before the European Court of Human Rights by the government of Ireland in a landmark case in which it was alleged that suspects had been subjected to torture, cruel, inhuman and degrading treatment or punishment. It became known as the 'hooded men' case as the men were subjected to military interrogation practices.[2] The decision of the court that the men had experienced degrading treatment, led to a government inquiry into interrogation practices in Northern Ireland (Bennett 1979).

At about the same time, another government inquiry had examined the convictions of three youths for the murder of a male transvestite (Fisher 1977). All three youths had made admissions in the presence of their parent or guardian. Yet one of the youths was proved to have been attending a Salvation Army youth club at the time of death and so his confession was unreliable. The inquiry by a senior judge identified that all three youths had various forms of psychological vulnerabilities, indeed one youth had learning difficulties and had attended a special needs school. Irving, a psychologist, gave evidence to the inquiry drawing attention to these factors.

Although these cases led to the need for a Royal Commission on Criminal Procedure being identified, there has been a continuous stream of miscarriage of justice cases. Gudjonsson (2003) identifies 22 landmark British Court of Appeal cases as follows:

- 1989 Guildford Four
- 1991 Birmingham Six
- 1991 Tottenham Three
- 1992 Judith Ward
- 1992 Stefan Kiszko
- 1992 Jaqueline Fletcher
- 1992 UDR Four
- 1992 David MacKenzie
- 1992 Darvell Brothers
- 1992 Cardiff Three
- 1994 Idris Ali
- 1995 George Long
- 1997 Case of murder of Carl Bridgewater
- 1997 Patrick Keane
- 1997 Andrew Evans
- 1998 Derek Bentley
- 1999 John Roberts
- 1999 Ashley King
- 1999 Darren Hall
- 2000 Donald Pendleton
- 2000 Iain Hay Gordon
- 2001 Peter Fell[3]

Psychological evidence relating to suggestibility and compliance was considered seriously by the court in each of these cases. For example, in the recent case of Pendleton (2001) the House of Lords said,

> In light of these uncertainties and this fresh psychological evidence it is impossible to be sure that this conviction is safe, and that is so whether members of the House ask whether they themselves have reason to doubt the safety of the conviction or whether they ask whether the jury might have reached a different conclusion. (Gudjonsson 2003[4])

There is an increasing willingness for the courts to accept expert evidence from forensic psychologists such as Gudjonsson 'including that relating to' suggestibility and compliance.

The Police and Criminal Evidence Act 1984

When the Police and Criminal Evidence Act 1984 was implemented, it provided a legislative framework for the regulation of custodial questioning. Under Section 76 of PACE, it is no longer up to the defence to show that something had happened in the interrogation that would render the statement unreliable, it was up to the prosecution to show that nothing had happened to make the statement unreliable. Under Section 78 of the Act, the trial judge can exclude anything that is deemed 'unfair' such as deception by the interviewing officers or providing misleading information. In R. *v.* Heron the judge acquitted the defendant when, *inter alia,* the interviewing officers misled the accused regarding identification evidence in a homicide case.[5]

Section 66 of the Act provides for a Code of Practice. The codes are in the process of being revised but the extant codes cover four areas of police activity:

- the exercise by police officers of statutory powers of stop and search
- the searching of premises by police officers and the seizure of property found by police officers on persons or premises
- the detention, treatment and questioning of persons by police officers
- the identification of persons by police officers.

The Act entitled suspects to free legal advice and also provided for the tape recording of interviews with suspects.

The important contribution of technology to regulating custodial questioning

Early research into the quality of the police interviews, which was possible through the analysis of video and audio tape recordings, revealed that interviewing skills were generally poor. The interviewers appeared inept, nervous, ill at ease and lacking in confidence. Questioning was conducted on the basis of assumption of the suspect's guilt. Suspects were given very little opportunity to speak and when they did so, the interviewing officer(s) constantly interrupted them. The officers had a fragile grasp of the legal points needed to prove the offence. The interviewing style was harrying and aggressive. There were examples of unfair inducements (Baldwin 1992). This reflected a continuing over-reliance on confession evidence under the new legislation. The reliance on confession evidence also meant that witnesses and victims were frequently not interviewed thoroughly and so were unable to provide all the information they were capable of giving as evidence. The role of the police in the investigation of offences was still one of persuading suspects to confess rather than engaging in a process of inquiry, which was a search for the truth.

In an analysis of over 1,000 tape recorded interviews in London, Moston *et al.* (1992) found that there was a strong correlation between the strength of the evidence and the outcome of the interview (see Moston 1992). Where the evidence was weak, 77 per cent of suspects denied the allegation and where the evidence was strong, 67 per cent of suspects made admissions (Table 8 from Moston *et al*, reproduced below).

Table 3.1   Strength of evidence by interview outcome

	Strength of Evidence and Outcome of interview			
Strength of Evidence	No. of cases	% of admissions	% of denials	% neither admit nor deny
Weak	274	9.9	**76.6**	13.5
Moderate	363	36.4	45.2	18.5
Strong	430	**66.7**	16.3	17.0
Total cases	1067	–	–	–

(taken from Moston *et al.* (1992) Table 8)

Clearly, there was a need for a change of culture to meet the aspirations of the new legislation and to prevent challenges to the evidence obtained through questioning. This resulted in the creation of a national committee on investigative interviewing that involved police officers, lawyers and psychologists. The committee produced the Principles for Investigative Interviewing which were circulated to all police forces in Home Office circular 22/1992:

- The role of investigative interviewing is to obtain accurate and reliable information from suspects, witnesses or victims in order to discover the truth about matters under police investigation.

- Investigative interviewing should be approached with an open mind. Information obtained from the person who is being interviewed should always be tested against what the interviewing officer already knows or what can reasonably be established.

- When questioning anyone a police officer must act fairly in the circumstances of each individual case.

- The police interviewer is not bound to accept the first answer given. Questioning is not unfair merely because it is persistent.

- Even when the right of silence is exercised by a suspect, the police still have a right to put questions.

- When conducting an interview, police officers are free to ask questions in order to establish the truth, except for interviews with child victims of sexual or violent abuse which are to be used in criminal proceedings, they are not constrained by the rules applied to lawyers in court.

- Vulnerable people, whether victims, witnesses or suspects, must be treated with particular consideration at all times.

The circular marked the start of a very successful programme, which led to changing interviewer behaviour in the UK. A new national training programme was developed and this has now become a mandatory part of the curriculum for the training of all police officers. The Youth Justice and Criminal Evidence Act 1999 allows videotaping of interviews with vulnerable witnesses, which can then be used as evidence-in-chief. The Association of Chief Police Officers has conducted a national review of investigative interview training that will recommend further training to take place at five levels:

- recruit training
- detectives investigating volume crime
- detectives in serious crime
- specialist interviews (e.g. children)
- supervisors.

Effective representation for suspects at public expense has also contributed to a growth in professionalism. The Law Society has created training courses whilst an accreditation system for legal advisors has ensured that legal representation is of a good quality (Bridges and Choongh 1998).

The Police and Criminal Evidence Act provided various rights for detainees. They have the right to inform someone of their arrest (Section 5), and to consult privately with a legal representative (Section 6) which can only be waived with the authority of a Superintendent. This waiver only applies where there is fear of immediate harm, so in practice, it is rarely exercised; detainees have a right to access to the Codes of Practice. Custody officers dealing with their detention must provide a written notice of their rights. They must be informed of the grounds for their detention.

The codes also contain provision for special groups of detainees. Interpreters must be provided for those who only speak a foreign language or are deaf. Juvenile detainees must have a parent or guardian informed of their detention. Detainees with a mental handicap have the right to have someone who is experienced in dealing with learning difficulties called an 'Appropriate Adult' attend the interview in addition to the person providing legal advice.

The conditions under which detainees are held are also regulated. There must only be one person per heated, cleaned and ventilated cell, which must have light. There must be access to washing and toilet facilities. Detainees must be provided with two light meals and one main meal per day. Dietary and religious needs must be observed. Detention is a documented process and complaints and requests for medical attention and medicines are to be recorded and actioned.

The duration for which the police can detain a person is strictly regulated. A detained person can make representation to an Inspector regarding detention for more than eight hours and to a Superintendent after 24 hours. Suspects can only be detained after 72 hours on the order of a Magistrates Court. They must be charged as soon as the police have sufficient evidence to prosecute. There must be no further questioning after charge.

Disclosure of prosecution evidence

The government has introduced legislation covering disclosure by the prosecution of all material collected during the course of the inquiry. This has provided a new level of openness and accountability subjecting the investigation process to new levels of scrutiny. The Criminal Procedure and Investigations Act 1996 (Section 23) provides the basis for the disclosure of material gathered during the course of an investigation. Primary prosecution disclosure involves material in the possession of the prosecution, which might undermine the case against the accused. Secondary prosecution disclosure involves material which might assist in a defence disclosed in a defence statement. The prosecution can make application to the court for the agreement not to disclose sensitive material, such as the identity of an informant. The disclosure process works by separating the roles of the Senior Investigating Officer from that of the disclosure officer. The Investigating Officer is required to follow all lines of enquiry whether they point to or away from the suspect.

All information obtained during an investigation must be recorded. This includes negative information, for example the number of people in a particular place at a particular time who said that they saw nothing. There is a duty to retain all material including that casting doubt on the reliability of a confession or on the reliability of a witness. All material is to be listed in a Schedule of Non-sensitive material.

Criminal Cases Review Commission

The Criminal Appeal Act 1995 created the Criminal Cases Review Commission whose function is to review all allegations of miscarriages of justice. So far, over 100 cases have been referred to the Court of Appeal. The Commission has reviewed over 4,000 cases and currently has 450 cases under review. A similar review commission has been established in Scotland.

Safer UK justice?

It is argued that the combined effect of the Police and Criminal Evidence Act 1984 with the codes of practice, the introduction of an independent Crown Prosecution Service, legal representation for suspects at public expense, disclosure and the introduction of the Criminal Cases Review Commission should lead to safer criminal justice in the UK and to fewer miscarriages of justice. A recent Parliamentary Home Affairs Select Committee has examined the conduct of investigations into past cases of abuse in children's homes. It dealt with allegations of physical and sexual abuse when the adult complainants were children resident in the homes. It was not within the remit of the Committee to examine individual cases, but a large number had been drawn to its attention. It concluded, 'We share the general view that a significant number of miscarriages of justice have occurred' (HASC 2002, para.1.35). They were particularly concerned that the interviews with complainants had not been recorded. They also found that the test for referring alleged miscarriages to the Court of Appeal was too narrow as the legislation required that there had to be new evidence. They recommended that the test should be broadened, in line with the Scottish Criminal Review Commission, to make a referral where the Commission believed that a miscarriage of justice may have occurred. In the evidence of one solicitor specialising in such cases, 'in excess of 100 care workers and teachers have been wrongly convicted' (Saltrese, p. Ev.105 Home Affairs Select Committee 2002). Safer justice? Yes, for some. A total of 21 recommendations was made by the Select Committee to plug the loopholes in legislation that the inquiry had uncovered.

Miscarriages of justice in the United States of America

Using the English system as a template and applying it to the justice system in the United States, it will be seen that similar lessons can be learned from a study of miscarriages of justice in that country.

The United States has a federal constitution and so there is no equivalent of PACE covering the whole of the country. Laws relating to investigation, where they exist, are passed at the local or State level. The American constitution guarantees its citizens certain rights. The US Supreme Court set out in Miranda *v.* Arizona the rights of citizens who were being questioned by the police. This includes the right to legal representation. However since Miranda, the US Supreme Court has consistently watered down the rights articulated therein. In Gideon *v.* Wainwright, under the Sixth Amendment to the Constitution, indigent defendants have a right to a lawyer to provide 'effective assistance' in trials for serious offences. Effective assistance has been considered by the courts to include lawyers who are drunk, asleep, on drugs, or who in capital cases were unable to name a single Supreme Court decision on the death penalty (Cole 1999: 88/96; Scheck, Neufeld and Dwyer 2000: 183/192).

The US government spends $97.56 billion on the criminal justice system of which 50 per cent is spent on the police and prosecution and only 1.3 per cent on indigent defence. Eighty per cent of all defendants are indigent. In Griffin *v.* Illinois 1956 the defendant could not pay for a transcript in order to prepare his appeal. This was considered to be a denial of his right to indigent defence. However the right to indigent defence now only applies after formal proceedings have begun and the encounter is at a critical stage. It does not relate to pre-charge questioning. There is no provision on post-conviction proceedings even in death penalty cases (Pennsylvania *v.* Finlay (1987) 481. US 51). There has until recently been no provision for defendants with learning difficulties although this may have changed as a result of a Supreme Court decision in June 2002.

The standards of 'effective defence' can be gauged from death penalty cases in the State of Alabama. Death penalty cases last four days on average and the death penalty phase only 3.5 hours. In Schlup *v.* Delo (1995) 115 S. Ct. 851 the trial lasted two days. The lawyer spent a total of 75 minutes with his client, who was convicted. A review found that there was a videotape of the defendant in a café when the homicide occurred and there were 20 witnesses to this, whom the lawyer had failed to interview. It is particularly worrying that procedural faults of this kind and omissions of the defence lawyer are visited on their clients. Many of the American miscarriage of justice cases have been identified through the work of Death Penalty Resource Centres and Innocence Projects. However in 1995, Congress cut off the funding for Death Penalty Resource Centres ostensibly because they were 'too effective'. Good representation is possible in the US but it is based on class and income. This class based disparity falls disproportionately on minorities because they are the poorest.

Race and the death penalty

In 1972 the Supreme Court declared the death penalty unconstitutional because it was 'arbitrary and capricious.' This was reversed in 1976 reflecting widespread public support for the death penalty. Between 1976 and 1998 six white men were executed for killing black victims whereas 115 black men were executed for killing white victims. In a study by Baldus *et al.* (1994) of 2,000 murder cases in Georgia it was found that where the attack had been by a black person on a white person the death penalty was given in 22 per cent of cases but where the attack was by a white person on a black person the death penalty was give in only three per cent of cases. The United States government conducted a review of 28 death penalty studies. It concluded that in 82 per cent of cases the race of the victim was related to the death penalty.[6]

In McClesky *v.* Kemp (1987) 481 US 279.327, it was argued that the strong statistical evidence of racial bias in death penalty cases should lead to the abolition of the death penalty. The court said that the statistical evidence on its own was not sufficient and that there would have to be an admission of racial bias. Clearly this was unlikely to occur. However the court did concede that the statistics represent a 'challenge to the validity of capital punishment in a multi-cultural society', but considered that this issue was best addressed by legislation.

There are now at least 110 people who were on death row who have been released and totally exonerated as a result of new DNA forensic evidence showing that they could not have committed the offence. In April 2002, Governor Ryan of the State of Illinois published the Report of a Committee, which he established to review the death penalty in Illinois. It found that almost half of the defendants should not have been convicted. The commission made a total of 80 recommendations including the creation of a state-wide panel to review prosecutor requests for the death penalty; banning death sentences on the mentally retarded (sic.); significantly reducing the number of death eligibility factors; videotaping interrogations of homicide suspects; and controlling the use of jail house informants. The members of the committee were split over the issue of abolition of the death penalty but made a series of recommendations which they argued would make the death penalty safer and be applied more scrupulously. In Illinois and a number of other States, there is currently a moratorium on the use of the death penalty. At present, there are at least 83 people on death row for homicides committed when they were juveniles.

On examination of these miscarriage of justice cases where the defendants in 74 cases are actually innocent, the main contributory factors appear to be:

- 81 per cent mistaken ID
- 69 per cent 'junk' forensic science
- 50 per cent police misconduct
- 45 per cent misconduct by prosecutor
- 22 per cent false confessions
- 20 per cent false witnesses
- 19 per cent informants.

(Scheck, Neufeld and Dwyer 2000: 361)

Although 'junk' science was a factor in the Court of Appeal decision in the case of the Birmingham Six, there has been much less criticism of forensic science in Britain than in the USA. In England, the forensic science laboratories have been removed from the control of the police and are now a stand-alone government agency.

USA and UK similarities and differences

The political debates on criminal justice in both countries appears to be becoming more punitive and less tolerant. This constrains what politicians and elected officials can achieve through reform of the existing system. This is particularly true in the United States where judges, prosecutors and senior law enforcement officials are elected and so reflect public attitudes to punishment. There are fewer opportunities for ethical leadership.

The response in Britain to miscarriages of justice has been through legislation to put in place a rigorous regulatory regime, which has been strictly enforced by the judges. Technology has been adopted to ensure that custodial questioning is open, transparent and that what is said during questioning is said freely and recorded accurately. In the USA, reaction to miscarriages of justice is still in the denial phase and has not yet created the pressure necessary for reform.

In the United States, the laboratories are mainly under the control of law enforcement agencies.

Within the US Federal Constitution, there is no means of providing national legislation or delivering training to improve investigative standards to a national standard.

In the US, there is an absence of public high profile champions for change.

The retention by the US of the death penalty marks a significant difference between the two jurisdictions. Had Britain retained the death penalty, there is little doubt that the Guildford Four, the Birmingham Six and Judith Ward would probably have been executed. The lack of safeguards in the criminal justice system presents powerful evidence for abolition of the death penalty, a step that had been taken by the end of 2000 by 75 countries and territories. A further 13 countries had abolished it for all but exceptional crimes such as wartime crimes. At least 20 countries were abolitionist in practice: they had not carried out any executions for the past ten years or more and were believed to have an established practice of not carrying out executions. Commenting on a scheduled execution in Virginia, USA, Guiliano Amato, Prime Minister of Italy, said on 14 September 2000:

> The death penalty is disgusting, particularly if it condemns an innocent. But it remains an injustice even when it falls on someone who is guilty of a crime (Amnesty International: 14). According to Amnesty International, in 2000 there were 85 judicial executions in the USA. (Amnesty International 2001: 15)

Conclusions: minimising miscarriages of justice – opportunities for forensic psychologists

There would appear to be a number of steps that societies can take in order to minimise miscarriages of justice. Good pre-trial investigation and custodial questioning processes will reduce the over-reliance on confession evidence and encourage a search for the truth. Making better use of forensic evidence and more thorough questioning of victims and witnesses to enable them to give their best evidence will be more likely to enable courts to reach the truth. Greater sensitivity in interviewing those who are vulnerable would prevent many future miscarriages of justice. Quality legal representation for accused at public expense and disclosure of prosecution evidence are important safeguards. Formal systems for reviewing alleged miscarriages of justice are an important investment. Independent status for forensic science laboratories should prevent some of the 'junk' science that has been a feature in miscarriage of justice cases. Given the propensity for error in adversarial systems of justice, it is important to continue challenging the validity of capital punishment. There needs to be greater recognition that truth and justice suffer when criminal justice systems become too adversarial. As Stephenson (1992) identified, many of the current systems are fundamentally flawed. This should provide an incentive and broad range of opportunities for forensic psychologists to continue to identify the weaknesses and propose reform based on scientific research of the kind that has been so valuable in minimising miscarriages of justice. Much has been achieved which could be adopted as international best practice. Much remains to be done.

Notes

1   See Simmons, Jon (2002) Crime in England and Wales 2001/2002, Table 8.02 showing the current level to be 13 per cent.
2   Ireland *v.* United Kingdom 1978 2 EHRR 25.
3   Presentation to Wrongful Convictions conference, the Criminal Justice Institute, Harvard Law School, 19 April 2002.
4   Gudjonsson (2003) provides a comprehensive analysis of the cases listed above. See also Mullin, C. (1990) *Error of Judgement: The truth about the Birmingham bombings.* Revised Edition Dublin: Poolbeg and Victory, P. (2002) *Justice and Truth. The Guildford Four and Maguire Seven.* London: Sinclair-Stevenson.
5   Unreported, Leeds Crown Court 18 October 1993.
6   U.S. Gen. Accounting Office, *Death Penalty Sentencing: Research indicates pattern of racial disparities,* 6 (1990).

References

Amnesty International (2001) *Annual Report for 2001.* London: Amnesty International Publications.
Baldus, D.C., Woodworth, G. and Pulaski, C.A. Jr. (1994) *Reflections on the 'Inevitability' of Racial Discrimination in Capital Sentencing and the 'Impossibility' of its Prevention, Detection and Correction.* 51 Wash. and Lee L. Rev. 359.386 n.115 (1994).

Baldwin, J. and McConville, M. (1981) *Confessions in Crown Court Trials*. Research Study No 5 Royal Commission on Criminal Procedure (1981). Cmnd 8092 London: HMSO.

Baldwin, J. (1992) *Video taping police interviews with suspects – an evaluation*. Police Research Series Paper 1. London: The Home Office.

Bennett, H.G., Q.C. (1979) *Report of the Committee of Inquiry into Police Interrogation Procedures in Northern Ireland*. Cmnd 7497 London: HMSO.

Bottomley, A.K. and Coleman, C.A. (1980) 'Police effectiveness and the public: the limitations of official crime rates', in R.V.G. Clarke and J.M. Hough (eds) *The Effectiveness of Policing (1980)*. Farnborough: Gower.

Bridges, L. and Choongh, C. (1998) *Improving Police Station Legal Advice*. London: Jointly by Legal Aid Board and Law Society.

Cole, D. (1999) *No Equal Justice. Race and class in the American criminal justice system*. New York: The New Press.

Fisher, H., Sir (1977) *Report of an Inquiry by the Hon. Sir Henry Fisher into the circumstances leading to the trial of three persons on charges arising out of the death of Maxwell Confait and the fire at 27, Doggett Road, London SE6*. London: HMSO.

Gudjonsson, G.H. (2003) *The Psychology of Interrogations and Confessions. A handbook*. Chichester: Wiley.

Home Affairs Select Committee (2002) *The conduct of investigations into past cases of abuse in children's homes*. HC 8361 London: House of Commons.

Irving, B. (1981) *Police interrogation. A case study of current practice*. Research Study No 2 Royal Commission on Criminal Procedure (1981) Cmnd 8092. London: HMSO.

Jones, T., MacLean, B. and Young, J. (1986) *The Islington Crime Survey, Crime Victimization and Policing in Inner-City London*. London: Gower.

Macpherson of Cluny, Sir W. (1999) *The Stephen Lawrence Inquiry*, Cm 4262-1. London: HMSO.

Mawby, R. (1979) *Policing the City*. Farnborough: Saxon House.

McConville, M., Sanders, A. and Leng, R. (1991) *The Case for the Prosecution: Police suspects and the construction of criminality*. London: Routledge.

Moston, S., Stephenson, G.M. and Williamson Thomas, M. (1992) The effects of case characteristics on suspect behaviour during police questioning. *British Journal of Criminology*, 32 (1): Winter 1992.

Mullin, C. (1990) *Error of Judgement. The truth about the Birmingham Bombings*. Dublin: Poolbeg.

Philips, C., Sir (1981) *The Royal Commission on Criminal Procedure*. Cmnd 8092. London. HMSO.

Runciman, Viscount, of Doxford, CBE. FBA (1993) *The Royal Commission on Criminal Justice*. Cm 2263. London. HMSO.

Ryan, G.H. (2002) *The Governor's Commission on Capital Punishment*. Office of the Governor, State of Illinois, USA (www.idoc.state.il.us/ccp).

Scheck, B., Neufeld, P. and Dwyer, J. (2000) *Actual Innocence. Five days to execution, and other dispatches from the wrongly convicted*. New York. Doubleday.

Simmons, J. (2002) *Crime in England and Wales 2001/2002*. Home Office Statistical Bulletin. London: Home Office.

Smith, D.J. (1983) *Police and People in London. I. A survey of Londoners*. London: Policy Studies Institute.

Smith, D.J. and Gray, J. (1983) *Police and People in London. IV. The police in action*. London: Policy Studies Institute.

Softley, P. (1981) *Police Interrogation: an observational study in four police stations*. Research Study No 4 *Royal Commission on Criminal Procedure* (1981). Cmnd 8092. London: HMSO.

Steer, D. (1981) *Uncovering Crime: the police role*. Research Study No 7 Royal Commission on Criminal Procedure (1981) Cmnd 8092. London: HMSO.

Stephenson, G.M. (1992) *The Psychology of Criminal Justice*. Oxford. Blackwell.

Wright, A. (2002) *Policing: An introduction to concepts and practice*. Cullompton: Willan.

Zander, M. (1994) 'Ethics and crime investigation by the police', *Policing*, 10 (1).

Chapter 4

The interpretation and utilisation of offender profiles: a critical review of 'traditional' approaches to profiling

Laurence Alison and Emma Barrett,
Birmingham University

Acknowledgements

Support for the preparation of this chapter was provided by Economic and Social Research Council Grant PTA-030-2002-00482 awarded to the second author.

In this chapter one of the most prominent approaches to constructing 'offender profiles' is reviewed and the social psychological reasons for its continued but, we argue, largely unwarranted, popularity are explored. It is important to emphasise at the outset that this review considers the type of profiling that has been most prominent in the last decade and has attracted the most media attention. The profiling we review involves the extrapolation of lists of characteristics of offenders, based upon an evaluation of a 'type' of offender as derived from a profiler visiting a crime scene. Hereafter, we refer to this as the 'traditionalist' perspective. Other recent papers consider the many positive steps forward in behavioural investigative advice (Alison, West and Goodwill in press; Bennell and Canter 2002; Fritzon and Ridgway 2001; Keppel and Weis 1993) but we do not concentrate on this activity here. The interested reader will find that these and a number of other papers highlight different approaches to the provision of advice, recognising the need for systematic research, justification of the claims made and the requisite ethical standards. Indeed, recent ACPO (Association of Chief Police Officers) requirements in the UK (ACPO 2000) have resulted in significant restrictions on the way in which advice is provided to and employed by the police, thereby making traditional profiling methods more and more difficult to apply in practice. Why then is it important to review a form of profiling that is probably in 'recession'?

Firstly, in the mind of the public, and, indeed, many practitioners, profiling is typically associated with an approach in which typologies of offenders are derived from observations of a crime scene (Douglas, Ressler, Burgess and Hartman 1986). Yet there is, as we show, a lack of evidence for the utility of this type of advice, as well as a host of theoretical reasons why it is likely to prove unproductive (Alison, Bennell, Mokros and Ormerod 2002). In this chapter we consider why such profiles nevertheless hold so much appeal for police and public alike. Canter and Youngs (in press) have termed this the 'Hollywood effect' and it is clear that its seduction extends to students who are eager to learn about profiling. We therefore hope that this chapter will serve as a 'reality check' for students who might otherwise hold unrealistic views both of the present state of profiling, and of what is taught on forensic and investigative psychology courses.

Secondly, we suggest that much of the advice contained within traditional perspectives is ambiguous, unverifiable and contains many erroneous 'lay' beliefs about the consistency of human behaviour and the ability to classify individuals into discrete 'types' (Alison, Smith, Eastman and Rainbow 2002). As such, it affords us the opportunity to highlight some interesting psychological phenomena that relate to the way in which individuals perceive human behaviour.

Finally, enquiries in which profiles are sought are, by definition, serious and complicated cases. When faced with complex and ambiguous investigative data, investigators tend to engage in the generation of one or more narratives to make sense of the data (Innes 2002). We suggest that profiles, by offering plausible 'explanations' of an offender's actions by reference to the supposed psychological aetiology of such behaviour, and by providing otherwise elusive hints as to an offender's characteristics, help to fill important gaps in these narratives. Furthermore, these explanations and hints are particularly compelling because they tend to be consistent with generally held beliefs about behavioural consistency and the lay perception that behaviour can be explained by reference to types, despite the empirical evidence that context has a strong impact upon behaviour (Cervone and Shoda 1999). The creative interpretation of a profile may thus lead to a more favourable assessment of ambiguous, unverifiable and potentially erroneous accounts than is warranted by the evidence (Alison, Smith and Morgan 2002). We further suggest that lay beliefs concerning the 'types' of offenders, their motivations and behaviours, may be highly influential in many other decisions in criminal investigations. The content and structure of such beliefs is therefore an appropriate and important area for further psychological enquiry.

The plausibility of traditional approaches to offender profiling

Offender/behavioural/investigative/criminal profiling has variously been referred to as '... a technique for identifying the major personality and behavioural characteristics of an individual based upon an analysis of the crimes he or she has committed' (Douglas, Ressler, Burgess and Hartman 1986: 405); the '... process of inferring distinctive personality characteristics of individuals responsible for committing criminal acts' (Turvey 1999: 1) where, according to Pinizzotto and Finkel (1990), an offender profile '... focuses attention on individuals with personality traits that parallel traits of others who have committed similar offences' (p. 216) and where the '... interpretation of crime scene evidence can indicate the personality type of the individual(s) who committed the offence' (Rossmo 2000: 68). According to Douglas, Burgess, Burgess and Ressler 1992, 'The crime scene is presumed to reflect the murderer's behavior and personality in much the same way as furnishings reveal the homeowner's character' (p. 21).

However, as Alison, Bennell, Mokros and Ormerod (2002) have pointed out, the concept that reliable 'personality traits' of an offender(s) are based on observations of a crime scene is at odds with contemporary conceptualisations of personality and behaviour, where, in contrast, behaviour is explained in terms of conditional patterns that depend on the individual and his or her specific situation (Shoda, Mischel and Wright 1994).

Assumptions underlying traditional approaches to profiling

Some of the most widely recognised and oft-employed experts in the USA, the UK and several other European countries have previously made claims that clusters of behaviours can be derived from crime scenes and converted into some taxonomic framework. Further, from this classification, background characteristics may be derived (Åsgard 1996; Boon 1997; Britton 1997; Douglas, Burgess, Burgess and Ressler 1992; Douglas et al. 1986). It has been argued that the inferential process can be represented in the question series, 'What to Why to Who'? (Pinizzotto and Finkel 1990). Based on the crime scene material (What), a particular motivation for the offence behaviour is attributed to the perpetrator (Why). This, in turn, leads to the description of the perpetrator's likely characteristics (Who). This simple 'What to Why to Who' inference assumes that the supposed specific motivations that drive the initiation of the offence are consistently associated with specific types of background characteristics of the offender (e.g., '… if motivation X then characteristics A, B, C and D').

The idea of inferring background characteristics from crime scene actions relies on two central assumptions about offence behaviour. The first is the assumption of *behavioural consistency:* the variance in the crimes of serial offenders must be smaller than the variance occurring in a random comparison of different offenders. This is exemplified in the definitions of profiling outlined at the outset of this paper and in statements such as 'profiling rests on the assumption that at least certain offenders have consistent behavioural traits. This consistency is thought to persist from crime to crime and also to affect various non-criminal aspects of their personality and lifestyle, thus making them, to some extent, identifiable' (Homant and Kennedy 1998: 328). Similarly, the traditional view of personality dispositions leads to the assumption that, 'individuals are characterised by stable and broadly generalised dispositions that endure over long periods of time and that generate consistencies in their social behaviour across a wide range of situations' (Mischel 1990: 112).

However, as Mischel (1968) points out, there is little evidence to support this notion. As long ago as 1928, a number of studies examining behavioural consistency (tested by observing people's social behaviour as it occurred across a variety of natural settings) demonstrated that inter-correlations among behaviours comprising a particular trait concept tend to be low (Dudycha 1936; Hartshorne and May 1928; Newcomb 1929). This led many theorists to question not only popular trait theories (e.g., Mischel 1968; Peterson 1968; Vernon 1964), but the concept of personality itself (Epstein 1979). More recently, studies such as the often-cited Carleton College study also failed to allow predictions of behaviour across specific situations (Mischel and Peake 1982).

In terms of consistency in offence behaviour, a number of studies have revealed some evidence, albeit rather weak in most cases, that offenders are somewhat consistent. Most of this research has been conducted on samples of rapists (Bennell 1998; Grubin, Kelly and Ayis 1997; Mokros 2002) although there is also some evidence of behavioural consistency in other offences such as domestic burglary (Goodwill 2000). What is most revealing about these studies though is the finding that individual behaviours are subject to some fluctuation from crime to crime, due, perhaps, as many of the authors argue, to situational influences and the dynamic features of reoffending. The most significant aspect of behavioural consistency appears to relate to location, with proximity being the most effective element for linking and the actual behaviours occurring within the crime the least effective.

The second assumption is the *homology assumption* (Mokros and Alison 2002). In its most basic form, the assumption is that the more similar two offenders are in terms of characteristics, the more similar their behavioural style during the commission of the offence. Thus, two rapists who are, for example, both married, have pre-convictions for robbery and a history of alcohol abuse should be more likely to commit an offence in the same way than if their offence style was compared to an offender who is unmarried, has no pre-convictions and no history of alcohol abuse.

Davies, Wittebrood and Jackson (1998) had some success in linking specific actions to particular characteristics. For example, they found that rapists who break into a victim's house are five times more likely to have a previous conviction for burglary than those who do not enter a victim's house by force. However, Davies *et al.*'s attempt to integrate sets of crime scene variables into logistic regression models in order to predict the characteristics of rapists was unsuccessful. Similarly, House (1997) generated four thematic foci (*aggression, criminality, pseudo-intimacy* and *sadism*) from a sample of 50 rapists and, whilst achieving some success in linking particular behaviours to particular actions, was unable to develop lists of probable characteristics (specifically pre-convictions) of offenders based on the thematic foci. Neither study tested whether particular configurations of crime scene actions are associated with particular configurations of characteristics other than pre-convictions.

In Knight *et al.*'s (1998) clinically orientated classification scheme (the Massachusetts Treatment Center Rapist Typology Version 3; MTC:R3), typologies are derived on the basis of primary motivations. Motivations include *opportunity, pervasive anger, sexual gratification* and *vindictiveness*. These are further differentiated through the degree of social competence and the amount of sadism implicit in the offence. Whilst these have been used productively for clinical interventions, Knight *et al.* concede that one of these data sets contains, 'extensive coding of crime-scene in-formation but minimal offender data', while the other one comprises 'extensive offender data but minimal crime-scene data' (Knight *et al.* 1998: 46). So, for clinical reasons and as a result of its focus on motivation, the taxonomy does not consider the types of characteristics commonly outlined in offender profiles. For example, it does not link actions to age, socio-demographic status or previous convictions – all characteristics that are most likely to be of use in actual investigations (Annon 1995; Ault and Reese 1980; Grubin 1995; Homant and Kennedy 1998).

In an attempt to investigate the homology assumption, Mokros and Alison conducted a study on a sample of rapists ($N = 100$), for whom they had access to details both of the behaviours in the offence and the background characteristics of offenders. In terms of support for the homology assumption, results were not encouraging: neither age, socio-demographic features, nor previous convictions could be reliably linked to themes within offence behaviour.

In summary, there seems to be little evidence for the consistency and homology assumptions. Why, then, does 'offender profiling' in this form appear to enjoy such public and investigative attention?

The interpretation of profiles

Evaluations of offender profiling have commonly focused on police officers' claims of satisfaction with the advice received (Britton 1992; Copson 1995; Douglas 1981; Goldblatt 1992; Jackson, Van Koppen and Herbrink 1993). These reviews concluded that there was some perceived utility in using such reports but that they rarely led to the identification of the offender.

In a US study, Pinizzotto (1984) examined 192 profiled cases, 88 of which had been solved. Of these, a profile was perceived to have helped in the identification of a suspect in 15 cases (17 per cent). In a number of other cases, the responding agencies reported that profiling helped to focus the investigation or to locate or prosecute a suspect. Over a decade later, Bartol (1996) conducted a survey of 152 police psychologists. In this study, 70 per cent of the police psychologists did not feel comfortable with profiling and seriously questioned its validity and usefulness. Another study examined UK police officers' perceptions of usefulness of profiles and found that fewer than a quarter were judged as being of any assistance in solving the case, and profiles were perceived as opening new lines of enquiry in fewer than one in five cases (Copson 1995). Despite this, in over 60 per cent of cases, profiles were perceived as furthering officers' understanding of the offender and in over half of the cases, they reassured the officers' own judgements about the offender. There is, therefore, mixed evidence from these studies: whilst police officers may not regard profiling as crucial to their investigations, a large number appear to find the advice of profilers useful.

Alison, Smith and Morgan (2002) have argued that a contributory factor in the perception of usefulness of traditional profiles, despite evidence to the contrary, concerns the psychological processes involved in interpreting the information. Even when the identity of an offender is unambiguously determined, there exists a distinctly subjective element in deciding how well any given person fits an offender profile. In a recent small-scale study of 21 profiles, drawn from the last decade, Alison, Smith, Eastman and Rainbow (2002) demonstrated that 24 per cent of the profiling predictions were ambiguous and open to subjective interpretation (such as, 'the offender will have poor heterosocial skills'). Further, 55 per cent of statements in profiles would be extremely difficult to verify, even if the offender was caught (for instance, 'the offender will have fantasised about the act in the weeks leading up to offence'). They suggested that one of the possible dangers of such ambiguous and unverifiable information is that it facilitates 'creative interpretation' on the part of the investigator.

To explore this notion, Alison *et al.* conducted two pilot studies. Participants included police officers, individuals involved in the legal profession and forensic clinicians. The participants in the first study were all police officers. A profile was constructed that contained ambiguous and unverifiable information and was provided to participants who were to imagine that they were investigating a murder. Participants were given details of an actual offence,[1] the constructed profile and a suspect. Two groups of participants each received the same profile but different suspects. In one group, participants received a brief outline of the actual offender (genuine suspect), whilst in the other group participants were given a hypothetical suspect constructed for the study (bogus). The bogus suspect was constructed so as to be quite different on key demographic features whilst still enabling him to be a possible suspect (the suspect had to be male and of an age where it was physically possible to have committed the offence). Participants were asked to rate the accuracy of the profile based on the suspect that they were given. Despite being given quite different suspects (one was twice as old as the other; one had many pre-convictions, the other none, one had a history of psychiatric problems, the other did not, etc.), the mean accuracy rating for both groups was 5.3 (where 1 = very inaccurate, and 7 = very accurate). The median for both groups was 6; the mode for the genuine suspect was 5, and for the bogus suspect it was 6. Over 40 per cent (nine of the 22) of the 'genuine' group rated the profile as a generally-very accurate fit, whilst just over 50 per cent (13 of the 24) in the 'bogus' group rated the profile as generally-very accurate. None of the participants rated the profile as either generally or very inaccurate. Alison *et al.* also examined the qualitative justifications for the scores given. One group focused on relationship issues and the offender's sexuality (as mentioned in the profile), whilst relationship issues and the motivation of the offender appeared to justify scores given in the other group.

In a second exploratory study, based on police officers and individuals involved in the legal profession, Alison *et al.* employed a profile used in an actual enquiry. In this study, they also asked whether the profile would be useful in an enquiry. Twenty-nine of the 33 participants in study two stated that the profile would be useful if they were investigating the crime, with the most common justification relating to the idea that the profile could narrow down a suspect search. Using a similar design (two suspects: one bogus, one genuine, different demographic features in each) overall mean accuracy scores were 5.4 for the genuine offender and 5.2 for the fabricated offender with no differences between ratings for the two contrasting suspects.

Both studies indicated that the majority of participants rated the profile as at least somewhat accurate despite the distinctly different suspects that they were given. Of course, there are many limitations of this type of study, including the questionable ecological validity of paper and pencil tests of this sort, the fact that there is a non difference between groups, the relatively low numbers in each group and so on. However, Alison *et al.* argue that these preliminary studies highlight the need to conduct further research to test more comprehensively the hypothesis that participants were selectively noting aspects of the profile that can be easily applied to the suspect, ignoring those aspects that are not applicable, and constructing meaning from ambiguity. If this is the case, then such 'creative interpretation' of ambiguous information is reminiscent of the so-called 'Barnum Effect' in which people tend to accept vague and general personality descriptions as being specific to themselves (Forer 1949; Furnham and Schofield 1987; Meehl 1956).

Previous research has examined the role of the Barnum Effect in how individuals interpret feedback from psychometric tests, horoscopes, as well as handwriting analysis (Dickson and Kelly 1985; Fichter and Sunerton 1983; Snyder, Larsen and Bloom 1976). The effect is particularly prominent when the information provided is ambiguous, vague, difficult to verify yet comes from an authoritative source. This effect, and the closely related process of 'personal validation', in which individuals classify information that could be applied to anyone as being particularly descriptive of their own qualities, has much in common with processes of attribution theory (Ross 1977); the notion of scripts and schemas (Schank and Abelson 1977, 1995) and narrative approaches to personality (McAdams 1993). In each case, researchers argue that in attempting to make the world more predictable, individuals rely on pre-existing, case-based experiences when interpreting new information. Incoming information is thus structured according to familiar patterns and beliefs that have been informed by personal experiences, social cultural norms and the media, and which include beliefs about the regularity of human behaviour. Beyond the application of these processes to profiling, we believe that such issues may be of significance to the wider arena of investigative decision-making.

Thus far, our studies have focused on the use of traditional profiles in isolation, as one particular source of information available to investigators engaged in a complex criminal investigation. However, we believe that similar processes are at work as investigators attempt to make sense of a whole range of complex, ambiguous and incomplete information in the course of their enquiries. In the following section, we present evidence from a range of psychological research dealing with the cognitive mechanisms by which individuals deal with complex information. This evidence indicates that the general mechanism by which individuals make sense of such information, in particular social information, is one of story generation. The creative interpretation of offender profiles by investigators may be a specific application of a more general story generation mechanism, employed as a heuristic strategy for dealing with ambiguous and complex information.

The process of investigation

The idea that people use stories both to store and to explain information about the world has received much attention from researchers in a variety of fields, including cognition (e.g. Schank and Abelson 1995), social psychology (e.g. Read 1987; Wyer and Radvansky 1999) and personality psychology (e.g. McAdams 1993). The discussion here is largely confined to the notion of story generation as a cognitive heuristic employed when attempting to comprehend an otherwise confusing situation.

Schank and Abelson, in an update and extension to their seminal work on scripts, suggest that stories, by which they mean stereotypical event-based scripts that involve purposeful actors and incorporate notions of causality, intention and outcomes, are the fundamental building blocks of human knowledge and memory (Schank and Abelson 1977, 1995). Furthermore, they argue that story-based knowledge provides a template for individual decision-making and action: the process of 'understanding' a situation is a process of matching features of an ongoing situation with an old story in long term memory. Thus, an individual's repertoire of stories guides their understanding and consequent action in a particular environment.

The 'knowledge-as-stories' theory has considerable and long-established empirical support. For instance, Bartlett's classic studies on the nature of remembering demonstrated that individuals appear better able to recall information that is organised as a narrative with a clear plot compared to descriptive information without a story-like structure (Bartlett 1932). Since Bartlett, a number of other studies have demonstrated similar results. For example, Graesser and his colleagues found that narrative texts were read twice as fast as expository texts, yet facts in them were recalled twice as well (Graesser and Ottati 1995). Results such as these lend support to the idea that stories are a natural basis for memory and understanding.

The suggestion that individuals construct stories as a means of understanding a situation has also received support from the study of Naturalistic Decision Making (NDM), an area of research concerned with the ways in which individuals and teams use their experience to make meaningful decisions in dynamic, uncertain and often time-pressured situations (Zsambok 1997). According to one of the most prominent and widely tested NDM models, Klein's Recognition-Primed Decision Model, when tackling complex and ambiguous problems, a decision maker engages in story building to create a mental representation of the problem situation, drawing on existing case-specific, domain-specific and general knowledge from long term memory, and integrating it with perceived information (Klein 1999). This theory has much in common with constructionist approaches to discourse comprehension (e.g. Graesser, Mills and Zwaan 1997) that also deal with the comprehender's attempt to construct meaningful, coherent mental representations from relatively sparse perceived information.

Much of the work of NDM researchers has focused on decision making and problem solving in fields such as fire-fighting (e.g. Klein 1999), military command and control (e.g. Pascual and Henderson 1997) or piloting civilian aircraft (e.g. Orasanu 1997). However, the stories that firefighters construct in order to understand the cause and progression of a fire in a building, or those that a military analyst generates when deciding whether to treat a blip on a radar screen as friend or foe, are rather different to those of a police investigator. Achieving an effective and accurate mental representation of an investigative problem requires the ability to understand and predict the behaviour of others. Solving investigative problems thus requires the police investigator to deploy an understanding of the behaviour and actions of many types of individual: cunning or dim-witted offenders, vulnerable or culpable victims, well-meaning or malicious witnesses, helpful or obstructive journalists, genuine or malevolent informers, well-motivated or embittered members of their own team, and so on. An understanding of the multiplicity of potential goals, actions and reactions of every one of the individuals involved in a serious crime investigation is important to investigative situation, assessment, and action. Moreover, the investigator needs to be aware of how the actions s/he takes could affect these individuals. In sum, criminal investigations require both a deep and a broad understanding of the properties of social systems that are inherently complex and unpredictable.

A number of researchers have argued that story generation is a particularly useful tool for understanding social information. For instance, in his approach to causal reasoning, Read argues that in order to comprehend the behaviours of others, individuals need to have an understanding of how conditions initiate particular goals and how people's actions are performed as part of plans to achieve those goals (Read 1987; Read and Miller 1993, 1995). In Read's account, when someone observes an interaction, they begin by categorising the actors in that interaction. This activates particular schemata and associated scripts, which, for our purposes, can be thought of as generalised story structures, from long term memory. As the sequence of events unfolds, the observer tends to interpret new actions within the framework imposed by the activated story. The process of comprehension is thus one of constructing a causal scenario in which a sequence of actions is explained by the inference of cause-effect relationships between those actions.

Story generation also appears to be a mechanism that individuals use to make sense of complex forensic-related social information. In a series of important studies, Pennington and Hastie (1986, 1992) showed that when mock jurors, who had seen a simulated trial, were asked to verbalise their thoughts when considering a verdict, they tended to construct stories around the evidence that they had heard, often filling in any gaps with assumptions and inferences. Moreover, these assumptions frequently related to the inferred psychological states or likely behaviour of the actors involved in the crime (e.g. 'sometimes when people drink they get nasty', 'normally a person wouldn't carry a big knife in his pocket' (Pennington and Hastie 1986: 247)). Such information added to narrative coherence but had not been mentioned explicitly in any of the trial evidence. Furthermore, when the order of evidence presented was varied, so as to make story construction difficult for one verdict and easy for the other, participants consistently favoured the verdict for which story construction was easiest (Pennington and Hastie 1992). These striking findings lend considerable support to the notion that story construction is an important means by which individuals arrive at conclusions about the meanings of criminal events.

Both Schank and Abelson (1995) and Read (1987) suggest that existing knowledge plays an important part in shaping understanding of a new situation. Research by Weiner, Richmond, Seib, Rauch and Hackney (2002) lends support to this notion in a forensic context. Their work indicates that the nature of crime-related schemata has an important influence on the construction of jurors' explanatory stories: it appears that people rely on underlying prototypical crime scripts when processing trial-like information.

In sum, there is good reason to believe that people rely on story construction to help them understand complicated information, both in general and in the more specific case of information about crimes and criminals, because stories summarise important data about the development of other people's goals and the execution of their plans, and help us understand what underlies conflicts between individuals with differing goals and plans. As such, story generation can be thought of as an heuristic strategy by which we make sense of complex and ambigious information. Despite the focus on 'biases' in Kahnemann and Tversky's well-known 'heuristics and biases' programme (e.g. Kahnemann, Slovic and Tversky 1982), heuristic strategies should not be seen as inherently irrational (Gigerenzer and Todd 1999). Indeed, there is a significant body of work that suggests that the use of heuristic strategies is essentially adaptive. Thus, heuristic use is 'ecologically rational' (Gigerenzer and Todd 1999; Payne, Bettman and Johnson 1993; Simon 1990). Story generation is a good example of an adaptive heuristic: in general, events follow one another in an understandable sequence, outcomes have causes, and, in a general sense, people often do predictable things in well-defined circumstances. Thus far, the evidence suggests that 'people's decisions based on heuristics are pretty good, pretty often' (Markman and Medin 2002: 424).

Whilst heuristic use has important benefits, it can also have significant costs: stories may be helpful vehicles for understanding social information, but they are not necessarily accurate. If the perception of new information is faulty, or if the existing knowledge with which it is combined is unsound or incomplete, flawed mental models of the situation will result. Equally, defective social situation models may result if the comprehender holds biased or erroneous views on the meanings of particular behaviours, or if they fail to take account of important factors such as situational variables (e.g. Cervone 1999).

Stories and profiles

Our argument has important implications for our understanding of the cognitive processes that often lead investigators to hold a favourable view of traditional offender profiles, despite a lack of evidence for their utility. Firstly, the readiness to believe that psychologists, popularly believed to be 'experts' in the study of human behaviour, may have something to offer in a police investigation probably owes a lot to police officers' recognition that the understanding of the behaviour of others is crucial in an investigation. Believing a source of information to be both credible and useful is, of course, likely to predispose officers favourably towards the information itself.

Secondly, the use of a 'story generation' heuristic strategy may be an inevitable consequence of the complexity of the task at hand. Bringing coherence to the sort of intricate and ambiguous material available in a criminal investigation involves significant cognitive effort. Thus, it may be unsurprising that investigators will tend to fill gaps with assumption-based reasoning and to rely on the informed speculation of others, particularly those considered 'experts', to bring coherence to an otherwise confusing situation. These suggestions have some empirical support: for instance, Horowitz, Bordens, Victor, Bourgeois and Forster-Lee (2001) report that when presented with trial-like information of increasing complexity, mock jurors appear less able to process such information systematically.

Thirdly, it is possible that the overly positive view individuals hold of the type of profiles and profilers frequently mentioned in the press is, in part, influenced by the use of 'technical' psychological terms in such profiles. Horowitz *et al.*'s participants seemed to find expert witnesses to be more credible when the language they used was more technical, probably because such language use conforms to lay expectations about the nature of expert testimony.

Fourthly, there is some evidence that highly stressful, highly ambiguous situations tend to promote superstitious beliefs and the readiness to invoke simplistic views of behaviour (Vyse 1997).

Finally, it should be acknowledged that there are pragmatic reasons why police might commission profiles even if they believe them to have little or no value. In the UK, the Criminal Procedure and Investigations Act 1996 imposes on the police a statutory responsibility to pursue 'all reasonable lines of enquiry'. Add to this the public pressure that is so often brought to bear on the police in high profile cases and it is perhaps understandable that the police often make significant efforts to be seen to have employed every possible investigative resource, no matter how sceptical they might be in private about the efficacy of a particular technique.

Case-based reasoning in criminal investigation: novice and experts

To this point we have made no clear distinction between experienced and novice investigators when considering their interpretation of information from profiles, and, indeed, other investigative information. Further research is needed to determine whether and in what ways experienced investigators' greater store of domain-relevant information may facilitate effective processing of complex forensic information. For instance, the acquisition of experience may allow investigators to develop a richer and more diverse set of stereotypes upon which they rely heuristically when processing investigative material, thus reducing the need to rely on untested expert information when doing so. Equally, greater experience may lead to an increased ability to resist the temptation to interpret investigative material (including profiles) creatively, and to recognise flaws in assumption-based reasoning.

However, experience is not necessarily synonymous with expertise: as Yates points out, it is quite possible for an individual to achieve 'experienced incompetence' (2001: 24) by repetitive use of poor strategies. What, then, does it mean to be an expert in an investigative context? An increased ability to think critically about investigative material, including profiles, may not be a natural consequence of an increase in domain-relevant experience but may depend in part on the development of a particular set of meta-cognitive skills. Indeed, there is evidence from related fields that experts operating in highly pressured and ambiguous situations undergo a process of critiquing the stories that they generate to help them understand such situations (Cohen, Freeman and Thompson 1998). By correcting unreliable assumptions and filling gaps with carefully considered evidence, as opposed to speculation, such experts construct more reliable and accurate stories, which allow them to take more effective action.

To summarise, we suggest that investigators attempt to generate a mental representation of an investigative problem situation, consisting of a coherent, convincing and evidentiary sound story explaining the circumstances of the crime. Such a story consists of a series of episodes in which are embedded arguments about the actors (offenders, victims and witnesses) and their motivations and plans, their actions and the cause-effect relationships between them. An investigator's mental model, the narrative of the crime, must be complete and coherent. Where arguments are based on assumptions, they must be valid, and robust enough to withstand the scrutiny of the court. Where they exist, alternative stories should be shown to be implausible, incoherent or unreliable. The process of constructing such a representation is the process of investigation.

The clearer the incoming investigative data, and the more skilled the investigator at interpreting it, the more effective the process is likely to be. Returning to the principal topic of this chapter, ambiguous and unverifiable information is particularly dangerous when it masquerades as scientific fact. Therefore, the concerns that have arisen in the past few years with regards to clarity in profiles and the increasing recognition that offenders cannot be neatly fitted into types based on an analysis of the crime scene, is a welcome development. Work is gradually emerging within the social sciences that will contribute to our understanding of criminal behaviour for the purpose of assisting investigations. This now burgeoning field, which has begun to embrace both experience and systematic research as a way forward, promises stronger links between practitioners and academics and a stronger footing upon which advice may be provided (Alison, West and Goodwill, in press). However, it is important to articulate clearly the reasons why the type of profiles that have had a very lengthy media honeymoon have been so successful. Such knowledge may help inform subsequent research into investigative decision making and into the guidelines for constructing investigative advice.

Note

1. The offence involved the abduction, sexual assault and murder of a male youth in the 1970s.

References

ACPO (2000) Association of Chief Police Officers. *ACPO Crime Committee, Behavioural Science Sub-committee*. Internal report.

Ainsworth, P.B. (2001) *Offender Profiling and Crime Analysis*. Cullompton: Willan.

Alison, L., Bennell, C., Mokros, A. and Ormerod, D. (2002) 'The personality paradox in offender profiling. A theoretical review of the process involved in deriving background characteristics from crime scene actions', *Psychology, Public Policy and Law*, 8: 115–35.

Alison, L.J., West, A. and Goodwill, A. (in press) 'The academic and the practitioner: Pragmatists' views of offender profiling', *Psychology, Public Policy and Law*.

Alison, L.J., Smith, M.D. Eastman, O. and Rainbow, L. (2003) 'Toulmin's philosophy of argument and its relevance to offender profiling', *Psychology, Crime and Law*, 9 (2): 173–83.

Alison, L.J., Smith, M.D. and Morgan, K. (2003) 'Interpreting the accuracy of offender profiles', *Psychologty, Crime and Law*, 9 (2), 185–95.

Annon, J.S. (1995) 'Investigative profiling: A behavioural analysis of the crime scene', *American Journal of Forensic Psychology*, 13: 67–75.

Åsgard, U. (1996) *International Symposium: Methods of case analysis and offender profiling*. Wiesbaden: Bundeskriminalamt.

Åsgard, U. (1998) 'Swedish experiences in offender profiling and evaluation of some aspects of a case of murder and abduction in Germany', in Case Analysis Unit (BKA) (eds) *Method of Case Analysis: An international symposium* (pp. 125–30). Weisbaden: Bundeskriminalamt Kriminalistisches Institut.

Ault, R.L. and Reese, J.T. (1980) 'A psychological assessment of crime profiling', *FBI Law Enforcement Bulletin*, 49: 22–5.

Bartlett, F.C. (1932) *Remembering: A study in experimental and social psychology*. Cambridge: Cambridge University Press.

Bartol, C. (1991) *Criminal Behavior: A psychosocial approach* (3rd edn). Toronto: Prentice-Hall.

Bennell, C. (1998) *Linking Serial Sex Offences*. Unpublished M.Sc. thesis, Department of Psychology, University of Liverpool.

Bennell, C. and Canter, D. (2002) 'Linking commercial burglaries by modus operandi: Tests using regression and ROC analysis', *Science and Justice*, 42.

Boon, J. (1997) 'Contribution of personality theories to psychological profiling', in J.L. Jackson and D.A. Bekarian (eds) *Offender profiling: Theory, research and practice* (pp. 43–59). Chichester: Wiley.

Britton, P. (1992) *Review of Offender Profiling*. London: Home Office.

Birtton, P. (1997) *The Jigsaw Man*. London: Bantham Press.

Canter, D. and Youngs, D. (in press) 'Beyond "offender profiling": The need for an investigative psychology', in R. Bull and D. Carson (eds) *Handbook of Psychology and Legal Contexts*. Wiley and Sons.

Cervone, D. (1999) 'Bottom-up explanation in personality psychology: The case of cross-situational coherence', in D. Cervone and Y. Shoda (eds) *The coherence of personality: Social-cognitive bases of personality consistency, variability, and organization* (pp. 303–341). New York: Guilford Press.

Cervone, D. and Shoda, Y. (eds) (1999) *The Coherence of Personality: Social-cognitive bases of consistency, variability and organization*. London: Guilford Press.

Cohen, M.S., Freeman, J.T. and Thompson, B. (1998) 'Critical thinking skills in tactical decision making: A model and a training strategy', in J.A. Cannon-

Bowers and E. Salas (eds) *Making decisions under stress*. Washington, DC: American Psychological Association.

Copson, G. (1995) *Coals to Newcastle? Part One: A study of offender profiling*. Police Research Group Special Interest Series (Paper no.7). London: Home Office Police Department.

Davies, A., Wittebrood, K. and Jackson, J.L. (1998) *Predicting the Criminal Record of a Stranger Rapist*. London: Home Office, Policing and Reducing Crime Unit.

Dickson, D.H. and Kelly, I.E. (1985) 'The "Barnum Effect" in personality assessment: A review of the literature', *Psychological Reports*, 57: 367–82.

Douglas, J.E., Burgess, A.W., Burgess, A.G. and Ressler, R.K. (1992) *Crime classification manual: A standard system for investigating and classifying violent crime*. New York: Simon and Schuster.

Douglas, J., Ressler, R., Burgess, A. and Hartman, C. (1986) 'Criminal profiling from crime scene analysis', *Behavioural Sciences and the Law*, 4 (4): 401–21.

Douglas, J.E. (1981) *Evaluation of the (FBI) psychological profiling programme*. Unpublished manuscript.

Dudycha, G.J. (1936) 'An objective study of punctuality in relation to personality and achievement', *Archives of Psychology*, 204: 1–319.

Epstein, S. (1979) 'The stability of behavior I: On predicting most of the people most of the time', *Journal of Personality and Social Psychology*, 37: 1097–126.

Fichter, C.S. and Sunerton, D. (1983) 'Popular horoscopes and the "Barnum Effect"', *Journal of Psychology*, 114: 123–24.

Forer, B. (1949) 'The fallacy of personal validation: A classroom demonstration of gullibility', *Journal of Abnormal and Social Psychology*, 44: 118–23.

Furnham, A. and Schofield, S. (1987) 'Accepting personality test feedback: A review of the Barnum Effect', *Current Psychological Research and Reviews*, 6: 162–78.

Fritzon, K. and Ridgway, J. (2001) 'Near death experience: The role of victim reaction in attempted homicide', *Journal of Interpersonal Violence*, 16: 679–96.

Gigerenzer, G. and Todd, P.M. (1999) 'Fast and frugal heuristics: The adaptive toolbox', in Gigerenzer, G., Todd, P.M. and the ABC Research Group (eds) *Simple Heuristics that Make us Smart*. New York, NY: Oxford University Press.

Goldblatt, P. (1992) *Psychological offender profiles: How psychologists can help the police with their enquiries*. Unpublished manuscript.

Goodwill, A. (2000) *Suspect Prioritisation in Linking Burglary Offences*. Dissertation for M.Sc. Investigative Psychology. Internal Document: University of Liverpool.

Graesser, A.C., Mills, K.K. and Zwaan, R.A. (1997) 'Discourse comprehension', *Annual Review of Psychology*, 48: 163–89.

Graesser, A.C. and Ottati, V. (1995) 'Why stories? Some evidence, questions and challenges', in *Advances in Social Cognition: Volume 8. Knowledge and memory: The real story*. R.S. Wyer (ed.). Hillside, NJ: Laurence Erlbaum Associates.

Grubin, D. (1995) 'Offender Profiling', *Journal of Forensic Psychiatry*, 6: 259–63.

Grubin, D., Kelly, P. and Ayis, S. (1997) *Linking Serious Sexual Assaults*. London: Home Office Police Research Group.

Hartshorne, H. and May, M.A. (1928) *Studies in the nature of character (Volume 1): Studies in deceit*. New York: Macmillan.

Hickey, E.W. (1997) *Serial Murderers and their Victims* (2nd edn). New York: Wadsworth Publishing Company.

Homant, R.J. and Kennedy, D.B. (1998) 'Psychological aspects of crime scene profiling: Validity research', *Criminal Justice and Behavior*, 25: 319–43.

Horowitz, I.A., Bordens, K.S., Victor, E., Bourgeois, M.J. and Forster-Lee, L. (2001) 'The effects of complexity on jurors' verdicts and construction of evidence', *Journal of Applied Psychology*, 86 (4): 641–52.

House, J.C. (1997) 'Towards a practical application of offender profiling: The RNC's criminal suspect prioritization system', in J.L. Jackson and D.A. Bekerian (eds) *Offender profiling: Theory, research and practice* (pp. 177–190). Chichester: John Wiley and Sons.

Innes, M. (2002) 'The "process structures" of police homicide investigations', *British Journal of Criminology*, 42: 669–88.

Jackson, J.L., Van Koppen, P.J. and Herbrink, C.M. (1993) *Does the service meet the needs: An evaluation of consumer satisfaction with specific profile analysis and investigative advice as offered by the Scientific Research Advisory Unit of the National Criminal Intelligence Division (CRI), The Netherlands*. Unpublished manuscript.

Kahneman, D., Slovic, P. and Tversky, A. (eds) (1982) *Judgement Under Uncertainty: Heuristics and biases*. Cambridge: Cambridge University Press.

Keppel, R.D. and Weis, J.G. (1993) *Improving the Investigation of Violent Crime: The homicide investigation and tracking system*. USA: US Department of Justice.

Klein, G. (1999) *Sources of Power: How people make decisions*. Cambridge, MA: MIT Press.

Knight, R. Warren, J., Reboussin, R. and Soley, B. (1998) 'Predicting rapist type from crime scene characteristics', *Criminal Justice and Behavior*, 25: 46–80.

McAdams, D. (1993) *The Stories We Live By*. New York, NY: The Guilford Press.

Markman, A. B. and Medin, D.L. (2002) 'Decision making', in D.L. Medin and H. Pashler (eds) *Stevens Handbook of Experimental Psychology (3rd Edn.), Volume 2* (pp. 413–466). New York: John Wiley and Sons.

Meehl, P.E. (1956) 'Wanted – A good cookbook', *American Psychologist*, 11: 262–72.

Mischel, W. (1968) *Personality and Assessment*. New York: John Wiley and Sons.

Mischel, W. (1990) 'Personality dispositions revisited and revised: A view after three decades', in L. Pervin (ed.) *Handbook of Personality: Theory and research* (2nd edn) (pp. 111–134). New York: Guilford Press.

Mischel, W. and Peake, P.K. (1982) 'Beyond déjà vu in the search for cross-situational consistency', *Psychological Review*, 89: 730–55.

Mokros, A. (1999) *The centroid as a grouping variable for offences: A cluster-analytical approach*. Unpublished internal document, Department of Psychology, University of Liverpool.

Mokros, A. and Alison, L. (2002) 'Is offender profiling possible? Testing the predicted homology of crime scene actions and background characteristics in a sample of rapists', *Legal and Criminological Psychology*, 7: 25–43.

Newcomb, T.M. (1929) *Consistency of certain extrovert-introvert behavior patterns in 51 problem boys*. New York: Columbia University, Teachers College, Bureau of Publications.

Orasanu, J. (1997) 'Stress and naturalistic decision making: Strengthening the weak links', in R. Flin, E. Salas, M. Strub and L. Martin (eds) *Decision Making Under Stress*. Aldershot, Hants: Ashgate.

Pascual, R. and Henderson, S. (1997) 'Evidence of Naturalistic Decision Making in military command and control', in C.E. Zsambok and G. Klein (eds) *Naturalistic Decision Making*. Mahwah, NJ: Lawrence Erlbaum Associates Inc.

Payne, J.W., Bettman, J.R. and Johnson, E.J. (1993) *The Adaptive Decision Maker*. Cambridge: CUP.

Pennington, N. and Hastie, R. (1986) 'Evidence evaluation in complex decision making', *Journal of Personality and Social Psychology*, 51 (2): 242–58.

Pennington, N. and Hastie, R. (1992) 'Explaining the evidence: tests of the story model for juror decision making', *Journal of Personality and Social Psychology*, 62 (2): 189–206.

Peterson, D.R. (1968) *The Clinical Study of Social Behavior*. New York: Appleton-Century-Crofts.

Pinizzotto, A.J. (1984) 'Forensic psychology: Criminal personality profiling', *Journal of Police Science and Administration*, 12: 32–40.

Pinizzotto, A.J. and Finkel, N.J. (1990) 'Criminal personality profiling: An outcome and process study', *Law and Human Behavior*, 14: 215–33.

Read, S.J. (1987) 'Constructing causal scenarios: A knowledge structure approach to causal reasoning', *Journal of Personality and Social Psychology*, 52 (2): 288–302.

Read, S.J. and Miller, L.C. (1993) 'Rapist or "regular guy": Explanatory coherence in the construction of mental models of others', *Personality and Social Psychology Bulletin*, 19 (5): 526–41.

Read, S.J. and Miller, L.C. (1995) 'Stories are fundamental to meaning and memory: For social creatures, could it be otherwise?', in R.S. Wyer (ed.) *Advances in Social Cognition: Volume 8. Knowledge and memory: The real story*. Hillside, NJ: Laurence Erlbaum Associates.

Ross, L. (1977) 'The intuitive psychologist and his shortcomings: Distortions in the attribution process', in L. Berkowitz (ed.) *Advances in Experimental Social Psychology* (vol. 10). New York: Academic Press.

Rossmo, D.K. (2000) *Geographic profiling*. Boca Raton: CRC Press.

Schank, R.C. and Abelson, R.P. (1977) *Scripts, plans, goals and understanding*. Hillside, NJ: Laurence Erlbaum Associates.

Schank, R.C. and Abelson, R.P. (1995) 'Knowledge and memory: The real story', in R.S. Wyer (ed.) *Advances in Social Cognition: Volume 8. Knowledge and memory: The real story*. Hillside, NJ: Laurence Erlbaum Associates.

Shoda, Y., Mischel, W. and Wright, J.C. (1994) 'Intra-individual stability in the organization and patterning of behavior: Incorporating psychological situations into the idiographic analysis of personality', *Journal of Personality and Social Psychology*, 67: 674–87.

Simon, H. (1990) 'Invariants of human behavior', *Annual Review of Psychology*, 41: 1–19.

Snyder, C.R., Larsen, D.K. and Bloom, L.J. (1976) 'Acceptance of personality interpretations prior to and after receiving diagnostic feedback supposedly based on psychological, graphological and astrological assessment procedures', *Journal of Clinical Psychology*, 32: 258–65.

Turvey, B. (ed.) (1999) *Criminal profiling: An introduction to behavioural evidence analysis*. New York: Academic Press.

Vernon, P.E. (1964) *Personality assessment: A critical survey*. New York: Wiley.

Vyse, S. (1997) *Believing in Magic: The Psychology of Superstition*. Oxford University Press.

Weiner, R.L., Richmond, T.L., Seib, H.M., Rauch, S.M. and Hackney, A.A. (2002) 'The psychology of telling murder stories: Do we think in scripts, exemplars or prototypes?', *Behavioral Sciences and the Law*, 20: 119–39.

Wyer, R.S. and Radvansky, G.A. (1999) 'The comprehension and validation of social information', *Psychological Review*, 106: 89–118.

Yates, J.F. (2001) '"Outsider": Impressions of Naturalistic Decision Making', in E. Salas and G. Klein (eds) *Linking Expertise and Naturalistic Decision Making*. Mahwah, NJ: Lawrence Erlbaum Associates, Inc.

Zsambok, C.E. (1997) 'Naturalistic decision making: Where are we now?', in C.E. Zsambok and G. Klein (eds) *Naturalistic Decision Making*. Mahwah, NJ: Lawrence Erlbaum Associates Inc.

Section 3

Testimony and Evidence

The two chapters in this section complement each other and supplement the debate about the reliability of eyewitnesses. They do not rehearse the ubiquitous arguments about whether eyewitness evidence is or is not reliable in and of itself. The starting point for this section is how best we can reduce the likelihood of errors in testimony and where they are most likely to occur in the first place.

In Chapter 5, Mark Kebbell and Elizabeth Gilchrist explore the ramifications of a fundamental part of our adversarial legal system. What are the effects of cross examination on the accuracy and quality of the evidence that is being given? In our system, the job of counsel, whether prosecution or defence, is not to coax out the maximum amount of accurate evidence from the witness. Rather, it is to elicit those fragments of recall that will best serve the narrative being constructed by their side.

In contrast, it is the job of the police to gain as much accurate evidence as possible. This is then passed forward to the Crown Prosecution Service and they make decisions as to whether a case is there to be answered. It may be tempting for police to construct a tale that supports their original theories about a particular criminal incident. However, as the case will be challenged in court, they should always look for alternative explanations and test competing hypotheses. As such, they need to gather the best evidence possible and accurate statements from witnesses are very important. In this context, the older witness is an interesting case. The more senior members of society may well want to help the police and are more likely than younger people to have faith in the police as an effective service. Yet, there are questions as to how useful their evidence may be as there is the widespread belief that as we get older, our memory becomes less reliable. In Chapter 6, Amina Memon, Fiona Gabbert and Lorraine Hope show us where the ageing witness may be likely to make errors and what we can do to improve their testimony, where needed.

Chapter 5

Eliciting evidence from eyewitnesses in court

Mark R. Kebbell, James Cook University and Elizabeth L. Gilchrist, University of Coventry

Background

Eyewitnesses are central to most court cases (Kebbell and Milne 1998; Zander and Henderson 1993). For example, a witness might state, 'That is the man who robbed me, I'm certain of it!' This is powerful evidence that provides not only information concerning who committed the offence but also the nature of the offence. Research shows that jurors rely heavily on eyewitness accounts to determine whether to convict or to acquit (e.g., Cutler, Penrod and Dexter 1990). However, research into false convictions, for example where subsequent DNA evidence exonerates a convicted individual, shows that the usual reason for a false conviction is erroneous witness evidence (Connors, Lundregan, Miller, and McEwan 1996; Huff, Rattner and Sagarin 1996). Therefore, it is essential that accurate evidence is presented in court.

Examination in court

The Anglo-Saxon justice system used in most of the English speaking world to elicit evidence is 'adversarial'. A central premise of this system is that a person is innocent unless proven guilty or they admit guilt. In adversarial systems, a trial does not establish whether the accused is innocent but whether the prosecution evidence is sufficient beyond reasonable doubt, to prove guilt to the jury (Davies, Croall and Tyrer 1995). The principal way in which the guilt of the accused is established is through verbal witness evidence.

Evidence-in-chief occurs first and is supposed to be a relatively open account of what the witness saw elicited by the lawyer who called the witness. The open nature of the account is so as to prevent the lawyer from biasing the witness who is already assumed to be favourable to the lawyer who called him or her (Evans 1995; Murphy and Barnard 1994; Stone 1995).

Cross-examination follows evidence-in-chief and is conducted by the opposing lawyer. If a witness was called by the Prosecution, cross-examination would be conducted by the Defence and vice versa. In his popular guide to advocacy, Evans (1995) identifies four broad objectives of lawyers' cross-examination. These are: laying the foundation; putting your case; eliciting extra and useful facts, and, discrediting the evidence.

The lawyer is not allowed to comment on matters that have not been touched on during evidence. Consequently, laying the foundation and putting your case involves asking questions concerning the case that test the cross-examining lawyer's alternative explanation of events. Eliciting extra and useful facts concerns the cross-examining lawyer attempting to elicit evidence that is favourable to his or her case. However, arguably the most important aspect of cross-examination, as identified by Evans, is discrediting the evidence and he points out, 'it is not a procedure which is aiming to find out the truth' (p. 150). Re-examination sometimes occurs when the lawyer who conducted evidence-in-chief wishes to ask additional questions about information that was provided in cross-examination.

In sum, the aim of examining witnesses in court is for evidence to be elicited so the jury can determine if the evidence is sufficient beyond reasonable doubt to establish guilt. To achieve this aim, the jury must try to determine the accuracy of the evidence provided by the witnesses.

Factors having an impact on witness accuracy

One crucial factor relating to the accuracy and completeness of eyewitness testimony is the type of question asked (Clifford and George 1996; Fisher, Geiselman and Raymond 1987; Memon and Vartoukian 1996). Open questions (e.g., 'describe your attacker'), closed questions (e.g., 'what colour was his shirt?'), and yes/no questions (e.g. 'was the colour of his shirt red?') can have a dramatic influence on the accuracy of witness answers (Clifford and George 1996; Davies, Westcott and Horan 2000; Fisher, Geiselman and Raymond 1987; Hutcheson, Baxter, Telfer and Warden 1995; Memon and Vartoukian 1996; Memon, Vrij and Bull

1998; Memon, Holley, Milne, Koehnken and Bull 1994; Milne and Bull 1999). People tend to provide the most accurate answers (i.e., where the proportion of correct to incorrect information is greatest) to open questions. The more closed questioning strategies, mentioned above, can reduce the accuracy although they can add detail. As a general proposition, as questions become more and more specific, responses become less accurate (Kebbell and Wagstaff 1999).

The influence of these questions can be understood in terms of the relative demands of the questions. For more open questions, the task is to tell the questioner what the witness *can* remember. For more specific, closed questions, however, the task changes to one of providing the interviewer with what he or she *wants* the witness to remember. One result of this is that witnesses tend to provide less accurate answers to specific questions because they fill memory gaps with distorted or inaccurate material. In other words, they may become suggestible to the demands of the interviewer (Gudjonsson 1992; Kebbell and Wagstaff 1999). Answers to 'yes or no' questions may be particularly inaccurate because of the tendency of an individual to answer questions with a 'yes' irrespective of the content: 'acquiescence' (Gudjonsson 1990, 1992).

Suggestibility (the tendency to provide the answer believed to be required by the questioner) may also be a particular problem with leading questions. Leading questions suggest the response required (e.g. 'Did you see the man's red jumper?' This suggests that the man wore a red jumper). Witnesses are more suggestible to leading questions than neutrally worded questions (e.g. Loftus 1979; Loftus and Zanni 1975). For example, in a classic study by Loftus and Palmer (1974), participants were shown a film of a car accident. Later they were asked, 'About how fast were the cars going when they smashed into each other?' Alternative versions of the questions used the words 'collided', 'bumped', 'hit', or 'contacted'. Although the words all refer to the coming together of two objects, they differ in what they imply about the speed and force of the impact. Participants who received the 'smashed' version estimated the speed at 40.8 mph compared with participants given the 'contacted' version who estimated the speed at 30.8 mph, on average. Clearly, the implication of this is that if witnesses are questioned using inappropriate strategies, their accuracy is likely to suffer.

Research by Kebbell, Hatton and Johnson (2004) investigated the frequency of the above question types in the examination of 16 alleged victims of rape, sexual assault and assault. The trials were held at eight different English courts from 1994 to 1999. The frequency of open and closed questions, questions that were leading, and questions that could be answered with a yes or no were documented. In evidence-in-chief:

30 per cent of questions were open; 14 per cent were closed; 51 per cent could be answered with a yes or no; and three per cent were leading. In cross-examination, the frequency of the different question types was significantly different from evidence-in-chief: only 16 per cent of questions were open and four per cent were closed. There was a significant increase in yes or no questions and leading questions, when compared with evidence-in-chief, making up 87 per cent and 25 per cent of the questions in cross-examination respectively (questions could be coded into more than one category, see also Kebbell, Deprez and Wagstaff 2003).

Overall, these results show that the constraining nature of questioning in court even in evidence-in-chief is likely to result in many of the problems that have previously been identified concerning police interviewing (Fisher *et al.* 1987; Kebbell and Hatton 1999). That is, the pattern of questioning is likely to break the concentration of an eye-witness, impairing his or her ability to remember information. The use of such constraining questioning also means that the examination takes the form of the lawyer asking a question and the witness giving a brief answer, the lawyer asking another closed question, and so on. This format allows only a short time between a question's answer and the next question, giving little opportunity for the witness to elaborate an answer. Also, and importantly, the format ensures that the evidence is directed by the lawyer rather than the witness so the only information that is elicited is that which is requested. Therefore, if the lawyer forgets to ask a certain question, or does not realise that certain information is important, no information in that area is elicited for the jury. The large number of leading, potentially suggestive questions asked in cross-examination are also disturbing because a substantial literature shows that they can lead to inaccurate answers (Loftus and Zanni 1975; Loftus, Miller and Burns 1978).

Problems for witnesses are not confined to constraining and leading questions. Questions involving negatives, double negatives, and multiple questions can also pose difficulties to witnesses (Danet 1980; Kebbell and Johnson 2000; Perry, McAuliff, Tam, Claycomb, Dostal and Flanagan 1995). Negatives are questions involving the word 'not' (e.g. 'Did the man *not* tell you to be quiet?'). Double negatives are questions involving using the word 'not' twice (e.g. 'Did John *not* say that he would *not* go to the shops?'). These may cause problems because witnesses may have difficulty understanding the question. For instance, evidence from child witness studies shows that with respect to children, 'don't know' responses are often given to questions that are not understood. However, if the question is put to them in a simplified form, they often know the answer (Brennan and Brennan 1988; Perry *et al.* 1995). Alternatively, and additionally, instead of saying 'I don't know', witnesses may be tempted to 'guess' the right answer. Kebbell, Hatton and Johnson (under review) found that negatives accounted for two per cent of questions asked in evidence-in-chief and 15 per cent of questions asked in cross-examination. For double negatives, the frequency was much less, less than one per cent for both evidence-in-chief and cross-examination, indicating this form of questioning is unlikely to pose regular problems for witnesses.

Multiple questions are those involving two or more parts that have different answers (e.g. 'At 11 o'clock were you in the bar? Was John at the garage?'). Again, in experimental simulations, these kinds of questions cause eyewitnesses problems because they may fail to understand the question and usually only give one answer to the last question rather than an answer to both questions (Brennan and Brennan 1988; Kebbell and Johnson 2000; Perry *et al.* 1995). Kebbell, Hatton and Johnson (2004) found two per cent of questions asked in evidence-in-chief were multiple questions compared with six per cent in cross-examination.

A number of researchers have identified other types of questions that lawyers frequently use in court that create difficulties for eyewitnesses. Lawyers may ask questions with advanced vocabulary and/or legal terminology (e.g. 'Was the perpetrator of the crime occluded by any vehicles?') and with complex syntax making them difficult to process (e.g. 'At any time before or after she cried did the vehicle move either forwards or backwards?') (Danet 1980; Kranat andWestcott 1994; Perry *et al.* 1995; Walker 1993; Westcott 1995).

Kebbell and Johnson (2000) investigated the effect of the confusing questions often used by lawyers in court. Participants viewed a videotaped film and were individually questioned about the event a week later. Half the participants were asked questions using six categories of confusing questions (negatives, double negatives, leading, multiple questions, complex syntax and complex vocabulary). The remaining half were asked for the same information using simply phrased equivalents. Confusing questions reduced witness accuracy from 76 per cent in the simply phrased condition to 56 per cent in the confusing lawyers' questions condition (see also Perry *et al.* 1995).

Other lawyers' strategies in cross-examination are more subtle, less clearly defined and documented. These include the techniques of 'pining out', 'prefatory remarks', and 'slippery slopes' (Carson 2000; Cooke 1990; Evans 1995). The process of 'pining out' under cross-examination gets the witness to commit him or herself to a position before the advocate comes to the main focus of the argument. For example, the lawyer may get the witness to state that they are not shy then point out that the witness did not tell anyone about the offence until much later so discrediting their testimony (for an example see Westcott and Page 2002).

Another method that might be used during cross-examination is the prefatory remark. With this technique the lawyer makes a statement prior to asking a question. If the witness fails to make a comment on the statement it appears that he or she agrees with the statement. For example, the lawyer may say, 'I am sure we all agree you don't get into a man's car you've just met at a nightclub without expecting some sexual element, so could you please tell the court when you got into the car with Mr Smith?' Lawyers may also use the 'slippery slope' approach. Here the lawyer tries to redefine the witness's comments to make the lawyer's account seem more likely. As the following example illustrates.

Lawyer In your statement, you say my client is definitely the robber?
Witness Yes
Lawyer So my client might be the robber?
Witness Yes
Lawyer So, let me get this clear, you feel that there is the possibility that he is the robber?
Witness Yes

Of course lawyers may additionally resort to more direct approaches to discredit witness evidence. For example, they may attack the witness's integrity, innocence, and portray the witness as responsible for the crime (Westcott and Page 2002). All these factors are likely to have an impact on witness credibility, to which we now turn.

Witness credibility

Clearly, the literature reviewed so far shows that many of the questioning strategies adopted by lawyers can have an adverse influence on witnesses' answers. The implication of this is that evidence distorted or constrained by lawyers' questions might result in miscarriages of justice; either false convictions or, alternatively, false acquittals could occur. However, this problem might not be as damaging as it first appears. Jurors and other triers of fact rely heavily on witness confidence to judge the accuracy of evidence (Cutler, Penrod and Dexter 1990; Cutler, Penrod and Stuve 1988; Fox and Walters 1986; Leippe,

Manion and Romanczyk 1992; Lindsay, Wells and O'Connor 1989). So a witness who says 'I'm absolutely certain that the man had a gun' is more likely to be perceived as accurate than the witness who says 'I think he may have had a gun'. If witnesses' accuracy is impaired by lawyers' questions but confidence in those inaccurate answers is also reduced then false-convictions would be unlikely. Conversely, the implications for miscarriages of justice are severe if eyewitness accuracy is low but eyewitnesses are highly confident in their inaccurate answers.

Research shows a reasonable, positive confidence–accuracy relationship can be produced (e.g., Kebbell, Wagstaff and Covey 1996; Lindsay, Read, Sharma 1998; Sporer, Penrod, Read and Cutler 1995 although this issue is controversial, see Elliott 1993; Kassin, Ellsworth and Smith 1994). However, research also shows that confidence–accuracy relationships can be distorted easily (e.g., Luus and Wells 1994; Shaw and McLure 1996). Leippe (1980) suggests this is because the integrative, cognitive processes used to report memory and to report confidence are often unconscious and can be independent of each other. Thus, eyewitness accuracy can be reduced while confidence remains high (e.g., Wells, Ferguson and Lindsay 1981) or confidence can be increased or decreased whilst memory remains the same (e.g., Luus and Wells 1994).

In the previously mentioned study by Kebbell and Johnson (2000), where lawyers' confusing questions were compared with simplified alternatives, mock witnesses were also required to give confidence judgements for each answer they provided on a ten point Likert scale from 'pure guess' (1) to 'absolutely certain' (10). The difference between confidence regarding correct and incorrect answers in the simplified condition was 3.03 compared with only 1.59 when confusing lawyers' questions were used. This implies that using confusing questions is likely to reduce still further jurors' ability to discriminate between accurate and inaccurate answers.

In the few studies where the effectiveness of cross-examination has been directly tested, its efficacy in terms of enhancing jurors' ability to discriminate between accurate and inaccurate witnesses has not been good. Wells, Lindsay and Ferguson (1979) showed mock witnesses a staged theft of a calculator. Witnesses were then required to identify the 'thief' from photo-spreads. Mock jurors were unable to distinguish between accurate and inaccurate witnesses subjected to cross-examination, although interestingly, asking leading questions in cross-examination improved jurors' accuracy.

Kebbell, O'Kelly and Orchard (2001) also investigated the effectiveness of cross-examination by showing witnesses a simulated crime. Half the 'witnesses' were challenged about their accuracy as occurs during cross-examination and their testimony was shown to mock-jurors. The other half was not challenged. Challenging witness accuracy increased the believability of witnesses in the eyes of jurors, without increasing jurors' sensitivity for correct and incorrect answers. This effect is likely to be due to questioning occurring within a social context. Witnesses may react to what they see as a calculated attempt to reduce their accuracy and confidence through challenges by increasing their confidence, even at the expense of reducing the relationship between confidence and accuracy. This could be predicted from the Gudjonsson and Clark (1986) suggestibility model. Challenges are likely to reduce the interpersonal trust between the lawyer and witness. This is likely to lead witnesses to have a suspicious cognitive set that, Gudjonsson and Clark say, will encourage a resistant behavioural response. In the experiment, one resistant behavioural response would be to maintain confidence, despite the confusing questions.

Of course, some witnesses may be deliberately lying and cross-examination also has the aim of uncovering this deceit. Consequently, it is worth discussing the effectiveness of cross-examination for detecting deception. Detection of deception in forensic environments has attracted considerable attention (e.g., Vrij 2000) and there are a number of reasons why deception should be detectable. For example, those who are deceiving are likely to experience cognitive and emotional processes that may influence their verbal and non-verbal responses (Vrij 1998). Nevertheless, an extensive literature now indicates that when required to discriminate between honest and deceiving experimental partici-pants, people are not able to discriminate reliably at above chance between those who are deceiving and those who are telling the truth. The reason for this appears to be that cues to nervousness are often confused with cues for deceit (for reviews see Vrij 1998, 2000). However, these studies have not included cross-examination as a factor.

In what is, to our knowledge, the only study to look at the influence of cross-examination on the detection of deception (Kebbell, Brodie, Muspratt, Patterson, Quatermaine, Riolo and Stevenson 2002) 20 mock-defendants stole a wallet while 20 mock-defendants did not. All defendants were subsequently cross-examined concerning whether they had stolen the wallet. The 20 who had stolen the wallet were required to lie and say they did not. The cross-examinations of the deceitful and honest defendants were shown to mock jurors. Jurors were unable to determine at a level greater than chance whether defendants were honest or deceitful. However, Kebbell *et al.* (2002) did find that defendants who had stolen the wallet rated themselves as significantly less credible than those who did not, suggesting an important role of cross-examination may be to discourage lying in court even if it is unlikely to expose deceit directly to jurors.

Conclusions

Thus far, it has been implied that witnesses should be questioned in a manner that may elicit complete and accurate accounts in a similar manner to the way that police interviews should be conducted (see Milne and Bull 1999). For instance, with open-ended, specific questions and very few leading questions, as Davies, Westcott and Horan (2000) found was the case with interviews with children. However, important distinctions exist between police interviews of eyewitnesses and lawyers' questioning of eyewitnesses in court. Specifically, the police are interested in constructing a complete, accurate description of the critical event. By comparison, once the case reaches the courtroom, lawyers question witnesses for the purpose of convincing the jury or judge that their side of the argument is correct. If an accurate recollection does not serve the purpose of convincing the jury, then it does not further the lawyer's cause. It may even militate against the lawyer's argument. As a result, lawyers are not necessarily interested in eliciting complete, accurate recollections.

Nevertheless, it may be in a lawyer's best interests to elicit a complete and accurate account in evidence-in-chief for several reasons. Firstly, as Bell and Loftus showed, jurors perceive more complete and detailed accounts to be more credible (Bell and Loftus 1989). Secondly, a complete and accurate account in evidence-in-chief will mean less inaccurate and contradictory statements will be able to be challenged in cross-examination. Thirdly, an initial accurate recall attempt may improve witness memory for an event and inoculate against the distorting and damaging effects of leading questions asked in cross-examination (Geiselman, Fisher, Cohen and Holland 1986). Thus, the potential negative impact of the questioning used in cross-examination may be compounded by poor questioning in evidence-in-chief.

At this point, it is worthwhile asking the question, 'Why do lawyers attempt to constrain witnesses' responses in evidence-in-chief?' One reason could be that they are trained with the maxim, 'you should never ask a question to which you do not know the answer' (Evans 1995, p.118). Further, they are trained to believe that an accurate and complete account of events might damage their case (Evans 1995; Murphy and Barnard 1994). However, this may not necessarily be correct. For instance, if a defendant is guilty, then obtaining a complete and accurate account from a prosecution witness is potentially more likely to result in a conviction than eliciting an incomplete, inconsistent, and distorted account that may raise doubts in the jury's or judge's minds, and leave the witness open to damaging cross-examination. Thus, an important point is the frequency of a defendant's guilt. If most defendants are innocent, there might be some advantage for a prosecution lawyer to distort a prosecution witness's account to secure more convictions. However, the strict criteria needed before a prosecution is brought by the Crown Prosecution Service in England and Wales (Rose 1996) and the high numbers of convictions suggests that the majority of defendants in Crown Courts are guilty (Home Office 1995). Thus, an open evidence-in-chief designed to maximise the completeness and accuracy of a witness's evidence might be more likely to lead to just convictions.

However, while changing to a more open form of evidence-in-chief may be in a lawyer's best interests, a less distorting cross-examination is often not in an opposing lawyer's best interests and lawyers are likely to be reluctant to change. Thus, the combative nature of an adversarial criminal justice system means a 'rigorous' cross-examination relying on closed, constraining and leading questions seems to a large extent unavoidable (Bartlett and Memon 1995; McEwan 1995).

Nevertheless, many of the problems associated with cross-examination identified here have little to do with challenging, testing the evidence and suggesting alternatives. For example, the use of multiple questions, negatives, complex vocabulary and syntax achieve none of these aims but may unfairly discredit the witness because of the confusion they create. It is difficult to see how justice is served by asking witnesses multiple questions using language they do not understand. Many of these problems can be minimised through appropriate intervention by the judge who is obliged not only to have regard to the need to ensure a fair trial for the defendant, but also to the reasonable interests of other parties to the court process (for a detailed discussion see O'Kelly, Kebbell, Hatton and Johnson 2003). This is particularly true of vulnerable witnesses who are obliged to relive the ordeal to which they have allegedly been subjected (see Carson 1995; Davies and Noon 1991; Sanders, Creaton, Bird and Weber 1997; Youth Justice and Criminal Evidence Act, Home Office 1999; Westcott 1995). It is the judge's duty to do everything possible to minimise the trauma suffered by other participants (Murphy 1997). The Court of Appeal has also sanctioned the stopping of cross-examination which is repetitive and in which the witness becomes extremely distressed (R v. Brown 1998). The judge has a great deal of power. The following examples show how judges can intervene to ensure the 'best' evidence is elicited from witnesses, in these instances involving people with learning disabilities.

Lawyer Did you get the impression that Andrew was being gregarious, sort of a party person at that time?
Judge Did you think he was getting friendly with everybody, was he?

Lawyer As you went into the kitchen, he picked up the wrench to defend himself against you? Because you have attacked Terry in the past, have you not?
Judge Can we perhaps get an answer to the first question? Did Terry pick up the wrench to defend himself from you?

Lawyer Alan thought you had something in your hand.
Judge That is not a question.

Lawyer All right, but my question is a slightly different one. Did you feel upset when you arrived at the discotheque? Well let me put this to you. You appeared your normal, happy self when you got there and in no way distressed because nothing had happened.
Judge You must separate these questions. You cannot have a multiple question.

Lawyer And exactly the same question for the second time that you have told the court about. Is the answer still yes? Do you want me to put the question another way? Mohamed, is it right that on the second occasion, the day after, when you were washed by that same man, you did not mind him washing your penis and your genitals. Is that right?
Judge Mr Power, I know you are cross-examining and you have a right to put that. I wonder if it is helpful to say: 'On the second occasion, did you mind him washing you there', rather than putting the negative and he can answer yes or no to that.

The clear implication of this is that judges should be advised of the issues concerning confusing questions we have outlined here, to ensure simple questions are asked in language the witness understands.

Whilst the adversarial criminal justice system of England and Wales relies upon the stringent questioning of witnesses, justice is not served by denying the witness an opportunity to give a detailed account of what they witnessed and by asking several questions at a time, using language a witness does not understand. Further, it appears that cross-examination is poor for determining witness accuracy. Supplementary measures, such as alternative sources of evidence, should be sought if justice is to be served.

References

Bartlett, D. and Memon, A. (1995) 'Advocacy', in R. Bull and D. Carson (eds) *Handbook of Psychology in Legal Contexts* (pp. 543–554). Chichester: John Wiley and Sons.

Bell, B.E. and Loftus, E.F. (1989) 'Trivial persuasion in the courtroom: The power of (a few) minor details', *Journal of Personality and Social Psychology*, 56: 669–79.

Brennan, M. and Brennan, R.E. (1988) *Strange Language: Child victims under cross-examination* (3rd edn). Wagga Wagga, NSW: Charles Sturt University-Riverina.

Carson, D. (1995) 'Regulating the examination of children', *Expert Evidence*, 4: 2–9.

Carson, D. (2000) 'Developing witness skills'. Unpublished manuscript: University of Southampton.

Clifford, B.R. and George, R. (1996) 'A field evaluation of training in three methods of witness/victim investigative interviewing', *Psychology, Crime and Law*, 2: 231–48.

Connors, E., Lundregan, T., Miller, N. and McEwan, T. (1996) *Convicted by Juries, Exonerated by Science: Case studies in the use of DNA evidence to establish innocence after trial*. Alexandria, VA: National Institute of Justice.

Cooke, D.J. (1990) 'Do I feel lucky? Survival in the witness box', *Neuropsychology*, 4: 271–85.

Cutler, B.L., Penrod, S.D. and Dexter, H.R. (1990) 'Juror sensitivity to eyewitness identification evidence', *Law and Human Behavior*, 14: 185-91.

Cutler, B.L., Penrod, S.D. and Stuve, T.E. (1988) 'Juror decision making in eyewitness identification cases', *Law and Human Behavior*, 12: 41–55.

Danet, B. (1980) 'Language in the legal process', *Law and Society Review*, 14: 445–564.

Davies, G.M. and Noon, E. (1991) *An Evaluation of the Live Link for Child Witnesses*. London: Home Office.

Davies, G.M., Westcott, H.L. and Horan, N. (2000) 'The impact of questioning style on the content of investigative interviews with suspected child abuse victims', *Psychology, Crime and Law*, 6: 81–97.

Davies, M., Croal, H. and Tyrer, J. (1995) *Criminal Justice. An introduction to the criminal justice system in England and Wales*. London: Longman.

Elliott, R. (1993) 'Expert testimony about eyewitness identification: A critique', *Law and Human Behavior*, 17: 423–37.

Evans, K. (1995) *Advocacy in Court: A beginner's guide* (2nd edn). London: Blackstone.

Fisher, R.P., Geiselman, R.E. and Raymond, D.S. (1987) 'Critical analysis of police interview techniques', *Journal of Police Science and Administration*, 15: 177–85.

Fox, S.G. and Walters, H.A. (1986) 'The impact of general versus specific expert testimony and eyewitness confidence upon mock-juror judgement', *Law and Human Behavior*, 10: 215–28.

Geiselman, R.E., Fisher, R.P. Cohen, G. and Holland, H.L. (1986) 'Eyewitness responses to leading and misleading questions under the cognitive interview', *Journal of Police Science and Administration*, 14: 31–9.

Gudjonsson, G.H. (1990) 'The relationship of intellectual skills to suggestibility, compliance and acquiescence', *Personality and Individual Differences*, 11: 227–31.

Gudjonsson, G.H. (1992) *The Psychology of Interrogations, Confessions and Testimony*. Chicester: Wiley.

Gudjonsson, G.H. and Clarke, N.K. (1986) 'Suggestibility in police interrogation: a social psychological model', *Social Behaviour*, 1: 83–104.

Home Office (1995) *Digest: Information on the Criminal Justice System in England and Wales*. London: HMSO.

Home Office (1999) *Youth and Criminal Evidence Act*. London: HMSO.

Huff, C.R., Rattner, A. and Sagarin, E. (1996) *Convicted But Innocent: Wrongful conviction and public policy*. London: Sage.

Hutcheson, G., Baxter, J., Telfer, K. and Warden, D. (1995) 'Child witness statement quality: Question type and errors of omission', *Law and Human Behavior*, 6: 631–48.

Kassin, S.M., Ellsworth, P.C. and Smith, V.L. (1994) 'Deja-vu all over again. Elliott's critique of eyewitness experts', *Law and Human Behavior*, 18: 203–10.

Kebbell, M.R., Brodie, S., Muspratt, S., Patterson, L., Quartermaine, R., Riola, V. and Stevenson, J. (2002) *The usefulness of cross-examination in detecting deception*. Unpublished manuscript James Cook University.

Kebbell, M.R. and Hatton, C. (1999) 'People with mental retardation as witnesses in court', *Mental Retardation*, 3: 179–87.

Kebbell, M.R., Hatton, C. and Johnson, S.D. (2001) 'Witnesses with mental retardation in court: What questions are asked and what influence do they have?', *Legal and Criminological Psychology*.

Kebbell, M.R. and Johnson, S.D. (2000) 'The influence of lawyers' questions on witness confidence and accuracy', *Law and Human Behavior*, 24: 629–41.

Kebbell, M.R., O'Kelly, C.M.E. and Orchard, K.J. (2001) *The effect of lawyers' confusing questions and accusations of lying on jurors' perceptions of eyewitness credibility*. Unpublished manuscript. James Cook University, Australia.

Kebbell, M.R. and Milne, R. (1998) 'Police officers' perception of eyewitness factors in forensic investigations: A survey', *The Journal of Social Psychology*, 138: 323–30.

Kebbell, M.R. and Wagstaff, G.F. (1999) *Face Value? Factors that influence eyewitness accuracy*. London: Police Research Group, Home Office.

Kebbell, M.R., Hatton, C. and Johnson, S.D. (2004) 'Witnesses with intellectual disabilities in court: What questions are asked and what influence do they have?', *Legal and Criminology Psychology*, 9: 1–13.

Kebbell, M.R., Deperez, S. and Wagstaff, G.F. (2003) 'The examination and cross-examination of alleged rape-victims and defendants in court', *Psychology Crime and Law*, 9.

Kebbell, M.R., Wagstaff, G.F. and Covey, J.A. (1996) 'The influence of item difficulty on the relationship between eyewitness confidence and accuracy', *British Journal of Psychology*, 87 (4): 653–62.

Kranat, V.K. and Westcott, H.L. (1994) 'Under fire: Lawyers questioning children in criminal courts', *Expert Evidence*, 3: 16–24.

Leippe, M.R. (1980) 'Effects of integrative and memorial processes on the correspondence of eyewitness accuracy and confidence', *Law and Human Behavior*, 4: 261–74.

Leippe, M.R., Manion, A.P. and Romanczyk, A. (1992) 'Eyewitness persuasion: How well do fact finders judge the accuracy of adults' and children's memory reports', *Journal of Personality and Social Psychology*, 63: 181–97.

Lindsay, D.S., Read, J.D. and Sharma, K. (1998) 'Accuracy and confidence in person identification. The relationships is strong when witnessing conditions vary widely', *Psychological Science*, 9: 215–18.

Lindsay, R.C.L., Wells, G.L. and O'Connor, F.J. (1989) 'Mock juror belief of accurate and inaccurate eyewitnesses: A replication and extension', *Law and Human Behavior*, 13: 333–39.

Loftus, E.F. (1979) *Eyewitness Testimony*. London: Harvard University Press.

Loftus, E.F., Miller, D.G. and Burns, H.J. (1978) 'Semantic integration of verbal information into a visual memory', *Journal of Experimental Psychology: Human Learning and Memory*, 4: 19–31.

Loftus, E.F. and Palmer, J.C. (1974) 'Reconstruction of automobile destruction: An example of the interaction between language and memory', *Journal of Verbal Learning and Verbal Behavior*, 13: 585–89.

Loftus, E.F. and Zanni, G. (1975) 'Eyewitness testimony: The influence of the wording of a question', *Bulletin of the Psychonomic Society*, 5: 86–8.

Luus, C.A.E. and Wells, G.L. (1994) 'The malleability of eyewitness confidence: Co-witness and perserverance effects', *Journal of Applied Psychology*, 79: 714–23.

McEwan, J. (1995) 'Adversarial and inquisitorial proceedings', in R. Bull and D. Carson (eds) *Handbook of Psychology in Legal Contexts* (pp. 495–508). Chichester: Wiley.

Memon, A., Holley, A., Milne, R., Koehnken, G. and Bull, R. (1994) 'Towards understanding the effects of interviewer training in evaluating the cognitive interview', *Applied Cognitive Psychology*, 8: 641-59.

Memon, A. and Vartoukian, R. (1996) 'The effects of repeated questioning on young children's eyewitness testimony', *British Journal of Psychology*, 87: 403–15.

Memon, A., Vrij, A. and Bull, R. (1998) *Psychology and Law: Truthfulness, accuracy and credibility*. London: McGraw-Hill.

Milne, R. and Bull, R. (1999) *Investigative Interviewing: Psychology and Practice*. Chicester: Wiley.

Murphy, P. (ed.) (1997) *Blackstone's Criminal Practice,* 7th edn. London: Blackstone.

Murphy, P. and Barnard, D. (1994) *Evidence and Advocacy,* 4th edn. London: Blackstone Press.

O'Kelly, C.M.E., Kebbell, M.R., Hatton, C. and Johnson, S.D. (2003) 'When do Judges intervene in cases involving people with learning disabilities?' *Legal and Criminological Psychology,* 8: 229–40.

Perry, N.W., McAuliff, B.D., Tam, P., Claycomb, L., Dostal, C. and Flanagan, C. (1995) 'When lawyers question children. Is justice served?', *Law and Human Behavior,* 19: 609–29.

Regina *v.* Brown (1998) *Criminal Appeal Reports,* 2: 364.

Rose, D. (1996) *In the Name of the Law.* London: Jonathan Cape.

Sanders, A., Creaton, J., Bird, S. and Weber, L. (1997) *Victims with Learning Disabilities: Negotiating the Criminal Justice System.* Oxford: Centre for Criminological Research, University of Oxford.

Shaw, J.S. III and Mc Clure, K.A. (1996) 'Repeated postevent questioning can lead to elevated levels of eyewitness confidence', *Law and Human Behavior,* 20: 629–53.

Sporer, S.L., Penrod, S.D., Read, J.D. and Cutler, B.L. (1995) 'Choosing, confidence, and accuracy: A meta-analysis of the confidence-accuracy relation in eyewitness identification studies', *Psychological Bulletin,* 118: 315–27.

Stone, M. (1995) *Cross-examination in Criminal Trials* (2nd edn). London: Butterworths.

Vrij, A. (1998) 'Nonverbal communication and credibility', in A. Memon, A.Vrij and R. Bull (eds) *Psychology and Law: Truthfulness, accuracy and credibility* (pp. 32–58). Maidenhead: McGraw-Hill.

Vrij, A. (2000) *Detecting Lies and Deceit.* Chichester: Wiley.

Walker, A.G. (1993) 'Questioning young children in court: A linguistic case study', *Law and Human Behavior,* 17: 58–81.

Wells, G.L., Ferguson, T.J. and Lindsay, R.C.L. (1981) 'The tractability of eyewitness confidence and its implications for triers of fact', *Journal of Applied Psychology,* 66: 688–96.

Wells, G.L., Lindsay, R.C.L. and Ferguson, T.J. (1979) 'Accuracy, confidence, and juror perceptions in eyewitness identification', *Journal of Applied Psychology,* 64: 440–48.

Westcott, H.L. (1995) 'Children's experience of being examined and cross-examined: The opportunity to be heard?', *Expert Evidence,* 4: 13–19.

Westcott, H.L. and Page, M. (2002) 'Cross-examination, sexual abuse and child witness identity', *Child Abuse Review,* 11: 137–52.

Zander, M. and Henderson, P. (1993) 'Crown Court study', *Royal Commission on Criminal Justice. Research studies, 19.* HMSO: London.

Chapter 6

The ageing eyewitness

*Amina Memon, Fiona Gabbert and
Lorraine Hope, University of Aberdeen*

Acknowledgements

The research reported in this chapter was supported by grants from the National Science Foundation and the Economic and Social Research Council. We would like to thank our research collaborators James Bartlett, Ray Bull, Lynn Hulse, Rachel Rose and Jean Searcy for their contribution to this work.

Eyewitness evidence plays a key role in the administration of justice and identification errors can lead to miscarriages of justice (Huff 1987; Rattner 1988; Scheck, Neufeld and Dwyer 2000). To address these concerns, researchers have attempted to identify the conditions under which eyewitnesses may be mistaken (for a review see Memon, Vrij and Bull 2003; Memon and Wright 2000). In some jurisdictions, safeguards are in place to reduce the likelihood of error (see Davies and Valentine 2000; Wells *et al.* 1998). However, the bulk of the literature on eyewitnesses is based on studies of young adults (typically college students) and children. There has been a lack of research on individuals over the age of 60 years. This raises concerns about the generalisability of earlier eyewitness findings. The ageing population profile of developed countries and the fact that senior citizens are more active now than ever before led to our interest in the older witness.

Where straightforward comparisons have been made between different age groups, young adults have been found to be significantly superior to older adults in many eyewitness skills, for example, in accuracy of recall for perpetrator characteristics, environmental details, and for details of actions and events (see Yarmey 2001, for an overview of literature regarding older eyewitnesses). This applies to both free recall (where the witness provides a narrative account from their own perspective) and to cued recall (where the witness responds to interviewer questions, see Yarmey and Kent 1980; Yarmey, Jones and Rashid 1984). Yarmey averaged the results across three studies (Yarmey 1982; Yarmey and Kent 1980; Yarmey *et al.* 1984) to explore age differences further and found that young adults (mean age of 21 years) were 20 per cent more accurate in free recall, 13 per cent more accurate in cued recall, and 15 per cent more complete in their descriptions of suspect than older adults (mean age of 70 years). Other studies have shown that older adult witnesses provide fewer descriptions of the perpetrator (physical and clothing characteristics) than younger witnesses (Brimacombe, Quinton, Nance and Garrioch 1997).

The age of a witness can also relate to memory performance in recognition situations. For example, the typical finding in laboratory studies of unfamiliar face recognition (the recognition of faces seen only once before) is that older adults (60–80 years) are more likely to 'false alarm' to new faces. In other words they are more likely to falsely 'recognise' a face they had not seen previously (Searcy, Bartlett and Memon 1999). In the eyewitness identification setting, older adults are also more prone to making false choices. This chapter will examine some of the difficulties facing the older eyewitness and review studies of young and older adults conducted in our laboratory. The nature of the age related memory errors, the underlying mechanisms and practical implications of the findings will be also be discussed.

Eyewitness errors in the recall of event details

One of the most common sources of eyewitness error is when witnesses' memories become contaminated by information they have acquired since they witnessed the event (Wright and Loftus 1998). When this post-event information is misleading or errant, it is referred to as *misinformation*. In studies of the misinformation effect, participants are exposed to an event (e.g. a simulated crime), then later misinformed about some aspect of it (e.g. an erroneous newspaper report about the crime). The typical finding is that participants exposed to misinformation will often incorporate misleading details into their memory reports (e.g. Wright and Loftus 1998).

Research in the field of cognitive ageing suggests that older adults *should* be more prone to misinformation effects. For example, research indicates that older adults often have deficits in source monitoring (Johnson, Hashtroudi and Lindsay 1993; Schacter, Kihlstrom, Kaszniak and Valdiserri 1993). In other words, older adults may experience difficulty in distinguishing what they have witnessed themselves as opposed to what they may have heard from someone else (i.e., a problem identifying the precise *source* of the information). Source confusion has been shown to play a major role in susceptibility to post-event misinformation (Mitchell, Johnson and Mather, in press; Zaragoza, Lane, Ackil and Chambers 1997), and older adults are particularly prone to making this kind of error (Schacter *et al.* 1993). A typical consequence of source confusion is that the suggested information is erroneously reported as if it was part of the original memory (Johnson *et al.* 1993; Karpel, Hoyer and Toglia 2001; Mitchell *et al.* 2003; Wegesin, Jacobs, Zubin, Ventura and Stern 2000; Zaragoza *et al.* 1997).

Mitchell *et al.* (2003) explored age differences in source monitoring performance using a standard misinformation paradigm and found that older adults were more likely than young adults to say that they saw information that was actually only suggested to them. They were also more confident in their source misattributions than were younger adults. Similarly, Karpel *et al.* (2001) found that older adults were more likely to report items falsely that had only been suggested. Again, it was found that older adults were more confident about the falsely recognised items. Cohen and Faulkner (1989) and Loftus, Levidow and Duensing (1992) have also demonstrated that older adults are more likely to retrieve misinformation than younger adults.

Gabbert, Memon and Allan (2003) employed a novel procedure to examine the effects of misinformation. In their study, younger (18–30 years) and older (60–80 years) adults were led to believe that they were seeing the same video of a crime scene. Although the two video clips contained exactly the same sequence of events, they were filmed from different angles to simulate different witness perspectives. Critically, this manipulation allowed different features of the event to be observed for each participant. After viewing the event, participants were asked to recall the event either alone or in (same-age) pairs. Thus, each person had an opportunity to (unintentionally) introduce items of mis-information into the discussion. In other words, details of the event visible only from their perspective and details that were not seen by the other witnesses. An individual recall test was then administered to examine the effects of the discussion on subsequent memory reports. A significant proportion (71 per cent) of witnesses who had discussed the event reported details acquired during the discussion (i.e. details they simply could not have seen given their witness perspective). Age differences emerged in the amount of correct items of information reported about the event (means = 18.00 and 15.95 for the young and older age-groups respectively). However, no age-related differences in susceptibility to the items of misinformation were demonstrated.

This finding contrasts with the conclusions of studies reviewed earlier that found an age-related increase in susceptibility to misinformation. Perhaps this is because the act of being able to discuss memories provides older adults with additional memory cues about event details, as well as focusing their attention to the event (see Gabbert et al. 2003).

Two further studies have also demonstrated that older adults are *not* more susceptible to misinformation than their younger counterparts. In a study comparing the performance of young adult witnesses with that of children and older adults, Coxon and Valentine (1997) found no significant differences in the suggestibility of young and older adults. Similarly, Searcy, Bartlett and Memon (2000) asked younger and older adults to view a videotape of a simulated crime, then presented them with misinformation about the criminal's physical features in the form of post-event narratives. In line with Coxon and Valentine (1997), they found the younger group were equally susceptible to the misleading physical cues as the older group. It is possible that differences between experimental procedures may explain the inconsistent results regarding age differences in susceptibility to misinformation (e.g. in samples of participants or task demands). At present, research examining age differences in recall within the eyewitness literature is sparse. Therefore, although a growing number of studies suggest an age-related increase in susceptibility to misinformation, no firm conclusions can be drawn.

Eyewitness recognition errors

One of the earliest studies to examine the effects of ageing on eyewitness recognition performance was that of Yarmey et al. (1984). They exposed younger and older participants to a simulated crime to investigate age differences in ability to identify accurately a suspect among a line-up of photographs. It was noted that there were no age differences in the correct identification of a suspect from suspect-present line-ups. However, if a suspect was absent from a line-up, older witnesses made more false identifications. This finding is reminiscent of the typical finding in laboratory studies of face recognition. For example, Bartlett, Strater and Fulton (1991) reported that while young and older adults did not differ in the rates of correct recognition of previously seen unfamiliar faces, they made more false alarms to faces that had not seen before.

More recently, Searcy *et al.* (1999) compared the performance of young (18–30 years) and older adults (60–80 years). Participants were shown a crime video followed by a photo-line-up. Older participants made more erroneous foil choices regardless of whether the target was present or absent. In a second line-up task, participants were asked to identify a person who appeared in a brief video interview shown prior to the crime tape. Again, the older participants made more false choices across target present and absent line-ups. The age related increase in false identifications was replicated in subsequent studies (Memon and Bartlett 2002; Memon and Gabbert 2003; Searcy *et al.* 2000; Searcy, Bartlett, Memon and Swanson 2001). Follow-up studies set about trying to understand the conditions under which age differences in eyewitness performance are attenuated and the factors responsible.

Four studies of ageing and eyewitness identification were recently completed in our laboratory at Aberdeen University. There were a number of similarities between the studies. For example, all but the final study involved showing unsuspecting witnesses a videotaped crime event followed by a six item photo-line-up. Delay between exposure to the event and identification varied from approximately 40 minutes to 48 hours. Participants in all studies received unbiased line-up instructions informing them that the target witnessed in the video may or may not be present in the line-up. Younger participants (17–30 years) were recruited from the undergraduate population at the University of Aberdeen. Older participants (60–81 years) were healthy, active members of the local community.

Study 1: exposure to mug-shots and accuracy of a subsequent identification

One factor that may be responsible for the age related increase in false alarms to faces that have not been seen before is that older adults rely on 'familiarity' as opposed to 'recollection' of the context in which the face was previously seen as a basis for responding (Bartlett *et al.* 1991; Searcy *et al.* 1999). As indicated earlier, accurate recollection of source information is critical in an eyewitness setting, especially when witnesses are exposed to a number of faces during the course of a police investigation. A person who has previously engaged in a similar criminal activity in the locality may appear in a police mug-book as well as a formal identification parade. Consider the case of Gary Graham who was convicted of murder in Texas in 1999. The Graham case relied primarily on eyewitness evidence but only one of eight witnesses actually made a positive identification from a line-up. This identification occurred one day after the witness had seen the same suspect's face in a photo array. We cannot say whether or not the witness in the Graham case was accurate, but research has shown that exposure to a suspect's face prior to a formal identification (e.g. a facial composite shown in the media, a face seen in a mug-shot album or in an earlier line-up) can affect the likelihood of an accurate identification. Gary Graham was executed in June 2000.

The results of several studies suggest that when witnesses view a line-up after they have examined mug-shots, they can be inclined, mistakenly, to identify a person whose mug-shot photograph they have previously seen (Brigham and Cairns 1988; Gorenstein and Ellsworth 1980). We refer to this phenomenon below as the 'mug-shot exposure effect'. There are two primary explanations for this effect. One explanation is that it is a source monitoring error of the kind described earlier – a face appears familiar because of a prior encounter. Another possibility is that once a witness reaches an identification decision and expresses it, he or she feels committed to that identification and may be less willing to change the decision later. The 'commitment' effect has recently been proposed to be one of the most important factors responsible for the mug-shot exposure effect (Dysart, Lindsay, Hammond and Dupuis 2001).

Our first study (Memon, Hope, Bartlett and Bull 2003) set out to see if older adults were more susceptible to mug-shot exposure effect. One hundred and sixty-nine young (mean = 22 years) and older (mean = 69 years) witnesses viewed a video of a crime. Participants were allocated to one of two conditions. One group were asked to look through a mug-shot album and asked if the thief (target) from the crime video was among the photographs. The mug-shot album consisted of 12 black and white 4″ × 3″ photographs of white males of a similar age to the main target depicted in the video event. Our mug-shot album modelled the 'witness book' format used in Scotland where instead of asking the witness to search through a large database of faces, the police frequently select fewer faces of suspects who have previously committed crimes that fit the category under investigation. The target's face did not appear in the mug-shot album. In the other condition, witnesses did not see the mug-shot album but engaged in a filler task. After a 48-hour delay all witnesses took part in a target absent photo identification parade comprised of large (10″ × 8″) coloured photographs presented in a 3 × 2 array. The line-up was comprised of six faces adopting the conventions of line-up procedures in Scotland where an identification parade generally consists of a suspect and between five and eight foils. Again, the target was absent but one of the faces from the mug-shot albums (an innocent face) appeared in the photo-line-up. We refer to this face as the critical foil.

Memon *et al*. (2003) report two main findings. Older adults showed a significantly greater tendency to make choices from the mug-shot album than young participants (71 per cent and 42 per cent respectively). Similarly, older adults were also more likely to make choices from the photo-line-up than younger participants (62 per cent and 33 per cent respectively). Given that these were choices of innocent foils, these are false identifications. But what about choices of our critical (innocent) foil face that appeared in both mug-shots and line-up? The results here were more complex. Witnesses who made *any* selection from the mug-shot album (whether it was a critical foil or a different foil) were more likely to make a false choice of the critical foil in the photo-line-up than those witnesses who made no mug-shot choice. Thus, the tendency to pick any face from the mug-shot (mug-shot choosing) seemed to be the most important factor in predicting critical foil choices. Participants' prior commitment to choosing the critical foil was not a necessary prerequisite for the mug-shot effect. This effect is interesting because it is somewhat counterintuitive. One might have predicted that a witness who is presented with a line-up in which the face he or she saw earlier is absent will not pick anyone from the line-up. Yet Memon *et al*. (2003) found that mug-shot choosers are highly likely to make line-up choices whether or not the previously chosen face was present.

The increase in choices of the critical (innocent) foil following prior exposure supports the hypothesis that source monitoring errors may in part be responsible for the tendency to choose that foil erroneously . The participants see the critical foil in the photo-line-up and he appears familiar. They misattribute this familiarity to the crime video. One problem with this account is that it would not have predicted that critical foil choices would depend on mug-shot choosing. Moreover, the literature on ageing and source memory problems (e.g. Brown, Jones and Davis 1995) would have led us to expect that that older adults would be more susceptible to choosing the critical foil but there were no age by condition interactions. However, we know that in healthy community samples of older adults, source memory deficits are not always observed (Glisky, Rubin and Davidson 2001), a point illustrated by our discussion of the next study reported in this chapter.

A more plausible explanation of the Memon *et al*. (in press, a) data is that the older adults were relying more on a familiarity strategy in making their choices from the mug-shot album task and photo-line-up task. This is consistent with the high rates of false choosing of all foil faces in both tasks (see Memon *et al.* 2003 for further details and alternative hypotheses). Thus, the conclusion so far is that older adults are more prone to choosing than younger adults. In the next study, we look more closely at our older age groups.

Study 2: identification abilities of young-old and old-old witnesses

In this study 32 young (m = 19.6 years) and 31 older participants (m = 69 years) were tested. All witnesses viewed a video of a man walking through a park engaging in relatively innocuous activities including a conversation with a young woman. One week later, all participants viewed a target absent line-up for the central male character around whom the film was based. The overall accuracy rate (correct rejections from the target-absent line-up) was 61 per cent. There was not a statistically significant difference in the accuracy rates of young and older adults (66 per cent and 55 per cent respectively). A median split was performed on the older group dividing the older participants into a younger-old and older-old group. Those of 69 years and above were placed in an Old-Old group (n = 16) while those aged 68 and under constituted the Young-Old group (n = 15). There were significant age differences in line-up performance between these two older age groups. Seventy-five per cent of the Old-Old group made false choices from the target-absent line-up, compared to only 13 per cent of the Young-Old group. This suggests that perhaps older adults (ages 69 and over) may be particularly vulnerable to the age related false choosing effect. It is possible that by placing all our older adults in one large group we have been masking individual differences (see also LaRue 1992). Indeed, in their recent research, Glisky *et al.* (2001) make the same point. They suggest that:

> it may be the case that many older adults do not experience significant memory declines with age. Failure to take account of these individual differences may mask findings that are important for understanding the deficits that do occur and the reasons for them. The important differences may not be between young and old adults but may be between different subgroups of older adults who are ageing differently. (p. 1146)

Study 3: duration of exposure and eyewitness recognition

One factor that may underlie age differences in memory is a deficiency in the quality of encoding of event details, resulting in poor memory representations that are difficult to retrieve (see Balota, Dolan and Duchek 2000, for a review). It has been suggested that reduced processing resources (e.g. a reduction in attentional capacity) can impair the ability of older adults to encode the elaborative information (Craik 1986; Naveh-Benjamin and Craik 1996). For example, specific contextual details about items that can facilitate later retrieval. As argued earlier, in an eyewitness setting, it is critical to retrieve an accurate representation of what was seen earlier to avoid source confusion errors.

In order to explore the impact of age differences in encoding on memory, the next study examined the relationship between duration on exposure to a face in an eyewitness setting, and identification accuracy and confidence in young and older adults (Memon, Hope and Bull 2003). Prior literature suggests that increases in the amount of time available for processing enhances face recognition (e.g. Winograd 1981). In line with this, Shapiro and Penrod (1986), in a meta-analysis of face recognition studies, reported a positive relationship between the amount of time spent viewing a face and accurate identification rates. However, false alarm rates also increased with longer viewing times. Only a handful of eyewitness studies have systematically examined the effects of exposure duration on face memory, despite its forensic importance. Memon *et al.* (2003) were particularly interested in the counterintuitive finding that extended exposure increases false alarms. There is some evidence to suggest that under conditions of 'longer' exposure, participants make use of meta-memorial information such as the 'availability' or 'ease' with which information can be brought to mind (Read 1995) and this can sometimes lead to false alarms. Read (1995) found that participants who interacted with store clerks for a longer duration (four to 15 minutes as compared to 30 to 60 seconds) made more correct choices when presented with a line-up in which the target was present (a target-present line-up) but more false choices when a target was absent. Recall that older adults are more likely to rely on 'familiarity' and 'availability' in making decisions (Searcy, Bartlett and Memon 2000). Memon *et al.* (2003) therefore predicted an increase in false alarms in the extended exposure condition.

One hundred and sixty four young (ages 17–25) and older (ages 59–81) adults viewed a simulated crime in which they saw the culprit's face for a short (12 second) or longer (45 second) duration. They were then tested with a line-up in which the culprit or target was absent (TA) or a line-up containing the target (TP) line-up. The longer exposure significantly boosted accuracy rates for both young and older participants particularly for target present line-ups but it also increased the correct rejection rate in target absent line-ups. These findings reinforce the common-sense view (and that expressed by the USA's Supreme Court in the case of Neil *v*. Biggers 1972) that extended exposure should aid subsequent recognition accuracy. In the short exposure condition, self reports of confidence in the decision made differed depending on whether the witness was accurate or not, with inaccurate witnesses expressing lower confidence. However, longer exposure to the target inflated the confidence ratings of younger and older adults. In the target present condition, witnesses were confident in the long exposure condition, even when they were wrong. Clearly, jurors and police officers should be aware of this undesirable effect of extended exposure to a culprit on witnesses' subjective confidence in their identification decisions.

With respect to recall of event details, there were age differences in the short exposure condition with the older adults recalling significantly fewer correct details. There were no age differences in the amount of recall errors and no age effects in the long exposure condition. The age differences in the short exposure condition fit with Craik's (1986) hypothesis that older adults may fail to encode in elaboration of details involving effort when attentional capacity is limited. However, when environmental support is provided, or conditions facilitate elaborative encoding, age differences are minimised (Craik, Byrd and Swanson 1987).

Study 4: context reinstatement and eyewitness identification

Research has shown that reinstating the context in which an event was experienced improves identification accuracy (See Malpass 1996 for a review of the effects of context reinstatement techniques). Context reinstatement may occur physically (returning to the scene of crime when performing the identification task) or, if that is not appropriate, mentally (imagining the scene of crime before performing the identification task). Context reinstatement is one of the principle components of the cognitive interview (Fisher and Geiselman 1992), a technique that can significantly increase the quantity and quality of information that can be obtained from a witness (Koehnken, Milne, Memon and Bull 1999).

A number of studies have reported that the reinstatement of original contextual cues can reduce false choosing in eyewitness tasks (Cutler, Penrod and Martens 1997; Gwyer and Clifford 1997; Kraffka and Penrod 1985; Malpass and Devine 1981; Smith and Vela 1992) although several other studies report null effects (Fisher, Quigley, Brock, Chin and Cutler 1990; Searcy, Bartlett, Memon and Swanson 2001). Searcy *et al.* (2001) included a younger and older age group in their study of the effects of an extended delay (one month) and cognitive interview on eyewitness identification accuracy. The cognitive interview had no apparent effects on the performance of young or older witnesses.

The study conducted in our laboratory employed a 2 (cognitive interview versus structured interview) × 2 (misinformation versus no misinformation) between subjects design. Sixty older adults (mean = 68 years) were randomly assigned to receive either the cognitive or structured interview and, within each interview type, received mis-information or no misinformation before the interview, resulting in four experimental groups. Witnesses met a confederate, in the course of an interaction during which they engaged in a brief conversation with the confederate. An hour later, they were asked if they could identify her from a target-absent line-up. Eighty-seven per cent of our senior citizens falsely identified a face from the line-up. The cognitive interview had no effect whatsoever on identification accuracy. Five people correctly rejected the lineup under cognitive interview conditions (eight per cent) while only three people correctly rejected the line-up under SI con-ditions (five per cent). Those participants interviewed with a cognitive interview produced significantly more correct details about the objects that the confederate was carrying than a structured interview. Contrary to prior studies (e.g. Memon, Wark, Holley, Bull and Koehnken 1996) there were no significant differences in number of misleading details recalled under the cognitive and structured interviews.

In line with prior studies (Fisher *et al.* 1990), the cognitive interview does not aid face recognition (see also Brown 2003). Of most concern is that we obtained an alarmingly high false identification rate with an extended exposure to a face during the course of a live interaction (compare with Study 3, in this chapter). The vast majority of our older witnesses made a false identification from a target absent line-up even though they had the option to say the person they had encountered earlier was not in the line-up.

In the final section of this chapter, we describe a post-line-up questionnaire that provides some additional data on the attributions and thought processes that may underlie decisions in eyewitness tasks.

Post-line-up questionnaire

Researchers have tended to overlook the fact that witnesses are individuals with their own belief systems. Their decisions may be influenced by prior experiences and attitudes. These factors may have an impact upon decisions independently of any techniques designed to improve accuracy.

A post-line-up questionnaire was developed to examine participants' post-identification cognitions regarding the line-up identification task. Our young and older adults were asked to provide a response to four questions relating to their beliefs about the line-up task. The questionnaire was administered immediately after the line-up task in all studies and we asked people to work through the questionnaire at their own pace. No feedback on the accuracy of their line-up decision was supplied until the final debriefing at the end of the study. Two questions were of particular interest: question one sought to determine whether witnesses expect that the guilty party will always be present and thereby assume their job is to identify him or her (rather than first of all discern whether the actual perpetrator is in fact present). A further question asked witnesses whether they thought they would have made the same identification decision in real life. Results across four studies (N = 636) indicated that 90 per cent of younger and older witnesses assumed the perpetrator was present in the line-up. This came as a surprise as all witnesses were provided with cautionary instructions which stated that the perpetrator may or may not be present in the line-up. When asked, 95 per cent of our younger participants and 93 per cent of our older participants recalled the instruction that the perpetrator may not be present. Only 17 per cent said they felt under pressure to choose from the line-up and 78 per cent indicated that they would be happy to make the same decision in real life. The overall accuracy rate was only 48% (i.e. only 48 per cent of participants made the correct identification decision).

A significant proportion of witnesses indicated that they would make the same decision in real life even though they were actually inaccurate in their identification decision. Forty-seven per cent of those who said they would make the same decision in real life were incorrect in their line-up decision (N = 220).

Our results clearly indicate that participants in all our studies approach the line-up task with a strong and consistent expectation about the identification, namely that the target (perpetrator) will be present in the line-up. This expectation is there despite the use of cautionary line-up instructions. Some of our witnesses commented that they hold the same beliefs and expectations regarding real life line-up identification parades.

Conclusion

In this chapter we have attempted to provide an overview of the ageing eyewitness. We began by looking at age differences in susceptibility to misinformation. Prior work was inconclusive on this issue. The overall conclusion we have drawn from our work is that there is there is no clear evidence to suggest an age-related vulnerability to misinformation. In terms of accuracy of recall, older adults tend to recall fewer correct details than younger adults particularly when they have only had a brief exposure to an eyewitness event. Studies of eyewitness recognition errors have shown that older adults are consistently more prone to making false identifications from line-ups. The results of Study 4 suggest that even when older witnesses have had extended interactions with strangers, they are still likely to identify falsely someone from a target absent line-up. What is also worrying, is that the majority of witnesses told us that they expected the target to be present in the line-up and would make the same decision were it a real life situation.

More research is warranted to examine the generalisability of the findings reported here and to examine further individual differences between older age samples (*cf.* Study 2, this chapter). Finally, the research presented in this chapter may raise concerns regarding whether or not eyewitness evidence obtained from older witnesses is given the same weight by investigating officers and jurors as the testimony of younger adults. To date, there is only one published study (Brimacombe *et al.* 1997) that has systematically examined the perceptions of young and older eyewitnesses in a simulated jury setting. The participants in that study (college students) did not display negative stereotypes of older adult eyewitnesses. However, further research using a more representative sample of 'jurors' will shed more light on this issue.

References

Balota, D.A., Dolan, P. and Duchek, J. (2000) 'Memory changes in healthy older adults', in E. Tulving and F.I.M. Craik (eds) *The Oxford Handbook of Memory* (pp. 395–425). Oxford: New York.

Bartlett, J.C. and Fulton, A. (1991) 'Familiarity and recognition of faces: The factor of age', *Memory and Cognition*, 19: 229–38.

Bartlett, J.C., Strater, L. and Fulton, A. (1991) 'False recency and false fame of faces in young adulthood and old age', *Memory and Cognition*, 19: 177–88.

Brigham, J.C. and Cairns, D.L. (1988) 'The effect of mug-shot inspections on eyewitness identification accuracy', *Journal of Applied Social Psychology*, 18: 1394–410.

Brimacombe, C.A.E., Quinton, N., Nance, N. and Garrioch, L. (1997) 'Is age irrelevant? Perceptions of young and old adults eyewitnesses', *Law and Human Behavior*, 21: 619–34.

Brown, A.S., Jones, E.M. and Davis, T.L. (1995) 'Age differences in conversational source monitoring', *Psychology and Ageing*, 10: 111–22.

Brown, J.M. (2003) 'Eyewitness memory for arousing events: Putting things into context', *Applied Cognitive Psychology*.

Cohen, G. and Faulkner, D. (1989) 'Age-differences in source forgetting – effects on reality monitoring and on eyewitness testimony', *Psychology and Ageing*, 4: 10–17.

Coxon, P. and Valentine, T. (1997) 'The effects of the age of eyewitnesses on the accuracy and suggestibility of their testimony', *Applied Cognitive Psychology*, 11: 415–30.

Craik, F.I.M. (1986) 'A functional account of age differences in memory', in F. Klix and H. Hagendorf (eds) *Human Memory and Cognitive Capabilities, Mechanisms and Performances* (pp. 409–422). North-Holland: Elsevier Science Publishers B.V.

Craik, F.I.M., Bryd, M. and Swanson, J.M. (1987) 'Patterns of memory loss in three elderly samples', *Psychology and Ageing*, 2: 79–86.

Cutler, B.L., Penrod, S.D. and Martens, T.K. (1997) 'Improving the reliability of eyewitness testimony: putting context into context', *Journal of Applied Psychology*, 72: 629–37.

Davies, G. and Valentine, T. (2000) 'Codes of practice for identification', *Expert Evidence*, 7: 59–65.

Dysart, J., Lindsay, R.C.L., Hammond, R. and Dupuis, P. (2001) 'Mug shot exposure prior to line-up identification: Interference, transference and commitment effects', *Journal of Applied Psychology*, 86: 1280–284.

Fisher, R.P. and Geiselman, R.E. (1992) *Memory-enhancing techniques for investigative interviewing: The cognitive interview*. Springfield, IL: Charles C Thomas.

Fisher, R.P., Quigley, K.L., Brock, P., Chin, E. and Cutler, B. (1990) The effectiveness of the Cognitive Interview in description and identification tasks. Paper presented at American Psychology Law Society, Williamsburg, VA.

Gabbert, F., Memon, A. and Allan, K. (2003) 'Memory Conformity: Can eyewitnesses influence each other's memories for an event?', *Applied Cognitive Psychology*, 17: 533–44.

Glisky, E.L., Rubin, S.R. and Davidson, S.R. (2001) 'Source memory in older adults: An encoding or retrieval problem?', *Journal of Experimental Psychology: Learning, Memory and Cognition*, 27: 1131–146.

Gorenstein, G.W. and Ellsworth, P.C. (1980) 'Effect of choosing an incorrect photograph on a later identification by an eyewitness', *Journal of Applied Psychology*, 65: 616–22.

Gwyer, P. and Clifford, B.R. (1997) 'The effects of cognitive interview on recall, identification, confidence and the confidence-accuracy relationship', *Applied Cognitive Psychology*, 11: 121–45.

Huff, C.R. (1987) 'Wrongful convictions: Societal tolerance of injustice', *Research in Social Problems*, 4: 99–115.

Johnson, M.K., Hashtroudi, S. and Lindsay, D.S. (1993) 'Source monitoring', *Psychological Bulletin*, 114: 3–28.

Karpel, M.E., Hoyer, W.J. and Toglia, M.P. (2001) 'Accuracy and qualities of real and suggested memories: Non-specific age differences', *Journals of Gerontology Series B – Psychological Sciences and Social Sciences*, 56: 103–10.

Koehnken, G., Milne, R., Memon, A. and Bull, R. (1999) 'A meta-analysis on the effects of the Cognitive Interview', *Special Issue of Psychology, Crime and the Law*, 5: 3–27.

Kraffka, C. and Penrod, S. (1985) 'Reinstatement of context in a field experiment on eyewitness identification', *Journal of Personality and Social Psychology*, 49: 58–69.

LaRue, A. (1992) *Ageing and Neuropsychological Assessment*. Plenum Press: New York.

Loftus, E.F., Levidow, B. and Duensing, S. (1992) 'Who remembers best? Individual differences in memory for events that occurred in a science museum', *Applied Cognitive Psychology*, 6: 93–107.

Malpass, R.S. (1996) 'Enhancing eyewitness memory', in S.L. Sporer, R.S. Malpass and G. Köhnken (eds) *Psychological Issues in Eyewitness Identification* (pp. 177–204). Mahway, NJ: Lawrence Erlbaum Associates.

Malpass, R.S. and Devine, P.G. (1981) 'Eyewitness identification – Line-up instructions and the absence of the offender', *Journal of Applied Psychology*, 66: 482–89.

Memon, A. and Bartlett, J.C. (2002) 'The effects of verbalisation on face recognition in young and older adults', *Applied Cognitive Psychology*, 16: 635–50.

Memon, A. and Gabbert, F. (2003) 'Improving the identification accuracy of senior witnesses: Do pre-line-up questions and sequential testing help?', *Journal of Applied Psychology*, 88 (2): 341–47.

Memon, A., Hope, L., Bartlett, J. and Bull, R. (2002) 'Eyewitness recognition errors: The effects of mug-shot viewing and choosing in young and old adults', *Memory and Cognition*, 30: 1219–27.

Memon, A., Hope, L. and Bull, R. (2003) 'Exposure Duration: Effects on eyewitness accuracy and confidence', *British Journal of Psychology*, 94: 339–54.

Memon, A., Vrij, A. and Bull, R.H.C. (2003) *Psychology and Law: Truthfulness, Accuracy and Credibility of victims, witnesses and suspects* 2nd edition. Chichester: John Wiley and Sons.

Memon, A., Wark, L., Holley, A., Bull, R. and Koehnken, G. (1996) 'Reducing suggestibility in child witness interviews', *Applied Cognitive Psychology*, 10: 503–18.

Memon, A. and Wright, D. (2000) 'Eyewitness testimony: Theoretical and practical issues', in J. McGuire, T. Mason and A. O'Kane (eds) *Behaviour, Crime and Legal Process*. Chichester: John Wiley and Sons.

Mitchell, K.J., Johnson, M.K. and Mather, M. (in press) 'Source monitoring and suggestibility to misinformation: Adult age-related differences', *Applied Cognitive Psychology*.

Naveh-Benjamin, M. and Craik, F.I.M. (1996) 'Effects of perceptual and conceptual processing on memory for words and voice: Different patterns for young and old', *Quarterly Journal of Experimental Psychology: Human Experimental Psychology*, 49a: 780–96.

Neil *v.* Biggers (1972) 409, U.S. 188.

Rattner, A. (1988) 'Convicted but innocent: Wrongful conviction and the criminal justice system', *Law and Human Behavior*, 12: 283–93.

Read, J.D. (1995) 'The availability heuristic in person identification – the sometimes misleading consequences of enhanced contextual information', *Applied Cognitive Psychology*, 9: 91–121.

Schacter, D.L., Kihlstrom, J.F., Kaszniak, A.W. and Valdiserri, M. (1993) 'Preserved and impaired memory functions in elderly adults', in J. Cerella, J., Rybash, W. Hoyer and M.L. Commons (eds) *Adult Information Processing: Limits On Loss* (pp. 327–350). San Diego: Academic Press, Inc.

Scheck, B., Neufeld, P. and Dwyer, J. (2000) *Actual Innocence*. New York: Random House.

Searcy, J.H., Bartlett, J.C. and Memon, A. (1999) 'Age differences in accuracy and choosing in eyewitness identification and face recognition', *Memory and Cognition*, 27: 538–52.

Searcy, J.H., Bartlett, J.C. and Memon, A. (2000) 'Relationship of availability, line-up conditions and individual differences to false identification by young and older eyewitnesses', *Legal and Criminological Psychology*, 5: 219–36.

Searcy, J.H., Bartlett, J.C., Memon, A. and Swanson, K. (2001) 'Ageing and line-up performance at long retention intervals: Effects of meta-memory and context reinstatement', *Journal of Applied Psychology*, 86: 207–14.

Shapiro, P.N. and Penrod, S. (1986) 'Meta-analysis of facial identification studies', *Psychological Bulletin*, 100: 139–56.

Smith, S.M. and Vela, E. (1992) 'Environmental context-dependent eyewitness recognition', *Applied Cognitive Psychology*, 6: 125–39.

Wegesin, D.J., Jacobs, D.M., Zubin, N.R., Ventura, P.R. and Stern, Y. (2000) 'Source memory and encoding strategy in normal ageing', *Journal of Clinical and Experimental Neuropsychology*, 22: 455–64.

Wells, G.L., Small, M., Penrod, S., Malpass, R., Fulero, S.M. and Brimacombe, C.A.E. (1998) 'Eyewitness identification procedures: Recommendations for line-ups and photospreads', *Law and Human Behaviour*, 22: 603–47.

Winograd, E. (1981) 'Elaboration and distinctiveness in memory for faces', *Journal of Experimental Psychology: Human Learning and Memory*, 7: 181–90.

Wright, D.B. and Loftus, E.F. (1998) 'How misinformation alters memories', *Journal of Experimental Child Psychology*, 71: 155–64.

Yarmey, A.D. (1982) 'Eyewitness identification and stereotypes of criminals', in A. Trankell (ed.) *Reconstructing the Past: The role of psychologists in criminal trials* (pp. 205–225). Stockholm, Sweden: Norstedt and Soners.

Yarmey, A.D. (2001) 'The older eyewitness', in M.B. Rothman, B.D. Dunlop and P. Entzel (eds) *Elders, Crime and the Criminal Justice System* (pp. 127–148). Springer.

Yarmey, A.D., Jones, H.T. and Rashid, S. (1984) 'Eyewitness memory of elderly and young adults', in D.J. Muller, D.E. Blackman and A.J. Chapman (eds) *Psychology and Law* (pp. 215–228). Chichester, UK: John Wiley and Sons.

Yarmey, A.D. and Kent, J. (1980) 'Eyewitness identification by elderly and young adults', *Law and Human Behavior*, 4: 359–71.

Zaragoza, M.S., Lane, S.M., Ackil, J.K. and Chambers, K.L. (1997) 'Confusing real and suggested memories: Source monitoring and eyewitness suggestibility', in N.L. Stein, P.A. Ornstein, B. Tversky and C. Brainerd (eds) *Memory for Everyday and Emotional Events* (pp. 401–425). New Jersey: Lawrence Erlbaum.

Section 4

Correlates of Criminality: Sensations and Substances

If we can predict who is likely to offend, then ultimately, we can aim to prevent that offending behaviour. We consider two areas of prediction in the next section of the book. Firstly, we take a classic social psychological approach by assessing whether attitudes, beliefs and, in this case 'sensational interests' predict behaviour. Thereafter, we move to a consideration of whether one set of potentially harmful behaviours, those related to substance abuse, are associated with forms of anti-social and other criminal activity. The first chapter by Vincent Egan, examines how an interest in sensational material has been used to predict risk of serious, violent behaviour. Newspaper reports of particularly heinous crimes are spiced up by reference to people's sensational (and sensationalised) interests. However, it is unclear how readily such interests may be associated with any actions at all, be they legal or illegal. In Chapter 7, we see case examples and empirical explorations that can help develop more meaningful predictive tools.

Chapters 8 and 9 move us into the realms of whether illicit drugs use is causally related to offending and how innovative criminal justice approaches can be used alongside other programmes to tackle problems of substance misuse. There are a plethora of publications on the personalities of offenders and causes of offending, yet there are few forensic psychological text books that explore illicit drug and substance abuse in any way other than to acknowledge them as statistical predictors of offending behaviour.

The production and trade in drugs clearly fall into the realms of social policy and anthropology as well as forensic fields. A substantial proportion of prison health care budgets are targeted at Mandatory Drugs

Testing and treatment. Women's prisons contain many of the world's most dispossessed who have been used as 'mules' or couriers. Neighbourhood disorder, prostitution and organised crime all have links to substance abuse. Yet, the majority of drug users in this country are probably not engaged in other offences and many are in legitimate, well paid jobs. However, those who do offend account for a significant proportion of crime. Unlike our colleagues in health, counselling and clinical psychology, it is fair to say that forensic psychologists should have paid more heed to substance abuse. In Chapters 8 and 9, the authors utilise techniques from criminology, policing, health, occupational and forensic psychology to provide a broad, multi-disciplinary approach to drugs related offending.

Chapter 7

The status of sensational interests as indicators of possible risk

Vincent Egan, Glasgow Caledonian University

One does not have to view the media coverage of unusual and serious offences for long, before the interest patterns of the offenders are commented on. In February 2001, David Mulcahy and John Duffy ('The Railway Rapists') were convicted of the rape and murder of three women. In their background, it was noted that 'Neither boy had girlfriends at school and they shared a fascination with martial arts, watching kung-fu films, collecting knives and books on how to maim and kill' (Bennetto, *The Independent*, February 2001). Also in February 2001, it was feared that some high-school students in Kansas were about to massacre members of their school in the same way Eric Harris and Dylan Klebold had carried out the shooting at Columbine High School in April 1999. The raid on the homes of the students revealed pipe-bombs, knives, white supremacist literature and an animal skull daubed with swastikas. Detective Steven Rupert of Jackson County Sheriff's Office stated 'We don't know how serious they were. We can't delve into their minds, [but] we just couldn't wait.' In October 2002, a white racist bodybuilder with a large arsenal of weapons and explosives (and plans to use these in an attack on a mosque) was convicted for 12 years (Morris 2002). At the end of that month, the Washington DC–Baltimore conurbation was plagued by a serial-killing sniper who killed at least 12 persons and taunted the police with a message on the tarot card depicting death.

Fortunately, such persons are exceptional, and many offenders have more conventional interests in sports, vehicles or popular music. However, such information is not regarded as salient to understanding those individuals. Rather, an offender's interest or active involvement in violent, morbid, and macabre topics with a physiologically arousing and mentally stimulating dimension (e.g. actual and surrogate violence, sexuality, ideologically-driven power fantasies) has been presented as if this had some causal or contributory role to the offence in question. The current review discusses the status of such sensational interests as indicators of possible risk of serious violent or sexual offending, reviewing systematic research to operationalise formally the underlying constructs. The chapter seeks to provide a more systematic and scientific psychological framework by which such interests and behaviours might be formally examined and used to guide thinking about risk.

What is the aetiology of the idea of the pathological status of sensational interests?

Based on his decades of clinical experience, Brittain (1970) wrote a paper called *The Sadistic Murderer* in which he stated that the stereotypical male sadistic sexual killer tended to be timid, withdrawn, introverted and solitary. Such offenders were thought to be over-controlled, and subject to obsessive rumination and were typically socially and behaviourally incompetent. Their poor sex life was attributed to either impoverished relationships or 'deviant sexuality'. This view is hugely generic for the many patients seen by the clinical services, let alone forensic services, and provides no differentiation of a person who may be mentally ill but harmless from one who may be dangerous. Brittain goes on to suggest that the interests of sadistic sexual murderers encompass many dramatic topics; sado-masochism and pornography; torture and atrocities; the depiction of true-life crime; weapons; Nazism and fascism; horror films; black magic and the occult; funerals; multiple murderers; and paganism. Into this face-valid selection of constructs, he also suggested that sadistic sexual murderers could be deeply preoccupied by their pets, or even going to church; clearly the latter somewhat drifts from what may be a legitimate clinical observation.

Brittain's 'sensational interests' model is not the only unhelpful 'back-of-envelope' model of psychopathology; a predictive triad of persistent enuresis, animal cruelty and fire-setting in children has also been deemed sufficient to predict adult violent behaviour (Hellman and Blackman 1966). Similarly, the loosened florid associations of psychoanalysis have spuriously linked arson to masturbation, despite little evidence to support this as a general phenomenon (Fritzon 2000). As with sensational interests, the forensic triad and 'eroticised arson' are behaviours with a range of possible causes and outcomes that have been regarded as quasi or actual medical symptoms. In both cases, grossly over-generalised models have been influenced by the selective observation or inclusion of a small number of highly disturbed individuals. The Brittain criteria, 'forensic triad', and fireside onanism were somehow neglected in the development of useful and predictive risk assessment instruments like the HCR (Webster *et al.* 1997) or the SVR-20 (Boer *et al.* 1997). This is unsurprising; sensational interests (let alone masturbation and bonfires) are of wide interest to many non-pathological samples as well as ordinary offenders and the specific symptoms are often too specific, readily subsumed within more general criteria such as anti-social offending, impulsivity or callousness. Of themselves and taken out of context, specific behaviours are predictive of little bar the dangers of over-simplifying human behaviour into symptomology. Behaviour can have many causes and outcomes. The diversity of 'normality' is rarely appreciated by those preoccupied with the pathological (Offer and Sabshin 1991).

Popular culture and sensational interests

That sensational interests are not generally causal to serious offending should be of little surprise to observers of contemporary popular culture. What begins as a marginal statement of individual choice in ethnic and urban subcultures – for example being tattooed or having a piercing – was once regarded as pathognomic. Such individuals were criminal, sexually deviant and indubitably 'other' (Ellis 1890). However, appropriated by the fashion and music industry, such signs of personal display quickly become common and exemplify the rate at which revolt becomes style. Anthropological studies show how important images of status and power are to diverse cultures, and such imagery is also seen in the status displays in western society. This is contrary to the objection that 'sensational' interests are influenced by time, place and cultural milieu. Indeed, the practicalities of bodily modification, violence, drug use, transgressive beliefs, and the valuing of paranormal and physical power are as likely to be seen in followers of the 'carnival of crime' (Presdee 2000) and 'the new primitivism' (Vale and Juno 1989) as in tribal settings.

There is a large general interest in the most dramatic forms of criminality (Biressi 2001), whether these are serial killers or sadistic sexual offenders, despite the relative paucity of such offences in real crime figures. This curiosity dates back to at least the 'Newgate Calendar', a hugely popular Victorian journal detailing the acts of sensational crimes and the state's punishment of the offenders (Thomas 1998). The louche and the picaresque remain popular today, with entire television channels sometimes appearing to serve such a need. Films depicting mass murder are highly successful and lucrative rather than off-putting to audiences. Contemporary modern art is also saturated with sensational interests (Home 1991). In 1997, London's Royal Academy had an exhibition called *Sensation*. In this, the audience was challenged by what the artists fancied was edgy, dangerous and transgressive; Jay Jopling sculpted his own head in frozen blood; Mat Collishaw's work *Bullet Hole* comprised a close-up photograph of a bullet in the brain. Tabloid newspapers expressed their alarm perhaps forgetting the nightmare visions of Hieronymus Bosch, Andy Warhol's screen-prints of car crashes, or Govert Bidloo's copperplate anatomical engravings in the *Anatomia Humani Corporis* (1685).

If there is one force driving the popular media to exploit the grotesque or violent for entertainment and profit (and perhaps even aesthetics), other forces perceive this as malign. Every few years a pop group appropriates violent, 'Satanic' or otherwise sensationalist images to sell more records or concert tickets, leading to a moral panic in conservative, often religiously motivated commentators. Public funding bodies may also over-react; thus it was that, thanks to the generosity of the US Congress, a youth-outreach programme in Missouri received $273,000 to combat 'Goth culture' (Dinan 2002). Not everyone views the noisy, hedonistic fancy dress party that is youth culture as ultimately transient and mostly harmless (Gaines 1992). One of the earliest examples of moral panic about topics that might be construed under the label of 'sensational interests' was *The Seduction of the Innocent* (Wertham 1955). This book linked American horror comics produced by EC to sadism, spelled out the latent (and not so latent) homosexual and fetishistic imagery of Batman and Robin, and posited both as associated with the rise in juvenile delinquency. In the 1980s 'heavy metal' music, often lyrically about violence, motorbikes, dungeons, dragons, devils and things that go bump in the night became of concern. It was found that the overt lyrical content and musical intensity of heavy metal does not generally lead to delinquency (Singer, Levine and Jou 1993). Nor do reverse presented and masked messages on heavy metal recordings influence the behaviour of listeners (Vokey and Read 1985). There are plenty of case studies of disturbed teenagers who commit serious violent or sexual offences. These persons are sometimes affiliated to subcultures that older and more conservative adults dislike (Victor 1994); however adolescence also marks the peak age of offending and for the development of lifelong mental illness.

Nevertheless, the causal significance of sensational interests popularly continues; the youths responsible for the Columbine massacre were found to have CDs by the latest glamour-wicked pop star, Marilyn Manson, and at one concert Manson was not allowed to perform unless he also read extracts from the Bible. Mr Manson read the most violent and blood-thirsty extracts from the Good Book, aware that this book, like many 'holy' books, is replete with sensationalist imagery which could (and has) inspired some individuals to harm others while being inspirational and positive to many others. What inspires a person to act in a destructive way towards others is often subjective; film director Alfred Hitchcock was asked about his irresponsibility in showing murder in his thrillers. He showed the enquiring journalist a press-cutting he kept about a man who strangled his girlfriend after they had seen Walt Disney's *Snow White and the Seven Dwarfs*.

It comes down to statistics; the base-rate for sensational interests is high, and the base-rate for serious offending is low. As a result, in the general population, such associations will never be sufficiently strong to reflect causality. Most people are unaware of basic maths when evaluating evidence (Scarr 1997). Nevertheless, for some individuals, or particular populations, such relationships may occur. Responsible researchers should not only examine the clinical or forensic populations where such associations may occur, but also ensure that such concepts are not excessively broadened to become meaningless or oppress individual freedom and diversity.

Mechanisms underlying sensational interests: arousal

Several mechanisms explaining why sensational interests are rewarding for some individuals can be advanced. Most derive from the broader personality and sensation seeking literature:

1 'Excitation-transfer' models: These suggest that exposure to particular stimuli generate excitational states that intensify post-exposure emotional responses (Zillman 1978, 1980). The physio-logical arousal generated by exposure to such stimuli is transferred (or labelled) by individuals in an effort to impose meaning to their experience. Thus viewing-induced arousal to graphic horror images may be converted into feelings of distress or delight (Sparks 1991). These stimuli may lead to the formation of internalised sustaining fantasies that provide cognitive consolation when an individual feels upset (Zelin *et al.* 1983).

2 'Optimal level of arousal' (OLA) theories: OLA theories develop Eysenckian models of arousal modulation as a function of the individual leading to their expressed personality (e.g., Eysenck 1990), and can explain an interest in experiential stimuli that elicit anxiety, anger and even disgust. According to this model, the person's need for novel and arousing experiences drives a desire to witness or read about 'sensational' events. The arousal of apparently negative emotions becomes positively reinforcing if it brings an individual to an optimal level of cortical arousal (or just beyond). Individuals seek intense and/or novel stimulation because they are generally under-aroused relative to those with a higher OLA (Zuckerman 1994, 1997).

3 Learning processes may also be important, as beyond arousal, some persons may habituate more rapidly to repeated exposure to arousing stimuli. The arousing potential of any stimulus is reduced by repetition, and some persons may seek novel experiences and activities in order to avoid the inevitable decline in arousal produced by familiarity.

4 Lastly, high sensation interests may reflect neurochemical states. Fabregat and Beltri (1998) associate sensation seeking levels with differing levels of catecholamines (catecholamines being monoamine neurotransmitters in the central nervous system such as noradrenaline, dopamine and serotonin, all of which are associated with brain mechanisms underlying behaviour in general). By modulating these neurotransmitters, an individual can arguably sustain his or her particular OLA (Zuckerman 1994).

Mechanisms underlying sensational interests: evolution and mating effort

When one thinks of causes underlying a psychological process, one has to consider ultimate and proximate causality. While the mechanisms above reflect proximate causal influences, the basic and ultimate cause of behaviour is often founded on evolutionary processes. If sensational interests reflect natural tendencies, as seen by comparable cross-cultural expressions of interest in violence, supernatural ritual and extreme bodily adornment, it is likely that they have some kind of adaptive value, and do not necessarily reflect 'anti-social' traits as such. One core construct in evolutionary psychology is that of status display, which generally reflects intra-sexual competition for mates. It has often been noted that offenders – disproportionately young and male – seek to assert their dominance via physical and material display (Ellis and Walsh 2000), and Quinsey (2002) suggests that this forensic constant reflects an evolutionary strategy: the intra-sexual competition for partners. This is known as mating effort, which reflects the degree to which an individual devotes resources to finding and guarding sexual partners (Rowe *et al.* 1997). A study of juvenile sex offenders (Hunter, Figueredo, Malamuth and Becker 2003) found that high mating effort led to a series of deviant behavioural strategies including hostile masculinity and general (non-sexual) delinquency, which culminated in sex offending. Other strategies may be used in intra-sexual competition by those high in mating effort including: resource acquisition by legal or illegal means, wholesome activities indicating health or intelligence, or fitness displays of more or less social acceptability (e.g., sports, physical combat, or active aggression). Sensational interests are inherently attention-getting and should thus reflect a behavioural strategy for individuals high in mating effort. This suggests that, while sensational interests may be a strategy for some offenders, individuals who are not at risk of offending may also use such interests. In both groups, sensational interests may be one means of intra-sexual competition within their behavioural repertoire.

Evidence linking fantasies, interests and behaviour

I have argued that sweeping generalisations about the contribution of some sensationalist topic or construct to psychopathology or crime in populations are limited. This does not mean that certain individuals do not interpret and internalise such material in a way that contributes to their desire to harm others. The selection and use of violent, morbid, and macabre material has been claimed to contribute to violent and pathological fantasies in some individuals (West, Roy and Nicholas 1978; Dietz and Hazelwood 1986; Prentky *et al.* 1989). MacCullough *et al.* (1983) noted that 13 of 16 patients held in special hospitals for serious sexual offences described recurrent sadistic fantasies linked to sexual arousal. In all 13 cases, the index offences were recognisably part of the fantasy sequence, which contributed to their reported sexual arousal and mental pleasure during the offence. All 13 patients described previous behavioural try-outs to enact a fantasy sequence. One of the main reasons for behavioural try-outs was to maintain the effectiveness of the fantasy as a source of arousal. In 11 of the 13 patients, behavioural try-out occurred less than one year after the development of the fantasies, and in seven cases, the patients acted out parts of their fantasies at a frequency of once or twice per week.

The mechanism between fantasies and behavioural try-outs in some serious sexual offences is thought to be associative (MacCulloch et al. 2000). However, non-offending men also report sexual fantasies that have controlling and sadistic elements (Crepault and Couture 1980), and this group are well able to distinguish fantasy and behaviour. Equally, some offenders may not have deviant fantasies underlying their deviant behaviours (Langevin, Lang and Curnoe 1998), for example opportunist child molesters who are not actually paedophilic. Studying the fantasies of a patient is complicated by the fact that fantasies are unobservable, and may well be minimised. Clients may equally be brow-beaten into saying what the therapist wants to hear, and therapists may use this information in their reports. An alternative strategy is to identify the images and content of an individual's fantasies by looking at her or his recreational choices and interests, reasoning that these give an analogue external validation to a person's internal preoccupations.

Personality and sensational interests

The research into sensational interests as defined by Brittain is modest, and has generally addressed individual topics of a 'sensational' nature rather than the full constellation of constructs. Hans Eysenck's book *Psychoticism as a Dimension of Personality* reports unpublished results by David Nias showing low but statistically significant correlations between psychoticism (P; tough-minded hostility) and an interest in crime, horror, and viewing war films in children (Nias 1975, in Eysenck and Eysenck 1976). There are reasonably well-recognised associations between schizotypy and a range of occult interests (Claridge 1997). However, it is the overlapping constructs of sensation-seeking (Zuckerman 1994) and trait P that are the personality dimensions best associated with sensational interests. Studies have found high scores on the Sensation Seeking Scale (SSS) associated with (unsurprisingly) drug use and misuse (Zuckerman 1994), a greater interest in risky sports (Jack and Ronan 1998); torture, execution, and corpses (Zaleski 1984) and the representation of death in the mass media (Potts, Dedmon and Halford 1996). Zuckerman and Little (1986) found that sensation-seeking and P correlated with self-reported interest in media depictions of violent, morbid and sexual events. Fabregat and Beltri (1998) replicated Zuckerman and Little's result, finding the SSS (especially Disinhibition and Thrill and Adventure Seeking) had a relationship with interests in sex and horror-related topics, and in actually going to see horror and sex films. Further studies in the field of media preferences for horror and filmed violence have replicated this association, typically demonstrating associations with Psychoticism and Extroversion (e.g. Weaver 1991; Weaver *et al.* 1993; Fabregat 2000).

For all their faults and perhaps questionable taste, none of the persons showing these associations were known sadistic sexual or mentally disordered offenders. Indeed one difficulty with this field is that most studies have addressed student populations, with inevitable limitations for extrapolating such results to clinical and forensic populations. There have not been systematic studies into associations between personality measures and topics such as the military, weapons, martial arts, or motorcycles. Neither has there been a systematic programme of research into sensational interests with standardised metrics, dissociation of confounds such as age and psychopathology, and links to the broader psychological mechanisms described above. Brittain himself stated:

> Deliberately, no attempt has been made to quantify the data used nor to explain in detail the features mentioned. The purpose is to try and give a factual description for practical use, not a theoretical formulation. (Brittain 1970: 198)

Gunn and Taylor (1993) concur that Brittain's 'classical description' has 'largely stood the test of time' (p. 391). Prins (1990) is one of the few to note the potential value of sensational interests despite the paucity of work upon them. He observed that the context and quality of a sensational interest, rather than the interest itself, might be important, as might be the qualitative nature of how the interest is expressed. These are interesting ideas deserving examination; however more basic questions might be more immediately tractable. It is thus peculiar that despite the numerous individuals held within secure settings, with sensational interests, who have committed violent or sexual offences, and the assumed salience of these interests to their psychopathology, little such research has been conducted.

Systematic research into the topic: validating a measure of sensational interests

Despite the implications of someone being falsely labelled as dangerous as a result of their interests, the empirical and conceptual basis of 'sensational interests' has not been examined in serious offenders. In identifying this need, the first requirement was to produce a checklist of items to measure sensational interests in a more systematic way. The Sensational Interests Questionnaire (SIQ; Egan *et al.* 1999) was developed to identify those items that best discriminate between individuals and fall together into meaningful clusters, thus providing the user with a means to assess an individual. We sought to exclude items that did not discriminate between individuals, and to discover which items reflected content overlap, so measuring facets of some underlying factor. The pilot SIQ comprised 60 items. These items included all the interests mentioned in the original Brittain paper, along with items examining conventional interests. Individuals rated whether they were 'greatly interested', 'slightly interested', 'indifferent', 'disinterested' or 'greatly disinterested' in the particular topic. This pilot instrument was given to 301 persons; 156 control participants from the normal population, including the cleaners and security staff of a regional secure unit. The scale was also completed by 53 individuals referred to the forensic clinical psychology out-patients service, and 54 individuals held within the same regional secure unit, all of whom were detained under the 1983 Mental Health Act. These individuals also completed a short measure of personality (the NEO-Five Factor Inventory; (NEO-FFI); Costa and McCrae 1992) and a measure of social desirability (the Crowne-Marlowe Social Desirability scale; Reynolds 1982). General demographic information (age, sex, social class, years of education) was also recorded.

With 300 subjects and 60 items, there was a 5:1 ratio between subjects and items, justifying an item factor-analysis. Inspection of the items found five meaningful factors, with the remainder being generated by chance associations from such an analysis. The 29 items contributing to these five factors were then re-factored (Table 7.1). These factors explained over 50 per cent of all the observed variance in the scale. These factors were:

1 Militarism (an interest in paramilitary groups, the Armed Forces, body-building, martial arts, weapons, sport and survivalism).

2 Violent-occultism (an interest in drug use, black magic, paganism, tattoos and body-piercing, and weapons).

3 Intellectual recreation (an interest in psychology and psychiatry, philosophy, medicine, making music and foreign travel).

4 Occult credulousness (an interest in the paranormal, flying saucers and astrology).

5   Outdoors activities (an interest in country and hill-walking, camping, gardening and the environment).

Analysis of these items as scales indicated that they all had Cronbach's alpha co-efficients of 0.68 and above, meaning they were of acceptable reliability.

Table 7.1   Items of possible forensic interest extracted from pilot research into the SIQ

Original 'sadistic' interest proposed by Brittain	Identified in Factor analysis of pilot SIQ?	Substitute item which loaded in pilot SIQ	Identified factor
Vampires and werewolves	Yes		1st PC, F2
Pets	No	The paranormal	1st PC
Martial arts	Yes		1st PC, F1
Dinosaurs	No	Motorbikes	1st PC, F1
Crossbows, knives and swords	Yes		1st PC, F1, F2
Serial killers	No	Flying saucers	1st PC
Attending religious services	No	Body-building	1st PC, F1
Philosophy	Yes		1st PC
Psychology and psychiatry	Yes		F3
Drugs	Yes		1st PC, F2
Black magic	Yes		1st PC, F2
Mercenaries and the SAS	Yes		1st PC, F1
Guns and shooting	Yes		1st PC, F1, F2
Science fiction and fantasy	No	Alternative medicine	F3, F4
Hitler and fascism	No	Tattoos and body-piercing	1st PC, F2
True crime	No	Astrology	F4
Horror films and stories	No	Survivalism	1st PC, F1
Detective films and stories	No		
Paganism	Yes		1st PC, F2, F4
Thinking about spirituality	No		
The Armed Forces	Yes		1st PC, F1
Funerals and death	No		

1st PC = loaded on 1st principal component; F1 = loaded on first varimax factor; F2 = loaded on second varimax factor; F3 = loaded on third varimax factor; F4 = loaded on fourth varimax factor

Scores for the five SIQ dimensions were summed and control individuals were compared to forensic clinical out- and in-patients. It was found there were no differences between any of the groups in age or social desirability. On the NEO-FFI, control individuals were predictably lower in Neuroticism and higher in Extroversion, Openness, Agreeableness and Conscientiousness than forensic in- or out-patients. Forensic patients (whether in or out) were significantly higher in sensational interests than control subjects for the Militarism and Violent-Occult SIQ scales, but there was no difference between forensic-in and forensic-out groups themselves. Correlations between SIQ scales and the general personality traits were also calculated; higher scores on total sensational interests and the militarism and violent-occult sub-scales were significantly but somewhat modestly associated with lower scores on Agreeableness and lower scores on Conscientiousness. Investigation of the NEO-FFI found this instrument had several psychometric flaws, perhaps artificially reducing this association (Egan, Austin and Deary 2000). Nevertheless, a useful metric for measuring sensational interests – the SIQ – had been derived.

Table 7.2 Correlations (Pearson's r) between the SIQ, and SSS for the entire sample

	SSS Total	P<	Dis	P<	ES	P<	TAS	P<	BS	P<	SPM	P<
SIQ total	0.55	***	0.56	***	0.29	n.s.	0.46	**	0.12	n.s.	0.02	n.s.
Militarism	0.44	**	0.43	**	0.16	n.s.	0.47	**	0.05	n.s.	−0.14	n.s.
Violent Occultism	0.50	***	0.52	***	0.20	n.s.	0.43	**	0.15	n.s.	0.05	n.s.

Note. n.s. = not significant; ** $p < 0.01$; *** $p < 0.001$.

Basic principles: sensation-seeking and intelligence (Egan *et al.* 2001)

The next sensational interests study examined what might be called basic principles; that intelligence has a Protean influence on all aspects of human behaviour (Brand 1996); and that sensation seeking – higher in both the mentally disordered and offenders, and associated with a range of individual sensational topics – would be independent predictors of sensational interests. The study comprised 42 residents of a regional secure unit, none of whom were symptomatic for any active mental illness, and all of whom had been detained under the UK 1983 Mental Health Act. This represented 80 per cent of the patients held at the unit at the time of the study. All individuals were tested on the SIQ, the Standard Progressive Matrices (a non-verbal measure of intelligence; SPM; Raven, Court and Raven 1996), and the SSS (Zuckerman 1994). The results of this study are presented in Table 7.2, and show that scores on the SIQ have no relationship with intelligence, but are significantly and substantially associated with the more pathological elements of the SSS; disinhibition and thrill and adventure seeking. This study excluded one possible reason for lower sensational interests (intelligence) and highlighted that particular, perhaps more pathological, facets of sensation-seeking predict higher scores on the measure.

Are sensational interests associated with DSM-IV personality disorder?

Individuals who commit serious offences who also have sensational interests are sometimes reported to have personality disorder, and it is the more negative aspects of general personality, whether indexed by the NEO-FFI or the SSS that have been shown to be associated with the SIQ. A larger study was conducted to examine potential associations between formal personality disorder classifications and the SIQ (Egan *et al.* 2003). This study was conducted with 155 participants (62 outpatients, 30 inpatients, 63 court referrals) recruited over two years. All were assessed using the self-report International Personality Disorder Examination (IPDE; Loranger 1999). This instrument bases questions around formal criteria for each of the ten personality disorders listed in the standard diagnostic manual for psychiatrists, *DSM-IV* (American Psychiatric Association 1994). In addition, all participants completed the NEO-FFI and the SIQ. The NEO-FFI was used to see the degree to which general personality traits and specific personality disorders indexed common constructs. As the NEO-FFI has previously been shown to be problematic if individual scaled scores were used, it was approached using a multivariate approach, enabling such difficulties to be resolved. Table 7.3 presents the results of a joint factor analysis of the NEO-FFI and the IPDE, and indicates that the two separate scales (comprising 13 variables but excluding the unreliable self-report measure of schizoid personality disorder, and the unrelated to personality disorder trait dimension of Openness) can be readily reduced to four factors. These four factors follow what is called the '4A' model of personality disorders

(Livesley, Jang and Vernon 1998; Austin and Deary 2000); Asocial (i.e. odd, aloof and withdrawn); Asthenic (i.e., highly anxious and neurotic), Antisocial (i.e., emotionally unstable, paranoid and criminal); and Anankastic (i.e., compulsive and narcissistic). The 4 A's provide an empirically derived typology of personality disorders, rather than the arbitrary (though face-valid) classification of personality disorders into the three clusters traditionally described as odd, dramatic and neurotic.

Table 7.3 Factor analysis of NEO-FFI and IPDE-SQ (n = 150): Rotated Principal Component Matrix (16 iterations)

(70% variance explained)

	Asocial	Aesthenic	Antisocial	Anankastic
N	.64	.44	.27	.16
E	−.85	.10	−.10	−.06
A	−.31	.06	−.75	−.29
C	−.55	−.29	−.40	.22
Paranoid personality disorder	.50	.11	.49	.41
Schizotypal personality disorder	.63	.35	.23	.31
Antisocial personality disorder	.09	.24	.83	.03
Histrionic personality disorder	−.11	.71	.47	.04
Narcissistic personality disorder	−.01	.13	.29	.70
Borderline personality disorder	.37	.59	.47	.28
Avoidant personality disorder	.63	.53	−.09	.22
Compulsive personality disorder	.20	.11	−.04	.83
Dependent personality disorder	.25	.83	−.01	.14

These merged personality trait/disorder factors were saved and used as variables to correlate with SIQ scores. Higher scores on the anti-social factor predicted a higher score on all three measures of sensational interests; no other dimension of personality disorder showed such systematic associations (Table 7.4). Given the foregoing 4A model of personality disorder, it was possible to conduct a confirmatory factor-analysis to test this model and the associations in a more systematic way. The model was specified according to the previously observed 4A model, then linked to scores from the SIQ. Within this model, there were two additional correlated variables, which were also built into the analysis; thus recognition was given to an association between anxious and anti-social personality dimensions, and to the high correlation

Table 7.4 Correlations between merged personality trait/ disorder factor scores and SIQ measures

	Total SIQ	P<	Violent Occult	P<	Militarism	P<
Asocial	0.08	n.s.	0.20	.01	0.03	n.s.
Aesthenic	−.09	n.s.	−.03	n.s.	−.07	n.s.
Antisocial	0.41	.001	0.47	.001	0.35	.001
Anankastic	0.07	n.s.	0.01	n.s.	0.10	n.s.

between SIQ militarism and SIQ violent-occult scores. The fit indices for this model were all highly satisfactory. Standardised regression co-efficients between the anti-social personality factor and the SIQ militarism and violent-occult sub-scales were 0.26 and 0.32, respectively. These results re-affirm, using progressively more rigorous analysis, the view that it is elements of personality disorder associated with anti-social behaviour and aspects of emotional dyscontrol within this construct that best predict sensational interests, and that no other aspect of personality disorder is significantly associated with such interests.

While personality traits and personality disorders are clearly interleaved such that personality traits and disorders are often seen as part of the same continuum, it does not follow that all personality measures are equal in predicting sensational interests. To examine whether having a high score on the SIQ (defined as being above the 25th percentile) was better predicted by high scores on an Eysenckian P proxy (the total of scores for Agreeableness and Conscientiousness on the NEO-FFI) or an antisocial personality disorder factor derived from a factor analysis of the IPDE sub-scales, a ROC analysis was conducted. As can be seen from Figure 7.1, the 'area under the curve' (AUC) statistic for the personality disorder measure is a better predictor of sensational interests than a proxy P derived from the NEO-FFI. These results suggest that for mentally disordered offenders, those measures examining more clinical aspects of personality are perhaps more sensitive to detecting extremes of sensational interests than are general instruments.

The SIQ and psychopathy

Psychopathy presents a second-order construct deriving from the conjunction of particular personality disorders. Narcissistic personality disorder is compatible with the core psychopathic traits of callousness

Figure 7.1 ROC curve comparing measures of personality disorder and a psychoticism-type personality trait as predictors of sensational interests.

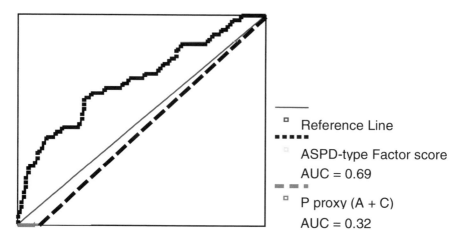

Reference Line

ASPD-type Factor score
AUC = 0.69

P proxy (A + C)
AUC = 0.32

and grandiosity indexed in factor 1 of the revised Psychopathy Checklist (PCL-R; Hare 1991). Anti-social personality disorder corresponds well with the lifestyle-driven criminality captured by a higher score on factor 2 of the PCL-R. Given the value of the PCL-R in predicting many other aspects of violence risk, associations between psychopathy and the SIQ have also been examined. This study comprised 40 men assessed for a personality disorder treatment unit at a regional secure unit. All persons were assessed with the PCL-R, IPDE, NEO-FFI, and the SIQ. The mean total PCL-R score for this population was = 20 (SD = 6.9). While psychopathy correlated in predictable manners with lower Agreeableness and Conscientiousness, a higher factor 1 PCL-R score correlated with higher self-rated scores of Narcissistic Personality Disorder, and higher scores on factor 2 of the PCL-R correlated with anti-social personality disorder, only one significant association was found between psychopathy and sensational interests: factor 2 of the PCL-R (lifestyle criminality) was correlated with SIQ militarism ($r = 0.29$, P<.05). Core psychopathy does not seem to predict a greater interest in sensational topics.

Evolutionary issues: Mating effort and sensational interests

Weiss, Egan and Figueredo (2004) tested the hypothesis that individual differences in sensational interests partially reflect intra-sexual competition for status and thus have an underlying evolutionary function. It was predicted that age and sex should be directly related to individual differences in mating effort; that mating effort should directly influence sensational interests; and that there should be direct effects of age and sex on sensational interests. To test these predictions, 972 university undergraduates were tested with the Revised Sensational Interests Questionnaire (SIQ-R) and the Mating Effort Scale (MES; Rowe *et al.* 1997). The difference between the SIQ and the SIQ-R is that the SIQ examines a full range of interest patterns which are rated on a simple 'interest to dislike' continuum; the SIQ-R focuses on sensational interests alone. Subjects rate their interest, knowledge and the putative relevance of this interest and knowledge, thus indexing salience and increasing measurement reliability. The SIQ is useful as a quick general measure, the SIQ-R is more focused and requires a more demanding subject response. They are highly correlated and cover much the same item content, but applicable to different contexts.

A structural equation model revealed that a single factor accounted for the majority of variance in the three SIQ-R sub-scales (Paranormal, Militaristic and Criminal Identity interests). The structural model found effects of age and sex on the MES and the effects of the MES on SIQ-R, indicating indirect effects of age and sex on SIQ-R. Model-fitting procedures were used to examine pathways between age, sex, mating effort and scores on the SIQ-R. Causal paths from the latent SIQ-R factor to Paranormal Interests, Militarism, and Criminal Identity sub-scales were significant and high, indicating that these sub-scales all measured a common sensational interests factor (SIQ-R). Our predictions concerning the relationships between (male) sex, (younger) age and (greater) mating effort were also supported. Our second prediction, that mating effort would be related to sensational interests and, hence, age and sex should be indirectly related to sensational interests, was supported by the significant relationship between the MES and the SIQ-R. Lastly, direct, positive effects of sex on the Militarism and Criminal Identity sub-scales indicated that sex contributed to these measures over and above the degree to which it was related to them via mating effort alone. It was concluded that, even in non-clinical samples, an affinity for sensational interests might serve a form of intra-sexual competition.

Does a high SIQ denote risk?

I have reviewed the background to the construct of sensational interests and described preliminary systematic research into the topic. I suggest that in clinical forensic populations, sensational interests are associated with the more pathological elements of personality indexed by emotionally dyscontrolled, lifestyle criminality. In the more general population, sensational interests are associated with mating effort and lower Agreeableness. What I have not addressed is what the specific degree of risk sensational interests denotes.

A case example

Figure 7.2 presents a drawing given to me by a prison officer concerned about a young offender. The young offender was on remand for having raped a woman in front of her child, the child being asked to hold the knife while the sexual act was carried out. The young man had also been reported as driving very dangerously whilst intoxicated, and when admonished by another road user, had left his car armed with a ball-pein hammer to threaten the remonstrating party. He disclosed a desire to slice his (supportive) mother's face with a pizza-cutter. Given his index offence, the young man was a serious offender, and was close to committing at least one other violent offence. His doodle depicts images of death, violence, and babies with half their faces blown away. Assessment indicated he met all seven criteria for antisocial personality disorder, six of the seven criteria for paranoid personality disorder, and seven of the nine criteria for borderline personality disorder. He was not actively mentally ill. He had SIQ scores 1.5 standard deviations above normal, despite possibly minimising his interests given the transparent nature of the checklist. He refused to engage in prison rehabilitative or educational programmes. I was advised of his desire to stab me on his release, should we meet in the future.

This brief example of an individual with sensational interests and his graphic expression of these is subject to criticisms raised of the somewhat anecdotal nature of sensational interests in the forensic literature. This is currently being addressed, but two unpublished studies perhaps indicate that more formal associations are possible.

Sustaining fantasies and sensational interests

One putative function of sensational interests is that they provide imagery as content for sustaining fantasies – fantasies that enable the person to console themselves at times of difficulty (Zelin *et al.* 1983). Ahmadi (1998) examined scores on measures of sensational interests, sustaining fantasies, personality and self-reported offending in young offenders. It was found that it was possible to predict violent behaviour from the linear combination of (low) Agreeableness, sensational interests

Figure 7.2 Drawing indicating possible sensational interests in a young offender.

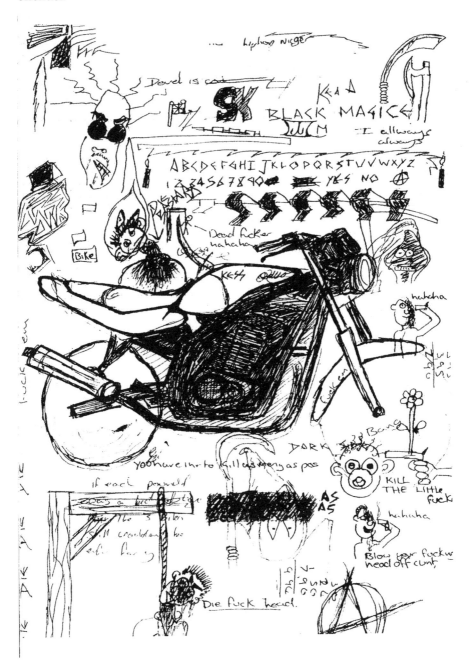

and negative sustaining fantasies on the Sustaining Fantasies Questionnaire (Zelin *et al.* 1983, *op cit*). Multiple regression found that these variables significantly and independently predicted a total of 49.6 per cent of the variance in violent behaviour (multiple R = 0.705, P<0.01). Agreeableness explained 33.3 per cent of the variance, sensational interests independently explained a further 10.3 per cent of the variance, and negative sustaining fantasies explained a further 6% of violence variance. Thus, in the case of young offenders, a simple model involving the action of low Agreeableness, Sensational Interests and negative Sustaining Fantasies constituted a highly significant prediction model for violence in young men.

Do sensational interests denote serious offenders?

Using data previously collected by Egan *et al.* (2001, 2003), Elliot (2000) examined whether higher scores on a measure of sensational interests were; a) linked with criminality; b) differentiated offender subgroups; and c) whether interest patterns linked to higher SIQ scores reflected more general psychological constructs associated with interests. It was found that offenders had a different pattern of sensational interests to control subjects, but that the sensational interests of offenders did not clearly differentiate offender subtypes. This is perhaps unsurprising; an offenders' offending histories are often arbitrary and subject to the point in their criminal history when they were arrested, and specialised offending is relatively uncommon (Simon 1997; Piquero 2000). Smallest space analysis was applied to the SIQ data and found that the interests in the SIQ formed a circumplex structure divisible into regions similar to those proposed by value-type theory (Schwartz 1992). Schwartz's values of hedonism (involving a bias to pleasure and selfish sensuous gratification) map onto the violent-occult factor of the SIQ, whilst SIQ militarism has affinities with self-direction, stimulation, achievement and power. These are all individualist rather than collectivist value orientations. When this model is applied to control subjects, a mixed model of individual and collectivist interests is seen, whereas the model for offenders who have offended against the person is far more individualistic.

The circumplex model identifies a progression in the continuum of sensational interests which ranges from socially acceptable but perhaps 'macho' interests, through to militarism and legitimised violence, and at the extreme of the continuum, violent occultism. Elliot's model suggests that perhaps persons with higher levels of sensational interests are thus more independent-minded. If this occurs without some sense of collectivist values (i.e., alienation from the greater social group) or a desire for achievement (i.e., lack of personal success via a demonstrated competency according to social standards), criminal behaviour may follow. The alienation and underachievement of most serious offenders – even those of normal intelligence and from adequate material and personal environments – work in conjunction with their strong sense of independence, perhaps rooted in the evolutionary and personality constructs identified as associating with sensational interests.

Conclusions

The present review has summarised the research into sensational interests up to the present, and linked the construct to aspects of personality and values. It is argued that sensational interests are underpinned by evolutionary processes, and that, like personality and values generally, these are not inherently criminal or psycho-pathological. If a person has large amounts of sensational interests it may reflect a strong independence of mind, but these may be checked by other interests of a more collective and conventional kind. Provided people are not alienated from the society (or a subsection of society) around them, and they have a desire for achievement via conventional means, they will be able to keep their sensational interests in perspective. This reflects the vast majority of individuals who may be interested in the military, or the occult, or, indeed have a tattoo, watch horror films, ride motorbikes, or practice martial arts. For those seeking systematically to measure sensational interests, the SIQ provides a valid and reliable measure of a range of sensational and non-sensational interests in both normal and offending populations, whereas the SIQ-R focuses on sensational interests alone. Both instruments identify those items described by Brittain that give the most useful information about an individual's interest patterns. Mentally-disordered offenders are more interested in Militaristic and Violent-Occult topics than normal persons, and scores on the SIQ are more associated with psychopathology than general personality or ability traits. Those individuals within the 'antisocial' cluster of personality disorder (rather than having ASPD alone) have the highest SIQ scores. However these individuals are inherently extreme. If the foregoing findings and interpretation are correct, individuals reasonably integrated into their society, with a normal level of achievement motivation, who have a diversity of interests, are unlikely to present an inherent risk. Alienated individuals with pathological individualism and polarised interests in hedonism and power may be potentially more problematic. It is easy to see how such persons could become involved in crime or violent terrorism.

References

Ahmadi, S. (1998) *Personality, sustaining fantasies, lurid interests and violent behaviour*. Thesis submitted for a BSc (Hons) in Applied Psychology, Cardiff University.

Aluja-Fabregat, A. (2000) 'Personality and curiosity about TV and films violence in adolescents', *Personality and Individual Differences*, 29: 379–92.

American Psychiatric Association (1994) *Diagnostic and Statistical Manual of Mental Disorders* (4th edn). Washington, DC: American Psychiatric Press.

Austin, E.J. and Deary, I.J. (2000) 'The "four As": A common framework for normal and abnormal personality?', *Personality and Individual Differences*, 28: 977–95.

Biressi, A. (2001) *Crime, Fear and the Law in True Crime Stories*. Basingstoke: Palgrave.

Boer, J.V., Hart, S.D., Kropp, P.R. and Webster, C.D. (1997) *Manual for Sexual Violence Risk 20: Professional Guidelines for Assessing Risk of Sexual Violence*. Vancouver, Canada: British Columbia Institute of Family Violence.

Brand, C.R. (1996) *The g Factor*. London: Wiley.

Brittain, R.P. (1970) 'The sadistic murderer', *Medicine, Science, and the Law*, 10: 198–207.

Claridge, G. (1997) *Schizotypy*. Oxford: Oxford University Press.

Costa, P.T. and McCrae, R.R. (1992) *The NEO PI-R Professional Manual*. Odessa, Florida: Psychological Assessment Resources.

Costa, P.T. and Widiger, T.A. (1994) *Personality disorders and the five factor model of personality*. Washington, DC: American Psychological Association.

Crepault, C. and Couture, M. (1980) 'Men's erotic fantasies', *Archives of Sexual Behaviour*, 9: 565–81.

Dietz, P.E. and Hazelwood, H.B.R.R. (1986) 'Detective magazines: Pornography for the sexual sadist?', *Journal of Forensic Sciences*, 31: 197–211.

Dinan, S. (2002) Pork list shows rise from 2001 spending. *The Washington Post*, 9 April 2002 (http://www.washtimes.com/national/20020409-90513512.htm).

Egan, V., Austin, E., Elliot, D., Patel, D. and Charlesworth, P. (2003) 'Personality traits, personality disorders and sensational interests in mentally disordered offenders', *Legal and Criminological Psychology*, 8: 51–62.

Egan, V., Auty, J., Miller, R., Amadi, S., Richardson, C. and Gargan, I. (1999) 'Sensational interests and general personality traits', *Journal of Forensic Psychiatry*, 10: 563–78.

Egan, V., Charlesworth, P., Richardson, C., Blair, M. and McMurran, M. (2001) 'Sensational interests and sensation seeking in mentally disordered offenders', *Personality and Individual Differences*, 30: 995–1007.

Egan, V., Deary, I.J. and Austin, E. (2000) 'The NEO-FFI: Emerging British norms and an item-level analysis suggest N, A and C are more reliable than O and E', *Personality and Individual Differences*, 29: 907–20.

Elliot, D. (2000) *Sensational interests: origin and structure*. Thesis submitted for an MSc in Investigative Psychology, Liverpool University.

Ellis, H. (1890) *The Criminal*. London: Walter Scott.

Ellis, L. and Walsh, A. (2000) *Criminology: A global perspective*. Toronto: Allyn and Bacon.

Eysenck, H.J. (1990) 'Biological dimensions of personality', in L.A. Pervin (ed.) *Handbook of personality: Theory and research* (pp. 244–76). New York: Guilford.

Eysenck, H.J. and Eysenck, S.B.G. (1976) *Psychoticism as a dimension of personality*. London: Hodder.

Fabregat, A.A. and Beltri, R.T. (1998) 'Viewing of mass media violence, perception of violence, personality and academic achievement', *Personality and Individual Differences*, 25: 973–89.

Fritzon, K. (2000) 'The contribution of psychological research to arson investigation', in D. Canter and L. Allison (eds) *Profiling Property Crimes* (pp. 147–84). Aldershot: Ashgate-Darmouth.

Gaines, D. (1992) *Teenage Wasteland*. New York: Harper-Collins.

Gunn, J. and Taylor, P.J. (1993) *Forensic Psychiatry: Clinical, legal and ethical issues*. London: Butterworth and Heinemann.

Hare, R.D. (1991) *The Hare Psychopathy Checklist – Revised*. Toronto: Multi-Health Systems.

Hellman, D.S. and Blackman, N. (1966) 'Enuresis, fire-setting and cruelty to animals: a triad predictive of adult crime', *American Journal of Psychiatry*, 122: 1431–435.

Home, S. (1991) *The Assault on Culture*. Stirling: AK Press.

Hunter, J.A., Figueredo, A.J., Malamuth, N.M. and Becker, J.V. (2003) 'Juvenile sex offenders: Toward the development of a typology', *Sexual Abuse: A Journal of Research and Treatment*, 15: 27–48.

Jack, S.J. and Ronan, K.R. (1998) 'Sensation seeking among high- and low-risk sports participants', *Personality and Individual Differences*, 25: 1063–083.

Langevin, R., Lang, R.A. and Curnoe, S. (1998) 'The prevalence of sex offenders with deviant fantasies', *Journal of Interpersonal Violence*, 13: 315–27.

Livesley, W.J., Jang, K.L. and Vernon, P.A. (1998) 'Phenotypic and genetic structure of personality disorder symptoms', *Archives of General Psychiatry*, 55: 941–48.

Loranger, A.W. (1999) *International Personality Disorder Examination*. Odessa, Florida: Psychological Assessment Resources, Inc.

MacCullough, M.J., Snowden, P.R., Wood, P.J. and Mills, H.E. (1983) 'Sadistic fantasy, sadistic behaviour and offending', *British Journal of Psychiatry*, 143: 20–9.

MacCulloch, M., Gray, N. and Watt, A. (2000) 'Brittain's sadistic murderer syndrome reconsidered: An associative account of the aetiology of sadistic sexual fantasy', *Journal of Forensic Psychiatry*, 11: 401–18.

Morris, S. (2002) 'Arsenal of arms to ignite a race war – the terrifying world of David Tovey', *The Guardian*, 4 October 2002: 3.

Offer, M. and Sabshin, M. (1991) *The Diversity of Normal Behaviour*. USA: Basic Books.

Piquero, A. (2000) 'Frequency, specialization, and violence in offending careers', *Journal of Research in Crime and Delinquency*, 37: 392–418.

Potts, R., Dedmon, A. and Halford, J. (1996) 'Sensation seeking, television viewing motives, and home television viewing patterns', *Personality and Individual Differences*, 21: 1081–084.

Prentky, R.A., Burgess, A.W., Rokous, F. and Lee, A. (1989) 'The presumptive role of fantasy in serial sexual homicide', *American Journal of Psychiatry*, 146: 887–91.

Presdee, M. (2000) *Cultural Criminology and the Carnival of Crime*. London: Routledge.

Prins, H. (1990) *Bizarre Behaviours: Boundaries of psychiatric disorder*. London: Routledge.

Quinsey, V.L. (2002) 'Evolutionary theory and criminal behaviour', *Legal and Criminological Psychology*, 7: 1–13.

Raven, J.C., Court, J.H. and Raven, J. (1996) *Standard Progressive Matrices: Manual for Raven's progressive matrices and vocabulary scales*. Oxford Psychology Press.

Reynolds, W.M. (1982) 'Development of a reliable and valid short form of the Marlowe-Crowne social desirability scale', *Journal of Clinical Psychology*, 38: 119–25.

Rowe, D.C., Vazsonyi, A.T. and Figueredo, A.J. (1997) 'Mating effort in adolescence: A conditional or alternative strategy', *Personality and Individual Differences*, 23: 105–15.

Scarr, S. (1997) 'Rules of evidence: A larger context for the statistical debate', *Psychological Science*, 8: 16–17.

Schwartz, S.H. (1992) 'Universals in the content and structure of values: theoretical advances and empirical tests in 20 countries', *Advances in Experimental Social Psychology*, 25: 1– 65.

Simon, L.M.J. (1997) 'Do criminal offenders specialize in crime types?', *Applied and Preventive Psychology*, 6: 35–53.

Singer, S.I., Levine, M. and Jou, S. (1993) 'Heavy metal music preference, delinquent friends, social control, and delinquency', *Journal of Research in Crime and Delinquency*, 30: 317–29.

Sparks, G. (1991) 'The relationship between distress and delight in males' and females' reactions to frightening films', *Human Communication Research*, 17: 625–37.

Thomas, D. (1998) *The Victorian Underworld*. London: John Murray.

Vale, V. and Juno A. (eds) (1989) *Research #12: Modern Primitives: An investigation of contemporary adornment and Ritual*. San Francisco, USA: Re/Search.

Victor, J.S. (1994) 'Fundamentalist religion and the moral crusade against Satanism: The social construction of deviant behaviour', *Deviant Behaviour*, 5: 305–34.

Vokey, J.R. and Read, J.D. (1985) 'Subliminal messages: Between the devil and the media', *American Psychologist*, 40: 11231–239.

Weaver, J.B. (1991) 'Exploring the links between personality and media preferences', *Personality and Individual Differences*, 12: 1293–299.

Weaver, J.B., Brosius, H.B. and Mundorf, N. (1993) 'Personality and movie preferences: A comparison of American and German audiences', *Personality and Individual Differences*, 14: 307–15.

Webster, C.D., Douglas, K.S., Eaves, D. and Hart, S.D. (1997) *HCR-20: Assessing Risk for Violence, Version 2*. Vancouver, Canada: Simon Fraser University Mental Health, Law and Policy Institute.

Weiss, A., Egan, V. and Figueredo, A.J. (2004) 'Sensational interests as a form of intra-sexual competition', *Personality and Individual Differences* (in press).

Wertham, F. (1955) *Seduction of the Innocent*. London: Museum Press.

West, D.J., Roy, C. and Nicholas, F.L. (1978) *Understanding Sexual Attacks on Women*. London: Heinemann.

Zaleski, Z. (1984) 'Sensation seeking and preference for emotional visual stimuli', *Personality and Individual Differences*, 5: 609–11.

Zelin, M.L., Bernstein, S.B., Heijn, C., Jampel, R.M., Myerson, P.G., Adler, G., Buie, D.H. and Rizzuto, A.M. (1983) 'The sustaining fantasy questionnaire: Measurement of sustaining functions in psychiatric patients', *Journal of Personality Assessment*, 47: 427–39.

Zillman, D. (1978) 'Attribution and misattribution of excitatory reactions', in J.H. Harvey, W.J. Ickes and R.F. Kidd (eds) *New Directions in Attribution Research, Vol. 2*. Hillsdale, NJ: Lawrence Erlbaum Associates.

Zillmann, D. (1980) 'Anatomy of suspense', in P.H. Tannenbaum (ed.) *The Entertainment Functions of Television* (pp. 133–163). Hillsdale, NJ: Lawrence Erlbaum.

Zuckerman, M. (1994) *Behavioural Expressions and Biosocial Bases of Sensation Seeking*. Cambridge University Press.

Zuckerman, M. (1997) 'The psychobiological basis of personality', in H. Nyburg (ed.) *The Scientific Study of Human Nature: Tribute to Hans J Eysenck at Eighty*. Pergamon.

Zuckerman, M. and Little, P. (1986) 'Personality and curiosity about morbid and sexual events', *Personality and Individual Differences*, 7: 49–56.

Chapter 8

Drug use and criminal behaviour: indirect, direct or no causal relationship?

Ian P. Albery, South Bank University;
Tim McSweeney and Mike Hough,
King's College, London

Links between substance use, addictive behaviour and criminal activity have been the subject of psychological, sociological and criminological research over a number of decades (see Anglin and Perrochet 1998; Ferri, Gossop, Rabe-Hesketh and Laranjeira 2002; Lowenstein 2001; Nurco *et al.* 1985, 1995; Yeoman and Griffiths 1996). At a public health level, legislation has aimed to counter the harmful effects of taking drugs or using alcohol excessively. Research has set out to understand those mechanisms that might be important in an individual undertaking highly risky and illegal behaviour as a result of their drinking or drug taking behaviour (e.g. Albery and Guppy 1996, 1995a, 1995b; Albery, Gossop and Strang 1998; Albery, Strang, Gossop and Griffiths 2000; Guppy and Albery 1997). This chapter aims to provide a review of the contemporary evidence in relation to the drugs-crime relationship.

Types of link

As will emerge, there is a clear *association* between illicit drug use and some types of crime. There is much overlap between those using illicit drugs and those who are involved in crime, with a pool of people who both use drugs and offend. This link can arise in several ways (see Best *et al.* 2001; Coid *et al.* 2000; Walters 1998, for fuller discussions):

- Illicit drug use may lead to other forms of crime e.g. to provide money to buy drugs or as a result of the disinhibiting effects of some drugs.

- Crime may lead to drug use e.g. providing the money and the contacts to buy drugs or serving as a palliative for coping with the stresses of a chaotic, criminal lifestyle.

- There could be a more complex interaction, whereby crime facilitates drug use, and drug use prompts other forms of crime.

- There may be an association arising from a shared common cause but no direct causal link between offending and drug use.

Each of the above four explanations will apply to *some* people at some times. In some cases, problem drug use – dependence on drugs such as heroin, crack/cocaine or amphetamines, or heavy binge use of these drugs – does trigger theft as a means of fund raising. Others would never have become drug-dependent if crime had not provided them with the means to buy large amounts of drugs. Some people will both be involved in crime and also use illicit drugs without there being any causal connection whatsoever between the two.

The fourth possibility deserves as serious consideration as the other three. Surveys of offenders' health show that they are much more likely to smoke nicotine than the general population (e.g. Singleton *et al.* 1999). No one would seriously argue that smoking causes crime, however, or that crime causes smoking. Rather, smoking and crime are likely to share *some* causal roots without themselves being causally related. The same is likely to be true of *some* links between illicit drug use and crime. For example, economic deprivation, inconsistent parenting, low educational attainment and limited employment prospects are risk factors not only for chaotic or dependent drug use but also for heavy involvement in crime (De Li Periu and MacKenzie 2000; Walters 1998). In a similar vein, Jessor and colleagues (e.g. Jessor and Jessor 1977; Jessor, Donovan and Costa 1991) have argued that behaviours such as drug use and criminal activity can be regarded as two of a constellation of effects of deviancy. That is to say, they have the same common cause but may not be causally related themselves.

Through large-scale, prospective, longitudinal research over the past 25 years or so, Jessor *et al.* (1991) have developed their problem behaviour theory to describe the development of deviant behaviour as well as the processes that underlie such deviance and associated behaviours. Basically, this theory argues that the likelihood of an individual acting in ways that may be deemed to oppose socially generated norms is influenced by three social psychological systems; the personality system, the environment system and the behaviour system.

Within each of these systems, there are built in controls and also built-in encouragement factors for problem behaviours. The balance between these controls and instigation of behaviour within any one individual is what Jessor *et al.* (1991) refer to as proneness to problem behaviour. Another way to conceptualise this may be in terms of underlying risk factors. Each system (personality, environment and behaviour) has an attached proneness continuum. As such, an individual can be seen to exist at some point along these continua. The combination of where a person is on each continuum defines their psychosocial proneness to deviancy, and also determines how conventional or unconventional a person appears. This conventionality-unconventionality dimension determines whether a person will act in general according to social norms or outside these norms. It is clear from this work that one reason why there may be an association between excessive drug use and criminal activity is not because of a causal relationship *per se*. Rather, the associations can best be conceptualised as a conglomeration of issues based on an individual's conventional status which, in turn, is determined by personality factors, environmentally based factors and past behavioural patterns.

Four types of study are relevant for the following discussion:

- Those examining illicit drug use and offending in the overall population.

- Those examining drug use in the offending population.

- Those examining offending amongst the 'problem drug using' population.

- Those examining patterns of drug use and crime amongst criminally involved problem drug users.

In the following pages, we gather together the research evidence under these four headings. At the end of the chapter we draw together the threads and discuss possible implications of the available evidence.

Simply in the interests of clarity and manageability, this chapter focuses primarily on an examination of the links between illicit drug use and property crime. It is not concerned with the links excessive drug consumption may have with violent crime. This is not to suggest that there are no such links. There is evidence that specific drugs can facilitate violent behaviour and that others can inhibit it (Anglin and Speckart 1988; Dobinson and Ward 1986; Harrison and Backenheimer 1998; Jarvis and Parker 1989). Nor is it concerned with the links between alcohol misuse and crime, significant though these may be.

Drug use and offending in the general population

The increasing numbers of individuals who report using illicit substances has heightened interest in drug use and criminal activity in the general population. Evidence from the British Crime Survey suggests that about 34 per cent of the adult population have used illicit substances during their life span and 11 per cent have used during the previous 12 months (Ramsay *et al.* 2001). These figures suggest a current drug using population of about four million in Great Britain. It also seems that this behaviour is largely restricted to younger individuals. Ramsay *et al.* (2001) report that over 50 per cent of young people aged 16-29 years old reported using an illicit substance in the previous 12 months. While the use of cannabis accounts for a significant proportion of these statistics, other drugs such as ecstasy, heroin and cocaine are also reported although in rather low numbers. Miller and Plant (1996) report similar figures for a cohort of 13–15 year olds.

The Youth Lifestyle Survey (YLS) makes broadly similar but slightly higher estimates (Flood-Page *et al.* 2000). The YLS found that about a fifth of young people admitted to some form of offending and that self-reported drug use was the strongest predictor of serious or persistent offending. However, for the majority of young people, there is no persuasive evidence that there is any direct causal linkage between offending and drug use. The association between drug use and offending in the YLS is best understood in terms of a common cause, which leads to two – not totally dissimilar – forms of hedonistic risk-taking. This interpretation concurs with Jessor's (1991) problem behaviour theory discussed previously.

Other evidence comes from Parker and colleagues' longitudinal studies that describe evolving patterns of drug use amongst young people in the North West of England (Measham *et al.* 2001; Parker *et al.* 1998). Experience of illicit drugs was widespread in their samples although most participants funded drug use through legitimate means. Respondents made a sharp distinction between acceptable and unacceptable drugs – with heroin and crack in the latter group and for which use of these drugs was low. Only a very small minority were heavily involved in crime, dependent drug use and other forms of delinquency.

143

Drug use in the known offending population

At any one time, there are very roughly 550,000 people in Britain who are persistently involved in crime, of whom slightly more than 100,000 are high-rate, persistent offenders (Home Office 2001). The majority of these offenders are known to the police. They are much more heavily involved in drug use, and in problematic drug use, than the general population. The largest relevant research study is the NEW-ADAM survey (Bennett 1998, 2000, 2001) in which drug testing and interviewing samples of arrestees was undertaken. The latest sweep of the survey found that 65 per cent of all arrestees tested (N=1,435) were positive for some form of illicit drug, with 24 per cent testing positive for opiates and 15 per cent for cocaine. The average weekly expenditure on drugs, for heroin and crack/cocaine users, was £290. The main sources of illegal income during the last 12 months were property crime (theft, burglary, robbery, handling stolen goods and fraud/deception) followed by drug dealing and undeclared earnings while claiming social security benefits. Heroin and crack/cocaine users had an average annual illegal income of around £15,000 – compared to an average annual illegal income of £9,000 for all interviewed arrestees. Bennett concludes that these findings suggest drug use and, in particular, the use of heroin and crack/cocaine is associated with higher levels of both prevalence and incidence of offending.

However, this study has some methodological limitations. The samples are small, and given that they are drawn from eight cities per sweep, they are unlikely to be representative of the country as a whole. Participation is voluntary and urine test data are not adjusted to take account of the differences in the half-life of drugs. For instance, amphetamines remain testable in urine for two days; opiates, cocaine and benzodiazepines for three days; and cannabis up to a month with chronic users. The results thus need cautious interpretation (see Stimson et al. 1998). Nevertheless, they give a good idea of the 'order of magnitude' of the relationships between illicit drug use, dependence and offending in this population.

Other studies have shown that levels of drug use among prisoners tend to be greater than in the general population (Farrell et al. 1998). Surveys of prison inmates indicate that a significant minority of the adult convicted population are dependent drug users prior to imprisonment (Maden et al. 1991; Singleton et al. 1999). Mason et al. (1997) report that 70 per cent of newly remanded individuals reported a history of illicit drug use, while 57 per cent had used illicit substances during the 12 months prior to incarceration. In addition Lader and colleagues in their study of psychiatric morbidity among young offenders aged between 16 and 20 years in England and Wales, found that six out of ten had used some drug before entering prison (Lader *et al.* 2000). Over half were being held for acquisitive crimes, although among women, drug offences were themselves more common (one in five being held for such offences). A large proportion reported a measure of dependency – 52 per cent of sentenced male offenders, 58 per cent of female offenders and 57 per cent of remanded male prisoners. In particular, opiate dependence in the year before coming into prison was reported by 23 per cent of women, 21 per cent of the male remanded and 15 per cent of the male sentenced group.

Recent evidence has emerged to suggest that not only are there a significant number of individuals who were problematic drug users before incarceration but that a proportion began using drugs in prison. For example, Boys *et al.* (2002) report findings from a large-scale investigation of psychiatric morbidity among 3,142 prisoners. Depending on choice of drug, between 38 (heroin use) and 77 (cannabis use) per cent reported lifetime use. In excess of 60 per cent of those who had ever used heroin or cannabis reported use in prison (64 per cent for cannabis, 62 per cent for heroin). In addition, more than a quarter of these users reported initiation into drug use while in prison.

Whilst many studies have found extensive drug use amongst persistent offenders, by no means everyone has concluded that there is a simple causal relationship, whereby dependent drug use fuels crime. This perspective has been labelled the 'addiction model' of the links between drugs and crime. The argument is that frequency of criminal activity is directly proportional to the frequency of drug use and also severity of dependence (Ball and Ross 1991). Further, that criminal activity is just one manifestation of the addictive disease (Hall, Bell and Carless 1993). In other words the greater the levels of use of a drug and its concomitant reflection in dependence levels, the more likely an individual is to take part in criminal activity. Support for this position comes from findings from investigations of opiate addicts that have shown that the frequency of criminal behaviour increases significantly during periods of dependence when compared to periods of abstinence (Ball *et al.* 1983). Other supportive evidence comes in the form a strong association between criminal activity and length of dependence episode (Ball *et al.* 1981). These studies also point to the overrepresentation of the proportion of acquisitive crime undertaken by heroin users.

However, Hammersley *et al.* (1989) examined opioid use amongst a group of offenders (in this case, people who had been sent to prison), contrasting them to a group of non-prisoners. They found that involvement in property crime predicted opioid use better than opioid use predicted property crime, and suggested that heavy heroin use could be understood as a function partly of the spending power of persistent offenders and partly of the criminal sub-cultures within which heroin use took place. Several researchers have also drawn attention to the ability of many people to use 'drugs of dependence' over long periods in controlled ways that do not amount to addiction. Ditton and Hammersley (1994) have argued this in relation to cocaine and Pearson (1987) in relation to heroin (also see Zinberg and Jacobson 1976; Harding *et al.* 1980).

These studies argue against the adoption of a simple 'addiction model' of the links between drugs and crime, whereby dependence inevitably follows the regular use of drugs, and where crime inevitably follows the onset of dependence. However, there is also the need for some realism in taking at face value the way in which a significant proportion of offenders say that they are drug-dependent, say that they commit crime to feed their habit, and are prepared to seek treatment to address their drug problems.

A strong association between drug use and known offending has also emerged from US research. Because the American criminal justice system has been actively targeting drug users for many years as part of the 'war on drugs', it is not surprising that such studies find large numbers of drug users amongst those arrested, dealt with by the courts or imprisoned (MacCoun and Reuter 1998).

Offending amongst the 'problem drug using' population

Extrapolating from the Home Office Addicts Index in 1996, Edmunds *et al.* (1998, 1999) estimated that problematic drug users in England and Wales number somewhere between 100,000 and 200,000 – less than 5 per cent of the four million or so of those who use illicit drugs each year. More recent estimates suggest that Class A problem users may number between 280,000 and half a million (Godfrey *et al.* 2002). The Scottish population would add around ten per cent to these estimates. In any one year, there may be around 50,000 in contact with treatment services, and several studies have considered the criminal involvement of those in treatment.

Kokkevi *et al.* (1993) showed that 79 per cent of their sample of heroin dependent individuals had been arrested in the past and 60 per cent had been convicted of a crime. Similarly, Stewart *et al.* (2000) showed that among a cohort of over 1,000 primarily opiate dependent users, acquisitive crime (in the form of shoplifting) was very common. Over 25,000 offences were reported by these participants in the three months prior to entry into the study. However, the majority of these crimes were accounted for by about ten per cent of respondents. Gossop *et al.* (1998) also found high levels of criminal behaviour among a large cohort of primarily opiate dependent individuals (Gossop *et al.* 1998). Sixty-one per cent of the sample reported committing crimes other than drug possession in the three months before they started treatment; when aggregated, they admitted to 71,000 crimes in this period. The most commonly reported offence was shoplifting. A smaller study of 221 methadone reduction and maintenance clients found over four-fifths had been arrested for some criminal offence in the past (Coid *et al.* 2000). However, offending prior to treatment had not always been undertaken solely to fund drug taking. Despite this, two-thirds believed there was a strong link between their current offending and their drug habit and half claimed that their current offending served solely to fund their drug habit. Best *et al.* (2001) examined 100 people entering drug treatment in London. Consistent with Gossop *et al.* (1998) and Coid *et al.* (2000), they found slightly more than half of the sample reported funding drug use through acquisitive crime.

Similar findings have emerged from American studies. Research on dependent opiate users have shown that the frequency of criminal behaviour increases significantly during periods of dependence when compared to periods of abstinence (Ball *et al.* 1983). Other supportive evidence comes in the form a strong association between criminal activity and length of dependence episode (Ball *et al.* 1981).

In addition, Kaye, Darke and Finlay-Jones (1998) have argued that excessive drug users are not a homogeneous group, and that different sub-groups may exhibit different sorts of links between drug use and criminal behaviour. They studied 400 methadone maintenance patients, some in community-based programmes and others in prison. They were able to distinguish between those for whom drug use preceded criminal behaviour, labelled 'secondary antisocials', and those whose criminal behaviour preceded excessive drug use, labelled 'primary antisocials'. These two groups differed on a number of dimensions. Primary antisocials were found to be younger, and were more likely to be male. They had committed more violent crime and were twice as likely to qualify for a diagnosis of antisocial personality disorder.

Patterns of drug use and offending amongst criminally involved problem drug users

There is now quite a significant body of research examining patterns of crime and drug use amongst problem users who are identified as such as they pass through the criminal process. Much of this work has involved evaluations of treatment or referral programmes targeting this group. The studies show that these problem drug users commit large amounts of acquisitive crime. For example, drug using offenders on probation in London were found to be spending an average of £362 per week on drugs prior to arrest, primarily raised by committing acquisitive crime, notably shoplifting. In the month before arrest, over half (51 per cent) of these probationers were using both heroin and crack (Hearnden and Harocopos 2000). The evaluation of a range of 'arrest referral schemes' designed to refer offenders to treatment also found similar levels of expenditure on drugs funded through property crimes such as burglary. Again most reported polydrug use with 97 per cent using either opiates or stimulants or both (Edmunds *et al.* 1999). Turnbull and colleagues described the drug use and offending behaviour of those offenders given Drug Treatment and Testing Orders. Three-fifths of those given the 210 pilot orders had never received any form of help or treatment for their drug use (Turnbull *et al.* 2000). Of 132 drug-using offenders interviewed, most (120 or 91 per cent) had been using opiates on a daily basis before arrest. They reported committing several types of property crime on a daily basis in order to fund an average expenditure of £400 per week on drugs. Almost half received their treatment and testing order following a conviction for shoplifting.

An important finding to emerge is that the criminal careers of this group usually pre-dated the onset of problematic or dependent drug use. Edmunds *et al.* (1999), for example, examining a sample drawn from arrest referral clients and probationers found that the average age at which illicit drugs were first used was 15 years. The average at first conviction (for any offence) was 17 years. The average age at which respondents recognised their drug use as problematic was 23 years, a full six years later.

A review of US research by Deitch *et al.* (2000) concluded that roughly two-thirds of drug using offenders report involvement in crime before the onset of drug use. This simple finding has led some to argue that drug use cannot be regarded as a cause. Obviously it cannot be the sole cause but may act as an amplifier for any deviant tendencies the individual may already possess (Harrison and Backenheimer 1998). Whilst dependent drug use may not have triggered the criminal careers of this group, it provides a mechanism by which they are locked into offending, and thus fail to mature out of crime in the way that characterises the majority of young offenders.

There are many studies that suggest that treating the drug problems of this criminally involved population has benefit. Both British and US research suggests that drug treatment can work to reduce offending as well as drug use (Coid *et al.* 2000; Edmunds *et al.* 1998 1999; Gossop *et al.* 1998; Hearnden and Harocopos 1999; Turnbull *et al.* 2000; also see Belenko 1998 and Lurigio 2000, for American reviews). Much of the research can be criticised on methodological grounds. Most have relied on urine test data for the period covering the treatment programme, few collected reliable outcome measures relating to re-offending, and fewer still have run for periods of time stretching beyond engagement with the programme, comparing treatment groups with comparison samples. Nevertheless, it cumulatively offers quite good evidence that appropriate drug services can help reduce drug use and related crime. The studies also have obvious implications about the links between dependent drug use and persistent offending. If reduced dependence results in reduced offending, this provides strong grounds for the existence of a causal link.

The nature of the drugs–crime relationship

So far, this review points to several conclusions about the links between drugs and crime in Britain:

- Around four million people use illicit drugs each year.

- Most illicit drug use is relatively controlled 'recreational' use of cannabis and ecstasy.

- People who try illicit drugs are more likely than others to commit other forms of law breaking.

- There is no persuasive evidence of *any* causal linkage between drug use and property crime for the vast majority of this group.

- A very small proportion of users – less than five per cent of the total – have chaotic lifestyles involving dependent use of heroin, crack/cocaine and other drugs.

- A proportion of this group – perhaps around 100,000 people – finance their use through crime.

- The majority of those who steal to buy drugs were involved in crime before their drug use became a problem for them.

- This group of criminally involved problem users commit very large amounts of shoplifting, burglary and other crime to finance drug purchases.

- If appropriate drug treatment is given to this group, they reduce their offending levels.

There are different explanations for the *association* between illicit drug use and crime for different groups of drug users. In considering the links, it is essential to be specific about these different groups.

The literature suggests that 'lifestyle' and 'sub-cultural' factors are important in explaining why those who try illicit drugs are also more likely than others to get involved in other forms of law-breaking. The search for novelty and excitement, and enjoyment of the rewards of risk-taking, are defining aspects of youth culture. It is hardly a surprise that large minorities of the population engage in the – relatively controlled – risks of both recreational drug use and minor crime at some stage of their adolescence and young adulthood.

For those individuals whose offending (and drug use) is more persistent and less controlled, other explanatory factors also need to be called into play. In the first place, chaotic drug users and persistent offenders – in contrast to controlled drug users and occasional petty offenders – have limited social and economic resources, and limited exposure to legitimate 'life opportunities' (see e.g. Harrison 1992; MacGregor 2000). The majority are from deprived backgrounds, with inconsistent parenting, poor access to housing and health care, low educational attainment and limited employment prospects. Given the scale of participation in *controlled* drug use, there is no reason to expect an obvious association with social exclusion. *Chaotic* or *dependent* use, by contrast, shares that constellation of risk factors that also predict heavy involvement in crime and exposure to many forms of social exclusion.

It has been argued that these risk factors predispose people both to uncontrolled drug use and to involvement in persistent offending. For instance, Walters (1998) and De Li Periu and MacKenzie (2000) have discussed how reciprocal causal relationships can begin to emerge, such that criminal involvement both facilitates and maintains drug use, and drug use maintains involvement in crime. Whilst some researchers (e.g. McBride and McCoy 1982) have argued for sub-cultural explanations of the drugs-crime link, the accounts of the offenders themselves are more consistent with a pathological perspective, where dependence provides the motive for acquisitive offending.

A number of authors have argued that undertaking criminal activities over time leads to drug use because of the their associations with deviant sub-cultures (Bean and Wilkinson 1988; McBride and McCoy 1982). In other words, one's involvement with criminal activities or excessive substance use will increase the likelihood of being drawn into a deviant sub-culture. This sub-culture acts to reinforce any form of deviant behaviour of which criminal behaviour and excessive drug use are two examples. As such, the sub-culture acts as a latent moderator of the relationship between crime and drug use (Bean and Wilkinson 1988). However, while there is empirical evidence to support this proposition (e.g. Bean and Wilkinson 1988), these same studies also indicate a more or less equal proportion of participants for whom drug use preceded criminal behaviour.

Studies of the impact of drug treatment also support this view. For instance, when users enter methadone maintenance, their criminal activity is in general decreased (Bell, Hall and Byth 1992; Ward, Mattick and Hall 1994). Those with continued criminal involvement tend to be also continuing their illicit drug use (Patterson, Lennings and Davey 2000) or else, show high scores on an antisocial personality inventory (Bovasso, Alterman, Cacciola and Rutherford 2002).

Over the past decade or so, successive political authorities have claimed a 'war on drugs' and as such that drug-related crime is one of the worst consequences of drug use. This chapter has presented theoretical and research evidence that calls into question this simple 'addiction model' of the relationship between drugs and crime whereby illicit drug use leads inexorably to dependence and thence to crime. The relationships are actually more complex. The vast majority of illicit drug users are, and remain, in control of their use. There is a small minority of illicit drug users who are dependent in their use and also chaotic in their lifestyles (Kaye *et al.* 1998). There is a strong probability that these will finance their drug use through property crime. The inter-relationships between illicit drug use, problematic drug use and persistent offending are set out schematically in Figure 8.1. This is intended to be illustrative rather than precise.

It makes sense to think of chaotic or dependent drug use and persistent offending sharing causal roots, but it is also important to understand how, once established, the two behaviours can be mutually sustaining. Drug dependence tends to amplify the offending rates of people whose circumstances may predispose them to becoming persistent offenders. There are important policy implications here. It

Figure 8.1 Relationship between illicit drug use, problem drug use and persistent offending in Great Britain

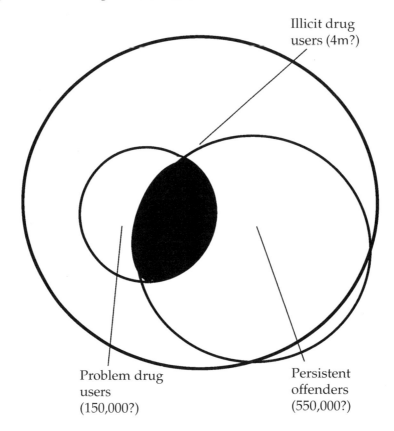

Illicit drug
users (4m?)

Problem drug
users
(150,000?)

Persistent
offenders
(550,000?)

makes excellent sense to provide treatment services for drug-dependent offenders. If successful, it should substantially reduce levels of crime. Indeed we have already seen some success from methadone programmes in this way (e.g. Strang *et al.* 2000). However, to maintain the lifestyle changes, which treatment may enable, it will also be necessary to address the factors that drew this group into persistent offending in the first place.

References

Albery, I.P. and Guppy, A. (1995a) 'Drivers' differential perceptions of legal and safe driving consumption', *Addiction*, 90: 245–54.

Albery, I.P. and Guppy, A. (1995b) 'The interactionist nature of drinking and driving: A structural model', *Ergonomics*, 38: 1805–818.

Albery, I.P. and Guppy, A. (1996) 'Drivers' biased perceptions of the adverse consequences of drink-driving', *Drug and Alcohol Review*, 15: 39–45.

Albery, I.P., Gossop, M. and Strang, J. (1998) 'Illicit drugs and driving: a review of epidemiological, behavioural and psychological correlates', *Journal of Substance Misuse*, 140–49.

Albery, I.P., Strang, J., Gossop, M. and Griffiths P. (2000) 'Illicit drugs and driving: accident involvement among a cohort of current excessive drug users', *Drug and Alcohol Dependence*, 58 (1–2): 197–204.

Anglin, M.D. and Perrochet, B. (1998) 'Drug use and crime: a historical review of research conducted by the UCLA Drug Abuse Research Center', *Substance Use and Misuse*, 33 (9): 1871–914.

Anglin, M.D. and Speckart, G. (1988) 'Narcotics and crime: a multi-sample, multi-method analysis', *Criminology*, 26: 197–233.

Ball, J. and Ross, A (1991) *The Effectiveness of Methadone Maintenance Treatment*. New York: Springer.

Ball, J.C, Rosen, L., Flueck, J.A. and Nurco, D.N. (1981) 'The criminality of heroin addicts: when addicted and when off opiates', in J.A. Inciardi (ed.) *The Drugs-Crime Connection* (pp. 39–65). New York: Sage.

Ball, J.C., Shaffer, J.W. and Nurco, D.N. (1983) 'The day-to-day criminality of heroin addicts in Baltimore: as study in the continuity of offence rates', *Drug and Alcohol Dependence*, 12: 119–42.

Bean, P.T. and Wilkinson, C.K. (1988) 'Drug taking, crime and the illicit supply system', *British Journal of Addiction*, 83: 533–39.

Belenko, S. (1998) *Research on Drug Courts: A critical review*. New York: The National Centre on Addiction and Substance Abuse at Columbia University.

Bell, J., Hall, W. and Blyth, K. (1992) 'Changes in criminal activity after entering methadone maintenance', *British Journal of Addiction*, 87: 251–58.

Bennett, T. (1998) *Drugs and Crime: The results of research on drug testing and interviewing arrestees*. HORS 183. London: Home Office.

Bennett, T. (2000) *Drugs and Crime: The results of the second development stage of the NEW-ADAM programme*. HORS 205. London: Home Office.

Bennett, T., Holloway, K. and Williams, T. (2001) *Drug Use and Offending: Summary results of the first year of the NEW-ADAM research programme*. Home Office Research Findings No. 148. London: Home Office.

Best, D., Sidwell, C., Gossop, M., Harris, J. and Strang, J. (2001) 'Crime and expenditure among polydrug misusers seeking treatment', *British Journal of Criminology*, 41: 119–26.

Bovasso, G.B., Alterman, A.I., Cacciola, J.S. and Rutherford, M.J. (2002) 'The prediction of violent and non-violent criminal behavior in a methadone maintenance population', *Journal of Personality Disorders*, 16: 360–73.

Boys, A., Farrell, M., Bebbington, P., Brugha, T., Coid, J., Jenkins, R., Lewis, G., Marsden, J., Meltzer, H., Singleton, N. and Taylor, C. (2002) 'Drug use and initiation in prison: results from a national prison survey in England and Wales', *Addiction*, 97: 1551–560.

Coid, J., Carvell, A., Kittler, Z., Healey, A. and Henderson, J. (2000) *Opiates, Criminal Behaviour, and Methadone Treatment*. London: Home Office.

De Li Priu, H. and MacKenzie, D. (2000) 'Drug involvement, lifestyles and criminal activities among probationers', *Journal of Drug Issues*, 30: 593–620.

Deitch, D., Koutsenok, I. and Ruiz, A. (2000) 'The relationship between crime and drugs: what we have learned in recent decades', *Journal of Psychoactive Drugs*, 32: 391–97.

Ditton, J. and Hammersley, R.H. (1994) 'The typical cocaine user', *Druglink*, 9: 11–12.

Dobinson, I. and Ward, P. (1986) 'Heroin and property crime: an Australian perspective', *Journal of Drug Issues*, 16 (2): 249–62.

Edmunds, M., May, T., Hough, M, and Hearnden, I. (1998) *Arrest Referral: Emerging lessons from research*. Home Office: Drugs Prevention Initiative Paper no 23.

Edmunds, M., Hough, M., Turnbull, P.J. and May, T. (1999) *Doing Justice to Treatment: Referring offenders to drug services*. DPAS Paper 2. London: Home Office.

Farrell, M., Howes, S., Taylor, C., Lewis, G., Jenkins, R., Bebbington, P., Jarvis, M., Brugha, T., Gill, B. and Meltzer, H. (1998) 'Substance misuse and psychiatric comorbidity: An overview of the OPCS National Psychiatric Morbidity Survey', *Addictive Behaviors*, 23: 909–18.

Ferri, C.P., Gossop, M., Rabe-Hesketh, S. and Laranjeira, R.R. (2002) 'Differences in factors associated with first treatment entry and treatment re-entry among cocaine users', *Addiction*, 97: 825–32.

Flood-Page, C., Campbell, S., Harrington, V. and Miller, J. (2000) *Youth Crime: Findings from the 1998/99 Youth Lifestyles Survey*. HORS 209. London: Home Office.

Godfrey, C., Eaton, G., McDougall, C. and Culyer, A. (2002) *The Economic and Social Costs of Class A Drug Use*. Home Office Research Study No. 249. London: Home Office.

Gossop, M., Marsden, J. and Stewart, D. (1998) *NTORS at One Year. The National Treatment Outcome Research Study. Changes in substance use, health and criminal behaviour at one year after intake*. London: Department of Health.

Guppy, A. and Albery, I.P. (1997) 'Survey of drivers to explain the reduction of drink-driving in the UK', *Journal of Traffic Medicine*, 25: 7–13.

Hall, W., Bell, J. and Carless, J (1993) 'Crime and drug use among applicants for methadone maintenance', *Drug and Alcohol Dependence*, 31: 123–29.

Hammersley, R.H., Forsyth, A., Morrison, V. and Davies, J.B. (1989) 'The relationship between crime and opioid use', *British Journal of Addiction*, 84: 1029–043.

Harding, W.M., Zinberg, N.E., Stelmack, S.M. and Barry, M. (1980) 'Formerly-addicted-now-controlled opiate users', *International Journal of the Addictions*, 15: 47–60.

Harrison, L.D. (1992) 'The drug-crime nexus in the USA', *Contemporary Drug Problems*, 19: 181–202.

Harrison, L.D. and Backenheimer, M. (1998) 'Research careers in unravelling the drug-crime nexus in the U.S.', *Substance Use and Misuse*, 33: 1763–2003.

Hearnden, I. and Harocopos, A. (1999) *Problem drug use and probation in London*. Home Office Research Findings No. 112.

Hearnden, I. and Harocopos, A. (2000) *Problem Drug Use and Probation in London*. Home Office Research Findings No. 112. London: Home Office.

Home Office (2001) Criminal justice: the way ahead. Presented to Parliament by the Secretary of State for the Home Department by Command of Her Majesty, February 2001. CM 5074.

Jarvis, G. and Parker H. (1989) 'Young heroin users and crime: How do the 'new users' finance their habits?', *British Journal of Criminology*, 29: 175–85.

Jessor, R., Donovan, J.E. and Costa, F.M. (1991) *Beyond Adolescence: Problem behavior and adult development*. Cambridge: Cambridge University Press.

Jessor, R. and Jessor, S.L. (1977) *Problem Behavior and Psychosocial Development: A longitudinal study*. New York: Academic Press.

Kaye, S., Darke, S. and Finlay-Jones, R. (1998) 'The onset of heroin use and criminal behaviour: does order make a difference?', *Drug and Alcohol Dependence*, 53: 79–86.

Kokkevi, A., Liappas, J., Boukouvala, V., Alevizou, V., Anastassopoulou, E. and Stefanis, C. (1993) 'Criminality in a sample of drug abusers in Greece', *Drug and Alcohol Dependence*, 31: 111–21.

Lader, D., Singleton, N. and Meltzer, H. (2000) *Psychiatric Morbidity among Young Offenders in England and Wales*. London: ONS.

Lowenstein, L.F. (2001) 'Recent research into the direct relationship between criminality and substance abuse', *International Journal of Adolescence and Youth*, 9: 257–72.

Lurigio, A. (2000) 'Drug treatment effectiveness and availability', *Criminal Justice and Behaviour*, 27: 495–528.

MacCoun, R.J. and Reuter, P. (1998) 'Drug control', in M. Tonry (ed.) *The Handbook of Crime and Punishment*. New York: Oxford University Press.

MacGregor, S. (2000) 'The drugs-crime nexus', *Drugs: Education, Prevention and Policy*, 7: 311–16.

McBride, D. and McCoy, C. (1982) 'Crime and drugs: the issues and literature', *Journal of Drug Issues*, 137–51.

Maden, A., Swinton, M. and Gunn, J. (1991) 'Drug dependence in prisons', *British Medical Journal*, 302: 880.

Mason, D., Birmingham, L. and Grubin, D. (1997) 'Substance use in remand prisoners: a consecutive case study', *British Medical Journal*, 315: 18–21.

Measham, F., Aldridge, J. and Parker, H. (2001) *Dancing on Drugs. Risk, health and hedonism in the British club scene*. London: Free Association Books.

Miller, P.M. and Plant, M. (1996) 'Drinking, smoking and illicit drug use among 15 and 16 year olds in the United Kingdom', *British Medical Journal*, 313: 294–297.

National Institute of Justice (2000) *1999 Annual Report on Drug Use Among Adult and Juvenile Arrestees*. Arrestee Drug Abuse Monitoring Program (ADAM). Washington DC: National Institute of Justice, NCJ 181426.

Nurco, D.N., Ball, J.C., Shaffer, J.W. and Hanlon, T.E. (1985) 'The criminality of narcotic addicts', *Journal of Nervous and Mental Disease*, 173: 94–102.

Nurco, D.N., Kinlock, T.W. and Hanlon, T.E. (1995) 'The drugs-crime connection', in J. Inciardi and K. McElrath (eds) *The American Drug Scene: An Anthology*. Los Angeles: Roxbury.

Parker, H., Aldridge, J. and Measham, F. (1998) *Illegal Leisure: The normalisation of adolescent recreational drug use*. London: Routledge.

Parker, H. and Newcombe, R. (1987) 'Heroin use and acquisitive crime in an English community', *British Journal of Sociology*, 38 (3): 331–50.

Patterson, S., Lennings, C. J. and Davey, J. (2000) 'Methadone clients, crime and substance use', *International Journal of Offender Therapy and Comparative Criminology*, 44: 667–80.

Pearson, G. (1987) *The New Heroin Users*. Oxford: Basil Blackwell.

Ramsay, M., Baker, P., Goulden, C., Sharp, C. and Sondhi, A. (2001) *Drug Misuse Declared in 2000: Results from the British Crime Survey*. HORS 224. London: Home Office.

Ramsay, M. and Partridge, S. (1999) *Drug Misuse Declared in 1998: Results from the British Crime Survey*. HORS 197. London: Home Office.

Singleton, N., Farrel, M. and Meltzer, H. (1999) *Substance Misuse Among Prisoners in England and Wales*. London: ONS.

Stewart, D., Gossop, M., Marsden, J. and Rolfe, A. (2000) 'Drug misuse and acquisitive crime among clients recruited to the national treatment outcome research study (NTORS)', *Criminal Behaviour and Mental Health*, 10: 10–20. I.

Stimson, G.V., Hickman, M. and Turnbull, P.J. (1998) 'Statistics on misuse of drugs have been misused', *British Medical Journal*, 317: 1388.

Strang, J., Marsden, J., Cummins, M., Farrell, M., Finch, E., Gossop, M., Stewart, M. and Welch, S. (2000) 'Randomized trial of supervised injectable versus oral methadone maintenance: report of feasibility and 6-month outcome', *Addiction*, 95: 1631–645.

Turnbull, P.J., McSweeney, T., Hough, M., Webster, R. and Edmunds, M. (2000) *Drug Treatment and Testing Orders: Final evaluation report*. HORS 212. London: Home Office.

Walters, G. (1998) *Changing Lives of Drugs and Crime*. Chichester: Wiley and Sons.

Ward, J., Mattick, R. and Hall, W. (1994) 'The effectiveness of methadone maintenance treatment', *Drug and Alcohol Review*, 13: 327–36.

Yoeman, T. and Griffiths, M. (1996) 'Adolescent machine gambling and crime', *Journal of Adolescence*, 19: 99–104.

Zinberg, N.E. and Jacobson, R.C. (1976) 'The natural history of "chipping"', *American Journal of Psychiatry*, 133L 37–40.

Chapter 9

Drug arrest referral schemes and forensic perspectives on the treatment of addiction

Andrew Guppy, Middlesex University;
Paul Johnson, North Yorkshire Police and
Mark Wallace-Bell, Christchurch School of
Medicine and Health Sciences

Drug use, misuse and problems

Initially, it is necessary to clarify what is meant by the concept of 'substance misuse' and the drugs involved. According to the American Psychiatric Association, misuse can include drug-related behaviour that may cause trouble in the short term through accidents, social or legal problems, though this behaviour need not have become a regular pattern. Two further categories of psychiatric disorder in relation to substance use are defined in the *DSM-IV*, (*Diagnostic and Statistical Manual of Mental Disorders*, American Psychiatric Association 1994).

'Substance Abuse' (APA 1994: 182) represents a 'maladaptive pattern of substance use leading to clinically significant impairment or distress, as manifested by one (or more) of the following occurring within a 12 month period.'

1 Recurrent substance use resulting in failure to fulfil major role obligations at work, school or home.
2 Recurrent use in risky situations (e.g. driving while impaired).
3 Recurrent substance-related legal problems.
4 Continued use despite persistent, or recurrent social or interpersonal problems, caused or exacerbated by substance-related behaviour.'

For the final category of 'substance dependence', the criteria are similar in nature to those of 'abuse', though more established patterns of behaviour relating to obtaining and using the substance may be present. Additionally, 'dependence' includes the possible presence of 'tolerance'

157

(diminished effect of the substance, leading to consumption of larger doses), 'withdrawal' (physical and psychological symptoms associated with a rapid, substantial decline in substance consumption) and an inability to control substance use, even when persistent or recurrent physiological or psychological problems exist which are caused or exacerbated by the substance.

The range of substances covered in the *DSM-IV* chapter includes alcohol, cannabis, cocaine, hallucinogens (e.g. LSD), inhalants, opiates (e.g. heroin) and sedative-hypnotics (e.g. benzodiazepines). All of these substances are seen as available for diagnoses of 'abuse' and 'dependence' and are detailed below.

Drugs guide

Drugs with stimulating properties

Amphetamines Short-term use results in feelings of energy and arousal. Long term and/or heavy use may result in delusions, hallucinations and feelings of persecution. Psychological dependence is possible, tolerance effects are common and it is detectable for up to three days after use.

Ecstasy (MDMA) Short-term use may be similar to LSD (calming, heightened senses) without hallucinations, larger doses may produce effects similar to amphetamines.

Cocaine (including crack) Short-term use produces feelings of well-being and exhilaration. Long-term and/or heavy use may result in feelings of restlessness, sleeplessness and persecution. Metabolite (benzoylecgonine) is detectable for three to five days.

Drugs with relaxing, depressing properties

Cannabis Short-term relaxant, enhances perceptions, impairs psychomotor skills. Heavy use may result in perceptual distortions. Detectable for between three to 30 days, depending on use.

Opiates (including heroin) Short-term use – feelings of contentment and warmth. Long-term heavy use – dependence may result. Physical harm is usually related to needle use. **Morphine** and **codeine** commonly prescribed, **heroin** usually illicit, **methadone** mainly prescribed as a heroin substitute, though can be obtained illegally (usually through misuse of the prescription system). Detectable for up to 72 hours.

Hallucinogenic drugs

Lysergic acid diethylamide (LSD) Short-term effects include heightened visual and auditory sensations, may include mystical, ecstatic or frightening experiences. True hallucinations are rare, impairment of psychomotor and cognitive performance are likely. Long-term effects relate to mental rather than physical well-being, prolonged serious disorders are rare, as yet.

Psilicybin (magic mushrooms) Short-term effects very much depend on dose taken but can follow a similar pattern to LSD.

Population use of alcohol and other drugs

Surveys suggest that 90 per cent of the British adult population consume alcoholic beverages on an occasional or regular basis (Wilson 1980; Goddard 1991). These surveys revealed that average weekly consumption in the UK was around 20 drinks per week for males and around seven drinks for females (a standard drink being equivalent to a single whisky, a small glass of table wine or a half pint of beer, all containing roughly 8–10g of ethanol). More usefully, surveys like these suggest that around five per cent of men and two per cent of women report alcohol-related problems in health, social and economic areas of life functioning.

For substances other than alcohol, the estimates vary considerably depending on legality, availability and reason for use. Generally speaking, the estimates on prevalence of use of illicit drugs in the United Kingdom are far from satisfactory and provide a tremendous range of possible values (Sutton and Maynard 1993) (see previous chapter). However, recent research has provided some basis for general prevalence estimates.

Ramsay *et al.* (2001) reported results from the British Crime Survey 2000 regarding current and lifetime use of illicit substances. They reported that 22 per cent of British 16–29 year olds reported using cannabis at least once during the 12 months prior to interview. Around five per cent of respondents reported using cocaine, with another 5 per cent reporting amphetamine use, only one per cent of the sample reported heroin use.

Among offender sub-populations, we may expect substance use to be higher than that in the general population. Bennett (1998) reported a detailed investigation of 839 arrestees who were interviewed in five police regions (Cambridge, London, Manchester, Nottingham and

Sunderland). About three-quarters of those interviewed were screened for a range of illicit drugs. Over 60 per cent of arrestees interviewed tested positive for drugs. Forty-six per cent of the tested sample were positive for cannabis, 18 per cent were opiate positive, with 10–12 per cent positive for each of amphetamines, cocaine and benzodiazepines. A further eight per cent of the sample showed positive for methadone. Interestingly, of those arrested as shoplifting suspects, 50 per cent tested positive for opiates, and 33 per cent positive for cocaine. A quarter of those suspected of car thefts tested positive for opiates and 10 per cent of those arrested on suspicion of burglary tested positive for opiates.

Thus it would seem clear that alcohol and drug use is substantial among researched cohorts of arrestees in relation to general population estimates. By the nature of the contact with the legal process, many of these substance users may become defined as substance misusers because their use is associated with a criminal act that has been detected. This acknowledgement of the link between patterns of substance misuse and involvement in crime does not imply causation. Offending behaviour can develop alongside illicit substance use or excessive alcohol use without being caused by them. However, the association alone has provided motivation for the development of a number of interventions aimed at offenders that sought to emphasise the importance of addressing substance use patterns.

Addressing the treatment needs of substance misusing offenders

Substance misuse intervention strategies can be described as operating at stages of prevention, detection and rehabilitation (Guppy and Albery 1997; Guppy and Marsden 2003). While such a process seems rather simplistic, it seems an accurate reflection of much of the activity in this field and serves to highlight the crossover between healthcare and criminal justice systems. A full exploration of strategic and operational details in this field is beyond the scope of this chapter and the reader is referred to sources such as the Drugs Prevention Advisory Service (e.g. Home Office 1999; Edmunds *et al.* 1999). However, it is felt that insight can be gained from examining a process designed to develop activity in detecting misuse and abuse and moving appropriate individuals towards appropriate interventions. The next section of the chapter focuses therefore on describing the process and participants of a current Drug Arrest Referral Scheme. The subsequent sections examine approaches to the rehabilitation of substance abusers and the likelihood of successful outcome.

Drug Arrest Referral Schemes

As well as those most heavily involved in drug misuse, the criminal justice system also comes into contact with many young people (especially in the 18–25 year old age group) who are at the early stages of drug misuse, the majority of whom appear in court for non-drug offences such as theft or soliciting. The development of Drug Arrest Referral systems provides a way of encouraging arrested drug users to access assessment and treatment resources at an early stage. Edmunds *et al.* (1998) labelled three different kinds of Drug Arrest Referral models as: 'information', 'pro-active' and 'incentive'. Information schemes simply provide information about drug misuse and treatment contacts to people passing through custody and is seen as a minimum contact approach. Pro-active schemes involve drug workers collaborating closely with the police such that certain arrestees may be contacted at the station and offered confidential assessment and advice interviews. The incentive model follows this approach, but also incorporates a means of significantly motivating particular sub-groups of arrestees to take up the offer of an interview with a drugs worker.

Edmunds *et al.* (1998) described the development and operation of three demonstration Drug Arrest Referral projects based in Brighton, Derby and Southwark. These schemes all followed the 'pro-active' model and showed substantial reductions in reported drug use and crime among those interviewed.

Over the last few years, most Police Forces/Services have operated some form of Arrest Referral Scheme. The majority have opted for the information and more recently, the pro-active models. However, the following section describes the operation of an incentive scheme, operated by North Yorkshire Police.

The development of Drug Arrest Referral in North Yorkshire

An information model had been operating in York from 1996, and a new scheme was also established that adopted an incentive approach. It was acknowledged from the beginning that there were obvious legal issues arising in such a model. However, these issues were clarified in a report by the Association of Chief Police Officers discussing Home Office advice upon Cautioning Plus and Referral Schemes. The report stated that once the arrested person has admitted the offence without any inducement, it is open to the police to invite offenders to demonstrate a commitment to address their underlying drug problems, for instance by making an appointment with a drug agency. The report acknowledged that there could be a benefit in allowing a pause in the due process to allow the arrest referral to have some benefit. This mirrored an approach already operational in the Kirklees area of West Yorkshire serving Huddersfield and Dewsbury.

This model capitalises upon the bail aspect of the judicial process. Once individuals have admitted to their offence, or offences, without inducement, they are offered the opportunity to address potential underlying drugs problems. This is not compulsory and they may decline the offer, should they so desire. In this eventuality, they will be dealt with in the normal way, without any further punishment being awarded. Should they decide to take up the offer, then they are bailed for 28 days with a non-enforceable proviso that they arrange an appointment with the agency within the first 14 days of that bail period and attend at the appointed time.

If people return after 28 days, without having attended, then they are dealt with for the offence in the normal way. If information is received from the agency that they have attended, then due consideration is given to this fact and one of a number of options is taken, including the decision not to prosecute. This new system was adopted by North Yorkshire Police and later extended to include a pro-active model (Scheme Two) which applied to a wider range of arrestees. (Please see box below for a step by step summary of these schemes.)

Case study: York Arrest Referral Scheme operations guide

Criteria for people being referred to Scheme 1

Where people are arrested in possession of drugs for their own personal use then, *assuming that they have not been on Scheme 1 previously* they can take up the offer of going on scheme 1.

Criteria for people being referred to Scheme 2

Any offenders, irrespective of the offence types, are given the opportunity to see the Arrest Referral Worker to discuss drug related matters that influence their offending.

How does Scheme 1 work?

Scheme 1 is only available to arrestees actually found in possession of drugs. The offender should be interviewed by way of tape-recorded interview and have fully admitted the offence of possessing drugs for personal use. The interview should cover all the points sufficient to prove that case. If the person does not comply with the scheme, then the case will still have to be proven. In the case of a juvenile, the appropriate adult still needs to be present.

A check with the Custody Officer will reveal whether the person is eligible to go on the scheme. Arrestees can only have one opportunity to go on this scheme. If the person is ineligible, see Scheme 2.

Ensure that it is appropriate to refer the offender (*i.e. not going on remand or before the court in breach of bail*). If the person is eligible, then the offer of Scheme 1 will be made. If refused, then the case proceeds in the normal way. If taken up, then the person is referred using the Scheme 1 Form and provided with information leaflets. People are then bailed for 28 days (in the case of a juvenile for 35 days).

What if the offender does not comply with Scheme 1?

If they have not contacted the Arrest Referral Worker in the allotted 15 days from the arrest date, the worker will inform the officer in the case. The Arresting Officer will prepare the case file in anticipation of the individual answering Police bail. The offender is then dealt with in exactly the same way as though he or she had never been offered the scheme.

How does Scheme 2 work? The pro-active model in York

Whilst Scheme 1 deals with offenders arrested in possession of drugs for personal use, Scheme 2 makes it possible for those people arrested for *any offence* to access the services of the Arrest Referral Worker. However, this scheme cannot offer anything by way of a reduced punishment if they choose to take up the option. *Scheme 2 can still be offered to those offenders that have already been on the Scheme 1 programme.*

Profile of York Drug Arrest Referrals

The following profile of referrals is taken from an early report on the York DARS activities. Four hundred and thirty cases were considered appropriate for referral in the 12-month period of evaluation. Regarding the source of these arrests, just over half (52 per cent) were direct police arrests, with 14 per cent being police arrests that were incidental to drug misuse. A surprisingly prominent (34 per cent) source of arrestees came from the Doorsafe Scheme operating in pubs and clubs around the city.

For the vast majority, the main drug concerned was cannabis (around 60 per cent of sample), with heroin accounting for around 20 per cent and amphetamines and ecstasy also accounting for nearly ten per cent each. A small number of individuals had cocaine as their primary drug of concern.

By far the bulk (86 per cent) of those arrested were male, with a generally youthful age profile, with 12 per cent being under 18 years of age, 32 per cent between 18 and 21 years, 22 per cent between 22 and 25 and 34 per cent aged 26 or over. While nearly half (47 per cent) of those arrested were unemployed, 41 per cent were in full or part-time employment with a further 12 per cent being in full-time education. Forty per cent of the arrested sample had no previous convictions. Of those with previous convictions, 70 had had ten or more previous convictions recorded.

Of the 430 people arrested, 360 (84 per cent) complied with the referral and 70 did not. Of the 360 interviewed, nine per cent admitted to funding their drug use through illegal income, with quite a high proportion of individuals (38 per cent) indicating that they also had problems with alcohol misuse. A sketch emerged of the more serious drug users in the cohort, based on information of their drug spending per week. Twelve per cent of those interviewed admitted to spending over £100 per week on drugs. This small sub-group tended to be older than the main sample, three-quarters were unemployed, and 80 per cent had previous convictions. Nearly 80 per cent of this group had heroin as their primary drug of arrest with around 75 per cent of the total sub-group being intravenous users.

Of the 360 individuals who complied with the referral, the vast majority (79 per cent) had only one appointment with the Arrest Referral Worker (ARW). Only 12 per cent had further appointments with the ARW, while another nine per cent had an onward referral to another agency. Thus the picture from this profile of participants of the York Drug Arrest Referral Scheme would seem to indicate that there were a significant number of individuals that could be the focus of further attention in terms of treatment, assistance or counselling. The following sections outline the range of intervention approaches that are usually available within the UK at the moment with a brief review of expected effectiveness.

Counselling substance misusers

Models of substance misuse and their implications for treatment

There are several different theoretical models prevalent in the drug and alcohol counselling field (e.g. see Miller and Hester 1986). One widely held view may be epitomised by Narcotics Anonymous (NA) and is designed to follow on from the approach pioneered by Alcoholics Anonymous (AA). This assumes that drug abuse is a pre-existing physical (biochemical) abnormality and it is almost as though some individuals have an incurable allergy to their substance of addiction (hence lifelong abstinence being the only answer). Another approach, particularly prevalent within the UK, views the important element as being the harm that is related to the drug misuse and seeks to minimise this by reducing risks, reducing intake (as opposed to cessation) and possibly changing to another substance with reduced harm implications. The third perspective views drug misuse as principally a pattern of inappropriate coping. This approach focuses on cognitive behavioural elements in order to recognise and deal with situations likely to lead to drug use, reduce unhelpful perceptions, improve feelings of efficacy and to increase the range of coping behaviours that may be used as an alternative to drugs. Obviously, there are any number of other approaches that are available and successful, but the following are probably the most commonly encountered within the UK at present.

Narcotics Anonymous

Although this kind of 'intervention' may appear to be different to usual forms of 'counselling', Narcotics Anonymous quite clearly provide a well known type of support for those with problems. The spread and level of activity of NA in the United Kingdom is considerably less than its sister organisation AA, however, the broad philosophy of this approach can also be found in a number of residential and outpatient treatment facilities.

The principles of the NA (and AA) approach are covered in the 'Twelve Steps'. These steps principally involve six stages. Firstly, there is an admission of powerlessness over substance use and that life has become 'unmanageable'. The second stage involves an acceptance of assistance from a 'higher power'. Stage three is about becoming aware of the 'nature of our wrongs' with the fourth stage working on removing 'defects of character' and 'shortcomings'. A penultimate stage is about promising to make amends to those who have been harmed and the final stage emphasises the maintenance of progress through prayer, meditation and a commitment to helping others in similar need. NA themselves summarise this process as including 'admitting to a drug problem, seeking help, self-appraisal, confidential self-disclosure, making amends (where possible) when harm has been done, achieving a spiritual awakening and supporting other drug addicts who want to recover.' This perhaps suggests a gradual change in the emphasis placed on the 'higher power principle' (more spiritual rather than religious). However, the principle that does not vary within the Twelve Steps approach concerns the goal behaviour of abstinence. This has some implications for those who are opiate abusers, where a common alternative involves methadone substitution (described below) which some may regard as incompatible with an abstinence approach.

Typical harm reduction approach

The essence of the harm reduction approach to substance misuse is a focus of service provision on meeting and working with drug users on their terms. It is a feature of such an approach that, at times, these terms may be out of line with mainstream social, government or service provision policy. Critics of this approach have long argued that by being supportive, in reality giving drugs to drug users, the services may be encouraging these individuals to maintain their current patterns of use, with no compelling reason to stop. Supporters of the harm reduction approach would argue that it is an attempt to bridge the gap between the expectations of drug users and service providers with realistic rather than moralistic methods of intervention.

Usually the first step in harm reduction involves the stabilisation of the clients' illicit use, this includes provision of sterile equipment and other harm reduction resources (e.g. condoms). The next step would normally involve reduction of use, sometimes paired with provision of a 'script' to top up the reduced quantity of illicit drug. A number of drug dependency units (DDUs) adopt a policy of only providing scripts when the client is illicit drug free (usually monitored by urine screening).

Generally, counselling is offered throughout this process but is particularly encouraged during periods of change (reduction in script).

Group counselling is generally available at most DDUs, however, the consistent uptake of counselling is generally felt to be low. Clients would normally keep close contact with a key worker whose remit includes social and welfare support as well as specific drug related matters. To some extent, problem oriented, directive, counselling occurs with this key worker. In many environments, this relationship may be maintained within a 'contract' situation where support from the key worker is dependent on the client complying with the 'script regime' (e.g. cessation of illicit use).

One of the primary benefits of this approach tends to be in the realistic perspective on relapse management. As the approach does not rely on abstinence as the only acceptable alternative to harmful use, the relapse event may be more accepted within the treatment regime and the re-establishment of the treatment process is much easier. However, one possible drawback to the most commonly encountered harm reduction approach is the potential lack of detailed counselling support. To some extent, the process may focus on the management of the intake reduction and ignore underlying deficiencies in terms of self perceptions and coping skills.

A typical psychological approach to substance misuse counselling

A number of community-based agencies focusing on alcohol and drug misuse could be seen as providing a mixture of intervention methods added to a more traditional counselling approach. Therefore, one may see agencies providing features core to the harm reduction approach, whilst advocating a move towards abstinence and featuring a range of group and individual sessions focusing on elements central to cognitive behavioural and rational emotive therapies.

The elements of harm reduction education and support in the provision of information and advice (as well as equipment in terms of syringes, etc) would normally occur early on in the process. Later, the discussion of eventual outcome goals could be approached. Specific input relating to unhelpful cognitions and behaviours would also be the focus of later sessions, particularly the use of group sessions focusing on the uptake of alternative (to substance use) behaviours in order to positively replace the effects of drug taking.

Beyond the drug specific information, the main difference in substance misuse counselling concerns the focus of activities (towards abstinence or 'controlled' use) rather than the actual activities themselves (e.g. role playing within a general social skills development package). It is common for some time to be devoted to obvious substance related issues as 'saying no'. Additionally, a lot of effort is directed towards 'relapse prevention' within the substance misuse field (see later). Within this general package, material focusing on stress management and assertiveness training could be included as would other exercises on self-awareness and the development of positive ways of spending leisure time (other than substance use).

Outcome effectiveness of substance misuse interventions

Whilst the range of potential measures for evaluating treatment outcome is extensive, it is clear that most studies focus on substance use, mental health, social functioning and criminal behaviour (Marsden *et al*. 1998). While large scale, prospective outcome studies are very expensive and thus quite rare, the process of outcome research is a necessary component of any treatment provision. Thus, there is a need to ensure that lessons learnt from large programmes of research are embedded within smaller projects to benchmark performance and inform developments in provision.

American research has indicated some positive findings in terms of outcome research across a range of treatment types. The Drug Abuse Reporting Programme (DARP) compared outcomes across methadone maintenance, therapeutic communities, outpatient abstinence-oriented counselling and outpatient detoxification intervention types. There was clear evidence that a minimum of three months treatment was associated with positive change and that longer treatment spells produced more positive outcome. However, no substantial differences in outcome were found between methadone maintenance, therapeutic communities and outpatient abstinence-oriented counselling. In terms of drug use, the long term follow-up (12 years) indicated that over 60 per cent of the sample had not used opioid drugs daily for at least three years, though criminal behaviour remained high (over 50 per cent) at this point even for those who were drug-free.

A similar positive outcome was evidenced at one year follow-up in the Treatment Outcome Prospective study (TOPS) for clients who had remained in treatment for at least three months. This study included three treatment modalities: methadone maintenance, residential, and outpatient drug-free counselling and again showed a positive relationship between length of time in treatment and outcome. The residential and methadone maintenance interventions were similarly effective, with over half of the clients abstinent from heroin at the 12 month follow-up.

More recently, Hubbard *et al.* (1999) reported initial findings from the Drug Abuse Treatment Outcome Study (DATOS) which covered outcomes in 3,000 clients from four intervention types (outpatient methadone, outpatient abstinence, short-term inpatient and long-term residential). In their summary of this research, Mueller and Wyman (1997) reported that 'Patients in programs surveyed for DATOS showed a marked reduction in drug use after treatment regardless of the type of treatment program in which they participated.' However the results for heroin users were only statistically significant for methadone maintenance and long-term residential programmes as the numbers of heroin users in other programme types were too low.

The National Treatment Outcome Research Study (NTORS) was the largest prospective outcome evaluation study yet undertaken in the UK. Gossop *et al.* (1998) reported on outcome data from 753 clients at the 12 month follow-up stage who had received a variety of treatment inputs (275 residential and 478 community-based). For clients treated in community settings, there was an increase in abstinence from illicit opiates (heroin and illicit methadone) from five per cent at intake to 22 per cent at 12 months. Also where 86 per cent of clients were regular users at intake, only 55 per cent remained so at follow-up. For residential clients, abstinence from illicit opiates increased from 22 per cent at intake to 50 per cent at 12 months. Regular use of illicit opiates dropped from 69 per cent to 40 per cent. However, it was reported that the best performing agencies reported reductions in heroin use in clients to around one third of intake levels whereas the worst performing agencies showed no average reduction in heroin use among clients at 12 months follow-up. The five year follow-up review of the NTORS programme (Gossop *et al.* 2001) indicated quite a stable picture in relation to the results obtained at 12 months. This was particularly the case for residential clients, though there was some evidence that further improvements occurred in relation to abstinence and regular heroin use among the community clients.

Additional measures for drug misusing offenders

One of the more innovative interventions that has been researched in the UK in recent years concerns Drug Treatment and Testing Orders (DTTOs) established under the Crime and Disorder Act 1998. From the introduction of DTTOs, offenders could be required to undergo substance misuse treatment as part of or in association with an existing community sentence. While DTTOs resembled the already existing opportunity to use Probation Orders with an additional requirement for treatment of alcohol or drug dependency, they also provided requirements for the courts to review offenders' progress regularly and for offenders to be regularly screened for drug use. Turnbull *et al.* (2000) reported an evaluation of three pilot DTTOs operated in three pilot sites and indicated some positive signs, although the actual quality of the data was severely compromised by the high variation in how procedures had been implemented across the sites. In particular, there were differences in how cases were reviewed and what measures were taken following the quite frequent failures to meet conditions. Whilst as many as 60 per cent of the DTTOs in any one site were revoked, there was strong evidence that illicit drug use had reduced substantially (other than cannabis) though acquisitive crime did not seem particularly reduced.

Belenko (1999, 2001) has reviewed the impact of the Drug Courts initiative across a number of states in the USA. The evidence from the first report was again undermined by a lack of consistency across the interventions and by poor research methodology. However, there were strong positive signs in relation to outcome which were felt to be associated with the relatively high programme completion rates (48 per cent) experienced across the drug courts. Belenko (2001) reviewed more recent developments in this field and concluded that completion rates remained high at 47 per cent on average. Where available, 12 month post-programme follow-up data revealed that recidivism was reduced for these interventions but that reductions varied in size across programmes. In general, there was little good research data available across a range of possible outcome measures including drug use, social and economic functioning.

Thus the evidence from the USA and the UK seems generally positive in supporting court-based referral to compulsory treatment contact. However, it is less clear that these approaches have substantial long-term impact above and beyond that which may be expected from normal treatment routes. It can therefore be concluded that such approaches should continue to be supported and researched.

Conclusions

The area of substance misuse in relation to offending behaviour is an important one that has moved towards the top of the agenda in many countries in recent years. There are clearly complex issues that have yet to be fully resolved in terms of the cause and effect nature of substance use, misuse and crime. There are also difficult grey areas that governments need to address between the criminal justice system and those systems that promote healthy lifestyles and treat those who suffer physical and mental health problems associated with long-term misuse. What can be said with some confidence is that those with substance misuse problems can be helped successfully. Those individuals with shorter, less chaotic and less severe substance misuse careers tend to respond more successfully to interventions. Thus early detection of problems, accompanied by referral to appropriate advice, support and treatment opportunities, is an important strategic goal. In some forms, an early opportunity may be provided within the criminal justice system and referral at this point may well hit the right moment in the client's life where desire to change may be strong. Drug Arrest referral may well function best if the gap between referral and take-up is kept short and does not seem likely to succeed where excessive waiting lists for appointments exist. With motivation and assistance, change can be achieved and substantial benefits to the individual and society may result. Our collective views on substance misuse and its relationship with criminal behaviour are evolving, perhaps more rapidly now than ever before. This would seem to be an important and interesting journey and may be encapsulated by the personal journey described in the following case study.

Case study: C's story

I have been using heroin for about ten years, but have had a habit for about eight years. When I first started using, I was seeing a guy who didn't use heroin. So half the week I would be with my mates smoking and the other half of the week I would be with my boyfriend. At first, I never used to take anything with me when I went to stay with him. This lasted for about two years, until one morning I woke up clucking and that was it, I had a habit. At first I was using a small amount. About five to ten pounds a day. But soon I needed at least a bag. Eventually towards the end this was more, four to five bags. It was easy when it was just a small amount as my Giro covered this, but as my habit got bigger I had to start shoplifting to support my habit. The guy I was seeing found out and helped me do a cluck at home. I didn't last long until I relapsed. I tried to clean up again a few months later but again I relapsed. My boyfriend at the time was dealing cocaine and we got busted. He was sent to prison for four years. Just before his sentence began we split up. By this time, I was smoking a lot of gear and had started smoking crack as well. I was shoplifting every day. I was caught a few times but managed to stay out of jail. I was losing weight rapidly and my periods stopped. I tried going into detox, but again I wasn't ready. I did it more for other people and again relapsed. The one thing about giving up heroin is you yourself have to really want to. For about the last 12 months I have been seriously thinking about getting clean. I went to a treatment agency after being caught shoplifting. I really thought that this time I would go to jail. They told me about a residential centre and I asked them to refer me. I had my first meeting a couple of months later. Soon after this I was back in court for my shoplifting case. I was given an extra six months on my already existing probation order and a 22 week 'Think First' course to address my offending behaviour. Even though I knew why I offended this course kept me out of prison. I had to complete this course and if I missed more than two sessions I had to start the whole thing again. So I thought the best thing for me to do was get this course out of the way before reapplying to the respite centre. I got back in touch with the respite centre about eight months after I had first contacted them and had two more interviews and a commitment letter. I was invited to my first stay and now I feel I can turn my life around. I am ready to do this. The respite centre is like a dream come true for me. I will be eternally grateful to them for giving me a chance to regain my self-respect and get my life back. Thank you.

References

American Psychiatric Association (1994) *Diagnostic and Statistical Manual of Mental Disorders* (4th edn). Washington, DC: American Psychiatric Association.

Belenko, S. (1999) 'Research on drug courts: a critical review 1999 update', *National Drug Court Institute Review*, II (2): 1–58.

Belenko, S. (2001) *Research on Drug Courts: A critical review 2001 update*. The National Center on Addiction and Substance Abuse, Columbia University.

Bennett, T. (1998) *Drugs and Crime: The results of drug testing and interviewing arrestees. Home Office Research Study 183*. London: Home Office.

Edmunds, M., May, T., Hearnden, I. and Hough, M. (1998) *Arrest Referral: Emerging lessons from research. Drug Prevention Initiative Paper 23.* London: Home Office Central Drugs Prevention Unit.

Edmunds, M., Hough, M., Turnbull, P. and May, T. (1999) *Doing Justice to Treatment: Referring offenders to drug services.* London: Home Office.

Goddard, E. (1991) *Drinking in England and Wales in the Late 1980s.* Office of Population Censuses and Surveys. London: HMSO.

Gossop, M., Marsden, J. and Stewart, D. (1998) *NTORS at One Year. The National Treatment Outcome Research Study: Changes in substance use, health and criminal behaviours at one year after intake.* London: Department of Health.

Gossop, M., Marsden, J. and Stewart, D. (2001) *NTORS after Five Years: Changes in substance use, health and criminal behaviour during the five years after intake.* London: Department of Health.

Guppy, A. and Albery, I. (1997) 'The deterrence of drinking and driving – the psychological signs of success', *Journal of Traffic Medicine,* 25: 7–13.

Guppy, A. and Marsden, J. (2003) 'Alcohol and drug misuse and the organization', in M. Shabracq, J.A. Winnubst and C.L. Cooper (eds) *Handbook of Work and Health Psychology* (2nd edn). Chichester: Wiley.

Home Office (1999) *Drugs Interventions in the Criminal Justice System.* London: Home Office.

Hubbard, R., Craddock, S., Flynn, P. and Anderson, J. (1999) 'Overview of one-year follow-up outcomes in DATOS', *Psychology of Addictive Behavior.*

Marsden, J., Gossop, M., Stewart, D., Best, D., Farrell, M., Lehmann, P., Edwards, C. and Strang, J. (1998) 'The Maudsley Addiction Profile (MAP): A brief instrument for assessing treatment outcome', *Addiction,* 93 (12): 1857–867.

Miller, W.R. and Hester, R.K. (1986) 'Matching problem drinkers with optimal treatments', in W.R. Miller and N. Heather (eds) *Treating Addictive Behaviors: Processes of change* (pp. 175–204). New York: Plenum Press.

Mueller, M. and Wyman, J. (1997) *Study sheds new light on the state of drug abuse treatment nationwide.* National Institute of Drug Abuse Notes. http://165.112.78.61/NIDA_Notes/NNVol12N5/Study.html

Ramsay M., Baker P., Goulden, C., Sharp, C. and Sondhi, A. (2001) *Drug Misuse Declared in 2000: Results from the British Crime Survey.* Home Office Research Study 224. London: Home Office.

Sutton, M. and Maynard, A. (1993) 'Are drug policies based on fake statistics?', *Addiction,* 88: 455–58.

Turnbull, P., McSweeney, T., Webster, R., Edmunds, M. and Hough, M. (2000) *Drug Treatment and Testing Orders: Final Evaluation Report.* Home Office Research Study 212. London: Home Office.

Wilson, P. (1980) *Drinking in England and Wales.* Office of Population Census and Surveys. London: HMSO.

Section 5

Persistent offending

In nearly every assessment of the aetiology of criminal behaviour, there is data presented depicting a version of the 'age crime' curve. The curve may have shifted upwards in recent years but, essentially, the finding is the same in most of the literature. As children grow into adolescents and young adults, so the amount of offending increases, peaking at somewhere between the late teens and early twenties, depending on which data set is used, and dropping down somewhat as age increases.

There has been some question as to how reflective such cohort descriptions are of individual criminal careers. Studies investigating pathways through crime suggest that for most, the age crime curve seems reasonable; they become involved in crime as children, committing most of their offences at somewhere around 17 years old, then gradually settle down and offend less. However, for some, this is simply not the case. A few people offend persistently and frequently and can be termed 'life course persistent offenders'. Chapter 10, sees Alex Piquero and Terrie Moffitt presenting and evaluating the developmental taxonomy that Moffitt has developed and applied to life-course-persistent offending. It is one of the first theoretical models proffered to account for the few persistent offenders who seem responsible for so many crimes.

Much of the life course persistent research focuses on career criminals, people who are versatile offenders, engaged in crime as a way of life. There are, however, a number of offences that are committed by people who do not always conform to this image. For example, those who stalk and harass others are frequently not known to the courts for other types of criminal behaviour. In Chapter 11, Lorraine Sheridan and Graham

Davies explore this phenomenon. By definition, stalking is a persistent, yet varied set of behaviours, making it particularly difficult to police and prevent. In their chapter, Sheridan and Davies give us empirical evidence that may help to predict who is likely to be victimised, and by whom. Placed within a framework of policy and practice, their chapter shows how vital it is that we adopt creative approaches to crimes of this nature as there are both advantages and disadvantages to the civil and criminal court procedures currently in place.

Chapter 10

Life-course persistent offending

*Alex R. Piquero, University of Florida and
Terrie E. Moffitt, University of London*

Of all facets of crime, perhaps none has received as much research attention as age. The relationship between age and crime is one of the most well-documented (Hirschi and Gottfredson 1983; Quetelet 1831) and contentious (Britt 1992; Steffensmeier *et al.* 1989) of all criminological findings. Researchers studying the relationship between age and crime have typically observed that the aggregate pattern is such that criminal activity tends to peak in the late teens (in early cohorts) through the mid twenties (in contemporary cohorts), then declines throughout adulthood.

At the same time that the relationship between age and crime has been reproduced, it raises the question of the degree to which the *aggregate* pattern displayed in the age/crime curve is similar to – or different from – the pattern of *individual* careers and whether conclusions about individuals can be validly drawn from aggregate data (Piquero, Farrington and Blumstein 2003). For example, how far does the observed peak of the aggregate age/crime curve reflect changes within individuals as opposed to changes in the composition of offenders? In other words, is the peak in the age/crime curve a function of active offenders committing more crime, or is it a function of more individuals actively offending at those peak years?

Farrington (1986) suggests that the aggregate peak age of offending primarily reflects variations in prevalence, and not frequency. If this is the case, then it suggests that although the majority of offenders are dropping out of a life of crime, some small select group remains criminally active well into adulthood. This notion of persistence, recognised by proponents of the criminal career paradigm as being one of the key dimensions of the criminal career (Blumstein *et al*. 1986), has been the subject of much empirical attention (Dean *et al*. 1996; Huesmann *et al*. 1984; Paternoster *et al*. 1997), yet has not received much theoretical attention; that is, until the last decade.

In this essay, we examine the ability of one particular theory, Moffitt's (1993) developmental taxonomy, to account for persistence in criminal activity. Her theory takes as its starting point the aggregate age-crime curve, and from it, explains the stability of criminal activity as a function of a particular group of offenders, termed life-course persistent, whose offending proclivities begin early in life and continue throughout the life-course. Herein, we review (1) the underlying theoretical arguments articulated in Moffitt's theory, (2) the research completed on her theory to date, and (3) the challenges levied against Moffitt's developmental taxonomy. Finally, we conclude with the identification of a number of unanswered research questions that will likely offer a number of important future research directions.

Moffitt's developmental taxonomy

Moffitt's taxonomy proposes two primary types of offenders, each of whom possesses a unique set of factors that cause criminal and antisocial activity, as well as a different patterning of criminal and antisocial activity over the life-course. A third group of individuals, the abstainers, is a small, select group who refrain from antisocial and criminal activity throughout the life-course.

The first group of offenders in Moffitt's theory, adolescence-limited, restrict their offending activity to the adolescent stage of life, occurring between puberty and when they attain adult social roles. The set of factors underlying adolescence-limited delinquency consists of the maturity gap and the peer social context. The maturity gap reflects the youngsters' experience of dysphoria during the relatively role-less years between their biological maturation and their access to mature privileges and responsibilities, while the peer social context reflects the observation that similarly-situated adolescents biologically and socially 'grow up' together, and as a result, look to each other for support during the time period when they are not allowed to be adults. During the adolescent time period, delinquent coping is appealing and involvement in delinquency surfaces as a way to demonstrate autonomy from parents and teachers, win affiliation with peers and hasten social maturation. Because adolescence-limited delinquency is typically social in nature, the offending manifestations constitute group-oriented activities and relatively minor and status-oriented offences, but not necessarily instrumental violence. Importantly, because their pre-delinquent development is normal, most adolescence-limited delinquents have the characteristics they need to desist from crime when they age into real adult roles, such as healthy personalities and cognitive abilities such as reading skill. They are able to return gradually to a more conventional lifestyle. For a select few adolescence-limited delinquents, their recovery may be delayed because of snares, which are experiences that can compromise the ability to make a successful transition to adult-hood. Examples of such snares include a criminal record, incarceration, drug and alcohol addiction, truncated education, and (for girls) unwanted pregnancy.

In contrast, the second group of offenders, the life-course-persistent, begins their antisocial activity early in the life-course, offends more while active, commits all sorts of crimes, including violence, and is very unlikely to desist from criminal activity in adulthood. Because peer influence is not a necessary condition for life-course persistent delinquency, some of the crimes engaged in by life-course persistent offenders are committed without the assistance of others, often referred to as 'lone offending'. According to the taxonomy, the child's risk for life-course persistent offending emerges from inherited or acquired neuro-psychological variation, initially manifested as subtle cognitive deficits, difficult temperament, or hyperactivity. The environment in which the child is reared is also an important contributory factor as inadequate parenting, disrupted family bonds, poverty, etc tend to compromise effective parenting efforts and in many cases exacerbate the child's vulnerabilities. The environmental risk domain expands beyond the family as the child ages, to include poor relations with people such as peers and teachers. Over the first two decades of development, trans-actions between individual and environment gradually construct a disordered personality with hallmark features of physical aggression and antisocial behaviour persisting to mid-life. The taxonomy antici-pates that antisocial behaviour will infiltrate multiple adult life domains including illegal activities, employment, marriage or family life, and intimate victimization. As could be expected, this infiltration diminishes the possibility of reform such that life-course persistent offenders have few (if any) opportunities for prosocial behaviour and opportunities for change. Fortunately, Moffitt anticipates that membership in this group is quite small, about five to eight per cent of the population.

How do race and gender fit into the taxonomy?

Moffitt's original statements asserted that the theory would describe the behaviour of females as well as it describes the behaviour of males. In particular, Moffitt (1994: 39–40) notes:

> The crime rate for females is lower than for males. In this developmental taxonomy, much of the gender difference in crime is attributed to sex differences in the risk factors for life-course persistent antisocial behaviour. Little girls are less likely than little boys to encounter all of the putative links in the causal chain for life-course persistent antisocial development. Research has shown that girls have lower rates than boys of symptoms of nervous system dysfunction, difficult temperament, late verbal and motor milestones, hyperactivity, learning disabilities, reading failure, and childhood conduct problems ... Most girls lack the personal diathesis elements of the evocative, reactive, and proactive person/environment interactions that initiate and maintain life-course persistent antisocial behaviour.
>
> Adolescence-limited delinquency, on the other hand, is open to girls as well as to boys. According to the theory advanced here, girls, like boys, should begin delinquency soon after puberty, to the extent that they (1) have access to antisocial models, and (2) perceive the consequences of delinquency as reinforcing ... However, exclusion from gender-segregated male antisocial groups may cut off opportunities for girls to learn delinquent behaviours ... Girls are physically more vulnerable than boys to risk of personal victimization (e.g., pregnancy, or injury from dating violence) if they affiliate with life-course persistent antisocial males. Thus, lack of access to antisocial models and perceptions of serious personal risk may dampen the vigour of girls' delinquent involvement somewhat. Nonetheless, girls should engage in adolescence-limited delinquency in significant numbers ...

In sum, Moffitt's (2003) taxonomy anticipates that (a) fewer females than males would become delinquent (and conduct disordered) overall, and that (b) within delinquents the percentage who are life-course persistent would be higher among males than females. Following from this, (c) the majority of delinquent females will be of the adolescence-limited type, and further, (d) their delinquency will have the same causes as adolescence-limited males' delinquency. Regarding race, Moffitt (1994: 39) hypothesises that:

> In the United States, the crime rate for Black Americans is higher than the crime rate for Whites. The race difference may be accounted for by a relatively higher prevalence of both life-course persistent and adolescence-limited subtypes among contemporary African Americans. Life-course persistent antisocials might be anticipated at elevated rates among Black Americans because the putative root causes of this type are elevated by institutionalised prejudice and by poverty. Among poor Black families, prenatal care is less available, infant nutrition is poorer, and the incidence of exposure to toxic and infectious agents is greater, placing infants at risk for the nervous system problems that research has shown to interfere with prosocial child development. To the extent that family bonds have been loosened and poor Black parents are under stress, ... and to the extent that poor Black children attend disadvantaged schools ... for poor Black children, the snowball of cumulative continuity may begin rolling earlier, and it may roll faster downhill. In addition, adolescence-limited crime is probably elevated among Black youths as compared to White youths in contemporary America. If racially-segregated communities pro-vide greater exposure to life-course persistent role models, then circumstances are ripe for Black teens with no prior behaviour problems to mimic delinquent ways in a search for status and respect. Moreover, Black young people spend more years in the maturity gap, on average, than Whites because ascendancy to valued adult roles and privileges comes later, if at all. Legitimate desirable jobs are closed to many young Black men; they do not shift from having 'little to lose' to having a 'stake in conformity' overnight by leaving schooling and entering the world of work. Indeed, the biological maturity gap [i.e., puberty] is perhaps best seen as an instigator of adolescence-onset delinquency for Black youths, with an economic maturity gap maintaining offending into adulthood.

In sum, Moffitt anticipates that, due to elevated levels of the risk factors for both life-course persistent and adolescence-limited crime, African-Americans will be somewhat more prevalent than White Americans in both offending typologies.

Research on Moffitt's taxonomy

A number of studies have sought to examine the viability of Moffitt's developmental taxonomy, and in particular have assessed some of the key hypotheses underlying the taxonomy. Before we review these research efforts, it is helpful at this point to recall the original hypotheses underlying the two offending groups. For life-course persistent antisocial activity, the predictors should include 'health, gender, temperament, cognitive abilities, school achievement, personality traits, mental disorders (e.g., hyperactivity), family attachment bonds, child-rearing practices, parent and sibling deviance, and socio-economic status, but not age' (Moffitt 1993: 695). For adolescence-limited antisocial activity, the taxonomy anticipates that

> individual differences should play little or no role in the prediction of short-term adolescent offending careers. Instead, the strongest predictors of adolescence-limited offending should be peer delinquency, attitudes toward adolescence and adulthood reflecting the maturity gap [such as desire for autonomy], cultural and historical contexts influencing adolescence, and age. (Moffitt 1993: 695)

What do we know about life-course persistent offending?

A number of the hypotheses associated with life-course persistent offending have been examined with data from the Dunedin Multi-disciplinary Health and Development Study, a 30-year longitudinal study of a birth cohort of 1,000 New Zealanders. In general, these studies have examined childhood predictors measured early in life and examined their relation to criminal and antisocial activity measured via self-report, informants such as mothers, teachers, and friends, and official records. These efforts have consistently shown that life-course persistent offending is differentially predicted by individual risk factors including under controlled temperament, neurological abnormalities and delayed motor development at age three, low intellectual abilities, reading difficulties, poor scores on neuropsychological tests of memory, hyperactivity, and slow heart rate (see Bartusch *et al.* 1997; Moffitt and Caspi 2001; Moffitt *et al.* 1994, 1996). In addition, life-course persistent offending is also differentially predicted by parenting risk factors including teen-aged single parents, mothers with poor mental health, mothers who were observed to be harsh or neglectful, as well as experiences of harsh and inconsistent discipline, much family conflict, many changes of the primary caretaker, low family SES, and rejection by peers in school (Moffitt and Caspi 2001).

Importantly, the main findings regarding life-course persistent offending uncovered with the Dunedin data have also been observed in other samples from different countries (see review in Moffitt 2001). For example, using data from the Philadelphia portion of the National Collaborative Perinatal Project (NCPP), Tibbetts and Piquero (1999) examined how the biosocial interaction of low birth weight and disadvantaged environment predicted early onset offending. Their results indicated that the biosocial interaction was significantly related to early onset of offending. Piquero and Tibbetts (1999) examined the interaction between pre/perinatal disturbances and disadvantaged familial environment in distinguishing between involvement in non-violent and violent offending. Their analysis indicated that, consistent with Moffitt's expectation, the biosocial interaction was predictive of violent but not non-violent offending (see also Arseneault *et al.* 2002). Piquero (2001) used the Philadelphia data to examine how neuro-psychological variation, using cognitive test scores, was related to three different manifestations of life-course persistent offending (early onset, chronic offending, and seriousness offending) by age 18. His results indicated that poor neuropsychological test scores were predictive of all three measures of life-course persistent offending in a manner consistent with Moffitt. Gibson *et al.* (2001) extended Piquero's analysis and found that neuropsychological risk also combines with poor familial environments to predict early onset of offending. Finally, Kratzer and Hodgins (1999) used data from a Swedish cohort to study how cognitive abilities related to offending from childhood to age 30. Their results indicated that early start offenders (i.e., life-course persistent offenders) committed more crimes and a greater diversity of crimes than other offending groups. Childhood problems and low global scores of intelligence distinguished these offenders from other offender types as well as non-offenders.

Several recent studies have tested expectations from Moffitt's theory with criminal populations. One such study was of 4,000 California Youth Authority inmates followed into their thirties, in which Ge and his colleagues (2001) found results consistent with Moffitt's theory. For example, significantly more early-starters than later-starters continued offending past age 21, past age 25 and past age 31. In addition, early-onset and low cognitive ability were significant predictors of offending that continued into the thirties. Piquero, Brame, and Lynam (2003) used another sample of California Youth Authority inmates to study how neuropsychological variation was related to the length of an offender's criminal career and found that a risk contrast, comprised of low cognitive abilities and disadvantaged environments, was related to career length such that individuals with low cognitive abilities and reared in disadvantaged environments during childhood tended to experience the longest careers. Finally, Piquero and his colleagues (2002) used yet another sample of California Youth Authority parolees to study how changes in life circumstances were related to changes in criminal activity in the twenties. Their analysis indicated that changes in several life circumstances, such as marriage and heroin dependency, were associated with changes in criminal activity such that marriage served to reduce crime while heroin dependency served to increase crime. Interestingly, the effect of local life circumstances also varied across offender typologies, such that the effects were apparent for some typologies but not others.

In sum, studies using a number of different samples from several different countries show that life-course persistent offending has the predicted neuro-developmental correlates as well as showing the importance of a biosocial interaction.

What do we know about adolescence-limited offending?

Unfortunately, much of the research on Moffitt's taxonomy has tended to focus on life-course persistent offending. Still, a few studies have examined adolescent-limited offending, and they are reviewed below.

Using a low SES sample from Minneapolis, Aguilar et al. (2000) found that adolescent-onset delinquents experienced elevated internalising symptoms and perceptions of stress at age 16, which may be consistent with Moffitt's assertion that these adolescents experience dysphoria during the maturity gap. Data from the Dunedin study also indicates that the offending of adolescence-limiteds is strongly associated with delinquent peers, as compared to the offending of life-course persistent offenders (Bartusch et al. 1997; Moffitt and Caspi 2001). In addition, Caspi and his colleagues (1993) showed that an increase in young teens' awareness of peers' delinquency pre-dates and predicts onset of their own later delinquency. Piquero and Brezina (2001) used data from 2,000 males participating in the Youth in Transition Survey to test the hypothesis that desires for autonomy promoted adolescent-onset offending. They found that the offences committed by adolescence-limited delinquents were primarily rebellious in nature (i.e., not violent), and that this rebellious offending was accounted for by the interaction between maturational timing and aspects of peer activities that were related to personal autonomy. However, one measure of youth autonomy did not yield a significant finding in their analysis.

To be sure, we cannot finish our discussion of adolescence-limited delinquency without reviewing what we know about those adolescents who refrain from delinquency, commonly referred to as abstainers. This is an important issue because, if as the theory says, adolescence-limited delinquency is normative, then the existence of teenagers who abstain from delinquency requires explanation.

Moffitt proffers four potential reasons for such abstinence. First, some youths may refrain from antisocial behaviour because they do not sense the maturity gap, and therefore lack the hypothesised motivation for experimenting with crime, or they may skip the maturity gap altogether because of late puberty. Second, some adolescents incur early initiation into adult roles, or at the very least, they have access to prosocial roles. Third, some adolescents encounter few opportunities for mimicking life-course persistent delinquent models. Fourth, and the 'explanation most central to [Moffitt's] theory' is that abstainers are excluded from opportunities to mimic antisocial peers because of some personal characteristic(s) that cause them to be excluded from the delinquent peer groups, which ascend to importance during adolescence (see also Moffitt *et al*. 1996: 419). Thus, under this hypothesis, some adolescents may possess certain personality characteristics that prevent them from being a part of the peer social context during adolescence.

Unfortunately, aside from a few exceptions (Moffitt *et al*. 1996; Shedler and Block 1990), the developmental histories of adolescents who abstain from delinquency have not been examined in great detail. Only one study, in fact, has tested the 'abstainer' hypotheses as articulated by Moffitt. Piquero, Brezina and Turner (2004) used data from the National Longitudinal Survey of Youth, a high-risk adolescent sample, to examine the abstainer hypothesis, and their results led to four major conclusions. First, across three different data sets, adolescent abstainers were comprised of a small group of individuals. Second, the correlates of abstention primarily included situational and social characteristics, with social factors exhibiting central importance. Individuals who were not part of the peer social context, and/or who spent less time with peers, were more likely to be abstainers. The results also revealed that many personality characteristics were not directly related to abstention. Third, bearing in mind the importance of access to the peer social context, Piquero *et al*. found that, consistent with Moffitt, several personality, emotional, structural and situational characteristics were related to involvement in the peer social context. Finally, split-gender analyses revealed more similarities than differences in the correlates of peer social context and abstention. Thus, Moffitt's writings and hypotheses over-estimated the importance of personality traits.

In sum, much less is known about the developmental patterning of adolescence-limited offending as well as the causes of abstention. The few studies that have been conducted appear, at first glance, to provide support for some of the key hypotheses put forth by Moffitt.

Outcomes of life-course persistent and adolescence-limited offenders: personality, crime types and persistence

The two offending typologies have been compared on a number of different outcomes. Herein, we focus on three particular outcomes: personality structures, crime types and persistence in crime into adulthood.

Regarding personality, Moffitt (1993: 684) argued that 'Over the years, an antisocial personality is slowly and insidiously constructed as the accumulating consequences of the youngster's behaviour problems prune away options for change.' A few studies have initiated investigations of this issue.

Moffitt and colleagues have employed the Dunedin data to examine the personality issue in great detail. In the first analysis, Moffitt *et al.* (1996) showed that the age-18 personality characteristics of individuals on the life-course-persistent path were differentially associated with weak bonds to family, and psychopathic personality traits of alienation, callousness and impulsivity. In contrast, the adolescence-limited path at age 18 was differentially associated with a tendency to endorse unconventional values, and with a personality trait called social potency. In their assessment of personality traits at age 26, self- and informant reports concurred that the life-course persistent men were more neurotic (stress-reactive, alienated, and aggressive) and less agreeable (less social closeness, more callous), compared to adolescence-limited men.

Ge *et al.* (2001) used personality data from 4,000 California Youth Authority inmates to examine this issue as well. Taxonomy comparison groups were defined as early-starters versus later-starters, and as chronic adult arrestees versus those arrested less often. The early-starter chronic arrestees were distinguished by extreme personality scale scores, in particular low communality, little concern with impression, irresponsibility, low control of emotions, low achievement motivation, low socialisation, low tolerance (hostile, distrustful) and low well-being.

Regarding crime types, several studies have sought to assess Moffitt's (1993: 695) hypothesis that life-course persistent offenders, as compared to adolescence-limited offenders, would engage in a wider variety of offence types, including 'more of the victim-oriented offences, such as violence.' Data from the Dunedin study up to age 18 reports that the life-course persistent path was differentially associated with convictions for violent crimes (Bartusch *et al.* 1997; Moffitt *et al.* 1996), while the adolescence-limited pathway was differentially associated with non-violent offences. In their investigation of neuropsychology and delinquency, Moffitt *et al.* (1994) found that pre-adolescent antisocial behaviour that was accompanied by neuropsychological deficits predicted greater persistence of crime and more violence until age 18. A follow-up of the Dunedin subjects at age 26 reinforced the finding that life-course persistent men, as a group, differed from adolescence-limited men in the realm of violence, including violence against women. For example, life-course persistent men tended to specialise in serious offences, whereas adolescence-limited men specialised in non-serious offences. Moreover, life-course persistent men accounted for five times their proportional share of the cohort's violent convictions, in addition to exhibiting elevated scores on self-reported and official conviction measures of abuse towards women.

Studies using other samples have tended to replicate these findings. For example, using the Philadelphia NCPP data, Piquero (2001) found that neuropsychological risk was related to several different mani-festations of life-course persistent offending such that poor cognitive scores predicted early onset and serious offending by age 18. Research comparing the predictors of violent crime versus non-violent crime indicates that violence is differentially predicted by birth complications (Raine *et al.* 1997), minor physical anomalies (Arseneault *et al.* 2000), and difficult temperament (Henry *et al.* 1994).

Regarding persistence into adulthood, one of the critical hypotheses emanating from Moffitt's typology is that life-course persistent offenders continue their antisocial proclivities into adulthood whereas adolescence-limited offenders desist, and several studies have attempted to address this question (e.g., Dean *et al.* 1996; White *et al.* 2001). Using the age-26 data from the Dunedin study, Moffitt (2003) found that the childhood-onset delinquents were the most elevated on psychopathic personality traits, mental-health problems, substance dependence, numbers of children sired, domestic abuse, financial problems, work problems, drug-related crimes and violent crimes. On the other hand, the adolescent-onset delinquents were less extreme but also elevated on property offences and financial problems.

Ge *et al.* (2001) used data on over 4,000 California Youth Authority inmates followed into their thirties to examine issues related to persistence. They found that significantly more early-starters than later-starters continued offending past age 21, past age 25, and past age 31. Moreover, early-onset and low cognitive ability were significant predictors of offending that continued into the thirties.

Piquero and White (2003) followed up the Philadelphia NCPP into the late thirties to study how cognitive deficits related to persistence. Their analysis indicated that cognitive deficits, measured at both ages 7/8 and 13/14, were related to adult convictions through the thirties.

What do we know about gender as it pertains to Moffitt's taxonomy?

Only a handful of studies have explored the role of gender in Moffitt's taxonomy. Moffitt and her colleagues (2001) reported a comprehensive analysis of gender differences in antisocial behaviour. A number of key findings emerged from their effort. First, the male:female difference was very large for the life-course persistent form of antisocial behaviour (10:1) but much smaller for the adolescence-limited form (1.5:1). Second, childhood-onset females had high-risk neuro-developmental and family background, but adolescent-onset females did not, which indicates that females and males on the same trajectories share the same risk factors. In related research, Moffitt and colleagues have found that the delinquency onset of girls is linked to the timing of their own puberty, that delinquent peers are a necessary condition for onset of delinquency among adolescent girls, and that an intimate relationship with an offender promotes girls' antisocial behaviours.

Other studies have also examined potential sex differences in Moffitt's taxonomy. In a study discussed earlier, Tibbetts and Piquero (1999) found that a biosocial interaction comprising low birth weight and disadvantaged environment predicted early onset of offending for males but not females. Fergusson *et al.* (2000), using data from Christchurch, found that a single model described male and female trajectories of antisocial behaviour, and the male to female ratio was 4:1 for early-onset, versus only 2:1 for late-onset subjects. In another study with these data, Fergusson and Horwood (2002) found that an identical five trajectory group applied for both males and females, and that the risk factors associated with trajectory group membership appeared to operate similarly for both males and females. The only sex differences to emerge indicated that females were more likely to exhibit low-risk or early onset adolescent-limited offending while males were more likely to exhibit chronic offending or later adolescent-limited onset. Kratzer and Hodgins' (1999) study of a Swedish cohort found similar childhood risk factors for males and females in the life-course persistent group, with a male:female ratio of 15:1 for early onset, and only 4:1 for late onset. Using data from the second Philadelphia Birth Cohort, Mazerolle and colleagues (2000) reported that early onset signalled persistent and diverse offending for males and females alike.

In sum, most studies indicate that females are seldom childhood-onset or life-course persistent offenders and more commonly follow the adolescent-limited pattern; however, when females do exhibit the risk factors for life-course persistent offending, their pathway is similar to that of males.

What do we know about race as it pertains to Moffitt's taxonomy?

As is the case with gender, only a few studies have explored the race implications of Moffitt's theory. Early research on this issue, with data from the Pittsburgh Youth Study, showed that childhood risk factors (low IQ and impulsive under-control) were associated with life-course persistent offending (early-onset frequent offending and physical aggression) among Black and White males alike (Caspi *et al.* 1994). However, research using the Pittsburgh data has not divided the Pittsburgh delinquents into childhood- versus adolescent-onset comparison groups.

Donnellan *et al.* (2003) examined how race was implicated in Moffitt's taxonomy using data from California Youth Authority inmates. On a number of different measures of cognitive abilities, life-course persistent offenders scored below adolescence-limited offenders. Interestingly, the predicted finding of differential cognitive risk applied to adjudicated Whites and Hispanics but not to adjudicated African Americans.

Piquero, Moffitt and Lawton (2003) used data from the Baltimore site of the NCPP to study race differences in the life-course persistent pathway. Their analysis showed that several variables helped to explain differences between Whites and Blacks in the level of chronic offending measured to age 33. However, although Black participants had higher mean levels of risk factors than Whites, the developmental processes predicting chronic offending were the same across groups defined by race. Specifically, low birth weight in combination with adverse familial environments predicted chronic offending from adolescence to age 33 among Whites and African Americans alike, although the effect size reached statistical significance only among African Americans.

Finally, in a study described earlier, Piquero, Brame, and Lynam (2004) studied how the life-course persistent explanation could account for criminal career length. Specifically, they split their sample of California Youth Authority inmates into White and non-White parolees, and examined how a risk contrast of cognitive abilities and disadvantaged environments related to career length. When the risk contrast was examined across White and non-White parolees, the results indicated that the risk contrast was more important for non-Whites. In particular, the data pointed to three sets of findings across race. First, among those parolees experiencing low risk in the risk contrast (i.e., no cognitive deficits and no disadvantaged environments), career duration was identical among White and non-White parolees (almost 17 years). Second, among non-Whites only, the risk contrast was related to career length such that non-White parolees experiencing cognitive deficits and disadvantaged environments exhibited the longest career lengths (almost 19 years). Third, among White parolees, the risk contrast was not related to career length; among Whites, career lengths varied between 16 and 17 years, regardless of the level of the risk contrast.

In sum, it is too early to tell how Moffitt's race hypotheses square with empirical research. With the exception of Donnellan *et al.*, the research, at this time, seems to suggest that the causal process appears more similar than different across race, with the exception that the mean levels of risk factors are higher among non-Whites than Whites.

Challenges to Moffitt's theory

Although some research efforts have produced, at times, somewhat contradictory results to Moffitt's typology (see in particular Aguilar *et al.* 2000), two key challenges have been put forth regarding the viability of Moffitt's taxonomy. The first concerns the number of offender typologies, and the second calls into question the taxonomy's applicability to females.

As originally outlined, Moffitt anticipated the existence of two groups of offenders. Empirical research using advanced statistical models that are designed to isolate relatively homogenous categories of offenders, however, has uncovered several additional groups of offenders (D'Unger *et al.* 1998; Nagin and Land 1993; Nagin *et al.* 1995). The most prominent of these additional groups is the 'low-level chronic'. Because of their particular pattern of offending, i.e., persistent, but low-level offending from childhood to adolescence and/or from adolescence to adulthood, this group of offenders does not 'fit' into either of Moffitt's offender typologies. Unfortunately, very little light has been shed on the personal characteristics associated with the low-level chronics.

The second challenge put forth against Moffitt's taxonomy concerns the role of gender. Silverthorn and Frick (1999) reviewed the literature on female antisocial/criminal activity and challenged Moffitt's developmental taxonomy. These authors suggest that, although girls' onset of delinquency is delayed until adolescence, there is no analogous pathway in girls to the adolescence-limited pathway in boys. In particular, they argue for a female-specific theory in which all delinquent girls will have the same high-risk causal backgrounds as life-course persistent males, but that their antisocial activity will start in mid adolescence as opposed to early adolescence/late childhood as in Moffitt's life-course persistent conception. Aside from Moffitt and colleagues' (2001) thorough analysis of sex differences in antisocial behaviour, a number of studies have begun to examine the Silverthorn and Frick challenge, and with the exception of results from Silverthorn *et al.* (2001), fail to find support for their challenge (see Fergusson and Horwood 2002; White and Piquero 2003).

The way forward: future research topics

Since the publication of Moffitt's theory, a number of research efforts have attempted to distinguish between the two offender typologies. Although much has been learned, much remains to be explored. Here, we identify a number of future research directions that may help continue the assessment of Moffitt's typology.

The first hypothesis concerns that of 'snares'. Moffitt contends that individuals (especially adolescence-limited offenders) may encounter 'snares', or life events, that lead to continuation of antisocial lifestyles. Examples of such snares include a criminal record, incarceration, addiction and so on. Moffitt anticipates that these snares should explain variation in the age at desistance from crime during the adult age period, especially among adolescence-limited offenders. Unfortunately, we know little about how snares are implicated in Moffitt's typology.

The second point for future research concerns the varied outcomes associated with membership in each typology. One example would be that, although Moffitt concentrates her discussion of outcomes within the antisocial domain, there is reason to believe that life-course persistent offenders exhibit risk in other domains as well. For example, life-course persistent offenders are believed to select undesirable partners and jobs, and would, in turn, expand their repertoire into domestic abuse and workplace crime, whereas adolescence-limited offenders would obtain good partners and jobs, in turn desisting from crime (Moffitt 1993: 695). Similarly, it would be reasonable to suspect that the behaviour of life-course persistent offenders would infiltrate multiple life domains such as employment and health. In this regard,

Moffitt (2003) has noted that the antisocial lifestyle of life-course persistent offenders is such that it will place them at greater risk in mid-life for poor health, cardiovascular disease and early mortality.

A third point for future research concerns the continued attention aimed at studying how race and gender are implicated in the developmental taxonomy. Still perilously little is known about race and gender differences (and similarities) within and between the two offender typologies. An interesting hypothesis, that has yet to be tested, concerns the effect of the maturity gap across race. Moffitt (2003) predicts that the maturity gap will last longer for African-American young men. Because of this, it may be difficult to distinguish the life-course persistent versus adolescence-limited groups on the basis of chronic offending into adulthood. Clearly, this warrants sustained empirical attention.

A fourth hypothesis, that has yet to be explored in detail, concerns the role of the neighbourhood environment. Although several studies have sought to examine how neighbourhoods are implicated in the developmental taxonomy (see Lynam *et al.* 2000; Moffitt 1997; Piquero, Moffitt and Lawton 2003), researchers have not examined how changing neighbourhood environments may (or may not) matter for expectations derived from the taxonomy.

Fifth, within the context of Moffitt's theory, researchers have not examined closely the role of co- and solo-offending over the life-course across the two typologies. Moffitt's theory anticipates that adolescence-limited offenders will tend to be co-offenders, but that life-course persistent offenders will tend to be solo-offenders. Unfortunately, data on co-offending is relatively sparse (Warr 2002), but this should not dissuade researchers from assessing this important prediction.

The final point for future research concerns the role of genetics. According to Moffitt's taxonomy, the genetic component of variation in early-onset antisocial behaviour, a marker for life-course persistent offending, may conceal effects of correlations between vulnerability, genes and risky environments, and interactions between them as well. Recently, Caspi *et al.* (2002) used the Dunedin data to study why some children who are maltreated grow up to develop antisocial behaviour, whereas others do not. They found that a functional polymorphism in the gene encoding the neurotransmitter-metabolizing enzyme monoamine oxidase A (MAOA) moderated the effect of maltreatment, such that maltreated children with a genotype conferring high levels of MAOA expression were less likely to develop antisocial problems. This result is particularly important because it provides some evidence that some genotypes can moderate children's sensitivity to environmental factors. The study also revealed that children with the at-risk genotype did not develop antisocial behaviour unless they were maltreated, showing that social experiences exert strong control over whether genes can influence behaviour. (Boys on the life-course persistent path in the Dunedin sample were particularly likely to have the combination of a maltreatment history and the at-risk MAOA genotype, but because this group was made up of a very small number of individuals, this finding did not attain statistical significance.) We envision much more work on this front, especially into the role that the interplay between genes and environmental experiences plays in crime over the life-course.

References

Aguilar, B.L., Sroufe, A., Egeland, B. and Carlson, E. (2000) 'Distinguishing the early-onset/persistent and adolescence-onset antisocial behaviour types: From birth to 16 Years', *Development and Psychopathology*, 12: 109–32.

Arseneault, L., Tremblay, R.E., Boulerice, B., Seguin, J.R. and Saucier, J.F. (2000) 'Minor physical anomalies and family adversity as risk factors for adolescent violent delinquency', *American Journal of Psychiatry*, 157: 917–23.

Arseneault, L., Tremblay, R.E., Boulerice, B. and Saucier, J.F. (2002) 'Obstetric complications and adolescent violent behaviours: Testing two developmental pathways', *Child Development*, 73: 496–508.

Bartusch, D., Jeglum, R., Lynam, D.R., Moffitt, T.E. and Silva, P.A. (1997) 'Is age important? Testing a general versus a developmental theory of antisocial behavior', *Criminology*, 35: 13–48.

Blumstein, A., Cohen, J., Roth, J.A. and Visher, C.A. (eds) (1986) *Criminal Careers and Career Criminals* 2 vols. Panel on Research on Criminal Careers, Committee on Research on Law Enforcement and the Administration of Justice, Commission on Behavioral and Social Sciences and Education, National Research Council. Washington, DC: National Academy Press.

Britt, C.L. (1992) 'Constancy and change in the US age distribution of crime: A test of the "Invariance Hypothesis"', *Journal of Quantitative Criminology*, 8: 175–87.

Caspi, A., McClay, J., Moffitt, T.E., Mill, J., Martin, J., Craig, I.W., Taylor, A. and Poulton, R. (2002) 'Role of genotype in the cycle of violence in maltreated children', *Science*, 297: 851–54.

Caspi, A., Moffitt, T.E., Silva, P.A., Stouthamer-Loeber, M., Schmutte, P. and Krueger, R. (1994) 'Are some people crime-prone? Replications of the personality-crime relation across nation, gender, race, and method', *Criminology*, 32: 301–33.

Caspi, A., Lynam, D., Moffitt, T.E. and Silva, P.A. (1993) 'Unraveling girls' delinquency: Biological, dispositional, and contextual contributions to adolescent misbehavior', *Developmental Psychology*, 29: 19–30.

Dean, C.W., Brame, R. and Piquero, A.R. (1996) 'Criminal propensities, discrete groups of offenders, and persistence in crime', *Criminology*, 34: 547–74.

Donnellan, M.B., Ge, X. and Wenk, E. (2000) 'Cognitive abilities in adolescence-limited and life-course-persistent criminal offenders', *Journal of Abnormal Psychology*, 109: 396–402.

D'Unger, A.V., Land, K.C., McCall, P.L. and Nagin, D.S. (1998) 'How many latent classes of delinquent/criminal careers? Results from mixed poisson regression analyses', *American Journal of Sociology*, 103: 1593–630.

Farrington, D.P. (1986) 'Age and crime', in M. Tonry and N. Morris (eds) *Crime and Justice: An Annual Review of Research, Volume 7*. Chicago: University of Chicago Press.

Fergusson, D.M., Horwood, L.J and Nagin, D.S. (2000) 'Offending trajectories in a New Zealand birth cohort', *Criminology*, 38: 525–52.

Fergusson, D.M. and Horwood, L.J. (2002) 'Male and female offending trajectories', *Development and Psychopathology*, 14: 159–77.

Ge, X.J., Donnellan, M.B. and Wenk, E. (2001) 'The development of persistent criminal offending in males', *Criminal Justice and Behaviour*, 28 (6): 731–55.

Gibson, C., Piquero, A.R. and Tibbetts, S.G. (2001) 'The contribution of family adversity and verbal IQ relate to criminal behavior', *International Journal of Offender Therapy and Comparative Criminology*, 45: 574–92.

Henry, B., Moffitt, T.E., Caspi, A., Langley, J. and Silva, P.A. (1994) 'On the remembrance of things past: A longitudinal evaluation of the retrospective method', *Psychological Assessment* 6: 92–101.

Hirschi, T. and Gottfredson, M.G. (1983) 'Age and the explanation of crime', *American Journal of Sociology*, 89: 552–84.

Huesmann, L.R., Eron, L.D., Lefkowitz, M.M. and Walder, L.O. (1984) 'Stability of aggression over time and generations', *Developmental Psychology*, 20: 1120–134.

Kratzer, L. and Hodgins, S. (1999) 'A typology of offenders: A test of Moffitt's theory among males and females from childhood to Age 30', *Criminal Behaviour and Mental Health*, 9: 57–73.

Lynam, D.R., Caspi, A., Moffitt, T.E., Wikstrom, P-O., Loeber, R. and Novak, S.P. (2000) 'The interaction between impulsivity and neighbourhood context on offending: The effects of impulsivity are stronger in poorer neighborhoods', *Journal of Abnormal Psychology*, 109: 563–74.

Mazerolle, P., Brame, R., Paternoster, R., Piquero, A. and Dean, C. (2000) 'Onset age, persistence, and offending versatility: Comparisons across gender', *Criminology*, 38: 1143–172.

Moffitt, T.E. (1993) 'Life-course-persistent and adolescence-limited antisocial behaviour: A developmental taxonomy', *Psychological Review*, 100: 674–701.

Moffitt, T.E. (1994) 'Natural histories of delinquency', in E. Weitekamp and H.J. Kerner (eds) *Cross-National Longitudinal Research on Human Development and Criminal Behaviour*. Dordrecht: Kluwer Academic Press.

Moffitt, T.E. (1997) 'Neuropsychology, antisocial behaviour, and neighbourhood context', in J. McCord (ed.) *Violence in the Inner City*. Cambridge: Cambridge University Press.

Moffitt, T.E. (2003) 'Life-course persistent and adolescence-limited antisocial behaviour: A research review and a research agenda', in B. Lahey, T.E. Moffitt and A. Caspi (eds) *The Causes of Conduct Disorder and Serious Juvenile Delinquency*. New York: Guilford.

Moffitt, T.E. and Caspi, A. (2001) 'Childhood predictors differentiate life-course persistent and adolescence-limited pathways, among males and females', *Development and Psychopathology*, 13: 355–75.

Moffitt, T.E., Caspi, A., Dickson, N., Silva, P.A. and Stanton, W. (1996) 'Childhood-onset versus adolescent-onset antisocial conduct in males: Natural history from age 3 to 18. *Development and Psychopathology*, 8: 399–424.

Moffitt, T.E., Caspi, A., Rutter, M. and Silva, P.A. (2001) *Sex Differences in Antisocial Behaviour: Conduct disorder, delinquency, and violence in the Dunedin longitudinal study*. Cambridge, UK: Cambridge University Press.

Moffitt, T.E., Lynam, D. and Silva, P.A. (1994) 'Neuropsychological tests predict persistent male delinquency', *Criminology*, 32: 277–300.

Nagin, D.S., Farrington, D.P. and Moffitt, T.E. (1995) 'Life-course trajectories of different types of offenders', *Criminology*, 33: 111–39.

Nagin, D.S. and Land, K.C. (1993) 'Age, criminal careers, and population heterogeneity: Specification and estimation of a nonparametric, mixed poisson model', *Criminology*, 31: 327–62.

Paternoster, R., Dean, C.W., Piquero, A., Mazerolle, P. and Brame, R. (1997) 'Generality, continuity, and change in offending', *Journal of Quantitative Criminology*, 13: 231–66.

Piquero, A.R. (2001) 'Testing Moffitt's neuropsychological variation hypothesis for the prediction of life-course persistent offending', *Psychology, Crime and Law*, 7: 193–216.

Piquero, A.R. and Brezina, T. (2001) 'Testing Moffitt's account of adolescence-limited delinquency', *Criminology*, 39: 353–70.

Piquero, A.R. and White, N. (2003) 'On the Relationship Between Cognitive Abilities and Life-Course-Persistent Offending Among a Sample of African Americans: A Longitudinal Test of Moffitt's Hypothesis', *Journal of Criminal Justice*, 31: 399–409.

Piquero, A.R., Brame, R. and Lynam, D. (2004) 'Studying the Factors Related to Career Length', *Crime and Delinquency*, forthcoming.

Piquero, A.R., Brezina, T. and Turner, M.G. (2004) 'Testing Moffitt's Account of Delinquency Abstention', *Journal of Research in Crime and Delinquency*, forthcoming.

Piquero, A.R., Farrington, D.P. and Blumstein, A. (2003) 'The criminal career paradigm: Background and recent developments', in M. Tonry (ed.) *Crime and Justice: A Review of Research, Volume 30*. Chicago: University of Chicago Press.

Piquero, A.R., Moffitt, T.E. and Lawton, B. (2003) 'Race Differences in Life-Course-Persistent Offending: Our Children, Their Children: Race/Ethnicity and Crime', edited by Darnell Hawkins and Kimberley Kempf-Leonard; Chicago: University of Chicago Press.

Quetelet, A. (1831) *Research on the Propensity for Crime at Different Ages*. Cincinnati, OH: Anderson Publishing Company (1984 Edition).

Raine, A., Brennan, P. and Mednick, S.A. (1997) 'Interaction between birth complications and early maternal rejection in predisposing individuals to adult violence: Specificity to serious, early-onset violence', *American Journal of Psychiatry*, 154: 1265–271.

Shedler, J. and Block, J. (1990) 'Adolescent drug use and psychological health', *American Psychologist*, 45: 612–30.

Silverthorn, P. and Frick, P.J. (1999) 'Developmental pathways to antisocial behaviour: The delayed-onset pathway in girls', *Development and Psychopathology*, 11: 101–26.

Silverthorn, P., Frick, P.J. and Reynolds, R. (2001) 'Timing of onset and correlates of severe conduct problems in adjudicated girls and boys', *Journal of Psychopathology and Behavioral Assessment*, 23: 171–81.

Steffensmeier, D.J., Allan, E.A., Harer, M.D. and Streifel, C. (1989) 'Age and the distribution of crime', *American Journal of Sociology*, 94: 803–31.

Tibbetts, S.G. and Piquero, A.R. (1999) 'The influence of gender, low birth weight, and disadvantaged environment in predicting early onset of offending: A test of Moffitt's interactional hypothesis', *Criminology*, 37: 843–78.

Warr, M. (2002) *Companions in Crime: The Social Aspects of Criminal Conduct*. Cambridge: Cambridge University Press.

White, H.R., Bates, M.E. and Buyske, S. (2001) 'Adolescence-limited versus persistent delinquency: Extending Moffitt's hypothesis into adulthood', *Journal of Abnormal Psychology*, 110: 600–09.

White, N. and Piquero, A.R. (2003) 'An empirical test of Silverthorn and Frick's delayed-onset pathway in girls: Evidence of criminal activity from birth to adulthood', unpublished manuscript.

Stalking

Lorraine Sheridan and Graham Davies,
University of Leicester

'Stalking' is a nebulous crime, comprising a set of behaviours that are difficult both to define and legislate against. In 1996, a consultation paper produced by the Home Office noted that stalking was not defined in the civil or criminal law in England and Wales, but stated that 'it can be broadly described as a series of acts which are intended to, or in fact, cause harassment to another person' (1.2). While this may be a useful in terms of illustrating what is broadly meant by 'stalking', it also highlights the definitional problem: the term may be applied to almost any behaviour, but only some behaviours will constitute stalking, as long as the behaviour is of a repetitive nature. Certainly, repetition, or persistence, is one of the key features of any stalking case and must usually be present to allow for criminal charges to be brought. The persistent nature of stalking behaviours means that they can be particularly difficult to eradicate. The current chapter will draw on empirical evidence to illustrate the nature of 'stalking' and seek to identify whom stalkers and their victims are most likely to be. The legislative history of stalking will be briefly discussed, before outlining the potential benefits and pitfalls associated with both legal sanctions and alternative modes of intervention.

A new crime?

Although stalking was labelled by the British media as 'the crime of the 1990s' (e.g. Daly 1996), it does not represent a new form of deviant behaviour (e.g. Meloy 1999, Mullen, Pathé and Purcell 2000). Despite many academic articles stating that stalking was first outlawed by California in 1990, it appears that Californian law had an ancient precedent. Book four of the Ancient Roman legal tome *Institutes of Justinianus* (approximately 550 AD) contains the passage '*Iniuria commititur … si quis matrem familias aut praetextatum praetextatumve adsectatus fuerit*' which roughly translated means that it is prohibited to inflict injury or cause hindrance by following a boy, girl or married woman. Neither is stalking behaviour new to popular fiction. Louisa Mae Alcott's nineteenth century novel *A Long Fatal Love Chase* also bears a strong resemblance to many contemporary accounts of stalking. John Fowles' first novel *The Collector* (1963) features a young art student who is obsessively pursued by an inadequate man. He observes her every activity, moves house in order to be closer to her, and engages in photographic surveillance before finally entrapping her and holding her hostage. What *is* new is the frequency of such behaviour, perhaps en-couraged by the greater empowerment and emancipation of women and ready access to mechanisms of surveillance and control, such as mobile phones and e-mail. Stalking is now a criminal act in most countries of the developed world.

Stalking is now widely considered to be a particular form of 'harassment'. In the past it has been linked to various mental conditions, notably De Clerambault's syndrome and erotomania. De Clerambault, a French psychiatrist, first identified a condition in 1927 that he labelled *psychose passionelle*. De Clerambault stated that sufferers were primarily females who laboured under the delusional belief that a man, with whom she may have had little or no contact, returned intense feelings of love for her. The target of affections were usually persons of much higher socio-economic status and likely to be unobtainable to the sufferer, such as a film star or a politician. Erotomania, a *DSM-IV* delusional disorder, has the same predominant theme, and research has suggested that diagnoses are primarily given to females (see Bruene 2001; Fitzgerald and Seeman 2002; Kennedy, McDonough, Kelly and Berrios 2002; Lloyd-Goldstein 1998). When stalking research burgeoned in the 1990s, it soon became apparent that the modal stalker was male, rather than female, and that women were more likely to be victims of stalking than men. Spitzberg (2002) conducted a meta-analysis of the stalking literature, reporting that across more than 40 samples, 79 per cent of stalkers were male and that 75 per cent of victims were female. It also became clear that stalkers are a heterogeneous, rather than a homogenous, group (e.g. Budd and Mattinson 2000; Meloy 1999; Mullen, Pathé and Purcell 2000). Children and adolescents, for instance, have been found to engage in stalking behaviour (McCann 1998, 2000, 2001, 2002).

What is stalking?

Now that the stalking-related literature encompasses more than 160 studies, reports, reviews and books, researchers and practitioners alike are equipped with a more realistic idea of what stalking constitutes than they were when legislation was first introduced in the 1990s. Essentially, 'stalking' encompasses an infinite range of behaviours that may be targeted at one individual by another. Some of these behaviours may be considered as sinister in nature and are likely to be already illegal in most Western legal systems. Threatening telephone calls, death threats and physical assaults are prime examples. Others may be quite innocuous in themselves, but when sufficiently repeated, are often likely to provoke feelings of harassment and intimidation in the target. Examples include walking past the target's home or workplace, and sending letters or flowers to the target. An important question that may be raised is: despite this ambiguity, can citizens distinguish reliably between stalking and other forms of socially intrusive behaviour? This has been examined in several related studies by the authors.

Sheridan, Davies and Boon (2001a) asked 348 women aged between 18 and 65 years to read through a list of 42 intrusive behaviours, and select all those that they personally considered to represent stalking behaviours. Participants were asked to think of the behaviours being performed solely by males towards a female 'target'. The 42 behaviours were designed to represent a continuum of likely stalking and non-stalking acts. Examples included: 'Confining the target against her will', 'Repeated excessive unwanted telephone calls – regardless of content', and 'A stranger engaging the target in an unsolicited conversation in a public place: such as at a bus stop'. The results revealed that there was no one behaviour on which there was unanimous agreement within the sample that it did or did not constitute a stalking behaviour. However, 22 of the 42 items saw agreement from at least 70 per cent of the sample that they were constituent of stalking ('stalking' behaviours). Further, 17 behaviours were seen as representative of stalking by less than 50 per cent of the sample ('non-stalking' behaviours).

A cluster analysis was performed on participants' 'yes/no' responses to the 42 intrusive items. This revealed that both the 'stalking' and 'non-stalking' behaviours could be broken down into sub-clusters. The 'stalking' cluster had four sub-clusters: The first of these, containing 17 items, was labelled 'classic' stalking behaviours. This is because these items were virtually identical to those most commonly revealed by the academic research that has recorded the behaviour of stalkers (see Sheridan and Davies 2001, for an overview) including 'Following the target' and 'Constantly watching/spying on the target'. The seven behaviours in the second sub-cluster were given the label of 'threatening' behaviours as five of them had an overtly threatening/ violent theme, for instance, 'Death threats' and 'Confining the target against her will'. The third 'stalking' sub-cluster comprised just three items and was labelled 'unpredictable' stalking behaviours as the three behaviours were threatening, but also unpredictable, when compared with the threatening but more controlled acts listed by the previous sub-cluster (e.g. 'Continuously acting in an uncontrolled, aggressive, or insulting manner upon seeing the target out with other men (friends or partners')). The final sub-cluster of 'stalking' behaviours (containing five items) was focused on 'attachment'. That is, means by which a stalker may seek to maintain maximally close contact with a target. Examples include 'A man the target is not involved with moves house closer to where she lives or places she frequents – just to be nearer to her' and 'Often purposefully visiting places he knows that the target frequents'.

The six items in the first sub-cluster of 'non-stalking' behaviours were collectively labelled 'courtship' behaviours. The common characteristic of these activities was that they could reasonably comprise part of the early stages of courtship, such as 'Telephoning the target after one initial meeting', and 'Agreeing with the target's every word (even when she is obviously wrong)'. The second 'non-stalking' sub-cluster contained just two items and was dubbed 'verbally obscene' behaviours, which is self-explanatory. The final sub-cluster (containing eight items) was labelled 'overbearing' behaviours. The common theme among these was that they illustrated ways by which one individual attempts to interfere in the affairs of another, but not to a degree that unequivocally constitutes harassment. Items included: 'Trying to become acquainted with the target's friends in an attempt to get to know her better' and 'Unasked for offers of help: lifts in his car, DIY, etc.'

This study supported previous work (Sheridan, Gillett and Davies 2000) and has since been largely replicated in a sample of 210 British males (Sheridan, Gillett and Davies 2002), and in a sample of 354 Trinidadian women (Jagessar and Sheridan 2002). Taken together, these research findings demonstrate that diverse groups share common beliefs concerning the type of activities that are and are not constituent of stalking. All four samples were able consistently to classify a range of acts to the extent that identifiable subgroups of stalking and non-stalking behaviours could be formed. So, although people may not personally be able to define stalking exhaustively, there does appear to be a consensus concerning which types of behaviours are acceptable and which are deviant. This suggests that people can reliably distinguish between the courtship behaviour of someone who is 'trying too hard' to secure a date, and the behaviour of someone whose activities reveal disturbing obsessive traits that require intervention. In all four studies, the real-world relevance of the 'stalking' and 'non-stalking' clusters was tested by also conducting a cluster analysis on the sample's *actual* experiences of the same behaviours. In all cases, the sub-clusters generated by participants' perceptions of stalking were found partially to map on to the sub-clusters generated by the same participants' actual experiences of harassing behaviours. Thus, both potential and actual victims shared a sophisticated perspective on exemplars of stalking behaviours that was grounded in the everyday real-world experiences of stalking victims.

The studies described above did not assess the frequency of stalking behaviours. It was pointed out earlier that virtually any seemingly innocuous activity can constitute stalking, as long as it is engaged in repeatedly. Stalking is unlike many other criminal or intrusive activities in that it does not consist of one isolated incident; rather stalking consists of a series of activities that occur over a protracted period. Past research has reported mean stalking episodes of 24 months (Pathé and Mullen 1997), 58 months (Blaauw, Winkel, Arensman, Sheridan and Freeve 2002) and as long as 76 months (Sheridan, Davies and Boon 2001b). Hall (1998) reported that 13 per cent of victims in her study had been stalked for more than five years, with one victim being stalked for more than 31 years. Similarly, the British Crime Survey found that 19 per cent of stalking victims had been harassed for over a year (Budd and Mattinson 2000). It is clear that although stalking is a long-term phenomenon, stalker activity may vary in terms of intensity within individual cases. Some victim studies have reported that the frequency with which stalking occurs is variable over time (Blaauw *et al.* 2002; Brewster 1997; Hall 1998; Sheridan 2001). For instance, Sheridan's (2001) study in which victims reported that over time, stalkers decreased the amount of time in which they were proximal to the victim, but that they also became more violent. Only two of 29 long-term stalking victims said that their stalker's activities became less intense over time.

The victims of stalking

Since we can conclude that stalking is not only protracted and repetitive in nature, but also unpredictable, it is particularly important to identify possible risk factors in potential victims. The most obvious risk factor is gender, given that the research has indicated that the majority of victims are female (75 per cent) and that the majority of stalkers are male (79 per cent) (see Spitzberg's 2002 meta-analysis). However, these findings may not be entirely reliable. One possibility is that the stalking of males, and/ or stalking by females go largely unrecorded. It has been suggested (Emerson, Ferris and Gardner 1998; Hall 1998; White, Kowalski, Lyndon and Valentine 2002) that males may be less likely to recognise or report 'stalking' behaviour as problematic, because they feel less threatened by it than would females. Sheridan *et al.* (2002) conducted a population study of 210 British males, asking them to indicate whether they had had personal experience of 42 intrusive behaviours and, if they had, to provide free narrative concerning their 'worst experience'. Males did report substantially less experience of intrusive experiences than did females and just five per cent were judged to have suffered 'stalking'. This was significantly less than the figure of 24 per cent obtained by Sheridan *et al.* (2001b), when conducting the same study with a wholly female sample, but it still represents a sizeable portion of the British male population. Of course, the way in which stalking is measured between studies will have an impact upon resultant estimates of its prevalence in a given population. Tjaden, Thoennes and Allison (2000) found that when male participants were allowed to self-define as victims of stalking, rather than be defined according to a legal definition, prevalence rates almost tripled. This finding would suggest that males are able to recognise themselves as victims of stalking, but it still may be the case that they are not as concerned about it as are female victims. A comparison of male and female stalkers, however, has suggested that the duration of stalking and the incidence of violent acts do not differ according to stalker gender (Purcell, Pathé and Mullen 2001).

In addition to gender, age has been mooted as a risk factor for stalking, with those aged 18–30 being reported to be most vulnerable (Hall 1998; Purcell, Pathé and Mullen 2002; Tjaden and Thoennes 1998). The 1998 British Crime Survey found 16–19 year olds to be most at risk, with 16.8 per cent of this age group reporting a recent incident of stalking. Those outside the 18–30 age range are by no means immune, however. Victims aged 2 (Sheridan *et al.* 2001b) and 6 years have been identified (Purcell *et al.* 2002), as have victims aged 76 (Purcell, Pathé and

Mullen 2002) and 82 years (Blaauw *et al.* 2002). Like gender then, age does not provide practitioners with a reliable indicator for predicting who is likely to become a victim of stalking, but both gender and age do offer a rough predictive guide pointing to vulnerable sections of the population. Another possible predictive factor is the victim's socio-economic status. Although victims have been found across the socio-economic spectrum, those most likely to report the crime appear to be more highly educated than victims of other interpersonal crimes, and similarly, they appear to be in higher-level professions (e.g. Brewster 1997; Hall 1998; Pathé and Mullen 2002, Sheridan *et al.* 2001a). This is not surprising when one considers that some stalkers have been said to be motivated by resentment (Mullen *et al.* 2000), may be erotomanic (see above), and are themselves often of higher social status than other criminal offenders (e.g. Meloy 1999). The British Crime Survey however, based on a sample of 9,988 persons, found stalking prevalence to be highest among victims with a relatively low household income (Budd and Mattinson 2000).

Stalking victims are more frequently found among single persons, although married persons and those in other partnerships are not exempt from stalking victimisation. The 1998 British Crime Survey identified single persons as those most likely to experience stalking (Budd and Mattinson 2000), particularly if they were students and living in privately rented accommodation. It must be noted that many risk factors will overlap to a large degree, however, making the identification of key risk factors rather difficult. What is clear is that virtually anyone may become a victim of stalking, but that risks appear to be greater for young single women in high status occupations. Since 1990, the media has contained numerous stories regarding the stalking of celebrities (see Lowney and Best 1995). Indeed, it may be argued that stalking was first criminalised in response to the media storm that centered around a number of high profile celebrity cases (e.g. Saunders 1998). Although celebrities are stalked, they form an overall minority of stalking victims, but are more likely than non-celebrities to suffer the attentions of multiple stalkers (e.g. Pathé and Mullen 2002).

A final risk factor that the research has shown to be closely linked to the stalking of female victims is a history of domestic violence. Many studies (e.g. Burgess, Harner, Baker, Hartman and Lole 2001; Logan, Leukefeld and Walker 2002; McFarlane, Mechanic, Weaver and Resick 2000) have testified to the strong inter-relationship that stalking has with domestic violence (see also Baldry 2002; Walker and Meloy 1998). It is clear that domestic violence does not necessarily end along with the conclusion of a relationship, but may continue in the form of stalking.

What is certain, is that particular groups of society are dispro-portionately vulnerable to stalking risk, and the most unequivocal risk factor would appear to be a previous history of domestic violence.

The perpetrators of stalking

Given that domestic violence is so strongly associated with stalking, it would strongly suggest that a high proportion of stalkers were previously in intimate relationships with their victim. Research indicates that this is indeed the case. Meloy (1999) described the 'modal stalker' as male and the 'modal victim' as his female ex-partner. One of the most reliable research findings in relation to stalkers is that the majority of victims had some form of prior contact with their stalker. Spitzberg (2002) suggests that across 47 studies, 77 per cent of stalkers had had some form of prior acquaintance with their victim, while just 18 per cent stalked strangers. It is generally agreed that the largest stalker-victim relational sub-group covers ex-intimates, but proportional estimates have been found to vary substantially as the following examples will illustrate.

In a sample of Dutch victims, 67 per cent reported being stalked by an ex-intimate (Blaauw *et al.* 2002), whilst Wallis' (1996) analysis of police records of English and Welsh stalking cases revealed that 38 per cent had been targeted by ex-partners. In the US, Tjaden and Thoennes (1998) conducted telephone interviews with a random sample, finding that of those who reported being a victim of stalking, 59 per cent of women had been stalked by ex-intimates, as had 30 per cent of men. Finally, Pathé and Mullen (1997) found that 29 per cent of their Australian victims revealed they had been stalked by ex-intimates. It is likely that estimates of the extent of ex-intimate stalking vary at least partly as a function of sampling techniques, the discipline of the researcher and the definition of stalking employed. Two things, however, are apparent: first, ex-intimate stalkers represent a significant proportion of all stalkers. Second, stalking by non-intimates also has a high prevalence rate. As regards violence, Meloy, Davis and Lovette (2001) found that prior sexual intimacy between victim and stalker resulted in at least an 11-fold increase in potential for violence.

As previously indicated, and as is the case regarding the perpetrators of most crimes of an inter-personal nature, the majority of stalkers recorded by the literature are males. Compared with the general criminal population, however, stalkers tend to be older. Meloy's review of the literature pertaining to stalkers (1996), for instance, found mean stalker ages within individual studies of, e.g. 35 and 40 years. Similarly, Mullen *et al.*'s (2000) classification of stalkers indicated that although mean stalker age varied across sub-categories, overall mean age was over 35 years. As regards socio-economic status, stalkers tend to be found more often in professional occupations than most other criminals (e.g. Hall 1998; Sheridan *et al.* 2001a) but they may be found at any point along the socio-economic continuum. Meloy *et al.* (2001) noted that although the 'modal' stalker will have an average or above average IQ, he will be unemployed. Mullen, Pathé, Purcell and Stuart (1999) found that 39 per cent of 145 stalkers were unemployed, and that the majority of stalkers were socially incompetent. Taken together, the research findings pertaining to the demographic characteristics of stalkers suggest that although certain demographic trends do exist, a high proportion of stalkers will fall outside these.

The relevant research has suggested that stalkers may or may not be mentally ill, and may or may not have criminal histories. Stalking has been associated with a variety of mental disorders including anti-social, histrionic, borderline and narcissistic personality disorders (e.g. Zona, Palarea and Lane 1998), depression (e.g. McCann 2001), delusional disorder, erotomania (see above), sadism (e.g. Boon and Sheridan 2001), schizophrenia (e.g. Mullen and Pathé 1994a) and substance abuse disorder (e.g. Zona *et al.* 1998). Clinicians have noted (e.g. Badcock 2002; Farnham, James and Cantrell 2000) that stalkers are likely to be co-morbid for a range of disorders. However, many stalkers have no history of any psychiatric disturbance. Similarly, although a number of studies have identified the most likely criminal histories with which stalkers will present, not all stalkers will have a criminal record. Meloy *et al.* (2001) examined archival data on 59 stalkers, 66 per cent of whom had been violent towards their victims. No significance was found for drug abuse, drug dependency or prior criminal history. Mullen *et al.* (2000), however, found that 30 per cent of their 145 stalkers suffered from delusional disorders.

The research findings covered by this section allow the conclusions that potential stalkers are difficult to identify, and that a victim will first come into contact with their stalker or future stalker in an almost infinite variety of contexts. Some victims may never actually meet their stalker – the victim studies of Hall (1998), Jones (1996) and Sheridan (2001) for instance, have all identified cases where evidence of stalking existed, but the stalker's identity was never established. It is clear that further investigations and meta-analyses are necessary to provide a more adequate picture of the likely characteristics of stalkers. What is also clear is that stalkers should be grouped into various sub-types according to their demographic characteristics, mental state, motivations, and the nature of their victims (see Boon and Sheridan 2001; Mullen *et al.* 2000, for fuller discussions of the benefits of such typologies).

Stopping stalking

Stalking and the law

Several stalker typologies have suggested that different stalker sub-types will display differing responses to various intervention and treatment strategies. Boon and Sheridan (2001) suggest that legal intervention is likely to curtail the activities of their 'infatuation harasser', whilst their 'sadistic stalker' will only view police inter-vention as a challenge to overcome whilst still maintaining control of the victim. Similarly, Mullen *et al.* (2000) note that treatment for their sexually deviant 'predatory stalker' will pose a significant challenge for the clinician, whilst their 'incompetent suitors' will often stop their stalking activities in response to counselling (although they may later re-offend by focusing on a different victim). The law, however, tends to treat stalkers as a more homogenous group. As has already been noted, stalking is notoriously difficult to define and, across the developed world, the legislatures of different states and countries have adopted somewhat different approaches when framing legislation to outlaw stalking.

Since California first outlawed stalking in 1990, all US states, as well as Australia, Austria, Belgium, Canada, England and Wales, Germany, Ireland, the Netherlands, Scotland, Switzerland and others have enacted anti-stalking legislation. In the US, 30 States enacted their anti-stalking laws in 1992 alone, and wide variation was seen between states in the 'stalking' actions covered by the new legislation. This variation was thought to at least partly result from a haste to enact legislation in order to appease public concerns, as well as from debates over the lack of constitutionality of anti-stalking and harassment laws. In response, the National Institute of Justice in 1993 was asked by Congress to develop a Model Stalking Code. Wallace and Kelty (1995) distilled the require-ments of the Code into the following definition:

> a knowing, purposeful course of conduct directed at a specific person that would cause a reasonable person to fear bodily injury or death to himself or herself or a member of his or her immediate family. (pp. 100–01)

Yet, significant variation is seen between the laws of various States. These differences primarily relate to the type of stalking behaviour that is outlawed, whether or not a threat or intent is required, and also in relation to the reaction required from the victim (US Department of Justice 2002). Most States offer a broad definition of what constitutes stalking, with some offering specific exemplars of stalking behaviour. For instance, in Michigan, stalking is not limited to, but may include: following or appearing in sight of the victim, approaching or confronting the victim in a public place or on private property, appearing at the victim's workplace or residence, entering into or remaining on property owned, leased or occupied by the victim, telephoning the victim, sending mail or electronic communications, and placing an object on the premises of or delivering an object to the victim. Even fewer States provide very narrow definitions of what constitutes unlawful stalking. In Wisconsin, for instance, a stalker must maintain a visual or physical proximity to the victim in order to contravene state law.

Outside the USA, similar variations exist between countries with regard to what legally constitutes stalking or harassment. In England and Wales, a broad approach has been adopted where 'a person must not pursue a course of conduct which amounts to harassment of another, and which he knows or ought to know amounts to harassment of the other' (section 1, Protection from Harassment Act 1997). 'Harrassment' is not, in turn, defined. In Ireland, however, a definition of harassment is provided as follows:

> any person who, without lawful authority or reasonable excuse, by any means including by use of the telephone, harasses another by persistently following, watching, pestering, besetting or communicating with him or her, shall be guilty of an offence. (section 10, Non-Fatal Offences Against the Person Act 1997)

Differences are also seen between countries in terms of the inclusion of threat and intent. For instance, no intent is required in England and Wales, where harassment is considered as having occurred

> if a reasonable person in possession of the same information would think the course of conduct amounted to harassment of the other. (section 2)

Conversely, Australia's Capital Territory prescribes that

A person shall not stalk another person with intent to cause (a) apprehension or fear of serious harm in the other person or a third person; or, (b) serious harm to the other person or a third person. (Australian Capital Territory, Crimes Act 1900 section 34A)

Most countries and states prescribe the inclusion of a credible threat, but as the Hong Kong Law Reform Commission (2000) note, this can be problematic. The behaviour of many stalkers may appear to be innocuous, such as the sending of unwanted flowers or regularly walking past the victim's place of work. However, these activities may still be threatening to the victim where they are unwanted and where they take place frequently. The Hong Kong Law Reform Commission further notes that stalkers who are familiar with the threat element of a particular anti-stalking law may purposefully refrain from delivering any specific threat, thereby avoiding prosecution. Some legislatures have circumvented this possibility by adopting the 'reasonable person' test. For example, the USA's 1993 Model Stalking Code, as mentioned above. Differences in the compass of stalking laws between countries have raised extensive debates. In Germany, Smartt (2001) notes that the debate peaked when the stalker of tennis player Martina Hingis was put on trial in Florida. The Australian stalker had harassed his victim at her home in Germany, yet Hingis was unable to curtail his activities via German or Swiss law. A Florida court sentenced the stalker to two years imprisonment with a further two years probation and applied an indefinite injunction banning him from contacting Hingis.

Prescriptive versus non-prescriptive legislation

The victims of stalking also play important roles in the way that stalking may be legally defined. Anti-stalking laws frequently require the victim to display negative effects of stalking, or else require that a reasonable person would be likely to experience negative consequences in the same situation (see Finch 2002). These negative effects may take the form of substantial emotional distress (e.g. under Californian law), serious alarm, annoyance, fright, or torment (e.g. District of Columbia), fear for personal safety (e.g. Florida), arousal of fear (e.g. South Australia), or reasonable mental anxiety, anguish, or fear (e.g. Alabama). Blaauw, Sheridan and Winkel (2002) compared five victim studies in an attempt to discover whether stalking behaviours were consistent between samples. Two of the five studies were conducted in the United States, one by Brewster (1997) who interviewed 187 female victims of ex-partner stalkers in Pennsylvania who were recruited through victim service and law enforcement agencies and one by Hall (1998) whose 145 self-defined stalking victims had made themselves known via regional voice mail boxes that had been set up in seven US target cities. In Australia, Pathé and Mullen's (1997) study was based on questionnaires completed by 100 stalking victims who independently contacted the authors or who were referred to the authors' clinic. Two European studies were also included in the comparison. In the United Kingdom, Sheridan et al. (2001b) distributed questionnaires among 95 individuals who had contacted a charity concerned with the promotion of personal safety, and in the Netherlands 261 completed questionnaires were received from members of the Dutch Anti-Stalking Foundation who had all experienced stalking.

Across the five studies, nine distinct stalker behaviours had been recorded and these were: telephone calls, harassing letters, surveillance of the victim's home, following, unlawful entry to the victim's home, destruction or theft of the victim's property, direct unwanted approaches, threats to harm or kill the victim, and physical assaults. Thus, stalking behaviours were found to be consistent between diverse samples from four different countries. Further, most of the nine stalker behaviours were fairly equally distributed across the different studies. For instance, the number of victims reporting that their stalker telephoned them ranged from 78 per cent to 90 per cent, instances of following ranged from 68 per cent to 83 per cent, and threats to kill or harm the victim were reported by between 41 per cent and 53 per cent of victims. Blaauw et al. (2002) concluded that this consistency suggests that anti-stalking legislation could prescribe a core of behaviours that constitute stalking. However, it may be argued that stalkers may easily circumvent such prescriptive legislation, with the result that some victims would have no legal recourse. A number of authors have noted that the particularly tenacious nature of many stalkers has led to ingenious methods of harassment designed to cause maximal distress in the victim whilst at the same time minimizing the offender's chance of getting caught. Prior to the introduction of the Protection from Harassment Act in 1997, Lawson-Cruttenden (1996) reported that the majority of stalkers known to him had sought meticulously to stay within the bounds of criminal law, despite the objectionable or harassing nature of their behaviour. A more measured suggestion may be for anti-stalking legislation to include behaviours such as the nine detailed above as examples of what may constitute illegal stalking in order to inform the police and courts of the nature of stalking crimes.

Given that stalking has only been criminalised relatively recently, it is likely that debates will continue within different jurisdictions as to how best to frame legislation to outlaw stalking and harassment. The questions of how to define stalking (if at all), and the inclusion of stalker intent, threat and impact upon victims will continue to be discussed, as will the fundamental constitutionality of anti-harassment laws. Because a very fine line can exist between excessive courtship behaviour, reasonable communication attempts and harassment, disparities even within legal systems are almost inevitable. Further, as with many criminal activities, technological progress makes amendments to intervention strategies necessary. Many anti-stalking laws are already broad enough to encompass cyber-stalking and other technologically aided harassment activities. Other anti-stalking legislation, such as that of California, has been amended to cover stalking via e-mail. In the case of California, the term 'credible threat' has now been extended to include

> that performed through the use of an electronic communication device, or a threat implied by a pattern of conduct or a combination of verbal, written or electronically communicated statements. (US Department of Justice 2002)

Stalker remedies

Legal intervention is not the only manner by which stalkers may be deterred from their harassment campaigns. In terms of treating stalkers, as previously noted, psychotherapeutic intervention may be the most effective course of action for some stalker sub-types, such as delusional stalkers. For other sub-types however, such as those with a teenage or mid-life 'crush' and certain ex-partner stalkers, police intervention would be more strongly advocated (Boon and Sheridan 2001).

Although there exists no effective treatment for stalking *per se*, many of the psychiatric conditions associated with stalking behaviour (such as personality disorders, depression, substance abuse disorders, delusional disorders and schizophrenia) may respond to relevant interventions (see Kropp, Hart, Lyon and LePard 2002). An important factor for a clinician faced with a stalker will be the recognition that as a group, stalkers are likely to be co-morbid for a range of disorders. Kropp *et al.* (2002) suggest that in the case of stalkers, 'treatment' will likely have a preventative aim, rather than a solely rehabilitative aim. Because of this, these authors advocate a multi-disciplinary approach to case management, with risk assessment forming the basis of their approach. Mullen *et al.* (2000) also suggest that although management of any existing mental disorder is imperative, this should not be the sole task of the clinician – for many stalkers, the stalking is an all consuming task and stalkers will need to be connected or re-connected with a real social world if successful intervention is to be achieved. It should be noted that because of the serious negative effects that stalking may have on its victims, victims too should be offered counselling or psychotherapeutic help. In the most extensive study of its kind to date, Davis, Coker and Sanderson (2000) found a strong link between stalking and poor mental and physical health in a sample of 6,563 women and 6,705 men. Both sexes reported a significantly greater likelihood of injury or chronic disease since they were first victims of stalking.

Conclusions

Stalkers engage in a range of harassing behaviours, many of which are common to a majority of stalkers. Although some stalker activities may appear ostensibly harmless, stalkers become a menace when their behaviour is repetitive and unwanted. Although basic similarities exist between some stalkers and between some victims, it would appear that virtually anyone might become a stalker or the victim of a stalker. Anti-stalking legislation takes a blanket approach to outlawing stalking behaviour, embracing a wide range of stalker sub-types – from those who are infatuated with their target and sincerely wish to start a relationship to sadistic stalkers who intend serious harm. In order to help prevent recidivism, treatment regimes should not take a blanket approach, but should be targeted towards specific sub-categories of stalkers. To help protect the public from the lasting damage that may be inflicted by stalkers, a multi-disciplinary approach is required where information is shared between the judiciary, police officers, clinicians and academics.

References

Alcott, L.M. (1996) *A Long Fatal Love Chase*. Waterville, ME: Thorndike.

Badcock, R. (2002) 'Psychopathology and treatment of stalking', in J.C.W. Boon and L. Sheridan (eds) *Stalking and Psychosexual Obsession: Psychological Perspectives for Prevention, Policing and Treatment* (pp. 125–139). Chichester: Wiley.

Baldry, A. (2002) 'From domestic violence to stalking: The infinite cycle of violence', in J.C.W. Boon and L. Sheridan (eds) *Stalking and Psychosexual Obsession: Psychological Perspectives for Prevention, Policing and Treatment* (pp. 83–104). Chichester: Wiley.

Blaauw, E., Sheridan, L. and Winkel, F.W. (2002) 'Designing anti-stalking legislation on the basis of victims' experiences and psychopathology', *Psychiatry, Psychology and Law*, 9 (2): 136–45.

Blaauw, E., Winkel, F.W., Arensman, E., Sheridan, L. and Freeve, A. (2002) 'The toll of stalking: The relationship between features of stalking and psycho-pathology of victims', *Journal of Interpersonal Violence*, 17: 50–63.

Boon, J.C.W. and Sheridan, L. (2001) 'Stalker typologies: A law enforcement perspective', *Journal of Threat Assessment*, 1: 75–97.

Brewster, M.P. (1997) 'An exploration of the experiences and needs of former intimate stalking victims', *Final Report Submitted to the National Institute of Justice*. West Chester, PA: West Chester University.

Bruene, M. (2001) 'De Clerambault's syndrome (erotomania): An evolutionary perspective, *Evolution and Human Behavior*, 22: 409–15.

Budd, T. and Mattinson, J. (2000) *Stalking: Findings from the 1998 British Crime Survey*. London: Home Office.

Burgess, A.W., Harner, H., Baker, T., Hartman, C.R. and Lole, C. (2001) 'Batterers' stalking patterns', *Journal of Family Violence*, 16: 309–21.

Daly, E. (17 December 1996) 'Sweeping penalties in new laws on stalkers', *The Independent*: 9.

Davis, K.E., Coker, A.L., Sanderson, M. (August 2002) 'Physical and mental health effects of being stalked for men and women', *Violence and Victims*, 17 (4): 429–43.

Emerson, R.M., Ferris, K.O. and Gardner, C.B. (1998) 'On being stalked', *Social Problems*, 45: 289–314.

Farnham, F.R., James, D.V. and Cantrell, P. (2000) 'Association between violence, psychosis and relationship to victim in stalkers', *The Lancet*, 355: 199.

Finch, E. (2002) 'Stalking: A violent crime or a crime of violence?', *Howard Journal of Criminal Justice*, 41 (5): 422–33.

Fitzgerald, P. and Seeman, M.V. (2002) 'Erotomania in women', in J.C.W. Boon and L. Sheridan (eds) *Stalking and Psychosexual Obsession: Psychological Perspectives for Prevention, Policing and Treatment* (pp. 165–179). Chichester: Wiley.

Fowles, J. (1963) *The Collector*. London: Little Brown and Co.

Hall, D.M. (1998) 'The victims of stalking', in J.R. Meloy (ed.) *The Psychology of Stalking: Clinical and Forensic Perspectives* (pp. 113–137). San Diego, CA: Academic Press.

Home Office (1996) *Stalking – the Solutions: A Consultation Paper*. London: HMSO.

Hong Kong Law reform Commission (October 2000) 'Stalking – The new offence', in *Stalking*. Hong Kong: Law Reform Commission of Hong Kong.

Jagessar, J.D.H. and Sheridan, L.P. (2004) 'A cross-cultural investigation into stalking', *Criminal Justice and Behaviour*.

Jones, C. (1996) 'Criminal harassment (or stalking)'. See: http://www.chass.utoronto.ca/~cjones/pub/stalking

Kennedy, N., McDonough, M., Kelly, B. and Berrios, G.E. (2002) 'Erotomania revisited: Clinical course and treatment', *Comprehensive Psychiatry*, 43: 1–6.

Kropp, P.R., Hart, S.D., Lyon, D.R. and LePard, D.A. (2002) 'Managing stalkers: Coordinating treatment and supervision', in J.C.W. Boon and L. Sheridan (eds) *Stalking and Psychosexual Obsession: Psychological Perspectives for Prevention, Policing and Treatment* (pp. 141–16). Chichester: Wiley.

Lawson-Cruttenden, T. (1996) 'Is there a law against stalking?', *New Law Journal*, 22 March 1996: 418–19.

Lloyd-Goldstein, R. (1998) 'De Clerambault on-line: A survey of erotomania and stalking from old world to the world wide web', in J. Reid Meloy (ed.) *The Psychology of Stalking: Clinical and Forensic Perspectives* (pp. 193–212). San Diego: Academic Press.

Logan, T.K., Leukefeld, C. and Walker, B. (2002) 'Stalking as a variant of intimate violence: Implications from a young adult sample', in K.E. Davis and I.H. Frieze *et al.* (eds) *Stalking: Perspectives on Victims and Perpetrators* (pp. 265–291). New York: Springer.

Lowney, K.S. and Best, J. (1995) 'Stalking strangers and lovers: Changing media typifications of a new crime problem', in J. Best (ed.) *Images of Issues: Typifying Contemporary Social Problems* (pp. 33–57). New York: Aldine de Gruyter.

McCann, J.T. (1998) 'Subtypes of stalking (obsessional following) in adolescents', *Journal of Adolescence*, 21: 667–75.

McCann, J.T. (2000) 'A descriptive study of child and adolescent obsessional followers', *Journal of Forensic Sciences*, 45: 195–99.

McCann, J.T. (2001) *Stalking in Children and Adolescents: The primitive bond.* Washington, DC: American Psychological Association.

McCann, J.T. (2002) 'The phenomenon of stalking in children and adolescents', in J.C.W. Boon and L. Sheridan (eds) *Stalking and Psychosexual Obsession: Psychological Perspectives for Prevention, Policing and Treatment* (pp. 125–139). Chichester: Wiley.

McFarlane, J., Campbell, J.C. and Watson, K. (2002) 'Intimate partner stalking and femicide: Urgent implications for women's safety', *Behavioral Sciences and the Law*, 20: 51–68.

Mechanic, M.B., Weaver, T.L. and Resick, P.A. (2002) 'Intimate partner violence and stalking behavior: Exploration of patterns and correlates in a sample of acutely battered women', in K.E. Davis and I.H. Frieze *et al.* (eds) *Stalking: Perspectives on Victims and Perpetrators* (pp. 62–88). New York: Springer.

Meloy, J.R. (1996) 'Stalking (obsessional following): A review of some preliminary studies', *Aggression and Violent Behavior*, 1: 147–62.

Meloy, J.R. (1999) 'Stalking: An old behavior, a new crime', *Psychiatric Clinics of North America*, 22: 85–99.

Meloy, J.R., Davis, B. and Lovette, J. (2001) 'Risk factors for violence among stalkers', *Journal of Threat Assessment*, 1: 3–16.

Mullen, P.E. and Pathé, M. (1994) 'The pathological extensions of love', *British Journal of Psychiatry*, 165: 614–23.

Mullen, P.E., Pathé, M. and Purcell, R. (2000) *Stalkers and their victims.* Cambridge: Cambridge University Press.

Mullen, P.E., Pathé, M., Purcell, R. and Stuart, G.W. (1999) 'Study of stalkers', *The American Journal of Psychiatry*, 156: 1244–249.

Pathé, M. and Mullen, P.E. (1997) 'The impact of stalkers on their victims', *British Journal of Psychiatry*, 170: 12–17.

Pathé, M. and Mullen, P.E. (2002) 'The victim of stalking', in J.C.W. Boon and L. Sheridan (eds) *Stalking and psychosexual obsession: Psychological perspectives for prevention, policing and treatment* (pp. 1–22). Chichester: Wiley.

Purcell, R., Pathé, M. and Mullen, P.E. (2001) 'A study of women who stalk', *American Journal of Psychiatry*, 158: 2056–060.

Purcell, R., Pathé, M. and Mullen, P.E. (2002) 'The incidence and nature of stalking in the Australian community', *Australian and New Zealand Journal of Psychiatry*, 36: 114–20.

Saunders, R. (1998) 'The legal perspective of stalking', in J.R. Meloy (ed.) *The Psychology of Stalking: Clinical and Forensic Perspectives* (pp. 28–49). San Diego: Academic Press.

Sheridan, L. (2001) 'The course and nature of stalking: An in-depth victim survey', *Journal of Threat Assessment*, 1: 61–79.

Sheridan, L. and Davies, G.M. (2001) 'Stalking: The elusive crime', *Legal and Criminological Psychology*, 6: 133–147.

Sheridan, L., Davies, G.M. and Boon, J.C.W. (2001a) 'Stalking: perceptions and prevalence', *Journal of Interpersonal Violence*, 16: 151–67.

Sheridan, L., Davies, G.M. and Boon, J.C.W. (2001b) 'The course and nature of stalking: A victim perspective', *Howard Journal of Criminal Justice*, 40: 215–34.

Sheridan, L., Gillett, R. and Davies, G.M. (2000) 'Stalking: Seeking the victim's perspective', *Psychology, Crime and Law*, 6: 267–80.

Sheridan, L., Gillett, R. and Davies, G.M. (2002) 'Perceptions and prevalence of stalking in a male sample', *Psychology, Crime and Law*, 8: 289–310.

Smartt, U. (2001) 'The stalking phenomenon: Trends in European and international stalking and harassment legislation', *European Journal of Crime, Criminal Law and Criminal Justice*, 9: 209–32.

Spitzberg, B.H. (2002) 'The tactical topography of stalking victimization and management', *Trauma, Violence and Abuse*, 3: 261–88.

Tjaden, P. and Thoennes, N. (1998) *Stalking in America: Findings from the national violence against women survey.* Washington, DC: National Institute of Justice and Centers for Disease Control and Prevention.

Tjaden, P., Thoennes, N. and Allison, C.J. (2000) 'Comparing stalking victimization from legal and victim perspectives', *Violence and Victims*, 15: 7–22.

US Department of Justice (January 2002) *Legal Series Bulletin 1: Strengthening Anti-Stalking Statutes.* US Department of Justice, Office of Justice Programs, Office for Victims of Crime.

Walker, L.M. and Meloy, J.R. (1998) 'Stalking and domestic violence', in J.R. Meloy (ed.) *The Psychology of Stalking: Clinical and Forensic Perspectives* (pp. 140–159). San Diego, CA: Academic Press.

Wallace, H. and Kelty, K. (1995) 'Stalking and restraining orders: A legal and psychological perspective', *Journal of Crime and Justice*, 18 (2): 99–111.

Wallis, M. (1996) 'Outlawing stalkers', *Policing Today (UK)*, 2 (4): 25–9.

White, J., Kowalski, R.M., Lyndon, A. and Valentine, S. (2002) 'An integrative contextual developmental model of male stalking', *Violence and Victims*, 15: 373–88.

Zona, M.A., Palarea, R.E. and Lane, J.C. Jr. (1998) 'Psychiatric diagnosis and the offender-victim typology of stalking', in J.R. Meloy (ed.) *The Psychology of Stalking: Clinical and Forensic Perspectives* (pp. 70–83). San Diego, CA: Academic Press, Inc.

Section 6

Intervention and Prevention

When we apply the word 'domestic' to violence, we minimise and relegate it to the private sphere. Over recent years, it has been acknowledged that both the police and the judiciary should do far more to challenge violence within the home and that perpetrated by family members against one another, wherever it takes place. However, it is not as simple as the police responding to every call, treating each call seriously and arresting the offender. A number of innovative intervention programmes are now in existence in many European and American jurisdictions. Despite this, the long-term effects of interventions and their ramifications on the families have not been assessed in a particularly systematic way. In Chapter 12, Elizabeth Gilchrist and Mark Kebbell seek to redress this and present an evaluation of current intervention strategies in this country.

Chapters 13 and 14 are linked together in that they both assess ways of intervening to prevent offending in the first place. For decades, social scientists have argued that our research findings should be used more systematically to design policy and practice. Within chapter thirteen, Brandon Welsh and David Farrington make a convincing case for certain types of interventions to prevent delinquency. They demonstrate long-term effectiveness on key measurable outcomes and, politically crucial, savings to the tax-payer. Chapter 14, provides a different emphasis to one type of intervention assessed in Chapter 13, the parenting programme. Within Chapter 14, Anthony Goodman and Joanna Adler bring the societal context into sharper focus. They explore the reality of parenting programmes for some of the parents who have participated in them already. It evaluates their experiences and sets the evolution of such programmes within a broader social context and political debate. These programmes clearly have much to offer society but care needs to be taken that neither the individual adults, nor children they are parenting, be alienated and further stigmatised. It has always behoved as to consider the context within which we work. Without such an understanding and recognition, forensic psychology may be in danger of losing currency and languish as little more than an academic curiosity.

Chapter 12

Domestic violence: current issues in definitions and interventions with perpetrators in the UK

Elizabeth L. Gilchrist, Coventry University and Mark Kebbell, James Cook University

> Given the unpalatable nature of wife abuse, it is perhaps inevitable that explanations are entangled with political, moral and inter-disciplinary issues. (Blackburn 1993)

There is a large body of literature, and a growing bank of empirical data, related to domestic violence, but we are far from establishing one unified theory of domestic violence that can explain why certain men do, or perhaps why others do not, abuse their female partners. There are also many current initiatives aimed at reducing the incidence or ameliorating the effects of domestic violence. However, they are heavily influenced by discipline or orientation and by theoretical and political approach. There are also substantial gaps in our knowledge. Many correlates of domestic violence have been identified, but the data are dominated by material collected in North America. Consequently, there is still a huge gap in what we know in Britain about the nature, needs and risks of such offenders. Even based upon the North American literature, our understanding of which factors are causal remains fragmented. Also, whilst the government and voluntary groups have been funding and supporting a variety of initiatives in this area, not much has been published as to whether these initiatives are effective, and even less about why.

What is clear, is that a number of areas of debate greatly influence current thinking and will influence future developments. It is those current themes and issues on which this chapter focuses. As the topic is so wide, this chapter will primarily address two areas: firstly, to explore some definitions of domestic violence and current theoretical debates and, secondly, to review in brief, current interventions with perpetrators in the UK and their efficacy.

Introduction

Survey data suggest that domestic violence is not at all uncommon in the United Kingdom. Indeed, domestic violence constitutes the largest single type of violence against women and accounts for 25 per cent of all violent crime in the UK (Home Office 2002). It is estimated that one in four women experience domestic violence at some stage in their lives. The British Crime Survey found that 23 per cent of the women interviewed for the 1996 survey reported having experienced a domestic assault during their lifetime (Mirrlees-Black 1999). Similar rates, ranging from 23 per cent to 28 per cent, have also been identified in the Netherlands, the US, Australia, New Zealand and Canada (Mirrlees-Black 1999, appendices). Data from a 'snapshot' survey in September 2000 show that the police in the UK received 1,300 calls reporting incidents of domestic violence in one day, and suggest that they would receive around 570,000 calls per year (Stanko 2000). This is less than the official estimate of numbers of domestic violence incidents for 1995, which was 6.6 million but implies a far larger hidden figure. [1] (Mirrlees-Black 1999).

The level of violence and even homicidal risk is also very high; two women per week are killed by their current or former partner. Also, the impact is wide, with suggestions that in addition to the women who suffer, thousands of children either witness or actually experience abuse within their family of origin. Also, the cost is high. It is estimated that the cost of supporting survivors of domestic violence in London alone would be as great as £278m per year, without accounting for prosecution and resultant child protection and child care costs (*Living Without Fear*, Home Office 1999).

Despite the prevalence and impact of domestic violence in the UK, not enough work has been done to clarify our conceptualisation and theoretical understanding of domestic violence nor to identify effective methods of tackling this problem. We know little about the characteristics of the male domestic violence offenders. There is actually not much, generalisable, UK data which provides appropriate detail about domestic violence offenders. There has been some interesting work done, but the studies have either tended to be descriptive studies, for example the Dobash work, (Dobash, Dobash, Lewis and Cavanagh

2000), which although excellent, did not assess the kinds of factors on which a psychologist would want to focus to assess risk, or they have been very general, for example the British Crime Survey (mentioned above) which established a great deal of general information about domestic violence incidents and victims, but not about perpetrators (Mirrlees-Black, Mayhew and Percy 1996).

There is little agreement about even the definition of domestic violence and less about what would constitute an appropriate response.

Definitions and debates

Debate and controversy surrounds the terminology used within this area. The debate over names may be partly due to the emotive nature of the topic and partly due to the tensions between the variety of disciplines that engage in research and intervention in this area. The differences in focus and philosophy underpinning the different labels applied mean that this issue is one that deserves some attention.

What's in a name?

In the 1970s, when this area initially became the focus of attention, the phenomenon was discussed under the term 'battered women' (e.g. Pizzey and Forbes 1974) However, this term has been identified as problematic as the focus was on the women, as if it were more a problem of abused women than a problem of abusing men. The focus shifted to 'couple violence' and 'family violence'. However, these terms were linked in with a particular approach to addressing the issue (Healey, Smith and O'Sullivan 1998), with the focus on problematic couple or family interaction and again not clearly identifying the problem as being one of abusing men. Also, 'violence' has been challenged as it restricts the attention to physical abuse rather than encompassing a more appropriate and wider range of abuses. So the term abuse or abuses or even 'constellation of abuses', a phrase coined by Dobash *et al.* (2000), would be more appropriate than violence. A similar criticism has been applied to the 'wife batterer' or 'spouse batterer' terms, which have been used in North America. Not only do these terms imply physical abuse only, but they restrict the focus to married couples.

Various alternative terms have been suggested. In Canada and the US often the term 'spouse abuse' is used to deal with these concerns (e.g.

Kropp and Hart 2000). This widens the focus to include a range of abuses. However, again there are issues with this, as it is gender neutral and could be seen as restricting the focus to only married couples. Also whilst abuse is more inclusive in terms of reflecting the reality of the experiences of women, it does not fit within a criminal justice context as most perpetrators will be convicted of an act of violence (direct or indirect), criminal damage or public disorder, rather than abuse.[2] Dobash *et al.* (2000) have criticised this term, as it is neutral in terms of gender. They suggest that 'wife beating' is a better term, but they have at points also explicitly limited their work to married couples, a distinction which is not suggested by the empirical data and so equally problematic in its own way.

The term 'domestic violence' has been widely used in the UK, but again this fails to state explicitly the relationship between gender and violence. It is not a term which appears to have been widely used in the States and it has been suggested that domestic violence is a term, similar to family violence, which could, and perhaps should encompass a wider range of violence, for example, child abuse, elder abuse, same sex relationship violence and female to male violence. It has also been suggested that 'domestic violence' fails to acknowledge the gendered nature of this type of abuse. These types of adult-to-adult violence, as measured by official figures and victim surveys such as the British Crime Survey, in the UK tends to be perpetrated by men against women.

Despite this, the term 'domestic violence' is one which is still commonly used in the UK, although it tends to be followed by a definition to clarify what the particular organisation or individual means by using this term. For example, the Home Affairs Select Committee (1993) defines domestic violence as: 'Any form of physical, sexual or emotional abuse which takes place within the context of a close relationship. In most cases, the relationship will be between partners (married, co-habiting, or otherwise) or ex-partners.' They do recognise the gender inequality in this offence, noting that 'in most cases, the abuser is male and the victim female and that lifetime prevalence, repeat victimization, injury, fear and threats are higher for women' (Home Affairs Select Committee 1993).

In the UK, 'domestic violence', despite the gender neutrality of the actual words, is generally held to refer to male abuse of women. 'Family violence' tends to be the label of choice of those who reject the gender inequality argument and who look at a wider range of abuses within a domestic setting.

Do women do as much as men?

Having identified that there have been debates about terminology, many focusing around issues of gender neutrality, we need to ask can a gendered definition of domestic violence be justified?

Much of the data available in the UK suggest that men perpetrate more violence against their intimate partners. Seven to 11 per cent of domestic homicide victims are men but 42 to 49 per cent of the victims are women and 76 per cent of violence in the home was 'wife beating', while only 1.2 per cent was 'husband beating' (BCS 1996). The ratios of perpetrators has been estimated as 80 per cent male to 20 per cent female (MVA 2000) and the impact and context of male abuse of women is identified as more problematic than female abuse of men (Dobash *et al.* 2000; Edleson and Tolman 1992; Mirlees-Black 1999).

With figures such as the ones quoted above, it may seem odd that there is any debate as to there being as much female to male violence as there is male to female violence, yet this argument continues. However, there are data on domestic homicide, which have suggested that, in the US, 45 per cent of victims of domestic homicides are men and 55 per cent are women. There are also data from large scale surveys from the US where the amount of violence reported by men and by women appears to be similar (e.g. Straus and Gelles 1990). This suggests a more equal pattern and provides some support for a gender-neutral approach. There are arguments from both extremes as to why the data collection tools employed and the populations approached mean that the evidence of gender asymmetry or gender symmetry remains unsubstantiated.

The 'family violence' camp has challenged many of the figures provided by feminist theorists and challenged the gendered nature of domestic violence, claiming that as much domestic violence is per-petrated by women against men as by men against women. There are US data, collected from a variety of surveys, mainly using the Conflict Tactics Scale, which suggest that the amount of violence reported by women in relationships is no greater than the amount of abuse reported by men. However, the Conflict Tactics Scale has been criticised, as it does not include any dimension of frequency of assault, so many claim it under-reports the reality of women's experiences, hides the amount of male violence, and does not include any measure of outcome of the violence. Hence, the impact of a woman hitting a man and a man hitting a woman are treated as the same, although data from other sources (emergency heath care) suggests that when men hit women, women suffer more (Dobash, Dobash, Wilson and Daly 1992).

There are further issues with the Conflict Tactics Scale as data from women involved in the Duluth initiative in the US, and from research conducted by Dobash *et al.* (2000) in the UK, suggests that if women are being physically abused within a relationship this is only one of a 'constellation of abuses' from which they suffer. Thus the coercive and unequal power-sharing context of the violence is not reflected. Data from these women suggest that the real problem is that the violence occurs within a psychologically, emotionally and socially controlling context, rather than the violence on its own. Also, using the Conflict Tactics Scale to measure physical violence does not recognise the wider context of that violence and the differential power of men and women at a societal level. (For a detailed discussion of issues with the Conflict Tactics Scale as a measure of domestic violence see Dobash *et al.* 1992).

One of the major features about this debate is that the two camps do appear to be taking their information from different sources and using different tools to define what it is that they are measuring. For example, the 'family violence' camp tends to use large-scale non-victim samples, in the sense that the respondents have not self-selected to be involved in the research and are not identified due to any link with the criminal justice system. The phenomenon is then measured using tools such as the conflict tactics scale and the results are interpreted as indicating a 'gender symmetry' in the violence/abuse. This is then used as a basis for suggesting family therapy as appropriate intervention and the focus of much of the work has been to explore family dynamics and arguments, assuming a neutral backdrop.

The 'feminist' camp tends to take information from women who have sought help from various agencies, or who have been identified as being a particular type of respondent, for example, those who have reported their partners to the police, those who have contacted a refuge and so on.[3] The information is then collected using different tools and questionnaires and perhaps using more qualitative methods to try to reflect the complexity of the women's experiences. This results in far more information about a range of abuses and a range of controlling behaviours experienced. It gives a picture of family violence which is men abusing women and women living in fear, and identifies little of the female violence as proactive and initiated by the woman. Busey (1993) identified four types of 'female defendants': self-defending victims, angry victims, mutually combatant women and primary physical aggressors. Combining the two latter categories, where the women could be seen as either equally or more responsible for initiating the violence, this amounts to a maximum of only five per cent of women arrested for domestic violence, at least in Denver. In a recent meta-analysis Archer (2000) found that if abuse was measured by recording specific acts, then women were more likely to self-report being violent, but when the consequences were taken into account, men were more likely to have injured their partners.

One way of resolving these differences is to consider that perhaps within this area there are two distinct phenomena and that they should be identified under separate terms. Johnson (1995) suggests that the couple violence which involves men using violence and abuse to control their female partners should be referred to as 'patriarchal terrorism' and a second form of couple violence which is a more gender neutral situation where a conflict might be inappropriately resolved by either party should be referred to as 'common couple violence'. The lack of clarity and lack of separation of these two different patterns may have contributed to confusion in this area, and this distinction may help to resolve this debate.

These debates as to appropriate terminology and the range and pattern of domestic violence across society, link quite closely with the range of theories which have been proposed in this area. We would suggest that a recognition of the two different phenomena being studied and explicit definition of the topic under discussion should allow current polarised positions to be reconciled in a more productive way, with researchers being able to engage in a quest for understanding rather than a quest for supremacy in definition.

It is 'patriarchal terrorism' to which we make reference under the term domestic violence and, as 'The overall pattern of intimate violence is dominated by men as abusers and by women as the abused' (Dobash *et al*. 2000: 3), we use the term domestic violence to mean adult, male abuse of female partners or ex-partners.

What are the theories?

There are a variety of levels of explanation, which have been proposed to explain domestic violence offending. They range from explanations at a societal/cultural level to those focusing on individuals and individual pathologies. Principally, research has focused on understanding intimate partner violence in terms of societal structure, at both a macro-systemic (society in general; global attitudes) or micro-systemic level (family; Edleson and Tolman 1992) although there appears to be a great deal of overlap between the two approaches (Dobash, Dobash,

Cavanagh and Lewis 2000). We will briefly review the varying levels.

Sociocultural: explanations at this level tend to argue that domestic violence is a product of a patriarchal society or an aggressive society. These types of society allow, and even support, male use of violence to control women, or the particular culture supports the use of violence in general as a means of problem solving.

Interpersonal: these explanations tend to situate the problem within family interactions, and cite factors such as stress and generally problematic family interactions as being linked to the incidence of wife beating and to other types of family violence. The major tenet is that it is the family interactions which are problematic, rather than the behaviour of any one individual within that family.

Individual/intrapersonal: there are a variety of factors which are linked to domestic violence at this level of explanation. For example, the social learning theory, incorporating the notion of modelling, which proposes that the use of violence against one's partner is learned through interaction with, and modelling on, one's own family of origin, one's peers and wider society. Once learned, the behaviour is then reinforced through positive short-term gratification and the general lack of negative sanctions following the behaviour (Hamberger, Lohr, Bonge and Tollin 1996). Other theories at this level have identified different types of psychopathology, for example, jealousy, dependency, attachment impulse control or self-esteem models as being associated with domestic violence offending. Finally, attitudinal or cognitive styles or deficits have been linked to the use of violence and similar arguments to the cultural acceptance of violence have been made. However, in this case, the attitudinal differences lie at the individual level (Cunningham *et al*. 1998).

What evidence is there? The empirical data

Whilst there has been a general view that domestic violence cuts across all classes and boundaries, research within the general sociological framework has linked increased risk of domestic violence with lower socio-economic status (Dobash *et al*. 2000, Healey *et al*. 1998), age, cohabiting status and employment (Stets 1995). These ideas have been extrapolated in the suggestion that increased stress or social isolation might explain the higher incidence of violence in lower socio-economic status and non-white couples (Gelles 1997). There are studies that suggest structural factors at a societal level may have an effect. For example, studies have identified higher levels of domestic violence in societies where women have less access to independent resources and to divorce (Alvazzi del Frate and Patrignani 1995; van Dijk, Mayhew and Killias 1994), where women have lower status (Bhatt 1998) and in societies where patriarchal attitudes are prevalent (Levinson 1989).

Alternatively, some data suggest that violence may be linked to structural factors at a family level, for example, cohabiting couples were found to be more likely than daters to use abusive behaviours (Magdol, Moffitt, Caspi and Silva 1998). Other researchers have found that there was some relationship between marital conflict styles and later violence by the male partner, although these were mediated by other factors such as the level of aggression in the male partner (Leonard and Senchak 1996).

However, if we are to intervene at a tertiary level with the individual perpetrators of intimate partner violence, particularly men who have been convicted of offences against their partner, and we are to hold these men accountable, within a criminal justice framework, then both sociological and family approaches offer limited scope within which to identify specific dynamic criminogenic needs (Andrews and Bonta 1994). Conversely, psychological and criminological research has identified numerous criminogenic needs of domestic violence offenders.

One of the most widely cited risk factors for perpetrating intimate partner violence is the experience, or witnessing, of physical abuse within their family of origin (Reitzel-Jaffe and Wolfe 2001). However, this intergenerational transmission of violence may be mediated by harsh parental discipline, ineffective parenting strategies and wider societal influences (Hotaling and Sugarman, Straus and Smith 1990; 1986; O'Hearn and Margolin 2000; Simons, Johnson and Conger 1995). Interpersonal dependency has been found to be higher in domestically violent, than non-domestically violent, men (Kane Staiger, and Ricciardelli 2000). Factors such as jealousy, poor attachment, poor impulse control and low self-esteem have been identified as elevated among domestic violence offenders (Dutton 1995). Attitudinal characteristics, such as seeing violence as acceptable (Saunders, Lynch, Grayson and Linz 1987) or holding beliefs which condone wife assault (Johnson 1995), have also been found to be important in the aetiology of domestic violence. Alcohol (Eberle 1982), substance abuse (Easton, Swan and Sinha 2000), anger and depression (Mairuo, Cahn, Vitaliano, Wagner and Zegree 1988) have all been identified as being linked with domestic violence.

Not all offenders exhibit all of these deficits and it has been suggested that there may be as many differences within groups of domestic violence offenders as between them and other groups. This has led to the exploration of potential sub-groupings or typologies of domestic violence offender.

Are there different types of domestic violence offender?

It is widely accepted that domestic violence offenders are a highly heterogeneous group (Hamberger *et al.* 1996; Tweed and Dutton 1998). In their theoretical typology, Holtzworth-Munroe and Stuart (1994) report that domestically violent men can be seen as varying on four dimensions. These dimensions are a) severity/frequency of violence; b) generality of the violence; c) psychopathology/personality disorder characteristics and d) distal/proximal antecedents to the violence. Three clearly discernible types of DV offender were hypothesised to exist depending on the extent to which each dimension identified was applicable. Family only perpetrators who were found to display low levels of marital violence, low extramarital violence, low depression, low substance misuse and moderate anger; Generally violent/antisocial perpetrators who were found to exhibit moderate/high marital violence, high extra familial violence, high substance misuse, low depression coupled with high anger and psychopathic characteristics as indicated by aspects of the MCMI-III (Millon 1994); Dysphoric/borderline perpetrators were found to display moderate/high marital violence, low/moderate extra family violence and criminal involvement, moderate substance misuse and high depression and anger.[4]

Holtzworth-Munroe and Stuart emphasise the potential benefits of matching treatment to type and offender heterogeneity has been found to have an impact upon treatment success (Dutton, Bodnarchuk, Kropp, Hart and Ogloff 1997; Saunders 1996). However, despite the support for this typology (Holtzworth-Munroe *et al.* 2000; Waltz, Babcock, Jacobson and Gottman 2000) we do not know to what extent these findings are applicable to UK populations.

Work funded by the Home Office is underway to explore the characteristics and criminogenic needs of domestic violence offenders in the UK.[5] This data will be available for early 2003 and should help practitioners in the UK develop our understanding and practice and identify how applicable some of the North American theories and interventions are in a British context.

As this brief review has shown, there are a variety of approaches to understanding domestic violence. The range of data is as wide as the range of theories. The 'evidence' gathered is as much a feature of the focus of a particular project, as it is the strength of any one level of theory. Despite this, we are now much more informed about domestic violence than previously. Indeed, some have even attempted to build integrated theories linking the levels of influence and explanation, suggesting that there are a number of influences on individuals and to understand, we need to incorporate all levels. For example, a nested ecological model has been applied to domestic violence (Dutton, D. 1994; Dutton, M. 1996; Edleson and Tolman 1992). This approach suggests that there are at least five different levels which all interact and affect whether domestic violence is a potential outcome. These levels are:

1 Individual level that considers a person's childhood socialisation, past experiences and personal perceptions of these.

2 Microsystem level that captures the immediate situation such as family, workplace, relationships, and so on.

3 Mesosystem level that involves interactions between an individual's microsystems.

4 Exosystem level that entails the structures and systems of the society one lives in.

5 Macrosystem level that involves the larger background of group history, culture and ethnicity. (Edleson and Tolman 1992)

The ecological approach is the start of a move which could address many of the issues discussed previously in this chapter and perhaps resolve some of the difficulties encountered by those who have previously sought a single factor explanation for this complex problem. One benefit of this type of approach is that it suggests interventions at multiple levels of social organisation. It therefore avoids the implications that only one response might provide an appropriate solution.

We would suggest that there are still debates as to how these levels interact. Further, that we must be clear about the message we give if we adopt a multi-level approach to explain domestic violence. Our concern is that if we are not clear about these interactions, we could fall into the trap that pathologises domestic violence and fail to hold men accountable. However, there is a way of conceptualising a multi-level approach which allows us to acknowledge the influence of factors such as socio-economic status, alcohol, personality disorder but also identifies one of the root causes as being societal structure. This blending of levels sometimes referred to as 'theory knitting' is a current theme in forensic psychological literature.

If patriarchy creates the conditions under which all men are potential perpetrators, yet many men do not offend, due to social, interpersonal or individual buffers, then we can see problems such as individual pathology, alcohol or substance abuse and so on, as breaking buffers that prevent domestic violence, rather than being the root causes. This is important in relation to changing men, as again, it would suggest that intervention at a variety of levels would be both appropriate and necessary for effective reduction of domestic violence.

Interventions

The dominant approach to domestic violence in the UK in the 1970s was to provide support for women and children to enable them to leave the violent relationship. Non-governmental organisations such as the Women's Aid Federation have been highly influential in establishing that there is a need for adequate provision and in seeking funds for those. Later developments have included the creation of many a 'domestic violence forum' throughout the UK. These groups have aimed to increase understanding and share best practice across the various agencies for whom domestic violence is relevant. The fora typically involve police, local authorities, housing, education departments, probation, health and so on. Much innovative and positive work has been carried out. In addition to these, a variety of alternative responses have been sought, from changes in the civil courts that allow a wider range of people to initiate proceedings to remove violent men from a house (Home Office 1999), to changes in police practice which encourage police to gather a wider range of evidence at the scene of a domestically violent incident which would then allow them to proceed with a prosecution without a victim if necessary. (For example, the use of Polaroid cameras in West Somerset, or the Brighton and Hove Intimidated Witness Support Service, see Home Office 2002). Professionals working in areas like health, housing or education are also adopting policies which will work towards enhancing the safety of women and children and avoid penalising them for having been in, choosing to remain in or choosing to leave a violent relationship (Home Office 1999). These developments are positive, but there is a great deal still to change as despite these initiatives, recent work has shown that professionals in the criminal justice system and in other areas continue to work with a stereotyped view of domestic violence. Their views affect their decisions as to how seriously to treat this type of offending and how to deal with the offenders, placing women and children at risk (Gilchrist and Blissett 2002).

One of the major interventions developed, has been that of the domestic violence perpetrator programme. It is on these programmes that this part of the chapter will focus, but the need to develop a range of responses and the need to maintain victim/survivor safety at the heart of all of those developments is something we support.

As the range of interventions developed in North America has been so influential in the UK, and as there is a dearth of information as to the effectiveness of provision here, data on the evaluation of North American programmes will be reviewed first. Subsequently, current approaches and outcome studies in the UK will be considered. It is hoped that by adopting this approach, the reader will feel able to adopt an informed critical view when considering appropriate future developments for the UK.

North American interventions with perpetrators

There are three dominant approaches to perpetrator intervention across the States: feminist psycho-educational group programmes, couple counselling and psychological approaches. These different approaches are first described, then the evaluation literature is briefly reviewed.

Pro-feminist groups

Many of the US programmes were influenced by feminist approaches to domestic violence. In 1986, it was estimated that 80 per cent of batterer programmes were 'pro-feminist' in orientation (Healey et al. 1998). One of the most influential exemplars of a pro-feminist approach is the Duluth model, which is a psycho-educational perpetrator group, with concurrent support for women and children. The original group was developed in Duluth, Minnesota and the group formed part of a co-ordinated community response to domestic violence. This group built upon information from women survivors of domestic violence to develop an educational programme designed to make men aware that they had been socialised into particular views and expectations which led on to feelings of entitlement which in turn linked to their use of violence and abuse.

Some of the key features of this type of programme are that men were held accountable for their abuse, they were challenged about underlying patriarchal views which drive their offending and the material was delivered in a didactic and confrontational style. It is held that this will allow men to change.

The strength of the Duluth model is that it does not allow victim-blaming, minimisation or denial, it holds the perpetrator accountable for his actions, it recognises the influence of culture on the violence and so reflects what the statistics tell us about domestic violence. It resonates with women's experiences and it does make it clear that there is an element of choice in many men's offending.

However, critics of this gender-influenced approach suggest that a feminist approach over-predicts domestic violence in society so cannot be justified. It also fails to identify specific issues for families or individuals that link into their own particular offending. The Duluth model may also be criticised for not incorporating what we know about effective methods of enabling and encouraging change into the model, for assuming that men will change purely through exposure to new ideas, and for assuming that it is culturally driven attitudinal problems which drive offending for all men. Also, many who have attempted to replicate the Duluth model have only replicated the perpetrator intervention and some support for women, rather than the community intervention. So, much of the strength of the original Duluth model may have been lost.

Couple counselling

Alternative approaches to intervention also developed in the USA, for example, the family systems model, which approaches individual problems with violence as being part of a dysfunctional system, in this case the family. It is the interaction that creates the violence, not the individual. The intervention of choice for proponents of this type of approach is couple counselling and the family systems approach would focus on promoting positive interpersonal skills for both parties to promote safety and reduce conflict.

The benefits are seen as being the focus on positives within the relationship but the negatives are seen as being that this approach does not hold violent partners accountable for their actions, the victims may not be safe to express themselves within the counselling sessions, and the sessions may inadvertently replicate power imbalances from the relationship. There is a greater potential for counsellors in this setting to collude with male perpetrators, minimising their offending, blaming the victim and not honestly reflecting the reality of the abuse.

There are still advocates of this type of approach and some very good practitioners in the UK who adopt this model, for example Reading Safer Families, but in general this approach is not currently favoured. Because of safety concerns, fears of therapist collusion and victim blaming, the majority of states in the US actively discourage the use of family therapies (Austin and Dankwort 1999; Healey, Smith and O'Sullivan 1998).

Psychologically informed interventions

A third approach, reflecting the three levels of theory, is the psychological approach. This has generally been seen as locating offending in individual psychopathology and holding that early child-hood trauma or personality disorder predisposes certain individuals to violence. Two types of psychological approach have dominated with either psychodynamic or cognitive-behavioural interventions being common. Psychodynamic approaches have used both individual and group-work formats whilst cognitive-behavioural interventions have tended to be delivered in groups.

The psychodynamic approach claims to address the underlying motivations for aggression and violence thereby leading to long-term change, whereas the cognitive-behavioural approach is situated in the present and is proffered as being capable of identifying patterns of problematic behaviour for individuals that can then be changed and replaced with non-abusive alternatives (Healey et al. 1998).

Critics of both psychological approaches suggest that locating the problem with individuals fails to recognise the structural component to offending and merely pathologises or medicalises the problem. These approaches have also been criticised as they can allow individuals to deny responsibility for their offending: psychodynamic approaches allowing individuals to sit back and wait to be cured rather than choosing to change or could allow men to fail to see the links between culturally driven expectations, situationally specific violence and abuse (i.e. only at home) and their behaviour.[6]

Alternative, but not widely recognised, approaches have been those of anger-management groups and self-help groups. Anger management groups have been criticised for failing to recognise that domestic violence is often not about being out of control, but rather of using abuse to re-establish or maintain control. Also, that men who are only abusive towards their female partners do not have a generalised anger problem, but they do have other deficits which this type of programme will not address. A further issue with anger management, is that it could send the wrong message to professionals and partners alike, as men who are domestically violent, without anger problems, who undertake this type of work will be no safer than if they did nothing (*ibid.*).

Self-help groups founded on principles similar to groups like Alcoholics Anonymous have run in the States. Again, they have been criticised as having the potential for collusion, not having clear change mechanisms and not being appropriate unless as part of a relapse prevention package that would protect women during their most vulnerable times (Healey *op cit.* 1998).

Interventions with perpetrators in the UK

In the UK there was some concern about working with men at all, and diverting critical resources away from the women and children. However, it became recognised that it was impossible to stop domestic violence without changing the perpetrators. Thus, the perpetrator programme became seen as an appropriate intervention. Programmes from the United States heavily influenced the early programmes in the UK, but did not all take the same approach. DVIP in London adopts a pro-feminist, but eclectic approach, being influenced both by Gestaltist group-work approaches and adopting some cognitive-behavioural techniques. 'CHANGE' in Scotland was developed as a pro-feminist programme (Dobash *et al.* 2000). It was also influenced by general developments in intervention at that time, hence the inclusion of motivational techniques and the adoption of some psychological foci, for example: looking at thoughts, feelings and emotions and identifying individual triggers for violence (Morran 2002).

Overall, pro-feminist treatment models are the most widely used in the UK (Scourfield and Dobash 1999). Domestic violence is seen as being a product of societal and systemic inequalities and the definitions include financial, sexual, physical and emotional abuse of women by men (Pence and Paymar 1993). These groups typically also incorporate some cognitive behavioural techniques and are delivered using a group work format. Using the 'power and control wheel' model of domestic violence, men are encouraged to accept responsibility for their violence, and are educated about egalitarian relationship skills (Cunningham *et al.* 1998).

Do these programmes work?

The 'what works' debate in the UK has identified cognitive behavioural programmes as being more effective and that there are certain 'quality' aspects of intervention which also affect effectiveness, for example, programme integrity and so on (McGuire 1985). In terms of measuring effectiveness of tackling domestic violence, the debates have mirrored the general debate, suffering from similar limitations in terms of experimental rigour and issues such as definitions of success, appropriate follow-up periods and appropriate measures of change. But, there are also further debates about what the appropriate outcome for a domestic violence programme, should be: reduction of violence? Can this be enough? Does it make any difference if the abuse only occurs once every six months rather than once every month? Is cessation of physical violence enough? If a man has beaten his partner up once and then stops, but the threat is always there, is her quality of life enhanced in any way? Can programmes aim to transform offenders into 'accountable men'? Can one justify imposing one particular set of standards and beliefs, which go well beyond 'no violence', on individuals from a range of cultures and backgrounds?

Hamberger and Hastings (1993) conducted a broad review of published studies evaluating interventions with perpetrators of domestic violence and suggest that it is almost impossible to say whether these programmes work. They identified problems with small sample sizes, non-random assignment to groups, no control groups, attrition, inadequate specification, differential follow-ups and outcome measures, inappropriate statistical analyses and lack of treatment of anomalous findings and suggested that this meant the area remained unclear. The studies they reviewed provided variable information about effects of treatment, some identifying recidivism rates for both treated and untreated groups, some identifying only recidivism rates for treated offenders and some did not report the effects in this way. It appeared that one could claim that certain programmes resulted in a 0 recidivism rate, whilst others only found that their completers had a reported recidivism rate of between 33–41 per cent and the drop-outs had a recidivism rate of between 46–48 per cent (Hamberger and Hastings 1993: 209).

Healey et al. (1998) produced a far more restricted review of the effectiveness of treatment programmes and they have suggested that the 'treatment effect' of perpetrator programmes could be between .946 (Dutton et al. 1986) and 0.108 (Dobash et al. 1996). They also examined research results of projects they termed 'true experiments'. The two reports here would suggest the effect size of perpetrator intervention could range from .287 (Davis and Taylor 1997) to 0.537 (Palmer, Brown and Barrera 1992). A study by Gondolf, evaluating a number of pro-grammes, suggests that the recidivism rates for those completing programmes are similar to those for men who drop out at the start and that the length and content of the programme had very little effect (Gondolf 1997, in Healey 1998). They also reviewed a study by Harrell (1991) whose rigorous research produced findings which suggested that those undertaking batterer intervention actually recidivated at a higher level than those in the control group. Despite this, they concluded that the majority of evaluations have found 'modest but statistically significant reductions in men participating in batterer interventions' (Healey *et al.* 1998, p8). This concurs with a review by Edleson and Tolman who concluded that the percentage of successful outcomes range from 53 per cent to 85 per cent and suggested that as this is across different programmes, and different evaluation methods, there is some favourable evidence for perpetrator programmes (Edleson and Tolman 1992).

Research results from Canada suggest that different programmes had very similar effects on recidivism rates with those who had completed any of the four treatment programmes (humanistic/existential, cognitive/behavioural, feminist psycho-educational and eclectic) all offending at a similar rate of around 17 per cent for a violent offence. This study found that the programme with the weakest programme implementation resulted in the highest recidivism rates, suggesting that it may be the 'quality' of the intervention provision, rather than the content or theoretical orientation, which is more important (Hanson and Wallace-Carpretta 2000).

Further, recent research in Canada has suggested a similar recidivism rate for three programmes evaluated, estimating between 13 per cent and 19 per cent and a combined recidivism rate after one year of 16 per cent, a range of 18 per cent–26 per cent and a combined rate of 23 per cent at two years and between 23 per cent and 33 per cent and a combined recidivism rate of 28 per cent at three years, for programme completers (Kropp and Bodnarchuk 2001). Again, this suggests that the content may be less important overall than the fact of treatment. However, there are further issues to consider.

Some of the emphasis has shifted from trying to establish whether groups 'work' to answering a slightly different question, 'which groups work best for which type of perpetrator? Further, what do we mean by "work"?' Another current issue is that we need more, good research into actual deficits shared by batterers and that we should use this knowledge to enhance the programmes which have demonstrated a small positive effect.

UK programmes and do they work?

Only three published evaluations of British domestic violence offender treatment programmes exist: Burton, Regan and Kelly 1998; Dobash *et al.* 2000; Skyner and Waters 1999.

Burton *et al.* evaluated the Violence Prevention Programme in London. This is a highly respected group which combines work with the men with a strong parallel support package for the partners as part of the DVIP initiative (see earlier). They found that the men who completed the programme were described as being less violent by their partners at the end of the first stage: 27 per cent were described as non-violent, 53 per cent had reduced their violence a lot and 25 per cent had reduced their violence a little and it was held that the programme had a positive effect.

The Dobash study of the CHANGE and Lothian Domestic Violence Probation Project compared men mandated to a domestic violence perpetrator group with men mandated to an alternative criminal justice sanction and found that the men who completed the programmes were much less likely subsequently to be violent (67 per cent at one year follow up compared with 25 per cent of the other criminal justice sanction group). If they were violent, then there were fewer incidents and the abuse within the relationship was reduced. (Dobash *et al.* 2000) Again it was held that the programme had a positive effect.

Skyner and Waters (1999) explored changes in offenders' attitudes to their offending following the Cheshire probation intervention and found statistically significant changes following this programme. This was also seen as having a positive effect.

However, these evaluations suffered the same set of limitations and problems as those from the States and the issues about evaluation remain (for a discussion of this see Bowen, Brown and Gilchrist 2002). What we can say is that the UK appears to follow a similar pattern to North America with the available limited data suggesting that these programmes do have a small significant effect. However, the groups evaluated here have been generally cognitive-behavioural and feminist informed and we know that there are many groups in the UK which do not run along those lines. We do not know what type of group is more effective, nor whether mandated or voluntary groups work best, but we might suggest that there may be less cause for optimism for the psychodynamic interventions in the UK linking in with the general lack of 'proof' that these type of interventions are effective[7] (Scourfield and Dobash 1999).

We can say that we need much more theoretically informed research in this area and await with interest the evaluations being conducted at the University of Birmingham and by the Home Office.[8]

Conclusions

The many debates in the area of intimate partner violence may not have been resolved but in the UK practitioners and some academics appear to have reached a tacit agreement around some central issues. Many of the debates as to the nature and direction of domestic violence are fuelled by claims from the US of evidence portraying domestic violence as gender neutral. This debate seems to arise from the two extremes in the States using different definitions of domestic violence (the Johnson distinction), using different tools to collect data and collecting the data from different populations.

The most common term used in the UK is 'domestic violence' and this is generally defined as violence and abuse by men directed at their ex- or current partner. This would be seen as fitting with Johnson's 'patriarchal terrorism' rather than coming under the 'common couple violence' category. The vast majority of data in the UK supports a gendered definition of domestic violence as victim surveys, official statistics, medical records and so on all indicate that men tend to be the perpetrators and women and children the victims.

The UK has followed the lead from North America, now seeing intervention with men as a critical component in the bid to reduce domestic violence and increase the safety of women and children in the UK. There have been a range of interventions available which have ranged from the Duluth informed feminist psycho-educational programmes, through family systems based couple counselling to group and individual psychological intervention and even anger management and self-help groups. Many of these approaches are out of favour due to concerns about the safety of women and children whose partners engage in such work and concerns about the underlying conceptualisation of domestic violence either explicitly stated or implicit within the programme focus and goals. The current interventions of choice in the US tend to be either Duluth programmes or feminist and psychology informed groups (e.g. EMERGE, AMEND).

Evaluations from the States suggest that these programmes do have a small but significant treatment effect, but there are concerns about how to deal with men from non-mainstream cultural backgrounds, how to deal with homosexual and female perpetrators and whether 'standard', 'one size fits all' programmes are appropriate. Many areas now advocate careful screening of participants for the groups, selecting only those at an appropriate level of risk and with deficits addressed by the particular programme, e.g. attitudinal issues, but excluding participants who would not benefit from the group or who would be detrimental to the group process. Some areas now mandate men to concurrent substance abuse treatment or individual counselling, recognizing that some perpetrators have a range of issues that must be addressed in order to reduce their risk. Some are looking at developing a range of programmes appropriate for different types and seriousness of abuser.

In the UK, perpetrator programmes have become quite common. Many areas now mandate men to domestic violence perpetrator programmes and a number of areas have 'voluntary' or 'partner mandated' programmes available for these men. The three evaluations currently available suggest that these groups are of benefit to the men who remain in treatment, but the effect on dropouts is less clear. However, these evaluations do suffer from very low participant numbers and they were not conducted along strict evaluation lines, so any outcomes must be considered as tentative. Also, we need to remain aware that, as the batterer programmes only have a small effect, they can only ever be a partial solution to the problem of abusive men. We need to continue to highlight the other areas, which can be developed to enhance the safety of women and children. For example, Babcock and Taillade (2000) suggest that police, prosecution and strong criminal justice sanctions are all necessary for effective change. We would go further and suggest that civil and social responses are also required to support this process.

The government has recently invested a great deal of money via the violence reduction programme and the police research programme into researching the needs of women and children and the effectiveness of new police, prosecution and support packages across the country. They have also funded research into serious violent offending in the UK, via the ESRC Homicide programme, the ESRC Violence Programme and Home Office directed research into criminogenic need in domestic violence offenders. This research suggests that perpetrators in the UK have both general and specific cognitive and attitudinal deficits indicating that a feminist informed, cognitive behavioural programme might be the most appropriate intervention for domestic violence offenders, at present.

Ongoing research evaluating the outcome for Duluth and cognitive behavioural interventions within the probation service will add to this knowledge. Similarly, a probation funded project is being conducted in the West Midlands examining the effectiveness of a feminist influenced domestic violence programme and this will also provide valuable information as to the nature of domestic violence in the UK and appropriate intervention. The prison service have been developing programmes for serious offenders, including spousal homicide offenders and exploring programmes and approaches from North America for possible implementation in the UK. We are starting to know more about what UK domestic violence offenders look like and what interventions might be effective, but we need to refine this knowledge so that we can start to identify what type of domestic violence offenders exist; start to develop a coherent and multi-level theory as to the causes of domestic violence; start to identify levels of risk posed by different types of offender and start to develop a range of interventions which can then be matched to the needs and level of risk posed by the offender. We have made a convincing start, but we need to maintain the current momentum.

Notes

1   The British Crime Survey suggest that only 12 per cent of incidents are reported to the police. On this basis the number of incidents of domestic violence for the year 2000 would be 4, 750,000.
2   Some men will be convicted for acts of public disorder or criminal damage, threats to kill and even harassment, which may not include direct violence but this is not as common as convictions for violence.
3   e.g. Dobash *et al.* (2000), information from partners of men mandated to intervention, Pence and Paymar (1993), Duluth data from female survivors in contact with support services.
4   They also found a fourth group of men who fell between the FO and the GVA groups. They named this group the Low-level antisocial group (LLA) (Holtzworth-Munroe *et al.* 2000). Holtzworth-Monroe *et al.* explained the emergence of a fourth type as being linked to their research drawing on men from community samples and clinical samples.
5   The work is being undertaken by Gilchrist, E. *et al.* at Coventry University and Birmingham University under a contract with the Home Office which commenced in 2001.
6   It is noted that many of the cognitive-behavioural programmes are actually 'feminist informed' or 'pro-feminist' so many of these potential problems do not arise.
7   The very nature of psychodynamic therapy means that 'evaluation' is problematic and difficult to quantify.

8 Current work being conducted by Erica Bowen and Elizabeth Gilchrist at Birmingham University and Clive Hollin and Emma Palmer at Arnold Lodge, will develop our knowledge in this area.

References

Alvazzi del Frate and Patrignani, A. (1995) *Women's Victimisations in Developing Countries*. Rome: UNICRI.

Andrews, D.A. and Bonta, J. (1994) *The psychology of criminal conduct*. Vancouver: Anderson Publishing Co.

Archer, J. (2000) 'Sex differences in aggression between heterosexual partners: A meta-analytic review', *Psychological Bulletin*, 126 (5): 651–80.

Austin, J.B. and Dankwort, J. (1999) 'Standards for Batterer Programs: A Review and Analysis', *Journal of Interpersonal Violence*, 14 (2): 152–68.

Babcock, J.C. and LaTaillade, J.J. (2000) 'Evaluating interventions for men who batter', in J.P. Vincent and E.N. Jouriles (eds) *Domestic Violence: Guidelines for research informed practice*. London: Jessica Kingsley Publishers.

Bhatt, R.V. (1998) 'Domestic violence and substance abuse', *International Journal of Gynaecology and Obstetrics*, 63: s25–s31.

Blackburn, R. (1993) *The Psychology of Criminal Conduct: Theory, Research and Practice*. London: Wiley.

Bowen, E., Brown, L. and Gilchrist, E. (2002) 'Evaluating probation based offender programmes for domestic violence perpetrators: A pro-feminist approach', *The Howard Journal*, 41 (3): 221–36.

Burton, S., Regan, L. and Kelly, L. (1998) *Supporting Women and Challenging Men: Lessons from the Domestic Violence Intervention Project*. University of Bristol: Policy Press.

Busey, T. (1993) 'Women defendants and reactive survival syndrome', *The Catalyst*, Winter: 6–7.

Cunningham, A., Jaffe, P.G., Baker, L., Dick, T., Malla, S., Mazaheri, N. and Poisson, S. (1998) *Theory Derived Explanations of Male Violence Against Female Partners: Literature Update and Related Implications for Treatment and Evaluation*. London: London Family Court Clinic.

Dobash, R., Cavanagh, K., Dobash, R. and Lewis, R. (2000) 'Domestic violence programmes: A framework for change', *The Probation Journal*: 18–29.

Dobash, R.E. and Dobash, R.P. (2000) 'Evaluating criminal justice interventions for domestic violence', *Crime and Delinquency*, 46 (2): 252–70.

Dobash, R.P., Dobash, R.E., Cavanagh, K. and Lewis, R. (1999) 'A research evaluation of British programmes for violent men', *Journal of Social Policy*, 28 (2): 205–33.

Dobash, R., Dobash, R., Lewis, R. and Cavanagh, K. (2000) *Changing Violent Men*. London: Sage.

Dobash, R.P., Dobash, R.E., Wilson, M. and Daly, M. (1992) 'The myth of sexual symmetry in marital violence', *Social Problems*, 39 (1): 71–91.

Dutton, D. (1995) *The Domestic Assault of Women*. California: Sage.

Dutton, D.G., Bodnarchuk, M., Kropp, P.R., Hart, S.D. and Ogloff, J. (1997) 'Wife assault treatment and criminal recidivism: An 11-year follow-up', *International Journal of Offender Therapy and Comparative Criminology*, 41: 9–23.

Easton, C., Swan, S. and Sinha, R. (2000) 'Motivation to change substance abuse among offenders of domestic violence', *Journal of Substance Abuse Treatment*, 19: 1–5.

Eberle, P.A. (1982) 'Alcohol and abusers and non-users: A discriminant analysis of differences between two subgroups of batterers', *Journal of Health and Social Behaviour*, 23: 260–71.

Edelson J.L. and Tolman R.M. (1992) *Intervention for Men Who Batter: An ecological approach*. California: Sage.

Gelles, R. (1997) *Intimate Violence in Families*. California: Sage.

Gilchrist, E. and Blissett, J. (2002) 'Magistrates' attitudes to domestic violence and sentencing options', *The Howard Journal*, 41 (4): 347–62.

Gilchrist, E., Johnson, R., Takriti, R., Weston, S., Beech and Kebbell, M. (forthcoming) *Characteristics, offence behaviours and criminogenic needs of domestic violence offenders on probation or referred for a pre-sentence report*. London: FINDINGS, HMSO.

Gondolf, E.W. (1997) 'Batterers' programs: What we know and what we need to know', *Journal of Interpersonal Violence*, 12 (1): 83–98.

Hamberger, L.K. and Hastings, J.E. (1993) 'Court mandated treatment of men who assault their partner: Issues controversies and outcomes', in N.Z. Hilton (ed.) *Legal Responses to Wife Assault: Current Trends and Evaluation*. London: Sage.

Hamberger, L.K., Lohr, J.M., Bonge, D. and Tollin, D.F. (1996) 'A large sample empirical typology of male spouse abusers and its relationship to dimensions of abuse', *Violence and Victims*, 11 (4): 277–91.

Hanson, R.K. and Wallace-Carpretta, S. (2000) *A multi-site study of treatment for abusive men. User Report 2000–05*. Ottowa: Department of the Solicitor General of Canada.

Healey, K., Smith, C. with O'Sullivan, C. (1998) 'Batterer intervention: Program approaches and criminal justice strategies', *Issues and Practices in Criminal Justice Series*. Washington DC: US Dept. of Justice.

Holtzworth-Munroe, A., Meeham, J.C., Herron, K., Rehman, U. and Stuart, G.L. (2000) 'Testing the Holtzworth-Munroe and Stuart (1994) batterer typology', *Journal of Consulting and Clinical Psychology*, 68 (6): 1000–1019.

Holtzworth-Munroe, A. and Stuart, G.L. (1994) 'Typologies of male batterers: Three subtypes and the differences among them', *Psychological Bulletin*, 116 (3): 476–97.

Home Affairs Select Committee (1993) *Government Policy Around Domestic Violence*. London: Crime Police Strategy Unit.

Home Office (1999) *Living Without Fear*. London: Central Office of Information.

Home Office (2002) Crime Reduction Programme: Violence Against Women Initiative, www.crimereduction.gov.uk

Hotaling, G.T. and Sugarman, D.B. (1986) 'An analysis of risk markers in husband to wife violence: The current state of knowledge', *Violence and Victims*, 1 (2): 101–24.

Johnson, M. (1995) 'Two forms of violence against women', *Journal of Marriage and the Family*, 57: 283–94.

Kane, T.A., Staiger, P.K. and Ricciardelli, L.A. (2000) 'Male domestic violence, attitudes, aggression and interpersonal dependency', *Journal of Interpersonal Violence*, 15 (1) 16–29.

Kropp, P.R. and Bodnarchuk, M. (2001*) Evaluation of Three Assaultative Men's Treatment Programs – Summary Report*. Vancouver: The British Columbia Institute Against Family Violence.

Kropp, P.R. and Hart, S.D. (2000) 'The Spousal Assault Risk Assessment (SARA) Guide: Reliability and validity in adult male offenders', *Law and Human Behaviour*, 24 (1): 101–17.

Leonard, K.E. and Senchak, M. (1996) 'Prospective prediction of marital aggression within newly wed couples', *Journal of Abnormal Psychology*, 105: 369–80.

Levinson, D. (1989) *Family in Cross-cultural Perspective*. Beverly Hills: Sage.

Magdol, L., Moffitt, T.E., Caspi, A. and Silva, P.A. (1998) 'Developmental antecedents of partner abuse: A prospective-longitudinal study', *Journal of Abnormal Psychology*, 107 (3): 375–89.

Maiuro, R., Cahn, T., Vitaliano, P., Wagner, B. and Zegree, J. (1988) 'Anger hostility and depression in domestically violent versus generally violent assaultative men and non-violent control subjects', *Journal of Consulting and Clinical Psychology*, 56: 17–23.

McGuire, J. (1985) *What Works: reducing reoffending guidelines from research and practice*. Chichester: John Wiley and Sons.

Millon, T. (1994) *Millon Clinical Multiaxial Inventory* – III. Minnaepolis, MN: National Computer Systems.

Mirrlees-Black (1999) *Domestic Violence: findings from a new British Crime Survey self-completion questionnaire. Home Office Research Study* 191. London: Home Office.

Mirrlees-Black, C., Mayhew, P. and Percy, A. (1996) *The 1996 British Crime Survey: England & Wales. Home Office Statistics Bulletin*. London: HMSO.

Morran, D. (2002) Personal communication, 12 November.

MVA (2000) *Violence in Scotland: Findings from the 2000 Scottish Crime Survey*. Edinburgh: Scottish Executive Central Research Unit.

O'Hearn, H.G. and Margolin, G. (2000) 'Men's attitudes condoning marital aggression: A moderator between family of origin abuse and aggression against female partners', *Cognitive Therapy and Research*, 24 (2): 159–74.

Pence and Paymar (1993) *Education Groups for Men Who Batter: The Duluth model*. New York: Springer.

Pizzey, E. and Forbes, A. (1974) *Scream Quietly or the Neighbours will Hear*. Harmondsworth: Penguin.

Reitzel-Jaffe, D. and Wolfe, D.A. (2001) 'Predictors of relationship abuse among young men', *Journal of Interpersonal Violence*, 16 (2): 99–115.

Saunders, D.G. (1996) 'Feminist-cognitive-behavioral and process-psychodynamic treatments for men who batter: Interactions of abuser traits and treatment model', *Violence and Victims*, 4: 393–414.

Saunders, D.G., Lynch, A.B., Grayson, M. and Linz, D. (1987) 'The inventory of beliefs about wife beating: the construction and initial validation of a measure of beliefs and attitudes', *Violence and Victims*, 2 (1): 39–57.

Scourfield, J.B. and Dobash, R.P. (1999) 'Programmes for violent men: Recent developments in the UK', *The Howard Journal*, 38 (2): 128–43.

Simons, R.L., Wu, C., Johnson, C. and Conger, R.D. (1995) 'A test of various perspectives on the intergenerational transmission of domestic violence', *Criminology*, 33 (1): 14–171.

Skyner, D.R. and Waters, J. (1999) 'Working with perpetrators of domestic violence to protect women and children: a partnership between Cheshire Probation Service and the NSPCC', *Child Abuse Review*, 8: 46–54.

Stanko, E. (2000) A Day to Count, www.domesticviolencedatasource.org

Stets (1995) 'Modelling control in relationships', *Journal of Marriage and the Family*, 57 (2): 487–501.

Straus, M. and Gelles, R. (eds) (1990) *Violence in American Families*. New Brunswick, NJ: Transaction Publishers.

Tolman, R.M. and Bennett, L.W. (1990) 'A review of the quantitative research on men who batter', *Journal of Interpersonal Violence*, 5 (1): 87–118.

Tweed, R.G. and Dutton, D.G. (1998) 'A comparison of impulsive and instrumental subgroups of batterers', *Violence and Victims*, 13 (3): 217–30.

van Dijk, J., Mayhew, P. and Killias, M. (1994) *Experiences of Crime Across the World*. Deventer: Kluwer.

Waltz, J., Babcock, J.C., Jacobson, N.S. and Gottman, J.M. (2000) 'Testing a typology of batterers', *Journal of Consulting and Clinical Psychology*, 68 (4): 658–69.

Wolfus, B. and Bierman, R. (1996) 'An evaluation of a group treatment program for incarcerated male batterers', *International Journal of Offender Therapy and Comparative Criminology*, 40 (4): 318–33.

Chapter 13

Effective programmes to prevent delinquency

Brandon C. Welsh, University of Massachusetts Lowell and David P. Farrington, University of Cambridge

The main aim of this chapter is to summarise briefly some of the most effective programmes for preventing delinquency and later offending whose effectiveness has been demonstrated in high quality evaluation research. Only programmes with outcome measures of delinquency, antisocial behaviour, or disruptive child behaviour are included; programmes were not included if they only had outcome measures of risk factors such as IQ or poor parenting. Some of the programmes did not have a direct measure of delinquency, because this would have required a long-term follow-up. However, there is considerable continuity between disruptive child behaviour and juvenile delinquency (e.g. Farrington 1998). Therefore, programmes that have immediate effects on disruptive child behaviour are likely to have long-term effects on delinquency and later offending.

Within the constraints of this chapter, it is not feasible to present an exhaustive or systematic review of interventions to prevent crime (Farrington and Petrosino, 2000). Systematic reviews are much more rigorous than more traditional narrative reviews of the literature. Whereas traditional reviews rarely include detailed information about why studies were included or excluded, systematic reviews provide explicit and transparent information about the criteria used for including or excluding studies. Systematic reviews focus on studies that have the highest methodological quality and use the most rigorous methods possible to combine results from different studies statistically to draw conclusions about what works. These reviews contain methods and results sections and are reported with the same level of detail that characterises high quality reports of original research. They include detailed summary tables of key features of studies such as design, sample sizes and effect sizes.

We will describe some of the most important and best-evaluated programmes, with special reference to programmes that have carried out a cost-benefit analysis. The conclusion from the Perry project (discussed later) that, for every dollar spent on the programme, seven dollars were saved in the long term (Schweinhart *et al.* 1993) proved particularly convincing to policy makers. The monetary costs of crime are enormous. For example, Brand and Price (2000) estimated that they totalled £60 billion in England and Wales in 1999. There are tangible costs to victims, such as replacing stolen goods and repairing damage, and intangible costs that are harder to quantify, such as pain, suffering and a reduced quality of life. There are costs to the government or taxpayer for police, courts, prisons, crime prevention activities and so on. There are also costs to offenders – for example, those associated with being in prison or losing a job.

To the extent that crime prevention programmes are successful in reducing crime, they will have benefits. These benefits can be quantified in monetary terms according to the reduction in the monetary costs of crime. Other benefits may accrue from reducing the costs of associated social problems such as unemployment, divorce, educational failure, drug addiction, welfare dependency and so on. The widely accepted finding that offending is part of a larger syndrome of antisocial behaviour (West and Farrington 1977) is good news, because the benefits of a crime prevention programme can be many and varied. The monetary benefits of a programme can be compared with its monetary costs to determine the benefit:cost ratio. Surprisingly few cost-benefit analyses of crime prevention programmes have ever been carried out (Welsh and Farrington 2000; Welsh *et al.* 2001).

This chapter is organised around two main categories of programmes to prevent delinquency: 1) individual and family programmes, and 2) peer, school and community programmes.

Individual and family programmes

Four types of programmes are particularly successful: parent education (in the context of home visiting), parent management training, child skills training, and pre-school intellectual enrichment programmes (Farrington and Welsh 1999, 2002). Generally, the programmes are targeted on the risk factors of poor parental child-rearing, supervision or discipline (general parent education or parent management training), high impulsivity, low empathy and self-centredness (child skills training) and low intelligence and attainment (pre-school programmes).

General parent education

In the most famous intensive home visiting programme, David Olds and his colleagues (1986) in Elmira (NY) randomly allocated 400 mothers either to receive home visits from nurses during pregnancy, or to receive visits both during pregnancy and during the first two years of life, or to a control group who received no visits. Each visit lasted about one and a quarter hours, and the mothers were visited on average every two weeks. The home visitors gave advice about prenatal and postnatal care of the child, about infant development, and about the importance of proper nutrition and avoiding smoking and drinking during pregnancy.

The results of this experiment showed that the postnatal home visits caused a decrease in recorded child physical abuse and neglect during the first two years of life, especially by poor, unmarried, teenage mothers; four per cent of visited versus 19 per cent of non-visited mothers of this type were guilty of child abuse or neglect. This last result is important, partly because children who are physically abused or neglected have an enhanced likelihood of becoming violent offenders later in life (Widom 1989). In a 15-year follow-up, the main focus was on lower class, unmarried mothers. Among these mothers, those who received prenatal and postnatal home visits had fewer arrests than those who received prenatal visits or no visits (Olds *et al.* 1997). Also, children of those mothers who received prenatal and/or postnatal home visits had less than half as many arrests as children of mothers who received no visits (Olds *et al.* 1998).

Several economic analyses show that the benefits of this programme outweighed its costs for the lower class unmarried mothers. The most important are by Karoly and colleagues (1998) and Aos and his colleagues (2001). However, both measured only a limited range of benefits. Karoly measured only benefits to the government or taxpayer (welfare, education, employment and criminal justice), not benefits to crime victims consequent upon reduced crimes. Aos measured only benefits to crime victims (tangible and intangible, based on Miller *et al.* 1996) and in criminal justice savings, excluding other types of benefits (e.g. welfare, education and employment). Nevertheless, both reported a benefit-to-cost ratio greater than 1 for this programme; 4.1 according to Karoly and 3.1 according to Aos. The benefit-to-cost ratio was less than 1 for the low risk part of the sample. This study and other similar evaluations (Kitzman *et al.* 1997; Larson 1980; Stone *et al.* 1988) show that intensive home visiting can help poor, unmarried mothers and reduce later antisocial behaviour of their children.

Pre-school programmes

The most famous pre-school intellectual enrichment programme is the Perry project carried out in Ypsilanti (Michigan) by Schweinhart and Weikart (1980). This was essentially a 'Head Start' programme targeted on disadvantaged African American children. A small sample of 123 children were allocated (approximately at random) to experimental and control groups. The experimental children attended a daily pre-school programme, backed up by weekly home visits, usually lasting two years (covering ages 3–4). The aim of the 'plan-do-review' programme was to provide intellectual stimulation, to increase thinking and reasoning abilities, and to increase later school achievement.

This programme had long-term benefits. Berrueta-Clement et al. (1984) showed that, at age 19, the experimental group was more likely to be employed, more likely to have graduated from high school, more likely to have received college or vocational training, and less likely to have been arrested. By age 27, the experimental group had accumulated only half as many arrests on average as the controls (Schweinhart et al. 1993). Also, they had significantly higher earnings and were more likely to be home-owners. More of the experimental women were married, and fewer of their children were born out of wedlock.

Several economic analyses show that the benefits of this programme outweighed its costs. The benefit-to-cost ratio was 2.1 according to Karoly et al. (1998) and 1.5 according to Aos et al. (1999), but both of these figures are under-estimates. The estimates of Aos et al. (1999) included only tangible, not intangible, victim costs; their later estimates including intangible victim costs (Aos et al. 2001) were based on a meta-analysis of several programmes rather than analysing each programme indi-vidually, so figures are not given for the Perry project alone. The Perry project's own calculation (Barnett 1993) was more comprehensive, including crime and non-crime benefits, intangible costs to victims, and even including projected benefits beyond age 27. This generated the famous benefit-to-cost ratio of 7.2. Most of the benefits (65 per cent) were derived from savings to crime victims. Desirable results were also obtained in other pre-school evaluations (Pagani et al. 1998; Webster-Stratton 1998).

Day care programmes

One of the very few prevention experiments beginning in pregnancy and collecting outcome data on delinquency was the Syracuse (NY) Family Development Research Programme of Lally and his colleagues (1988). The researchers began with a sample of pregnant women (mostly poor African American single mothers) and gave them weekly help with child-rearing, health, nutrition and other problems. In addition, their children received free full-time day care, designed to develop their intellectual abilities, up to age 5. This was not a randomised experiment, but a matched control group was chosen when the children were aged 3.

Ten years later, about 120 treated and control children were followed up to about age 15. Significantly fewer of the treated children (2 per cent as opposed to 17 per cent) had been referred to the juvenile court for delinquency offences, and the treated girls showed better school attendance and school performance. However, the benefit-to-cost ratio of this programme was only 0.3 according to Aos *et al.* (1999). This was largely because of the cost of the programme ($45,000 per child in 1998 dollars, compared with $14,000 for Perry and $7,000 for Elmira); providing free full-time day care up to age 5 was very expensive. Against this, it must be repeated that the Aos *et al.* (1999) benefit-to-cost ratios are under-estimates.

Desirable results were also obtained in a day care intervention in Houston by Johnson and Walker (1987) but not by McCarton *et al.* (1997) in the large-scale Infant Health and Development Program. This programme, implemented in eight sites across the United States, had encouraging results at age 3; however, the experimental and control children were not significantly different in behaviour problems at age 8.

Parent management training

Perhaps the best known method of parent training was developed by Gerald Patterson (1982) in Oregon. Parents were trained to notice what a child is doing, monitor behaviour over long periods, clearly state house rules, make rewards and punishments contingent on the child's behaviour, and negotiate disagreements so that conflicts and crises did not escalate. This treatment was shown to be effective in reducing child stealing and antisocial behaviour over short periods in small-scale studies (Dishion *et al.* 1992; Patterson *et al.* 1982, 1992).

Webster-Stratton and Hammond (1997) evaluated the effectiveness of parent training and child skills training with about 100 Seattle children (average age 5) referred to a clinic because of conduct problems. The children and their parents were randomly allocated to receive either (a) parent training, (b) child skills training, (c) both parent and child training, or (d) to a control group. The skills training aimed to foster prosocial behaviour and interpersonal skills using video modelling, while the parent training involved weekly meetings between parents and therapists for 22–24 weeks. Parent reports and home observations showed that children in all three experimental conditions had fewer behaviour problems than control children, both in an immediate and in a one-year follow-up. There was little difference between the three experimental conditions, although the combined parent and child training condition produced the most significant improvements in child behaviour at the one-year follow-up.

Scott *et al.* (2001) evaluated the Webster-Stratton parent training programme in London. About 140 children aged 3-8 who were referred for antisocial behaviour were allocated to receive parent training or to be in a control group. The programme was successful. According to parent reports, the antisocial behaviour of the experimental children decreased, while that of the control children did not change. Since this programme is relatively cheap (£571 per child for a 12-week programme), it is likely to be cost-effective. Other studies also show that parent training is effective in reducing children's antisocial behavior (e.g. Kazdin *et al.* 1992; Strayhorn and Weidman 1991).

Skills training

Perhaps the best known method of skills training was developed by Ross (e.g. Ross and Ross 1995). This programme aimed to teach people to stop and think before acting, to consider the consequences of their behaviour, to conceptualise alternative ways of solving interpersonal problems, and to consider the impact of their behaviour on other people, especially victims. It included social skills training, lateral thinking (to teach creative problem solving), critical thinking (to teach logical reasoning), values education (to teach values and concern for others), assertiveness training (to teach non-aggressive, socially appropriate ways to obtain desired outcomes), negotiation skills training, inter-personal cognitive problem-solving (to teach thinking skills for solving interpersonal problems), social perspective training (to teach how to recognise and understand other people's feelings), role-playing and modelling (demonstration and practice of effective and acceptable interpersonal behaviour).

Ross carried out his own 'Reasoning and Rehabilitation' programme in Ottawa, and found (in a randomised experiment) that it led to a large decrease in reoffending for a small sample of adult offenders in a short nine-month follow-up period. His training was carried out by probation officers, but he believed that it could be carried out by parents or teachers. This programme has been implemented widely in several different countries, including the United Kingdom. It forms the basis of many accredited cognitive-behavioural programmes used in the UK prison and probation services, including the Pathfinder projects (McGuire 2001). Other skills training programmes have also been successful (e.g. Schochet *et al.* 2000).

As an example, a similar programme, entitled 'Straight Thinking on Probation', was implemented in Glamorgan by Raynor and Vanstone (2001). Offenders who received skills training were compared with similar offenders who received custodial sentences. After one year, offenders who completed the programme had a lower reconviction rate than control offenders (35 per cent as opposed to 49 per cent), although both had the same predicted reconviction rate of 42 per cent. The benefits of the programme seemed to have worn off at the two-year follow-up point, when reconviction rates of experimentals (63 per cent) and controls (65 per cent) were similar to each other and to predicted rates. However, the reconvicted experimentals committed less serious crimes than the reconvicted controls.

Integrated or multiple component programmes are generally more effective than single component ones. The Montreal longitudinal-experimental study combined child skills training and parent training. Tremblay and his colleagues (1995) identified disruptive (aggressive/ hyperactive) boys at age 6, and randomly allocated over 300 of these to experimental or control conditions. Between ages 7 and 9, the experimental group received training designed to foster social skills and self-control. Coaching, peer modelling, role playing and reinforcement contingencies were used in small group sessions on such topics as 'how to help', 'what to do when you are angry' and 'how to react to teasing'. Also, their parents were trained using the parent management training techniques developed by Patterson (1982).

This prevention programme was successful. By age 12, the experimental boys committed less burglary and theft, were less likely to get drunk, and were less likely to be involved in fights than the controls (according to self-reports). Also, the experimental boys had higher school achievement. At every age from 10 to 15, the experimental boys had lower self-reported delinquency scores than the control boys. Interestingly, the differences in antisocial behaviour between experimental and control boys increased as the follow-up progressed. Unfortunately, no cost-benefit analysis of this programme has yet been published; it was included in the Aos *et al.* (2001) analysis of early childhood education but was not presented separately.

Peer, school and community programmes

Three types of programmes are particularly successful: school-based parent and teacher training, school-based anti-bullying curricula and education, and multi-systemic therapy (MST). Generally, the programmes are targeted on the risk factors of poor parenting and poor school performance (school-based parent and teacher training), bullying (school-based anti-bullying), and intra-personal (e.g., cognitive) and systemic (family, peer, school) factors associated with antisocial behaviour (MST).

Peer programmes

There are no outstanding examples of effective intervention programmes for delinquency or later offending based on peer risk factors. The most hopeful programmes involve using high-status conventional peers to teach children ways of resisting peer pressure; this has been effective in reducing drug use (Tobler *et al.* 1999). Also, in a randomised experiment in St Louis, Feldman and his colleagues (1983) showed that placing antisocial adolescents in activity groups dominated by prosocial adolescents led to a reduction in their antisocial behaviour (compared with antisocial adolescents in antisocial groups). This suggests that the influence of prosocial peers can be harnessed to reduce offending.

The most important intervention programme whose success seems to be based mainly on reducing peer risk factors is the Children at Risk programme (Harrell *et al.* 1997), which targeted high risk youths (average age 12) in poor neighbourhoods of five cities across the United States. Eligible youths were identified in schools, and over 670 were randomly assigned to experimental or control groups. The programme was a multiple-component, community-based, prevention strategy targeting risk factors for delinquency, including case management and family counselling, family skills training, tutoring, mentoring, after-school activities and community policing. The programme was different in each neighbourhood.

The initial results of the programme were disappointing, but a one-year follow-up showed that (according to self-reports) experimental youths were less likely to have committed violent crimes and used or sold drugs (Harrell *et al.* 1999). The process evaluation showed that the greatest change was in peer risk factors. Experimental youths associated less often with delinquent peers, felt less peer pressure to engage in delinquency, and had more positive peer support. In contrast, there were few changes in individual, family or community risk factors, possibly linked to the low participation of parents in parent training and of youths in mentoring and tutoring (Harrell *et al.* 1997: 87). In other words, there were problems of implementation of the programme, linked to the serious and multiple needs and problems of the families. No cost-benefit analysis of this programme has yet been carried out, but its relatively low cost ($9,000 per youth) and its targeting of high-risk youths suggest that its benefits may possibly outweigh its costs.

Peer tutoring was also involved in the Quantum Opportunities Programme, which was implemented in five sites across the United States (Hahn 1994, 1999). It aimed to improve the life course opportunities of disadvantaged, at-risk youth during the high school years and included peer tutoring for educational development and adult assistance with life skills, career planning and community service. Participants received cash incentives to stay in the programme, and staff received cash incentives for keeping youth in the programme.

Fifty adolescents aged about 14 were randomly assigned to experimental or control conditions in each site, making an initial sample size of 250. The programme was successful. Experimental adolescents were more likely to graduate from high school (63 per cent versus 42 per cent) and were less likely to be arrested (17 per cent versus 58 per cent). During the six-month follow-up period, experimental adolescents were more likely to have volunteered as a mentor or tutor themselves (28 per cent versus eight per cent) and were less likely to have claimed welfare benefits. Experiments using adult mentors have produced mixed results (Baker *et al.* 1995; O'Donnell *et al.* 1979).

A cost-benefit analysis of the Quantum Opportunities Programme (Hahn 1994) revealed substantial benefits for both the participants and taxpayers. There was a desirable benefit-to-cost ratio of 3.7. Monetary benefits were limited to gains from education and fewer children, with the benefits from fewer children accruing from reduced costs for health and welfare services for teenage mothers. The calculations by Aos *et al.* (2001) yielded a more conservative benefit-to-cost ratio of 1.9.

School programmes

One of the most important school-based prevention experiments was carried out in Seattle by David Hawkins and his colleagues (1991). They implemented a multiple component programme combining parent training, teacher training and child skills training. About 500 first grade children (aged 6) in 21 classes in eight schools were randomly assigned to be in experimental or control classes. The children in the experimental classes received special treatment at home and school which was designed to increase their attachment to their parents and their bonding to the school. Also, they were trained in interpersonal cognitive problem-solving. Their parents were trained to notice and reinforce socially desirable behaviour in a programme called 'Catch them being good'. Their teachers were trained in classroom management, for example to provide clear instructions and expectations to children, to reward children for participation in desired behaviour, and to teach children prosocial (socially desirable) methods of solving problems.

This programme had long-term benefits. O'Donnell et al. (1995) focused on children in low income families and reported that, in the sixth grade (age 12), experimental boys were less likely to have initiated delinquency, while experimental girls were less likely to have initiated drug use. In the latest follow-up, Hawkins et al. (1999) found that, at age 18, the full intervention group (receiving the intervention from grades 1–6) admitted less violence, less alcohol abuse and fewer sexual partners than the late intervention group (grades 5–6 only) or the controls. The benefit-to-cost ratio of this programme according to Aos et al. (2001) was 4.3.

Another important school-based prevention experiment was carried out by Kolvin and his colleagues (1981) in Newcastle-Upon-Tyne. They randomly allocated 270 junior school children (aged 7–8) and 322 secondary school children (aged 11–12) to experimental or control groups. All children had been identified as showing some kind of social or psychiatric disturbance or learning problems (according to teacher and peer ratings). There were three types of experimental programmes: (a) behaviour modification-reinforcement with the seniors, 'nurture work' teaching healthy interactions with the juniors; (b) parent counselling-teacher consultations with both; and (c) group therapy with the seniors, play groups with the juniors.

The programmes were evaluated after 18 months and after three years using clinical ratings of conduct disturbance. Generally, the experimental and control groups were not significantly different for the juniors, although there was some tendency for the nurture work and play group conditions to be better behaved than the controls at the three-year follow-up. For the seniors, those who received group therapy showed significantly less conduct disturbance at both follow-ups, and there was some tendency for the other two programmes also to be effective at the three-year follow-up. Other school-based prevention experiments have also been successful in reducing antisocial behaviour (Catalano *et al.* 1998).

School bullying, of course, is a risk factor for offending (Farrington 1993). Several school-based programmes have been effective in reducing bullying. The most famous of these was implemented by Olweus (1994) in Norway. It aimed to increase awareness and knowledge of teachers, parents and children about bullying and to dispel myths about it. A 30-page booklet was distributed to all schools in Norway describing what was known about bullying and recommending what steps schools and teachers could take to reduce it. Also, a 25-minute video about bullying was made available to schools. Simultaneously, the schools distributed to all parents a four-page folder containing information and advice about bullying. In addition, anonymous self-report questionnaires about bullying were completed by all children.

The programme was evaluated in Bergen. Each of the 42 participating schools received feedback information from the questionnaire, about the prevalence of bullies and victims, in a specially arranged school conference day. Also, teachers were encouraged to develop explicit rules about bullying (e.g. do not bully, tell someone when bullying happens, bullying will not be tolerated, try to help victims, try to include children who are being left out) and to discuss bullying in class, using the video and role-playing exercises. Also, teachers were encouraged to improve monitoring and supervision of children, especially in the playground. The programme was successful in reducing the prevalence of bullying by half.

A similar programme was implemented in 23 Sheffield schools by Smith and Sharp (1994). The core programme involved establishing a 'whole-school' anti-bullying policy, raising awareness of bullying and clearly defining roles and responsibilities of teachers and students, so that everyone knew what bullying was and what they should do about it. In addition, there were optional interventions tailored to particular schools: curriculum work (e.g. reading books, watching videos), direct work with students (e.g. assertiveness training for those who were bullied) and playground work (e.g. training lunch-time supervisors). This programme was successful in reducing bullying (by 15 per cent) in primary schools, but had relatively small effects (a five per cent reduction) in secondary schools. The effects of these anti-bullying programmes on offending need to be investigated.

Community programmes

There are a number of examples of successful community-based programmes. For example, Jones and Offord (1989) implemented a skills training programme in an experimental public housing complex in Ottawa and compared it with a control complex. The programme centred on non-school skills, both athletic (e.g. swimming and hockey) and non-athletic (e.g. guitar and ballet). The aim of developing skills was to increase self-esteem, to encourage children to use time constructively and to provide desirable role models. Participation rates were high; about three-quarters of age-eligible children in the experimental complex took at least one course in the first year. The programme was successful; delinquency rates decreased significantly in the experimental complex compared to the control complex. The benefit-to-cost ratio (focusing on taxpayer savings, excluding costs to crime victims) was 2.5.

One of the most important community-based treatment programmes is MST, which is a multiple component programme (Henggeler *et al.* 1998). The particular type of treatment is chosen according to the particular needs of the youth; therefore, the nature of the treatment is different for each person. The treatment may include individual, family, peer, school and community interventions, including parent training and child skills training. The treatment is delivered in the youth's home, school and community settings.

Typically, MST has been used with juvenile offenders. For example, in Missouri, Borduin *et al.* (1995) randomly assigned 176 juvenile offenders (mean age 14) either to MST or to individual therapy focusing on personal, family and academic issues. Four years later, only 29 per cent of the MST offenders had been rearrested, compared with 74 per cent of the individual therapy group. According to Aos *et al.* (2001), the benefit-to-cost ratio for MST is very high (28.3), largely because of the potential crime and criminal justice savings from targeting chronic, juvenile offenders.

Communities that care

In the interests of maximising effectiveness, what is needed is a multiple-component, community-based, programme including several of the successful interventions listed above. Many of the programmes reviewed in this chapter are of this type. However, Communities that Care (CTC) has many attractions (Farrington 1996). Perhaps more than any other programme, it is evidence-based and systematic: the choice of interventions depends on empirical evidence about what are the important risk and protective factors in a particular community and on empirical evidence about 'what works' (Sherman *et al.* 2002). It is currently being implemented in 20 sites in England, Scotland and Wales, and also in the Netherlands and Australia (Communities That Care 1997; Utting 1999; France and Crow 2001). While the effectiveness of the overall CTC strategy has not yet been demonstrated, the effectiveness of its individual components is clear.

CTC was developed as a risk-focused prevention strategy by Hawkins and Catalano (1992), and it is a core component of the US Office of Juvenile Justice and Delinquency Prevention's (OJJDP's) Comprehensive Strategy for Serious, Violent and Chronic Juvenile Offenders (Wilson and Howell 1993). CTC is based on a theory (the social development model) that organises risk and protective factors. The intervention techniques are tailored to the needs of each particular community. The 'community' could be a city, a county, a small town, or even a neighbourhood or a housing estate. This programme aims to reduce delinquency and drug use by implementing particular prevention strategies that have demonstrated effectiveness in reducing risk factors or enhancing protective factors. It is modelled on large-scale community-wide public health programmes designed to reduce illnesses such as coronary heart disease by tackling key risk factors (e.g. Farquhar 1985; Perry *et al.* 1989). There is great emphasis in CTC on enhancing protective factors and building on strengths, partly because this is more attractive to communities than tackling risk factors. However, it is generally true that health promotion is more effective than disease prevention (Kaplan 2000).

CTC programmes begin with community mobilisation. Key community leaders (e.g. elected representatives, education officials, police chiefs, business leaders) are brought together, with the aim of getting them to agree on the goals of the prevention programme and to implement CTC. The key leaders then set up a Community Board that is accountable to them, consisting of neighbourhood residents and representatives from various agencies (e.g. school, police, social services, probation, health, parents, youth groups, business, church, media). The Community Board takes charge of prevention on behalf of the community.

The Community Board then carries out a risk and protective factor assessment, identifying key risk factors in that particular community that need to be tackled and key protective factors that need enhancing. This risk assessment might involve the use of police, school, social or census records or local neighbourhood or school surveys. After identifying key risk and protective factors, the Community Board assesses existing resources and develops a plan of intervention

257

strategies. With specialist technical assistance and guidance, they choose programmes from a menu of strategies that have been shown to be effective in well-designed evaluation research.

The menu of strategies listed by Hawkins and Catalano (1992) includes prenatal/postnatal home visiting programmes, pre-school intellectual enrichment programmes, parent training, school organisation and curriculum development, teacher training and media campaigns. Other strategies include child skills training, anti-bullying programmes in schools, situational prevention, and policing strategies. The choice of prevention strategies is based on empirical evidence about effective methods of tackling each particular risk factor, but it also depends on what are identified as the biggest problems in the community. While this approach is not without its challenges and complexities (e.g. cost, implementation, establishing partnerships among diverse agencies), an evidence-based approach that brings together the most effective prevention programmes across multiple domains offers the greatest promise for reducing crime and building safer communities.

Conclusions

High quality evaluation research shows that many programmes are effective in reducing delinquency and later offending, and that in many cases the financial benefits of these programmes outweigh their financial costs. The best programmes include general parent education, parent management training, pre-school intellectual enrichment programmes, child skills training, teacher training, anti-bullying programmes and MST.

High quality experimental and quasi-experimental evaluations of the effectiveness of crime reduction programmes are needed in the United Kingdom. Most knowledge about the effectiveness of prevention programmes, such as cognitive-behavioural skills training, parent training and pre-school intellectual enrichment programmes, is based on American research.

There have been many commendable UK crime prevention initiatives in recent years. Following the review of research carried out as part of the Comprehensive Spending Review in 1997 (Goldblatt and Lewis 1998), the Home Office Crime Reduction Programme was established. Most of the initiatives were situational (e.g. focusing on burglary reduction) or probation/prison orientated (focusing on the treatment of offenders) until the On Track programme was launched at the end of 1999. This provided services for children aged 4–12 who were identified as at risk of being involved in crime in highly deprived communities.

The Youth Justice Board was established in 1998 and has been mainly concerned with providing services for offenders aged 10–17, for example through the Youth Offending Teams. However, it has established 70 Youth Inclusion Programmes, each aimed at the 50 young people aged 13–16 who are most at risk in particular deprived neighbourhoods. The Department for Education and Skills established the Sure Start programme for children aged 0–3 in deprived neighbourhoods, and New Deal for Communities and neighbourhood renewal funds have been established by the Department for the Environment.

While all of these initiatives are commendable, and all are being evaluated in some sense (at least by means of a process evaluation), what is largely missing in the UK at present is risk-focused primary prevention delivered at an early age and designed to reduce later offending and antisocial behaviour. Consideration should be given to implementing a multiple component, risk-focused, prevention programme – such as CTC – more widely throughout Great Britain. This integrated programme could be implemented by existing Crime and Disorder Partnerships. However, they would need resources and technical assistance to conduct youth surveys and household surveys to identify key risk and protective factors for both people and places. They would also need resources and technical assistance to measure risk and protective factors, to choose effective intervention methods, and to carry out high quality evaluations of the effectiveness of programmes in reducing crime and disorder.

The focus should be on primary prevention – offering the programme to all families living in specified areas – not on secondary prevention – targeting the programme on individuals identified as at risk. Ideally, the programme should be presented positively, as fostering safe and healthy communities by strengthening protective factors, rather than as a crime prevention programme targeting risk factors.

Nationally and locally, there is no agency whose primary mandate is the prevention of crime. For example, the very worthwhile intervention programmes being implemented by Youth Offending Teams are overwhelmingly targeted on detected offenders. Therefore, a national agency should be established with a primary mandate of fostering and funding the early prevention of crime.

This national agency could provide technical assistance, skills and knowledge to local agencies in implementing prevention programmes, could provide funding for such programmes, and could ensure continuity, co-ordination and monitoring of local programmes. It could provide training in prevention science for people in local agencies, and could maintain high standards for evaluation research. It could also act as a centre for the discussion of how policy initiatives of different government agencies influence crime and associated social problems. It could set a national and local agenda for research and practice in the prevention of crime, drug and alcohol abuse, mental health problems and associated social problems. National crime prevention agencies have been established in many other countries, such as Sweden (Ministry of Justice 1997; Wikström and Torstensson 1999).

The national agency could also maintain a computerised register of evaluation research and, like the National Institute of Clinical Excellence, advise the government about effective and cost-effective crime prevention programmes. Medical advice is often based on systematic reviews of the effectiveness of health care interventions organised by the Cochrane Collaboration and funded by the National Health Service. Systematic reviews of the evaluation literature on the effectiveness of criminological interventions should be commissioned and funded by government agencies.

Crime prevention also needs to be organised locally. In each area, a local agency should be set up to take the lead in organising risk-focused crime prevention. In Sweden, two-thirds of municipalities have local crime prevention councils. The local prevention agency could take the lead in measuring risk factors and social problems in local areas, using archival records and local household and school surveys. It could then assess available resources and develop a plan of prevention strategies. With specialist technical assistance, prevention programmes could be chosen from a menu of strategies that have been proved to be effective in reducing crime in well-designed evaluation research. This would be a good example of evidence-based practice.

Recent promising developments in the UK have clearly been influenced by recent research on risk factors and intervention strategies. The time is ripe to expand those experimental programmes into a large-scale evidence-based integrated national strategy for the reduction of crime and associated social problems, including rigorous evaluation requirements.

References

Aos, S., Phipps, P., Barnoski, R. and Lieb, R. (1999) *The Comparative Costs and Benefits of Programs to Reduce Crime* (version 3.0). Olympia, Washington: Washington State Institute for Public Policy.

Aos, S., Phipps, P., Barnoski, R. and Lieb, R. (2001) *The Comparative Costs and Benefits of Programs to Reduce Crime* (version 4.0). Olympia, Washington: Washington State Institute for Public Policy.

Baker, K., Pollack, M. and Kohn, I. (1995) 'Violence prevention through informal socialisation: An evaluation of the South Baltimore Youth Center', *Studies on Crime and Crime Prevention*, 4: 61–85.

Barnett, W.S. (1993) 'Cost-benefit analysis', in L.J. Schweinhart, H.V. Barnes and D.P. Weikart *Significant Benefits: The High/Scope Perry Pre-school Study through Age 27* (pp. 142–173). Ypsilanti, Michigan: High/Scope Press.

Berrueta-Clement, J.R., Schweinhart, L.J., Barnett, W.S., Epstein, A.S. and Weikart, D.P. (1984) *Changed Lives: The Effects of the Perry Pre-school Program on Youths Through Age 19*. Ypsilanti, Michigan: High/Scope Press.

Borduin, C. M., Mann, B.J., Cone, L.T., Henggeler, S.W., Fucci, B.R., Blaske, D.M. and Williams, R.A. (1995) 'Multisystemic treatment of serious juvenile offenders: Long-term prevention of criminality and violence', *Journal of Consulting and Clinical Psychology*, 63: 569–87.

Brand, S. and Price, R. (2000) *The Economic and Social Costs of Crime*, London: Home Office (Research Study No. 217).

Catalano, R.F., Arthur, M.W., Hawkins, J.D., Berglund, L. and Olson, J.J. (1998) 'Comprehensive community and school based interventions to prevent antisocial behavior', in R. Loeber and D.P. Farrington (eds) *Serious and Violent Juvenile Offenders: Risk factors and successful interventions* (pp. 248–283). Thousand Oaks, California: Sage.

Communities that Care (1997) *Communities that Care (UK): A new kind of prevention programme*. London: Communities that Care.

Dishion, T.J., McCord, J. and Poulin, F. (1999) 'When interventions harm: Peer groups and problem behavior', *American Psychologist*, 54: 755–64.

Dishion, T.J., Patterson, G.R. and Kavanagh, K.A. (1992) 'An experimental test of the coercion model: Linking theory, measurement and intervention', in J. McCord and R.E. Tremblay (eds) *Preventing Antisocial Behavior: Interventions from birth through adolescence* (pp. 253–282). New York: Guilford.

Farquhar, J.W. (1985) 'The Stanford five-city project: Design and methods', *American Journal of Epidemiology*, 122: 323–34.

Farrington, D.P. (1993) 'Understanding and preventing bullying', in M. Tonry and N. Morris (eds) *Crime and Justice*, vol. 17 (pp. 381–458). Chicago: University of Chicago Press.

Farrington, D.P. (1996) *Understanding and Preventing Youth Crime*. York: Joseph Rowntree Foundation.

Farrington, D.P. (1998) 'Predictors, causes and correlates of male youth violence', in M. Tonry and M.H. Moore (eds) *Youth Violence* (pp. 421–475). Chicago: University of Chicago Press.

Farrington, D.P. and Petrosino, A. (2000) 'Systematic reviews of criminological interventions: The Campbell Collaboration Crime and Justice Group', *International Annals of Criminology*, 38: 49–66.

Farrington, D.P. and Welsh, B.C. (1999) 'Delinquency prevention using family-based interventions', *Children and Society*, 13: 287–303.

Farrington, D.P. and Welsh, B.C. (2002) 'Developmental prevention programmes: Effectiveness and benefit-cost analysis', in J. McGuire (ed.) *Offender Rehabilitation and Treatment: Effective programmes and policies to reduce re-offending* (pp. 143–166). Chichester: Wiley.

Feldman, R.A., Caplinger, T.E. and Wodarski, J.S. (1983) *The St Louis Conundrum*. Englewood Cliffs, NJ: Prentice-Hall.

France, A. and Crow, I. (2001) *CTC – The Story So Far*. York: Joseph Rowntree Foundation.

Goldblatt, P. and Lewis, C. (1998) (eds) *Reducing Offending: An Assessment of Research Evidence on Ways of Dealing with Offending Behaviour*. London: Home Office (Research Study No. 187).

Hahn, A. (1994) *Evaluation of the Quantum Opportunities Program (QOP): Did the program work?* Waltham, Massachusetts: Brandeis University.

Hahn, A. (1999) 'Extending the time of learning', in D.J. Besharov (ed.) *America's Disconnected Youth: Toward a preventive strategy* (pp. 233–65). Washington, DC: Child Welfare League of America Press.

Harrell, A.V., Cavanagh, S.E., Harmon, M.A., Koper, C.S. and Sridharan, S. (1997) *Impact of the Children At Risk Program: Comprehensive Final Report, Vol. 2*. Washington, DC: The Urban Institute.

Harrell, A.V., Cavanagh, S.E. and Sridharan, S. (1999) *Evaluation of the Children at Risk Program: Results 1 year after the end of the program*. Washington, DC: National Institute of Justice.

Hawkins, J.D. and Catalano, R.F. (1992) *Communities that Care*. San Francisco: Jossey-Bass.

Hawkins, J.D., Catalano, R.F., Kosterman, R., Abbott, R. and Hill, K.G. (1999) 'Preventing adolescent health risk behaviors by strengthening protection during childhood', *Archives of Pediatrics and Adolescent Medicine*, 153: 226–34.

Hawkins, J.D., von Cleve, E. and Catalano, R.F. (1991) 'Reducing early childhood aggression: Results of a primary prevention program', *Journal of the American Academy of Child and Adolescent Psychiatry*, 30: 208–17.

Henggeler, S.W., Schoenwald, S.K., Borduin, C.M., Rowland, M.D. and Cunningham, P.B. (1998) *Multisystemic Treatment of Antisocial Behavior in Children and Adolescents*. New York: Guilford.

Johnson, D.L. and Walker, T. (1987) 'Primary prevention of behavior problems in Mexican-American children', *American Journal of Community Psychology*, 15: 375–85.

Jones, M.B. and Offord, D.R. (1989) 'Reduction of antisocial behavior in poor children by non-school skill development', *Journal of Child Psychology and Psychiatry*, 30: 737–50.

Kaplan, R.M. (2000) 'Two pathways to prevention', *American Psychologist*, 55: 382–96.

Karoly, L.A., Greenwood, P.W., Everingham, S.S., Hoube, J., Kilburn, M.R., Rydell, C.P., Sanders, M. and Chiesa, J. (1998) *Investing in Our Children: What we know and don't know about the costs and benefits of early childhood interventions*. Santa Monica, California: Rand Corporation.

Kazdin, A.E., Siegel, T.C. and Bass, D. (1992) 'Cognitive problem-solving skills training and parent management training in the treatment of antisocial behavior in children', *Journal of Consulting and Clinical Psychology*, 60: 733–47.

Kitzman, H., Olds, D.L., Henderson, C.R., Hanks, C., Cole, R., Tatelbaum, R., McConnochie, K.M., Sidora, K., Luckey, D.W., Shaver, D., Engelhardt, K., James, D. and Barnard, K. (1997) 'Effect of prenatal and infancy home visitation by nurses on pregnancy outcomes, childhood injuries, and repeated childbearing: A randomized controlled trial', *Journal of the American Medical Association*, 278: 644–52.

Kolvin, I., Garside, R.F., Nicol, A.R., MacMillan, A., Wolstenholme, F. and Leitch, I.M. (1981) *Help Starts Here: The maladjusted child in the ordinary school*. London: Tavistock.

Lally, J.R., Mangione, P.L. and Honig, A.S. (1988) 'The Syracuse University Family Development Research Program: Long-range impact of an early intervention with low-income children and their families', in D.R. Powell (ed.) *Parent Education as Early Childhood Intervention: Emerging directions in theory, research and practice* (pp. 79–104). Norwood, NJ: Ablex.

Larson, C.P. (1980) 'Efficacy of prenatal and postpartum home visits on child health and development', *Pediatrics*, 66: 191–97.

McCarton, C.M., Brooks-Gunn, J., Wallace, I.F., Bauer, C.R., Bennett, F.C., Bernbaum, J.C., Broyles, R.S., Casey, P.H., McCormick, M.C., Scott, D.T., Tyson, J., Tonascia, J. and Meinert, C.L. (1997) 'Results at age 8 years of early intervention for low-birth-weight premature infants: The Infant Health and Development Program', *Journal of the American Medical Association*, 277: 126–32.

McGuire, J. (2001) 'What works in correctional intervention? Evidence and practical implications', in G.A. Bernfeld, D.P. Farrington and A.W. Leschied (eds) *Offender Rehabilitation in Practice: Implementing and evaluating effective programmes* (pp. 25–43). Chichester: Wiley.

Miller, T.R., Cohen, M.A. and Wiersema, B. (1996) *Victim Costs and Consequences: A new look*. Washington, DC: National Institute of Justice.

Ministry of Justice (1997) *Our Collective Responsibility: A National Programme for Crime Prevention*. Stockholm: National Council for Crime Prevention.

O'Donnell, C.R., Lydgate, T. and Fo, W.S.O. (1979) 'The buddy system: Review and follow-up', *Child Behavior Therapy*, 1: 161–69.

O'Donnell, J., Hawkins, J.D., Catalano, R.F., Abbott, R.D. and Day, L.E. (1995) 'Preventing school failure, drug use, and delinquency among low-income children: Long-term intervention in elementary schools', *American Journal of Orthopsychiatry*, 65: 87–100.

Olds, D.L., Eckenrode, J., Henderson, C.R., Kitzman, H., Powers, J., Cole, R., Sidora, K., Morris, P., Pettitt, L.M. and Luckey, D. (1997) 'Long-term effects of home visitation on maternal life course and child abuse and neglect: Fifteen-year follow-up of a randomized trial', *Journal of the American Medical Association*, 278: 637–43.

Olds, D.L., Henderson, C.R., Chamberlin, R. and Tatelbaum, R. (1986) 'Preventing child abuse and neglect: A randomized trial of nurse home visitation', *Pediatrics*, 78: 65–78.

Olds, D.L., Henderson, C.R., Cole, R., Eckenrode, J., Kitzman, H., Luckey, D., Pettitt, L., Sidora, K., Morris, P. and Powers, J. (1998) 'Long-term effects of nurse home visitation on children's criminal and antisocial behavior: 15-year follow-up of a randomized controlled trial', *Journal of the American Medical Association*, 280: 1238–244.

Olweus, D. (1994) 'Bullying at school: Basic facts and effects of a school based intervention programme', *Journal of Child Psychology and Psychiatry*, 35: 1171–190.

Pagani, L., Tremblay, R.E., Vitaro, F. and Parent, S. (1998) 'Does preschool help prevent delinquency in boys with a history of perinatal complications?', *Criminology*, 36: 245–67.

Patterson, G.R. (1982) *Coercive Family Process*. Eugene, Oregon: Castalia.

Patterson, G.R., Chamberlain, P. and Reid, J.B. (1982) 'A comparative evaluation of a parent training program', *Behavior Therapy*, 13: 638–50.

Patterson, G.R., Reid, J.B. and Dishion, T.J. (1992) *Antisocial Boys*. Eugene, Oregon: Castalia.

Perry, C.L., Klepp, K-I. and Sillers, C. (1989) 'Community-wide strategies for cardiovascular health: The Minnesota Heart Health Program youth program', *Health Education and Research*, 4: 87–101.

Raynor, P. and Vanstone, M. (2001) 'Straight Thinking on Probation: Evidence-based practice and the culture of curiosity', in G.A. Bernfeld, D.P. Farrington and A.W. Leschied (eds) *Offender Rehabilitation in Practice: Implementing and evaluating effective programmes* (pp. 189–203). Chichester: Wiley.

Ross, R.R. and Ross, R.D. (1995) (eds) *Thinking Straight: The reasoning and rehabilitation programme for delinquency prevention and offender rehabilitation*. Ottawa, Canada: Air Training and Publications.

Schochet, P.Z., Burghardt, J. and Glazerman, S. (2000) *National Job Corps Study: The short-term impacts of job corps on participants' employment and related outcomes*. Princeton, NJ: Mathematica Policy Research.

Schweinhart, L.J., Barnes, H.V. and Weikart, D.P. (1993) *Significant Benefits: The High/Scope Perry Preschool Study through Age 27*. Ypsilanti, Michigan: High/Scope Press.

Schweinhart, L.J. and Weikart, D.P. (1980) *Young Children Grow Up: The effects of the Perry Preschool Program on Youths Through Age 15*. Ypsilanti, Michigan: High/Scope Press.

Scott, S., Spender, Q., Doolan, M., Jacobs, B. and Aspland, H. (2001) 'Multicentre controlled trial of parenting groups for child antisocial behaviour in clinical practice', *British Medical Journal*, 323: 194–96.

Sherman, L.W., Farrington, D.P., Welsh, B.C. and MacKenzie, D.L. (2002) (eds) *Evidence-Based Crime Prevention*. London: Routledge.

Smith, P.K. and Sharp, S. (1994) *School Bullying*. London: Routledge.

Stone, W.L., Bendell, R.D. and Field, T.M. (1988) 'The impact of socio-economic status on teenage mothers and children who received early intervention', *Journal of Applied Developmental Psychology*, 9: 391–408.

Strayhorn, J.M. and Weidman, C.S. (1991) 'Follow-up one year after parent–child interaction training: Effects on behavior of preschool children', *Journal of the American Academy of Child and Adolescent Psychiatry*, 30: 138–43.

Tobler, N.S., Lessard, T., Marshall, D., Ochshorn, P. and Roona, M. (1999) 'Effectiveness of school-based drug prevention programs for marijuana use', *School Psychology International*, 20: 105–37.

Tremblay, R.E., Pagani-Kurtz, L., Masse, L.C., Vitaro, F. and Pihl, R.O. (1995) 'A bimodal preventive intervention for disruptive kindergarten boys: Its impact through mid-adolescence', *Journal of Consulting and Clinical Psychology*, 63: 560–68.

Utting, D. (1999) (ed.) *A Guide to Promising Approaches*. London: Communities That Care.

Webster-Stratton, C. (1998) 'Preventing conduct problems in Head Start children: Strengthening parenting competencies', *Journal of Consulting and Clinical Psychology*, 66: 715–30.

Webster-Stratton, C. and Hammond, M. (1997) 'Treating children with early-onset conduct problems: A comparison of child and parent training interventions', *Journal of Consulting and Clinical Psychology*, 65: 93–109.

Welsh, B.C. and Farrington, D.P. (2000) 'Monetary costs and benefits of crime prevention programs', in M. Tonry (ed.) *Crime and Justice*, vol. 27 (pp. 305–361). Chicago: University of Chicago Press.

Welsh, B.C., Farrington, D.P. and Sherman, L.W. (2001) (eds) *Costs and Benefits of Preventing Crime*. Boulder, Colorado: Westview Press.

West, D.J. and Farrington, D.P. (1977) *The Delinquent Way of Life*. London: Heinemann.

Widom, C.S. (1989) 'The cycle of violence', *Science*, 244: 160–66.

Wikström, P-O.H. and Torstensson, M. (1999) 'Local crime prevention and its national support: Organisation and direction', *European Journal on Criminal Policy and Research*, 7: 459–81.

Wilson, J.J. and Howell, J.C. (1993) *A Comprehensive Strategy for Serious, Violent, and Chronic Juvenile Offenders*. Washington, DC: Office of Juvenile Justice and Delinquency Prevention.

Chapter 14

Parenting projects, justice and welfare

Anthony H. Goodman and Joanna Adler

In the previous chapter, Brandon Welsh and David Farrington provided a wide ranging review of the best demonstrated, most cost effective ways of preventing offending. It is our intention to provide the reader with more information about one kind of intervention that they highlighted, parenting training programmes. We take a different approach, seeking to provide an analysis of parenting programmes within a specific social context and to give a deeper flavour of people's experiences on those programmes. These two chapters have some similarities in terms of policy implications. We also think it likely that context specific, multi-faceted programmes, set within a better run system of crime prevention, and far improved social policies offer the best hope. Yet, we have concerns about how such polices will be effected and their implications for the individuals targeted. We therefore proffer this analysis of the historical, legal and psychological elements of youth justice and parenting in England and Wales.

Parental training is sometimes conducted in isolation of other interventions, sometimes as part of a more wide-ranging psycho-social set, such as within programmes like Communities That Care. In either form, parental skills training has found a place on the political agenda, with resources to match. This chapter provides an appraisal of what is now a major initiative of the British New Labour government; an initiative that takes the State into the very heart of the family in order to deal with parents deemed to be failing their children and society at large. The attempt has been made to engage with the parents/guardians of young people who either offend, fail to attend school, or in some way bring their nominal caregivers to the attention of the authorities as 'poor parents'.

Many parents are indeed worried, if not desperate, about the welfare and future of their children and some have appreciated the imaginative way that parenting programmes assist them to engage more constructively in the raising of their children. However, we are wary of forcing parents onto rigid, formulaic programmes under the guise of punishment for failing to control their children or send them to school regularly. To avoid the stigmatising effects of punishment, we would concur with the ideas in the previous chapter, regarding primary prevention. This would not, in and of itself alienate all our concerns. It is essential that intervention is sensitive to familial context and allows the parent to express feelings about their interactions with officialdom. We also contend that, as Cieslik and Pollock warn:

> The focus on 'problem youth' misrepresents the majority of young people's lives, fuelling the mediazed moral panics ... This in turn contributes to the development of often authoritarian and punitive social policy initiatives such as curfews, school exclusion and workfare type welfare programmes. (2002: 15)

As far as offending behaviour is concerned, parents are seen as part of the solution because they have been posited as part of the problem. Poor parenting can be seen as a reliably replicated predictive factor in delinquency studies, both longitudinal and cross sectional (e.g. Farrington 1995; Kolvin, Miller, Fleeting and Kolvin 1988; West 1982; Wilson 1987). Parental neglect and inappropriate parenting is associated with both young people's psychological distress and with offending behaviour in males (Chambers, Power, Loucks and Swanson 2001) and in females (Chesney-Lind and Shelden 1998).

A conceivable solution might be to remove the child from parental care, yet this is not normally a sensible course to take. In most countries, far from protecting them, child specific welfare/protection services have reputations that are less than salubrious and may further contribute towards the likelihood of delinquent activity (e.g. Haapasalo 2000). Keeping children within the family, but trying to 'improve' that family is to be preferred. This also maintains parental accountability for the actions of their offspring, in contrast to what happens if a child is actually taken into care. In most jurisdictions, there are exemptions in law towards state guardians of children removed from their families. The wards of court themselves are often protected by care orders. These young people tend to have the worst psycho-social experiences when growing up and are disproportionately involved in offending behaviour. In relation to the Australian law, Bessant argues strongly that 'differential justice' is thus in operation at the expense of parents and the family (Bessant and Hil 1998).

A rationale for supporting parents was laid down by the English Home Office, in the draft guidance issued on Parenting Orders made under the Crime and Disorder Act 1998. This catalogues the help that has been made available to parents: the Sure Start programme to support families in need and costed at £540 million, the Working Families Tax Credit targeted at 1.5 million families on low income and the Parenting Order. It commented:

> Parenting is a challenging job. Helping parents to develop good parenting skills is an effective way of ensuring that problems in a child or young person's behaviour or development are not allowed to grow unchecked into major difficulties for the individual, their family and the community. The Government is therefore aiming to increase the parenting support available to all parents ... (Home Office 1998a: 1)

The government decided that supporting parents should not be entirely voluntary but needed a coercive underpinning by way of statutory order. This New Labour policy can thus be seen as a return to the 30 year old Conservative notion of the 'cycle of deprivation' promulgated by Sir Keith Joseph. His thesis was that children who were not given adequate care, principally consistent love and guidance, would in turn become inadequate parents, producing the next generation of deprived children (Holman 1978).

Whilst the Conservatives were thus concentrating on the family, the Left were setting those families firmly within a societal context. Cohen argued for a minimalist approach from government 'a commitment to do less harm, rather than more good' (1979a). He drew heavily on Foucault to argue that the state was reproducing a complicated system to classify people that had typified nineteenth century penitentiaries. Cohen linked this to three aspects of community control that he called blurring, widening and masking. **Blurring** refers to an erosion of the boundaries of social control, with the implicit assumption that (new) community alternatives are less costly and more humane than custody. However, intensive community programmes may make it difficult to demarcate between the home and the institution. Concomitantly, **widening** refers to the expansion of the social control network. When instituted, community orders and the like are proffered as alternatives to custody. Yet when sentencing patterns are assessed, these programmes tend to be used for offenders at the 'shallow' end of offending, rather than at the heavy end, thereby extending the reach of judicial sanctions. Finally, **masking** is the process whereby interventions that are intended as benevolent endeavours are instead intrusive, with the threat of custody for failure to comply. Cohen's conclusion was that it was important to eradicate the factors that were incompatible with a moral society: 'overcrowding, slums, poverty, racism, deprivation, degrading education, unhappy family life' (1979b). This was important for all, not just offenders.

In the same year, Donzelot produced a book, the title of which made his viewpoint clear – *The Policing of Families*. He regarded the intervention of professionals or 'technicians' as intrusive and controlling:

> ... the family appears as though colonised. There are no longer two authorities facing one another: the family and the apparatus, but a series of concentric circles around the child: the family circle, the circle of technicians and the circle of social guardians. (1979: 103).

More recently, Petersen (1995) returned to much the same arena, making the case that policies such as Juvenile Intensive Probation Supervision (USA) or the Intensive Supervision and Surveillance Programme (England), ignore the societal context of delinquent activity. 'In essence, the experts are removing power from already powerless youths and citizens, and thus are placing it in the hands of a few who are viewed as knowing what is best for everyone.' This tone seems echoed in Lewis' views in a recent 'Head to Head' in *The Psychologist*, over the issue of general parenting classes and skills training where he states that 'It is easier to pathologise the poor and disadvantaged rather than to think about how to provide resources to help people meet their aspirations' (McGaw and Lewis 2002).

On the other side of this debate are those such as Walters and White (1988) who argue strongly against the cult of 'Disresponsibility'. This theme seems to have been picked up in England and Wales, where there have been more White Papers, Commissions and Bills before Parliament regarding crime, justice and delinquency over the past 25 years than ever before. The introduction to 'No More Excuses', one such White Paper, asserted that:

> For too long we have assumed that young offenders will grow out of their offending if left to themselves. The research shows that this does not happen. An excuse culture has developed within the youth justice system. It excuses itself for its inefficiency, and too

often excuses the young offenders before it, implying that they cannot help their behaviour because of their social circumstances. (Home Office 1997, preface)

The history of youth justice: the move from welfare to a justice model

The placing of responsibility back with offenders and their families would fit well with the philosophy of early writers on poverty like Charles Booth and Seebohm Rowntree, that individuals are able to control their 'environments and destinies'. The family became a vehicle for socialising children and when it failed, the state should have taken its place. Consequently, during the nineteenth century, the state formalised intervention. By 1866, vagrant children could be sent to industrial schools and by 1894, there were over 17,000 children in industrial schools and 4,800 young delinquents in reformatories (Morris *et al*. 1980).

The Children Act of 1908 established juvenile courts, separating young offenders from their adult counterparts. The Criminal Justice Act 1933, united industrial schools and reformatories and section 44 stated that:

> ... every court, in dealing with a child or young person who is brought before it, either as an offender or otherwise, shall have regard to the welfare of the child or young person and shall in a proper case take steps for removing him from undesirable surroundings or for securing that proper provision is made for his education and training. (Criminal Justice Act 1933)

More than 20 years later, the Ingleby Committee (Home Office 1960) was still trying to integrate the notions of punishment and welfare. It recommended raising the age of criminal responsibility to 14, with younger children being subject to care, protection or control proceedings.

The Children and Young Persons Act of 1963 raised the age of criminal responsibility to ten years, where it has remained. It concentrated on widening and defining the responsibilities of local authorities towards children and reflects the continuing tensions between punishment and welfare. It did, however, explicitly identify the family as a major cause of delinquency. A year later, the incoming Labour government set up a working party under Frank Pakenham, later Lord Longford, which produced a report entitled 'Crime – A Challenge to Us All'. In 1965, the

White Paper: 'The Child, the Family and the Young Offender' was published. This paper, like the 1968, 'Children in Trouble', laid great stress on the fact that juvenile delinquents are children. This can be compared with Leon Brittan, a Conservative junior minister at the Home Office in 1979, who contrasted bored youngsters who slip into crime with the deliberate totally uncaring or violent and identifiable minority for whom a deterrent sentence is justified. Thus, while Pakenham rediscovered the 'deprived' child, Brittan rediscovered the 'depraved' young offender. As 'Riff' had earlier posited, 'Hey, I'm depraved on account I'm deprived' (Laurents, Bernstein and Sondheim 1956).

The 1965 White Paper had recommended a revolutionary resolution to the justice versus welfare debate by abolishing the Juvenile Court, raising the age of criminal responsibility to 16 years and introducing family councils, comprising social workers and suitable experienced people, to deal with offenders and non-offenders after issues of guilt and innocence had been resolved.

> The maturing local authority childcare service undoubtedly represented the latest generation of 'child savers'. Their view was that delinquency was a symptom of emotional disturbance, created by a troubled family background and that, crudely speaking, criminal prosecution and punishment merely hid these causal factors, as well as failing to provide the necessary services to deal with them. (Thorpe *et al.* 1980: 5)

These radical changes did not take place, due to strong opposition from the police, magistrates, lawyers and probation officers. In 1968 'Children in Trouble' expressed the view that influences on a boy's behaviour were located in his, 'Genetic, emotional and intellectual factors, his maturity, and his family, school, neighbourhood and wider social settings' (paragraph 6, 1968). This White Paper was turned into statute, the 1969 Children and Young Persons Act. The Juvenile Court was retained, but limited in its operation. Power shifted from magistrates to social workers and Intermediate Treatment was introduced as a preventative measure. It marked a shift towards the treatment of the child. It also grafted a welfare approach on to a punitive system as Detention Centres and Borstals were retained. In doing so, it was not accepted in either Left or Right commentary.

The 1980 White Paper 'Young Offenders' completed the swing to control. In 1968: 'much behaviour by children [had been] part of the process of growing up, but some has more deep-seated causes'. By 1980, children were not referred to, instead: 'the Government share[d] the general public concern about the level of juvenile offending.' The 'short, sharp, shock' was met with vociferous approval at the Conservative Party conference. Later, when evaluated by the Home Office, it was demonstrated to have no significant effect on reconviction rates (Newburn 2002).

The 1982 Criminal Justice Act gave back power to the judiciary who would decide where young offenders should be placed, via care orders with residential requirements. It allowed conditions to be inserted into supervision orders and introduced community service for juveniles, a sanction not contingent upon social work. Borstal was abolished and custodial sentences were normally of determinate length. Punitive, Intensive Intermediate Treatment Schemes were funded by the Home Office to the sum of fifteen million pounds, to be run by the voluntary sector. The combination of both the White Paper and the Criminal Justice Act 1982:

> Attacked the root of the social welfare perspective underlying the 1969 Act … Both documents represented a move away from treatment and lack of personal responsibility to notions of punishment and individual parental responsibility … from the belief in the 'child in need' to the juvenile criminal – what Tutt called the 'rediscovery of the delinquent'. (Gelsthorpe and Morris 1994: 972)

The 1988 Criminal Justice Act replaced Detention Centres with Young Offenders' Institutions. This was a pragmatic decade in terms of juvenile penal policy, also marked by an increasing use of the caution and decrease in custody for young offenders. The right for legal aid for young offenders facing possible incarceration and the requirement that the reason for jailing young offenders had to be given in open court, helped to encourage restraint by sentencers.

Drawing in the parents: the legal context of children and parenting

The 1990 White Paper 'Crime, Justice and Protecting the Public' marked a major change by advocating a tripartite approach. For children under the age of 10, responsibility rested completely with the parent. For those aged between ten and 15, parents were expected to exercise some supervision over them and to know their children's whereabouts. The notion of *doli incapax*, that children aged between 10–13 had to be shown to have known that what they did was seriously wrong was not challenged. Children aged 16 and 17 were to be regarded as near adults, at an intermediate stage between childhood and adulthood, thus parental responsibility towards them was reduced. The White Paper pointed out that previously, parents were rarely asked to pay their children's fines or compensation orders. It advocated that parents 'be deemed fiscally responsible for the actions of their children.'

This drawing in of parents (and guardians) was formalised in the Criminal Justice Act 1991, s.58, when parents could be bound over in the sum of £1,000 to 'take proper care and exercise proper control over the child.' The effect of this was examined by Drakeford (1996) who found discrepancies in how the Act was implemented and that Bind Overs were used most heavily on mothers in court as opposed to both the mother and father or father alone. Parents interviewed in the small study felt that the imposition of the Bind Over had shifted power away from them and towards their child, leading to 'embitterment and erosion of productive family functioning' (1996: 254).

The 1991 Act was reinforced in the Criminal Justice and Public Order Act 1994 when minors' parents or guardians could themselves be made the subject of a Bind Over to ensure that the offenders complied with their sentence requirements. Yet, as Drakeford and McCarthy pointed out, parents are not eligible for legal representation and both the 1991 and 1994 Acts:

> Require those parents targeted to control behaviour which is not specified, by means which are equally unspecific. With both Orders there exists the potential for a criminal sanction, in terms of a fine, should parents fail to 'take responsibility' for their children. (2000: 98)

The Crime and Disorder Act 1998 gives four circumstances when a parenting order can be made:

(a) When a Child Safety Order is made in respect of a child.

(b) An Anti-Social Behaviour Order or Sex Offender Order is made in respect of a child or young person.

(c) A child or young person is convicted of an offence. Or

(d) A person is convicted of an offence under section 443 (failure to comply with school attendance order) or section 444 (failure to secure regular attendance at school of registered pupil) of the Education Act 1996 (CDA 1998, Section 8).

The Parenting Order can last for up to 12 months and may include attendance at counselling or guidance sessions. Failing to comply with a Parenting Order is not an arrestable offence but, if convicted in a magistrates' court, can result in a fine of up to £1,000. The court can impose any sentence available for a non imprisonable offence in addition to the fine i.e. absolute or conditional discharge, community rehabilitation order or curfew order (Home Office 1998a).

A Child Safety Order, available for children under 10 at the time of the making of the order, is expected to last for three months but can be for as long as a year. It can be made in four possible circumstances: when a child under the age of 10 commits an act which, had they been 10 or over would have constituted an offence; that the order is necessary to *prevent* the young person committing such an act (our emphasis); that the child has broken a local child curfew scheme (introduced in the same Act); finally that the child has acted in a way 'that caused or was likely to cause harassment, alarm or distress' to people outside of the child's household (Home Office 1998b). The Child Safety Order is consistent with the government's emphasis on early intervention and blurs the boundaries between social services and youth offending teams. The child safety order may be supervised by a local authority social worker or by a member of the youth offending team. Until then, children under 10 would have been worked with by local authority social services, not staff with an offending label. Should the order be breached for non-compliance, then a care order could be substituted, under the Children Act 1989.

The guidance document is illuminating regarding parental attendance when there is an application for a child safety order. Not least, as the parent or guardian may be a party to the court proceedings. It comments that the government believes that there is enough flexibility in the 'Rules':

> … to ensure that those who have the greatest influence on the child are involved in the proceedings. For example, where the child's parents are estranged and one of them exerts no influence on the child, then it would not only be inappropriate but wasteful of the court's time and resources to seek to contact them. (Home Office 1998b: 12–13).

It is naïve to imagine that absent parents have no influence on their children. Often, children are the witnesses and survivors of the conflict between parents. Indeed the absent parent may have had a malign influence on the child. It is often the parent who has been the victim of the matrimonial conflict who subsequently becomes the target of the court intervention and is seen as the 'faulty' parent. It comes as no surprise therefore, when the research on parenting orders discovers that it is the mother predominantly who is the subject of court intervention.

Parental views of the helping professionals are not neutral. Parents have expressed worries about the possibility of losing their children when social services became involved. They worried about being seen as failed parents or being pushed into unsatisfactory, short-term accommodation. Parents sometimes felt disempowered after professionals became involved (Department of Health 2000). The 'accessibility and quality of the initial response from social services' was seen as a source of concern by other agencies who looked to social services to provide leadership in the context of children in need of safeguarding. 'Duty systems were found to be impersonal and unresponsive … operating tight criteria for accepting referrals' (Department of Health 2002: 46–7). Even if concerned parents overcome their anxiety about the risk of approaching social services, they are liable to find unhelpful responses if they do not demonstrate a crisis level of need. Despite this, an earlier document stated: 'Parents … require and deserve support. Asking for help should be seen as a sign of responsibility rather than as a parenting failure. (Department of Health 1999: 1)

If these words are to be anything other than pious rhetoric, then a system of non-stigmatising support, that can be triggered well before major family crisis point, needs to be instigated.

Parenting projects in practice

In 1999 the Youth Justice Board for England and Wales funded 42 pilot parenting projects, that were independently evaluated. Each project developed in its own way, responding to local need and initiative. The projects were evaluated between June 1999 and December 2001. Two approaches that were found to be useful were the Webster-Stratton programme (see previous chapter) and the Hilton Davies model for working with isolated and vulnerable parents. In the latter approach, one-to-one work is used, not only to address parenting issues but to deal with social and welfare issues. This multi agency type approach requires patience and tact but above all, respect and empathy for the parents (Coleman, Henricson and Roker 1999). Webster-Stratton's techniques were mentioned in the previous chapter and the Policy Research Bureau's findings are similar to those in the United States. As the title of the Brestan and Eyberg 1998 paper asserts, they considered 82 studies over 29 years, based on 5,272 children and adolescents. They found that there were two types of intervention that could be deemed 'well established', social modelling type video based programmes first elucidated by Webster-Stratton and others (Webster-Stratton and Herbert 1994) and 'parent-training programs based on Patterson and Gullion's (1968) manual, Living With Children.' In terms of efficacy of the interventions (whether well established or not), they found that just under 25 per cent of the studies reviewed provided support for 'probably efficacious treatments' (Brestan and Eyberg 1998).

The sample in the evaluation of the English pilot schemes was 96 per cent white British, 81 per cent female and 49 per cent lone parents. The findings demonstrated that few projects engaged with the young people, focusing instead on the parents. Projects tended to be either 'preventative' (working with a wide group of parents) or 'therapeutic' (targeting 'higher tariff' parents in crisis) (Ghate and Ramella 2002). Most projects took a long time to move from inception to practice and typically offered a mixture of one-to-one group work. Interventions could start from crisis intervention and move to more structured work.

Findings from the evaluation were encouraging, with improved parent/child communication, supervision and monitoring; less conflict; better relationships; more influence; and better coping with the pressures of parenting. This was irrespective of whether the parent was on a statutory parenting order or if contact was voluntary. There were high levels of need for both emotional and practical support (Ghate and Ramella 2002).

It was apparent that overwhelmingly, it was the mothers who were seen by the project staff. One major complaint by mothers was that they had been made to feel like criminals in the courtroom, as if they had offended, not their children. As a consequence of this, project staff had to work hard in the early stages of contact with the parent/guardian to overcome the negative feelings engendered by the court experience. It was also difficult for the parents to acknowledge that they had developed dysfunctional relationships with their children or to accept that they had to relearn how to deal with conflicts. Through observing parenting groups and interviewing parents, it became clear that helpful coping and management strategies could indeed be taught without resorting to violence or rejection.

Children knew how to bring out the worst in the parent, exploiting tensions to get out of the house or to be 'bribed' back into co-operating with the parent. Also, as Buel reminds us, when designing a parenting programme, it is worth considering that children abuse and assault parents, it is not always *vice versa* (Buel 2002). Consistency in discipline and general parenting was a major problem at the outset of the schemes but could be taught. The essential premise on which such schemes are founded is that, as Feldman pointed out:

> Parenting is a learned skill like any other, 'instinct' is not enough. The current emphasis is on techniques and resources, and in general on the current family situation in which parents and children interact ... There is an increasing interest in the direction of effect being two-way: as well as parents influencing their offspring, children influence the way their parents behave towards them. (1993: 188)

As the government acknowledged in the Child Safety Orders guidance document, research by Graham and Bowling (1995) found that a number of factors have been identified as related to the onset of offending. These English findings mirror those of many previous studies that have included parenting as only one of a number of psycho-social risk (and protective) factors in delinquency (Chambers *et al.* 2001; Fergusson and Horwood 1998; Harris and Mertlich 2003; Holtzworth Munroe, Smutzler and Sandin 1997). The Home Office concentrated on: relationships with parents and family attachment; parental supervision; parent and sibling criminality; truancy; exclusion from school and association with delinquent peers. As Golombok comments:

> We must also remember that relationships between children and their parents do not take place within a social vacuum. Parents who are in conflict, or who have psychological problems themselves are less able to be effective mothers or fathers to their child. The social circumstance of the family, and the neighbourhood in which the family lives, also makes a difference to the quality of family life. Poverty, and the social disadvantages that accompany it, is one of the most detrimental and pernicious influences faced by children today. (2000: 102)

Whilst some parents neglect their children, others inappropriately punish, some are in conflict with each other, some are in conflict with the law. In other studies of the backgrounds of the most serious, repeatedly offending youth, their family situations have been found to be multi-problematic; disruptive, out of control, socially and criminally deviant. Further, different patterns of family problems were associated with different patterns of delinquent activity, even at the less serious levels

(Gorman-Smith, Tolan, Loeber and Henry 1998). Similarly, Smith and Stern concluded that the relationship between family life and offending is not a straightforward correlation and delinquency must be tackled in the proper familial and societal context (Smith and Stern 1997). Beyond parenting styles, other important considerations could include: peer activities; parental employment; school attainment and attendance; substance use; the personality or mental health of the child; gang membership; ethnicity; family nationality; and so on (e.g. Gavazzi *et al.* 2003; Moffitt, Caspi, Harrington and Milne 2002). For example, there is evidence that substance abusing mothers have themselves experienced a higher incidence of childhood abuse. Their substance reliance not only effects the way that they are perceived (and possibly copied) by their children but can affect their physical and psychological abilities to parent (Alison 2000).

Multi-systemic programmes or those taking an 'ecological' approach to school and family intervention (as discussed in the previous chapter) thus seem promising (e.g. Borduin 1999; Dishion and Kavanagh 2000). This appears particularly to be the case when dealing with violent youth where the 'most effective treatment and prevention' interventions are those that 'simultaneously address the multiple factors related to youth violence' (Kashani, Jones, Bumby and Thomas 1999). So what of parenting programmes in isolation? Family intervention can have an impact, even if this is the only official sanction, meta-anlysis has shown that successful intervention significantly reduces the time spent in institutions by children with conduct disorder and, or delinquent engagement (Woolfenden, Williams and Peat 2002).

A sound theoretical foundation for a parenting programme is a good start but is by no means sufficient, particularly if the individual is lost within the multiplicity of approaches. If we return to the English Pilot Projects, some mothers reported problems with their mental health; substance abuse; offending; chaotic home life and issues of neglect. There were others who did not have these experiences, yet were not successfully controlling their children. This brings us to a consideration of the children themselves, many of whom had special educational needs; were poor or non-school attendees; had behavioural problems and there were threats of eviction because of nuisance. In many instances, the relationship between the parents and the statutory services had degraded, with a high level of distrust on both sides.

Some of the histories of the parents are a testimony to their resilience and care for their family. They should certainly not be labelled irresponsible. One mother was so desperately worried about her teenage daughter that she described tucking another young child under her arm as she went round the streets at midnight trying to find her. Her interview highlights levels of loneliness and isolation but also her tenacity in trying to hold her family together. This mother was taught some useful techniques to engage with her child without losing her temper. By the end of her group sessions, they appeared to be working. Many parents expressed regret that the group process was too short. These concerns can be considered in the light of findings from the Syracuse Family Development Programme where 'enriched day care' was given over a five-year period. Levels of anti-social behaviour were reduced at 15 years, with only six per cent of the programme children being known to youth justice agencies compared to 22 per cent of a matched group (Little and Mount 1999: 94, also, please see previous chapter).

The four projects on which these findings were largely based were all very different and have endured beyond the end of the original funding period as the local authorities recognised their usefulness. One final observation is that when these 'problem families' were engaged, with a 'fresh pair of eyes', the outlook of the statutory agencies was challenged to the benefit of the parent and family. A family that is labelled as problematic can find themselves prevented from accessing support. The intervention of the parenting project worker forced the organisations to reappraise what they were doing with such families.

The research on the parenting projects in England and Wales is encouraging but the time period it ran for is very short, therefore any conclusions drawn from it must be tentative. Yet, it is impressive that the projects had succeeded in working with a high number of such disaffected families. This was irrespective of whether contact was voluntary or on an imposed parenting order. The accessibility of the project workers was most important and positively commented on by parents. They were seen as being neutral and different to previous officials. All the workers had been engaged as part of the pilot projects and were therefore not directly identified as being part of an existing formal agency.

Parenting classes, mothers and state responsibility: the future

There is a central incongruity at the heart of the Crime and Disorder Act 1998, around the concept of responsibility. The Act abolishes *doli incapax*, thereby effectively implying that from the age of 10, children have sufficient maturity to know right from wrong and are sufficiently rational to know the consequences of their actions. Parental authority decreases as the child grows older and the Gillick judgement points out that this parental authority must yield to the child when they have 'sufficient understanding and intelligence' to be able to make up their own mind (Jones and Bell 2000). Thus the loss of *doli incapax* is incompatible with holding the parent responsible for the wrongdoing of the child. Jones and Bell consider the continuing responsibility of the parent as 'problematic' but this has not stopped parents or more accurately mothers from being sent to prison for the non-attendance of their children at school.

It is important that parenting classes do not become the stick to beat parents who fail to send their children to school or co-operate with education staff. Charles Clarke, the Education Secretary, conflated the need to give respect to 'heads, teachers and other school staff' and the unacceptability of subjecting them to verbal or physical assault with the problem of truancy and those children given fixed term exclusions for bad behaviour. According to Passmore in the *Times Educational Supplement (TES)*:

> Ministers [as well as giving heads the ability to issue fixed-penalty fines] also propose a contract for parents whose children are given a fixed-term exclusion for bad behaviour and who do nothing to improve it. This would bind parents to go to classes to learn to manage their child better. If they refused to sign – or broke the contract – they could be taken to court and face a parenting order. (Passmore 2002: 1)

The danger is that the notion of parenting and constructive use of support and advice to parents becomes subsumed within the context of punishment and control, if the government wishes to maintain a populist approach to law and order. In this atmosphere, it will be very difficult to overcome the stigma involved in being the recipient of a parenting order and the effectiveness of working constructively with parents will be diminished. In practice, it is clear that the notion of engaging with the parent has resulted in work being undertaken with the mother. Surely, it will be more constructive avoid making parenting projects into part of the culture of punishment. This is the warning of Goldson and Jamieson, that 'the New Labour Government is preparing to grind out further interventionist and punitive routes into family life' (2002: 95).

It is easy to target and blame the single parent (typically single mother) family as if she is the cause of the problem. As has been indicated, the role of the father in the household is a complex area that has an impact on the child(ren), whether or not the father is actually living in the household. There is an extra dynamic present here and research from America and beyond indicates that:

> It is not uncommon to find battered mothers and exposed children who are mandated to have continuing contact with her abusive partner through visitation or the need to make arrangements for it. Research is needed to determine what types of parenting practices are used during visitation by battering fathers and how these are associated with child well being. (Rossman, Hughes and Rosenberg 1999: 29)

The effect and consequences on children of experiencing their parents' emotional conflicts is often acted out and has an impact on the parent left with day to day responsibility for child care. Adding low income, poor housing, lack of opportunity and all the other pressures on to the parent, it is not surprising that many children become disenfranchised and disillusioned. We welcome the idea of national and local agencies dedicated to crime prevention, yet we hope that the system will not lose sight of the individual, nor that it further stigmatises and disadvantages. Cohen's concepts of masking, widening and blurring are still relevant today in terms of drawing parents into the criminal justice system when previously this would not have been the case. The difficult trick is to be able to support and guide, without being judgmental and blaming. This takes time, patience and resources.

References

Alison, L. (2000) 'What are the risks to children of parental substance misuse?', in F. Harbin and M. Murphy (eds) *Substance Misuse and Child Care. How to understand, assist and intervene when drugs affect parenting.* Lyme Regis: Russell House Publishing.

Audit Commission (1996) *Misspent Youth: Young people and crime.* Abingdon: Audit Commission Publications.

Bessant, J. and Hil, R. (1998) 'Parenting on trial: State wards and governments accountability in Australia', *Journal of Criminal Justice*, 26 (2): 145–57.

Borduin, C.M. (1999) 'Multisystemic treatment of criminality and violence in adolescents', *Journal of the American Academy of Child and Adolescent Psychiatry*, 38 (3): 242–49.

Brestan, E.V. and Eyberg, S.M. (1998) 'Effective psychosocial treatments of conduct-disordered children and adolescents: 29 years, 82 studies, and 5,272 kids', *Journal of Clinical Child Psychology*, 27 (2): 180–89.

Buel, S.M. (2002). 'Why juvenile courts should address family violence: Promising practices to improve intervention outcomes', *Juvenile and Family Court Journal*, 53 (2): 1–16.

Chambers, J., Power, K., Loucks, N. and Swanson, V. (2001) 'The interaction of perceived maternal and paternal parenting styles and their relation with the psychological distress and offending characteristics of incarcerated young offenders', *Journal of Adolescence*, 24 (2): 209–27.

Chesney-Lind, M. and Shelden, R.G. (1998) *Girls, Delinquency and Juvenile Justice* (2nd edn). London: Wadsworth.

Cieslik, M. and Pollock, G. (eds) (2002) *Young People in Risk Society: The restructuring of youth identities and transitions in late modernity.* Aldershot: Ashgate.

Cohen, S. (1979) 'Some modest and unrealistic proposals', *New Society* 29 March: 731–34.

Cohen, S. (1979a) 'How can we balance justice, guilt and tolerance?', *New Society* 1 March: 475–77.

Cohen, S. (1979b) 'Community control – a new utopia', *New Society* 15 March: 609–11.

Coleman, J., Henricson, C. and Roker, D. (11 March 1999) *Parenting in the Youth Justice Context. A report by the Trust for the Study of Adolescence.* London: Trust for the Study of Adolescence.

Department of Health (1999) *Working Together to Safeguard Children.* London: Department of Health.

Department of Health (2000) *Assessing Children in Need and their Families: Practice guidance.* London: The Stationery Office.

Department of Health (October 2002) *Safeguarding Children: a joint Chief Inspectors Report on arrangements to safeguard children.* London: Department of Health Publications.

Dishion, T.J. and Kavanagh, K. (2000) 'A multilevel approach to family-centered prevention in schools: Process and outcome', *Addictive Behaviors*, 25 (6): 899–911.

Donzelot, J. (1979) *The Policing of Families: Welfare versus the state.* London: Hutchinson and Co. Ltd.

Drakeford, M. (1996) 'Parents of young people in trouble', *Howard Journal of Criminal Justice*, 35 (3): 242–55.

Drakeford, M. and McCarthy, K. (2000) 'Parents, responsibility and the New Youth Justice', in B. Goldson (ed.) *The New Youth Justice.* Lyme Regis: Russell House Publishing.

Farrington, D.P. (1995) 'The Twelfth Jack Tizard Memorial Lecture: The development of offending and antisocial behaviour from childhood: Key findings from the Cambridge Study in Delinquent Development', *Journal of Child Psychology and Psychiatry and Allied Disciplines*, 36: 929–64.

Feldman, P. (1993) *The Psychology of Crime.* Cambridge: Cambridge University Press.

Fergusson, D.M. and Horwood, L.J. (1998) 'Exposure to interparental violence in childhood and psychosocial adjustment in young adulthood', *Child Abuse and Neglect*, 22 (5): 339–57.

Gavazzi, S.M., Slade, D., Buettner, C.K., Partridge, C., Yarcheck, C.M. and Andrews, D.W. (2003) 'Toward conceptual development and empirical measurement of global risk indicators in the lives of court', *Psychological Reports*, 92 (2): 599–615.

Gelsthorpe, L. and Morris, A. (1994) 'Juvenile justice 1945–1992', in M. Maguire, R. Morgan and R. Reiner (eds) *The Oxford Handbook of Criminology*. Oxford: Oxford University Press.

Ghate, D. and Ramella, M. (September 2002) *Positive Parenting: The national evaluation of the Youth Justice Boards Parenting Programme*. London: Policy Research Bureau for the Youth Justice Board.

Goldson, B. and Jamieson, J. (2002) 'Youth crime, the parenting deficit and state intervention: A contextual critique', *Youth Justice*, 2 (2): 82–99.

Golombok, S. (2000) *Parenting: What really counts?* London: Routledge.

Gorman-Smith, D., Tolan, P.H., Loeber, R. and Henry, D.B. (1998) 'Relation of family problems to patterns of delinquent involvement among urban youth', *Journal of Abnormal Child Psychology*, 26 (5): 319–33.

Graham, J. and Bowling, B. (1995) *Young People and Crime*. Home Office Research Study 145 London: Home Office.

Haapasalo, J. (2000) 'Young offenders' experiences of child protection services', *Journal of Youth and Adolescence*, 29 (3): 355–71.

Harris, M.A. and Mertlich, D. (2003) 'Piloting home-based behavioral family systems therapy for adolescents with poorly controlled diabetes', *Childrens Health Care*, 32 (1): 65–79.

Holman, R. (1978) *Poverty: Explanations of social deprivation*. London: Martin Robertson.

Holtzworth Munroe, A., Smutzler, N. and Sandin, E. (1997) 'A brief review of the research on husband violence 2. The psychological effects of husband violence on battered women and their children', *Aggression and Violent Behavior*, 2 (2): 179–213.

Home Office (1960) *Report on the Committee on Children and Young Persons*. Cmnd 1191 [The Ingleby Report] London: HMSO.

Home Office (1965) *The Child, The Family and the Young Offender*. Cmnd 2742 London: HMSO.

Home Office (1968) *Children in Trouble*. Cmnd 3601 London: HMSO.

Home Office (1990) *Crime, Justice and Protecting the Public*. London: HMSO.

Home Office (1997) *No More Excuses – A new approach to tackling youth crime in England and Wales*. London: Home Office.

Home Office (1998a) *The Crime and Disorder Act Guidance Document: Parenting Order*. London: Home Office.

Home Office (1998b) *The Child Safety Order: Draft guidance document*. London: Home Office.

Jones, G. and Bell, R. (2000) *Balancing Acts: Youth, parenting and public policy*. York: York Publishing Services Limited for the Joseph Rowntree Foundation.

Kashani, J.H., Jones, M.R., Bumby, K.M. and Thomas, L.A. (1999) 'Youth violence: Psychosocial risk factors, treatment, prevention, and recommendations', *Journal of Emotional and Behavioral Disorders*, 7 (4): 200–10.

Kolvin, I., Miller, F.J., Fleeting, M. and Kolvin, P.A. (1988) 'Social and parenting factors affecting criminal-offence rates: Findings from the Newcastle Thousand Family Study (1947–1980)', *British Journal of Psychiatry*, 152: 80–90.

Laurents, A., Bernstein, L. and Sondheim, S. (1956) *West Side Story*. New York: Schirmer, Inc.

Little, M. and Mount, K. (1999) *Prevention and Early Intervention with Children in Need*. Aldershot: Ashgate.

McGaw, S. and Lewis, C. (2002) 'The changing family, head to head: Should parenting be taught', *The Psychologist*, 15 (10): 510–12.

Moffitt, T.E., Caspi, A., Harrington, H. and Milne, B.J. (2002) 'Males on the life-course-persistent and adolescence-limited antisocial pathways: Follow-up at age 26 years', *Development and Psychopathology*, 14 (1): 179–207.

Morris, A., Giller, H., Szwed, E. and Geach, H. (1980) *Justice for Children*. London: Macmillan Press Ltd.

Newburn, T. (2002) 'Young people, crime, and youth justice', in M. Maguire, R. Morgan and R. Reiner (eds) *The Oxford Handbook of Criminology* (3rd edn). Oxford: Oxford University Press.

Passmore, B. (13 December 2002) *Heads given the power to impose fines on parents*. Times Educational Supplement: 1.

Petersen, R.D. (1995) 'Expert policy in juvenile justice: Patterns of claims making and issues of power in a program construction', *Policy Studies Journal*, 23 (4): 636–51.

Rossman, B., Hughes, H. and Rosenberg, M. (1999) *Children and Interpersonal Violence: The impact of exposure*. Philadelphia: Brunner/Mazel.

Smith, C.A. and Stern, S.B. (1997) 'Delinquency and antisocial behavior: A review of family processes and intervention research', *Social Service Review*, 71 (3): 382–420.

Thorpe, D., Smith, D., Green, C. and Paley, J. (1980) *Out of Care: The community support of juvenile offenders*. London: George Allen and Unwin.

Walters, G.D. and White, T.W. (1988) 'Crime, popular mythology and personal responsibility', *Federal Probation*, 52 (1): 18–26.

Webster-Stratton, C. and Herbert, M. (1994) *Troubled Families–Problem Children: Working with Parents: A Collaborative Process*. Chichester: Wiley.

West, D.J. (1982). *Delinquency: Its roots, career and prospects*. Cambridge, MA: Harvard University Press.

Wilson, H. (1987) 'Parental Supervision re-examined', *British Journal of Criminology*, 27: 275–301.

Woolfenden, S.R., Williams, K. and Peat, J.K. (2002) 'Family and parenting interventions for conduct disorder and delinquency: a meta-analysis of randomised controlled trials', *Archives of Disease in Childhood*, 86 (4): 251–56.

Section 7

Punishment and Corrections

Our final section continues assessing practice and intervention. The different prison systems in the United Kingdom have been at the forefront of attempts to make regimes fairer and more humane; also, to make them more effective. Alongside performance indicators have come systematic reviews of programme efficacy and the establishment of a Unit responsible for Offending Behaviour Programmes. Within Probation, there has been a concomitant shift towards 'effective practice'. Gains have been made. However, we have the largest proportion of people in prison in Europe. We are imprisoning more women than ever before and are still guilty of imposing regimes and programmes upon them that were first designed for men.

In the penultimate chapter of this book, Nancy Loucks provides an appraisal of women's imprisonment. It is not a pretty picture and shows how overwhelmingly, we are imprisoning a disparate group of women in dire economic and personal circumstances. They can receive help and treatment within prison, but fundamental questions need to be asked as to when and why imprisonment became an intervention of choice.

Women, though, are a tiny minority of the prison population overall and incarceration is far from being the only punitive sanction at the disposal of the judiciary. In the final chapter, Graham Towl shows us how psychology is being deployed in the national probation and prison services in this country. It is clear that the uses of forensic psychology are varied and that other psychological disciplines may have an increasingly prominent role to play within these branches of forensic practice.

Chapter 15

Women in prison

Nancy Loucks

Women make up about five per cent of prison populations world-wide (Stern 1998). Most research has therefore focused on men, the majority population. However, it is precisely this minority status and marginalisation which increases the need to recognise women in prison as a distinct group with distinctive needs. A consistent picture of poverty, deprivation, victimisation and marginalisation makes up the basis of every female custodial population studied in every jurisdiction. The 'career' criminals and thrill-seekers common amongst male prisoners are virtually absent in women's prison, replaced instead by people in custody often through desperate circumstances or lives so chaotic that they failed to comply with community penalties or bail.

This chapter outlines the backgrounds, characteristics and issues surrounding women who end up in custody. Much of the information is based on the author's research in Scotland (Loucks 1998), but an international context is included where appropriate.

Backgrounds of women in custody

Women who end up in custody are distinctive for a number of reasons. Features such as addiction, psychological distress, abuse, poverty, and unemployment, while not exclusive to women in custody, characterise the vast majority of them (see for example Byrne and Howells 2002).

Drugs

Drug use is amongst the most common features of women in custody in many countries. In Scotland, 87.7 per cent of women in prison reported having used illicit drugs at some time in their lives. This rate is higher than in some countries (e.g. research in prisons in England by Fraser 1994; Morris *et al.* 1995; Johnson and Farren 1996; and Singleton *et al.* 1998); as a comparison, work by the Prison Service in HMP Holloway, London (King 1998) reported 31 per cent previous use of drugs. However, the higher rate is comparable to that found in other countries: one US study (Birecree *et al.* 1994), for example, recorded rates of 90 per cent. A project on young offenders in Scotland (Loucks *et al.* 2000) found the rate of prior drug use to be about 95 per cent, with no significant difference in reported experience of drug use between young men and women prior to custody.

Backgrounds of drug use among female prisoners tend to be heavy. In Scotland, a third had injected drugs at some stage, and over half the women (50.7 per cent) said they were addicted to drugs (based on self-assessment, medical interviews at reception and clinical scales). The rate of addiction in the Scottish sample was double that found in research in women's prisons in England and Wales, which showed rates of about a quarter (Maden *et al.* 1991; Gunn *et al.* 1991), but even the lower estimates suggest that addiction is a significant problem. A national survey of prisoners in the United States (Snell and Morton 1994) showed that women in prison used more drugs and used them more frequently than did male prisoners. Prior to custody, 41.5 per cent of female prisoners used drugs daily, compared to 35.7 per cent of male prisoners, and more were likely to be under the influence of drugs when they committed their offence (36.3 per cent compared to 30.6 per cent).

The available research suggests that few women begin their drug use in prison: only three women in the Scottish research did so, and more often than not they simply tried drugs once or twice, usually cannabis. Others began using different drugs in prison, for example where their normal drug of choice was not available, or where they chose to experiment. Drug use most commonly began for the women as teenagers.

Alcohol

Though not as common a problem as illicit drug use amongst female prisoners, a significant proportion of women in prison show evidence of alcoholism or alcohol-related problems. For example, 22.5 per cent of female prisoners in Scotland said they never drink, but 18.8 per cent said they drink daily outside custody. Based on the AUDIT scale (Fleming *et al.* 1991), ten to 15 per cent were addicted to alcohol. This is similar to rates of alcoholism amongst female prisoners in much of the past research, but a lower rate to that most recently reported in Singleton *et al.* (1998), which found a rate of 36 per cent amongst female prisoners in England. In the Scottish sample, binge drinking was more common than regular, heavy drinking. Female binge drinkers tended to combine drink and drugs, and a third had been drinking at the time of their offence, almost all of whom thought this contributed to their offence. These behaviours would not necessarily show up as addiction on clinical scales, nor did most of these women believe they had a problem with alcohol.

In contrast to the findings of previous research amongst female prisoners (e.g. Kendall 1993, in Canada), few women in Scottish prisons appeared to be cross-addicted to drugs and alcohol. Only one woman in the research in Scotland was found to be cross-addicted. Her story was important in other ways too, in that it exemplified the dire situation of many women when they enter custody. This woman had a substantial history of all forms of abuse: she grew up in an alcoholic family, ran away from physical and sexual abuse at home and was taken into care, where she was sexually abused by her foster father. She then entered a series of abusive relationships from which she had yet to escape. The following section shows that this woman's story was more often the norm than the exception amongst women in prison.

Backgrounds of abuse

Another recurring theme throughout the research into women in custody is the finding that so many of the women are victims as well as offenders. The research in Scotland showed that the vast majority of women in prison had been direct or indirect victims of physical, sexual, or emotional abuse, and often a combination of these: 82.2 per cent had suffered some form of abuse during their lives, and 66.7 per cent were directly aware of the abuse of others close to them. The rate of abuse in Scotland is similar to rates found in other female prison populations, such as in Canadian research by Lightfoot and Lambert (1992). A survey of 13,986 male and female prisoners in the United States (Snell and Morton 1994; also Morash *et al.* 1998) showed lower reported rates of abuse amongst women. Even so, the reported rates for female prisoners in their research (43 per cent) were almost four times higher than the comparable figure for men (12.2 per cent).

In the Scottish research, most women who reported being victims of abuse said this had taken place throughout their lives (as children, teenagers, and as adults), usually on a daily or virtually daily basis. Many were going back out to violent families or partners and for some, prison was the first 'safe' place they had been (see also Bradley and Davino 2002).

Health

Perhaps unsurprisingly in view of the above, female prisoners suffer more frequent and serious chronic disease, acute illness, and injuries; these can be attributed to factors such as poverty, poor nutrition, and lack of medical care, but also to drug use (Anderson, Rosay, and Saum 2002). Research in the US has found that women in prison show even higher rates of HIV/AIDS than do men in custody (Ingram Fogel and Belyea 1999; Zaitzow 2001). Ingram Fogel and Belyea reported a high proportion of high-risk behaviour amongst the women, including substance abuse, extensive past or ongoing violent experiences including sexual abuse, a high proportion of multiple partners (including prostitution) and low use of condoms.

Suicidal behaviour and emotional distress

Suicide and self-injury are common experiences for a significant proportion of female prisoners. In Scotland, over a third (37.7 per cent) had attempted suicide at some time in the past. Suicide attempts were more common outside custody than in prison: only seven of the 29 women who said they had tried to kill themselves had tried it while in prison. A notable proportion (16.9 per cent) had a history of deliberately injuring themselves, separate from those incidents that they considered as suicide attempts. None of the women did this for the first time in prison.

A history of treatment for mental health or emotional problems is also a common feature amongst this group. Research in England and Wales (Singleton et al. 1998), for example, showed that 40 per cent of women in custody had received help or treatment for a mental health or emotional problem in the year before they entered custody – double the proportion for male prisoners. Women in prison prior to conviction or sentence contained the highest proportion of prisoners ever admitted to a psychiatric hospital – 22 per cent, including six per cent admitted for six months or more and 11 per cent admitted to a secure ward. This compares to eight per cent of sentenced male prisoners, with two per cent admitted for six months or more and three per cent in a secure facility.

Education, employment and economic circumstances

Education amongst women in prison is generally limited. The research in Scotland found that over 90 per cent had left school at age 16 or under. Roughly three-quarters had a history of truancy, half had been suspended at some stage and a third had been expelled. A subsequent study (Henderson 2001) largely supported these findings, showing that only 14 per cent of women in prison had stayed in school beyond the statutory minimum age (16 in Scotland), and that 61 per cent left school with no qualifications. A recent study of female remand[1] prisoners in England assessed 59 per cent as having at least one mental disorder (excluding substance abuse) upon reception into custody, 11 per cent of whom were diagnosed as psychotic (Parsons, Walker and Grubin 2001).

Most of the women in prison in Scotland (80 per cent) were unemployed at the time of their imprisonment (Loucks 1998). Henderson (2001) found that, of those who had been employed, most were employed in unskilled manual work. For those who had held a job at any stage, the longest period of employment was usually less than a year. Because of these features, the main source of income for women in prison tends to be from social welfare services. In Scotland, two-thirds of the women in custody depended on state benefits (Income Support, Incapacity Benefit, Job Seekers' Allowance and so on) for their main income (Henderson 2001). Almost half of the 179 respondents believed their offence was related to financial need, with a similar proportion saying past offences were the result of a shortage of money.

Characteristics

The backgrounds of women in prison outlined above make them a distinctive population once in prison as well (Richie 2001). Even a brief glance at offence types, sentences, demographics and mental health sets female prisoners aside with very different needs from the vast majority of the population in prison.

Offences and sentences

As stated at the outset, women make up a very small proportion of the offending population (14 per cent of those convicted in Scottish courts) and an even smaller percentage of the prison population. The patterns of women's offending also differ quite substantially from those for men. Offending by women is disproportionately for relatively minor or non-violent offences, such as soliciting and shoplifting, and financial crimes such as fraud, forgery, and embezzlement. In the United States, a national survey of almost 14,000 male and female prisoners (Snell and Morton 1994) found that nearly half of all women in prison were serving sentences for non-violent offences and had past convictions only for other non-violent offences. One in three women in prisons in the United States is there for a violent crime, compared to roughly one in every two male prisoners (Chesney-Lind 1997).

Not surprisingly then, a higher proportion of women are in prison for very short sentences. In Scotland in 2001, 25 per cent of sentenced female adults and young offenders in custody on a given day were serving sentences of less than six months, compared to 11 per cent of their male counterparts (Scottish Executive 2002). Almost half of sentenced females received into prison in Scotland were received for non-payment of a fine – 45 per cent, compared to 37 per cent of male receptions. Further, a higher proportion of the female prison population on a given day is made up of people not yet convicted or sentenced (24 per cent v. 15 per cent of male prisoners). In Scotland, many of these unconvicted and unsentenced women end up without a custodial sentence. In 1998, for example, 525 convicted females were held in custody prior to sentencing. Of these, less than half (222 women, or 42.3 per cent) eventually received a custodial sentence (Scottish Court Services 2000).

Demographics

Imprisonment often begins early for women (in Scotland by age 16, and by age 15 in England). Female prison populations are therefore generally young: again in Scotland, roughly two-thirds are under the age of 30, and a fifth are under age 21. Many have been to court or even to prison several times. However, two-thirds of those serving sentences at any given time will have never spent time in custody before. Almost half of this group are first offenders. The majority of women in prison are parents, though in Scotland, only about two-thirds currently had custody of their children (some of whom had adult children).

A disproportionate number of incarcerated women in many countries (e.g. England and the United States) are from ethnic minorities. Indeed, recent surges in female prison populations in many countries have included an even greater proportion of women from ethnic minorities (Chesney-Lind 1997). In the United States, a higher prevalence of drug use amongst ethnic minorities is likely to be responsible for much of this, as increasingly harsh punishments for the use and sales of drugs such as crack cocaine have been imposed (see Huling 1995). In a number of countries, ethnic minorities and foreign nationals who have been used as drug couriers or 'mules', with and without their knowledge or consent, make up a substantial number of women in prison. The types of problems women in prison face (see 'Issues for women in custody', below) are even more extreme for foreign nationals, who are even further away from children, family, and social and community supports than are the other women.

Psychological distress

Psychological distress was clearly a common feature of women in custody, perhaps unsurprisingly in light of their extensive histories of suicidal behaviour, mental health problems, addiction and abuse. Levels of hopelessness, based on the Beck Hopelessness Scale (Beck *et al.* 1974), showed clinical levels of hopelessness for a high proportion of women. Prisoners often score highly for hopelessness using this scale: Zamble and Porporino (1988) found, for example, that a third of their subjects scored '6' or higher (out of 20 where higher scores indicate higher levels of hopelessness). In Scotland, the average score amongst women in prison was 6.3.

The most recent Prison Survey in Scotland (Scottish Prison Service 2002) noted that 44 per cent of women in custody said they felt depressed daily or almost daily. Over a third (35 per cent) said they never felt hopeful about the future, and almost half (47 per cent) said their sleep was restless on a daily basis. Distress was also evident from the results of the Hospital Anxiety and Depression Scale (HADS; Zigmond and Snaith 1983) administered during the research in 1997 (Loucks 1998). Only just over half of the women in prison in Scotland had scores for depression within the 'normal' range, and only a third had 'normal' scores for anxiety. Over a quarter of women were recorded as having moderate or severe depression, and over a third had such scores for depression.

Research in prisons in England and Wales showed similar patterns. According to Singleton and colleagues (1998), female prisoners were significantly more likely than male prisoners to suffer from a neurotic disorder: while 59 per cent of remand and 40 per cent of sentenced male prisoners in their sample were assessed as having a neurotic disorder, the proportions for women were 76 per cent and 63 per cent respectively. These were most commonly mixed anxiety and depressive disorders. Their research also suggested that psychotic disorders may be more common amongst female prisoners on remand (21 per cent, as assessed by lay interviews, compared to nine per cent of male remand prisoners, four per cent of male sentenced prisoners and ten per cent of female sentenced prisoners).

Issues for women in custody

Issues women face while in prison are in most cases similar to those of men. For example, both groups often have difficulty finding housing and employment upon release, both are separated from children and family, both may be struggling with addiction and the stress of imprisonment, and both may be faced with intimidation and violence while in prison. However, the proportion of male and female prisoners dealing with these issues differs, as does the impact on the two groups. This section outlines such issues in more detail.

Child care

As noted above, a high proportion of female prisoners have dependent children. Custody of children is generally of more concern for women in prison than it is for men: research in Scotland (Inspectorates of Prisons and Social Work Services 1998) found that only 17 per cent of fathers looked after their children while the mother was in custody. This compares to 87 per cent of mothers who care for the children when the father is in prison. Comparable figures in the United States showed that 25 per cent of the women's children, compared to 90 per cent of children of male prisoners, lived with the other parent during imprisonment (Morash *et al.* 1998). The picture in England and Wales was even more extreme, where only five per cent of the 8,100 children affected each year by their mother's imprisonment remained in their home and were looked after by the other parent (Wolfe 1999). Potential loss of custody of a child is therefore a very real concern for women who end up in prison.

Visits to women in prison can also be problematic. The low number of women held in custody means that few prisons or Young Offender Institutions exist which hold women. By definition, this means that many women will be located at a great distance from their families. Statistics from the Prison Reform Trust in London note that nearly a fifth of female prisoners in England and Wales are held over 100 miles away from their committal court town. In such circumstances, women in prison are less likely than male prisoners to have contact with their children. Research in the United States (Snell and Morton 1994) reported that over half of women with children under age 18 had never received a visit from their children while in prison. This is particularly the case where the women are foreign nationals: one study in England found that only 11 per cent of female foreign nationals had received a visit from their children while in prison (Caddle and Crisp 1997).

The research by Caddle and Crisp also noted a range of psychological effects on children whose mothers are imprisoned. This included problems with behaviour, sleeping, eating, bed-wetting, overall health, and with making and keeping friends. These issues were particularly acute when the children had to move home or go into care. While these problems may occur when the father is imprisoned, problematic behaviour among children has been found to be more common when the mother is taken into custody (Richards and McWilliams 1996).

Housing

As with child care, housing is another issue which differs for female prisoners. Again, statistics in Scotland show that women are more likely to lose their housing while in custody than are men (Inspectorates of Prisons and Social Work Services 1998). Research in England and Wales noted that a third of female prisoners lose their homes while in prison (Wolfe 1999). Women are more often single parents and have tenancy agreements in their own names; men, in contrast, are more likely to have a partner at home to maintain the tenancy.

Addiction

Some women use custody as an opportunity to withdraw from drugs. However, others continue to abuse licit and illicit drugs. The most recent Prison Survey in Scotland (Scottish Prison Service 2002) found that 32 per cent of women admitted to using illegal drugs in prison during the previous month, primarily opiates (82 per cent of those who said they had used drugs). Half of the women (51 per cent) reported the use of illegal drugs while in prison. Drug use amongst women in custody tends to differ from their use outside, usually because drugs are less readily available and, similarly, because their drug of choice may not be accessible. Because addiction is such a common feature of female prisoners prior to custody, withdrawal from addiction and its consequences poses tremendous problems for many women in prison. The difficulty of withdrawal for women in prison is usually more than the physical consequences. Rather, withdrawal forces many women to face issues they had blocked out with drugs, often for the first time, such as experiences of abuse or social realities such as poverty and loss of housing or custody of children.

Victimisation and custody

Victimisation has many implications for women in general, but perhaps particularly for those in custody. Increased substance abuse was one possible consequence, where people tried to block out memories of abuse (or, as one woman mentioned, violence from her partner hurt less if she was drunk). A small-scale study in the United States (Chiavaroli 1992) noted that treatment for drug abuse among victims of sexual abuse appeared to be more effective when it addressed both issues. Increased vulnerability during withdrawal from drugs or alcohol was therefore an important problem for victims.

People in custody often have feelings of shame, isolation, or self-blame as a result of their imprisonment, which in turn reduces their self-esteem. This is particularly the case for women who have been victims of abuse, where even standard prison procedures such as body searches or cell searches, and the loss of autonomy which is a basic part of prison life, can trigger feelings of helplessness and frustration common to the experience of abuse itself; in a sense prison 'retraumatises' them, albeit unintentionally, forcing them to relive past abuse.

Finally, prison staff are placed in a difficult position with victim/offenders: to what extent should professional staff in prisons 'open cans of worms' and help women address their past or ongoing abuse? This question is controversial, especially because the majority of the female prison population are short-term prisoners; whether it is safe or even responsible for a prison to start addressing issues which may take years to deal with is a question as yet unresolved. Some women are forced to address past abuse while they are in custody, for example if it is directly relevant to their offence or addiction, but these would primarily be longer-term prisoners who are more likely to have access to ongoing support while in custody.

Bullying

More direct victimisation can also take place in prisons: violence and bullying are not unusual amongst female prisoners. In Scotland, a quarter of prisoners said they had been bullied at some stage, though not necessarily during their current sentence. Physical assaults were also surprisingly common, with 15.1 per cent of prisoners saying they had been assaulted in a prison. These figures can however be misleading, as definitions of bullying and assaults are generally problematic. The most recent Prison Survey in Scotland (Scottish Prison Service 2002) reported much lower rates of bullying, with only nine per cent of women saying they had been bullied in the prison in the past month and 12 per cent saying they had feared for their safety in that time. Ironically, the proportion of recorded bullying, fights, and similar incidents doubled between the research in 1997 and the Survey in 2002 (HM Inspectorate of Prisons for Scotland 2002).

Bullying in women's prisons is often in the form of 'taxing' (where prisoners who are more dominant take things from those who are more vulnerable), intimidation, ostracism and extortion. Physical bullying (assaults, etc), in contrast, is generally more common amongst male prisoners. Bullying amongst female prisoners is often more insidious and therefore more difficult for staff to detect. As a result, some women complained during the research in Scotland that bullying frequently took place in front of staff, but that staff did nothing about it. Often, however, the behaviour was too ambiguous for staff to recognise it as bullying and to take appropriate action.

Bullying amongst female prisoners in Scotland was often related to competition for medication. The prison's detoxification programme meant that the vast majority of women were receiving prescription drugs, usually diazepam and dihydrocodeine. Prescriptions were also common for other problems such as mental disorder or poor health, with the result that about 97 per cent of the women were receiving some form of medication in the prison. With the relative shortage of illicit drugs coming into prison, the women would go to extreme measures to get prescription drugs from others. This included threats for people to give others their medication or telling people what to say to the medical staff to get extra. Measures designed to keep people from retaining their medication were being abused: women taking liquid medication would put cotton wool in their mouths to absorb it, or alternatively people would regurgitate their medication to pass on to other people. Despite the problems associated with medication, the physical and psychological distress of the vast majority of the women made it a necessary part of prison life.

Suicidal behaviour

Rates of suicide amongst women in custody are higher than amongst women in the population at large. One reason is that withdrawal from drugs and the stresses of imprisonment increase the risk of suicide and self-harm amongst a group already vulnerable to such behaviour (see for example Liebling 1996). Further, women use methods of suicide in custody that are more likely to be lethal than than those favoured outside prison: outside, women are most likely to resort to overdoses or 'cutting up', but inside prison, methods are generally limited to hanging, which is much more likely to succeed in causing death. Men tend to resort to 'more' lethal forms of suicide both in and out of custody (firearms or hanging outside prison, and again hanging inside custody). Amongst female prisoners in Scotland, suicide attempts were more often associated with addiction to alcohol than to drugs. The reason for this is less clear, though it may be because drug use was a feature of such a large proportion of the population resulting in a ceiling effect. Finally, clinical levels of hopelessness, anxiety, depression and poor problem-solving were notably high amongst the women in prison in Scotland – characteristics often related to suicidal behaviour.

What was very clear from the research in Scotland was that prison seems unlikely in itself to 'cause' suicidal behaviour. It can however be the 'last straw' in combination with problems outside. Such problems include the fact that many women will be withdrawing from drugs and will therefore be facing reality, perhaps for the first time in years. This reality can be intolerable, especially where extreme physical and sexual abuse are involved. In prison, women are away from their usual social supports. They may feel failure or shame, perhaps combined with bullying in custody and the loss of autonomy and (for victims of abuse) the retraumatisation that imprisonment can bring.

One question is whether the higher levels of distress amongst women in prison are all that surprising. Psychometric tests are designed to look at people's response to 'everyday' problems. However, the 'everyday' problems amongst women in prison are unusually severe compared to the 'average' population outside. If women are wrestling with daily drug use and addiction, daily physical, sexual, and emotional abuse, daily financial crises and housing problems, etc, their distress will understandably be high. This is not to say that women or even female offenders outside prison do not experience similar problems. What is clear, however, is that an "alarmingly high" proportion of women in prison show characteristics (such as the above) associated with risk of suicide (Liebling 1994).

Life events

Previous research has shown a consistent relationship between the number of stressful events in a person's life and that person's emotional and physical health (Holmes and Rahe 1967). That research measured the number of stressful events with a Life Change Scale (also known as the Holmes and Rahe Social Readjustment Rating Scale). With this in mind, the author of this chapter designed a short Prisoner Life Events Scale (PLES; Loucks 1999), developed specially for women in custody, during some research conducted in two women's prisons in England (Loucks 2001). The PLES is a 19-point scale, with an option for additional responses, designed to measure types of events other than custody itself which may influence a person's behaviour and ability to cope while inside.

The results derived from use of the scale showed quite dramatically the stressors which affect women in custody, above and beyond the stress of custody itself. Nearly half the women lost possession of their accommodation outside while they were in prison. Lack of visits from family were also common concerns. A high proportion in both prisons (roughly a third) had a close family member seriously ill while they were in custody. Having a close friend or family member go to prison during their time in custody and formal separation from partners were also common events, as were death or victimisation of family and friends. In total, the women reported an average range of 3.0–4.8 such events during their current period of custody.

Using a different scale of life events, research elsewhere reported an average of ten life events in the year prior to custody (Keaveny and Zauszniewski 1999). The authors reported a positive correlation between the number of life events and levels of depression.

A man's world

The small proportion of women in custody inevitably means that custodial culture is dominated by the needs of men. Programmes and activities in prisons are often designed with the needs and interests of male prisoners in mind (see Carlen 1983; Stern 1998). Stephanie Covington cites an example of the situation in the United States, but arguably the same situation exists in most jurisdictions:

> Despite this growing information on best practices for treating females, male-based programming remains the norm in many settings. Even female-only programmes are often merely copies of men's programmes, not based on research or clinical experience with women and girls. This problem is especially acute for juveniles. Boys far outnumber girls in the juvenile justice system, so programmes are designed with the needs of males in mind, and services for female adolescents simply replicate the male model. (Pepi 1998) (Covington 1998: 12–13)

Overall, female offenders are a vastly different group with different needs and problems to male offenders. The Criminal Justice System seems to have a very different effect on them, so policies and programmes directed towards men will often not be particularly useful (see also Easteal 2001).

Conclusion

Two inquiries into women's offending were conducted in Scotland (Inspectorates of Prisons and Social Work Services 1998) and in England (Wedderburn Committee 2000) specifically to understand and address the needs of women who end up in prison. The main emphasis of the recommendations from the two reports was on ensuring appropriate alternatives to custody for female offenders and on increasing the information available about the women and their needs. Importantly in Scotland, the recommendations secured a commitment by the government to halving the female prison population within two years and to keeping young women under the age 18 out of Prison Service custody. The logic behind this was that the problems these women are dealing with are best identified and addressed outside of custody, without complicating already difficult circumstances by the fact of imprisonment (also Radosh 2002). This is not to say that serious offending should be ignored, rather that it be prevented through more appropriate targeting of resources for female offenders. Unfortunately, the goals in both countries to reduce the population of female prisoners have failed to meet their targets, and the number of women who enter custody continues to rise.

Much of the information above is based on research in Scotland. However, the evidence available internationally shows an almost identical picture of female prisoners in every country (Stern 1998; McIvor 1999; Lemgruber 2001). Women consistently make up a tiny proportion of prisoners. They consistently come from backgrounds of poverty, unemployment, abuse and addiction. They are consistently young, uneducated and unskilled. Most are mothers of young children and are often single mothers. Most have committed a non-violent offence. The inquiry into female offenders in England and Wales (Wedderburn Committee 2000) described female prisoners as '... overwhelmingly, though not exclusively, drawn from a group who share all the characteristics of "social exclusion".' Overall, it is clear that the problems which female offenders face are unlikely to be solved by imprisonment and can, in reality, be made worse.

Note

1   Those held in custody prior to conviction or sentence.

References

Anderson, T.L., Rosay, A.B. and Saum, C. (2002) 'The impact of drug use and crime involvement on health problems among female drug offenders', *The Prison Journal*, 82 (1): 50–68.

Beck, A.T., Weissman, A.W., Lester, D. and Trexler, L. (1974) 'The assessment of pessimism: The hopelessness scale', *Journal of Consulting and Clinical Psychology*, 42: 861–65.

Birecree, E.A., Bloom, J.D., Leverette, M.D. and Williams, M. (1994) 'Diagnostic efforts regarding women in Oregon prison system – a preliminary report', *Journal of Offender Therapy and Comparative Criminology*, 38 (3): 217–30, fall 1994.

Bradley, R.G. and Davino, K.M. (2002) 'Women's perceptions of the prison environment: When prison is "the safest place I've ever been"', *Psychology of Women Quarterly*, 26 (4): 351–59.

Byrne, M.K. and Howells, K. (2002) 'The psychological needs of women prisoners: Implications for rehabilitation and management', *Psychiatry, Psychology and Law*, 9 (1): 34–43.

Caddle, D. and Crisp, D. (1997) *Imprisoned women and mothers*. Home Office Research Study 162. London: Home Office.

Carlen, P. (1983) *Women's Imprisonment: A study in social control*. London: Routledge and Kegan Paul.

Chesney-Lind, M. (1997) *The Female Offender: Girls, women, and crime*. Thousand Oaks: Sage Publications.

Chiavaroli, T. (1992) 'Rehabilitation from substance abuse in individuals with a history of sexual abuse', *Journal of Substance Abuse Treatment*, 9 (4): 349–54.

Covington, S.S. (1998) 'Women in prison: Approaches in the treatment of our most invisible population', *Women and Therapy*, 21 (1): 141–55.

Easteal, P. (2001) 'Women in Australian prisons: The cycle of abuse and dysfunctional environments', *The Prison Journal*, 81 (1): 73–86.

Fleming, M.F., Barry, K.L. and MacDonald, R. (1991) 'The alcohol use disorders identification test (AUDIT) in a College Sample', *The International Journal of the Addictions*, 26 (11): 1173–85.

Fraser, J. (1994) 'Drugs survey: An investigation into women prisoners' attitudes towards a proposed drug-free zone at Holloway and the experience of drug use', Psychology Department, HMP Holloway.

Gunn, J., Maden, A. and Swinton, M. (1991) *Mentally Disturbed Prisoners*. London: Home Office.

Henderson, S. (2001) *Women Offenders: Effective management and intervention.* Scottish Prison Service Occasional Papers 2001. Edinburgh: Scottish Prison Service.

HM Inspectorate of Prisons for Scotland (2002) *HMP and YOI Cornton Vale: Intermediate inspection 9–10 September 2002.* Edinburgh: Scottish Executive.

Holmes, T.H. and Rahe, R.H. (1967) 'The Social Readjustment Rating Scale', *Journal of Psychosomatic Research*, 11: 213–18.

Huling, T. (1995) 'African American women and the war on Drugs', Paper presented at the Annual Meeting of the American Society of Criminology Conference, Boston.

Ingram Fogel, C. and Belyea, M. (1999) 'The lives of incarcerated women: Violence, substance abuse, and at risk for HIV', *Journal for the Association of Nurses in AIDS Care*, 10 (6): 66–74.

Inspectorates of Prisons and Social Work Services (1998) Women offenders – a safer way. Review of Community Disposals and the use of custody for women offenders in Scotland: a summary.

Johnson, G. and Farren, E. (1996) 'An evaluation of prisoners' views about substance free zones', in N. Clark and G. Stephenson (eds) *Psychological Perspectives on Police and Custodial Culture and Organisation.* Division of Legal and Criminological Psychology, *Issues in Criminological and Legal Psychology,* 25: 30–8.

Kendall, K. (1993) *Literature Review of Therapeutic Services for Women in Prison: Companion Volume I to program evaluation of therapeutic services at the prison for women.* Correctional Services of Canada.

King, R. (1998) 'Females in custody: A profile', *Prison Research and Development Bulletin*, 6: 1.

Keaveny, M.E. and Zauszniewski, J.A. (1999) 'Life events and psychological well-being in women sentenced to prison', *Issues in Mental Health Nursing*, 20 (1): 73–89.

Lemgruber, J. (2001)'Women in the criminal justice system'. Keynote speech, in N. Ollus and S. Nevala (eds) *Women in the Criminal Justice System: International examples and national responses.* Proceedings of the workshop held at the Tenth United Nations Congress on the Prevention of Crime and the Treatment of Offenders, Vienna, Austria 10–17 April 2000. Helsinki: HEUNI.

Liebling, A. (1994) 'Suicide amongst women prisoners', *Howard Journal of Criminal Justice*, 33 (1): 1–9.

Liebling, A. (1996) 'Prison suicide: What progress research?', in A. Liebling (ed.) *Deaths in Custody: Caring for People at Risk* (pp. 41–53). London: Whiting and Birch Ltd.

Lightfoot, L. and Lambert, L. (1992) *Substance Abuse Treatment Needs of Federally Sentenced Women: Technical Report No. 2 (Draft).* Correctional Services Canada.

Loucks, N. (2001) *Evaluation of Improved Regimes for Female Offenders.* London: HM Prison Service for England and Wales, Women's Policy Group, unpublished.

Loucks, N. (1998) *HMPI Cornton Vale: Research into Drugs and Alcohol, Violence and Bullying, Suicides and Self-Injury, and Backgrounds of Abuse*. Scottish Prison Service Occasional Papers, Report No. 1/98. Edinburgh: Scottish Prison Service.

Loucks, N. (1999) *The Prisoner Life Events Scale*. Unpublished.

Loucks, N., Power, K., Swanson, V. and Chambers, J. (2000) *Young People in Custody in Scotland: The characteristics and perceptions of young people held in custody*. Occasional Paper 3/2000. Edinburgh: Scottish Prison Service.

Maden, A., Swinton, M. and Gunn, J. (1991) 'Drug Dependence in Prisons', *British Medical Journal*, 302 (6781): 880.

McIvor, G. (1999) 'Women, crime and criminal justice in Scotland', *Scottish Journal of Criminal Justice Studies*, 5 (1): 67–74.

Morash, M., Bynum, T. and Koons (1998) *Women Offenders: Programming needs and promising approaches*. National Institute of Justice.

Morris, A., Wilkinson, C., Tisi, A., Woodrow, J. and Rockley, A. (1995) *Managing the Needs of Female Prisoners*. London: Home Office Publications Unit.

Parsons, S., Walker, L. and Grubin, D. (2001) 'Prevalence of mental disorder in female remand prisons', *Journal of Forensic Psychiatry*, 12 (1): 194–202.

Pepi, C. (1998) 'Children without childhoods: A feminist intervention strategy utilizing systems theory and restorative justice in treating female adolescent offenders', in J. Harden and M. Hill (eds) *Breaking the Rules: Women in prison and feminist therapy*. New York: Haworth.

Radosh, P.F. (2002) 'Reflections on women's crime and mothers in prison: A peacemaking approach', *Crime and Delinquency*, 48 (2): 300–15.

Richards, M. and McWilliams, B. (1996) 'Imprisonment and family ties', *Home Office Research Bulletin* 38.

Richie, B.E. (2001) 'Challenges incarcerated women face as they return to their communities: Findings from life history interviews', *Crime and Delinquency*, 47 (3): 368–89.

Scottish Court Services (2000) Personal correspondence.

Scottish Executive (2002) *Prison Statistics Scotland, 2001. Statistical Bulletin*, Criminal Justice Series CrJ/2002/6. Edinburgh: Scottish Executive.

Scottish Prison Service (2002) *Prison Survey 2002: Prisoner Results – HMP Cornton Vale*. Edinburgh: Scottish Prison Service.

Singleton, N., Meltzer, H. and Gatward, R., with J. Coid and D. Deasy (1998) *Psychiatric Morbidity Among Prisoners: A survey carried out in 1997 by the Social Survey Division of ONS on behalf of the Department of Health*. London: Office for National Statistics.

Snell, T.L. and Morton, D.C. (1994) *Women in Prison*. Special report. Washington DC: Bureau of Justice Statistics.

Stern, V. (1998) *A Sin Against the Future: Imprisonment and the World*. London: Penguin.

Wedderburn Committee (2000) *Justice for Women: The need for reform*. Report of the Committee on Women's Imprisonment. London: Prison Reform Trust.

Wolfe, T. (1999) *Counting the Cost: The social and financial consequences of women's imprisonment*. Report prepared for the Wedderburn Committee on Women's Imprisonment. London: Prison Reform Trust.

Zaitzow, B.H. (2001) 'Whose problem is it anyway?: Women prisoners and HIV/AIDS', *International Journal of Offender Therapy and Comparative Criminology*, 45 (6): 673–90.

Zamble, E. and Porporino, F.J. (1988) *Coping, Behaviour, and Adaptation in Prison Inmates*. New York: Springer-Verlag.

Zigmond, A.S. and Snaith, R.P. (1983) 'Hospital Anxiety and Depression Scale', *Acta Psychiatrica Scandinavica*, 67: 361–70.

Chapter 16

Applied Psychological services in Prisons and Probation

Graham Towl, Home Office

The context

Punishment of offenders in the UK takes place by detention in secure facilities and through structured supervision in community settings. Whereas imprisonment is perhaps intuitively associated with 'punishment', this is not always the public perception of community based sentences. Indeed, as discussed earlier in this book, public attitudes towards punishment and criminal justice sanctions have posed problems for many governments. For the purposes of this chapter, the term punishment is taken to refer to the environments of prisons and to probation services delivered in the community. Thus, the 'punishment' element of prison and probation work is about the containment of prisoners in prison and the management of offenders in community settings.

In this chapter, the focus is on the work of applied psychologists in prison and probation services. By far the majority of such psychologists are from the forensic specialism (Towl 2003a). Although the work of forensic psychologists, in prisons, has been described elsewhere (for example, Towl and McDougall 1999; Towl 2000; Towl 2003a). Here, the work of forensic psychologists will be addressed in a context of possible future directions. The potential, and in some cases current, roles of other areas of applied psychological practice will also be covered. The potential to apply other psychological specialisms in delivering services in prisons and probation services has perhaps not been adequately addressed in the past. Increasingly, it is being recognised that an exclusive focus upon the forensic specialism in addressing the broad and varied needs of those involved in criminal and civil justice processes is unduly limiting (HM Prison Service and the National Probation Service 2003).

Background

The specialist Division of Forensic Psychology of the British Psychological Society has been one of the fastest growing in recent years. This has also been reflected in the employment market (Towl 2003a). The largest single employer of forensic psychologists both under training and amongst those trained is HM Prison Service (Towl 2002). In April 2000 a joint appointment of Head of Psychology for prisons and probation services was made (Towl 2000). The following year, the first joint recruitment of trainee forensic psychologists for prisons and probation services took place. There is a long tradition of psychological services in prisons. However, there is a far more varied picture in probation services. There are currently over 700 staff in psychological roles in prisons and over 30 who have been jointly recruited in probation services.

As has been mentioned, the overwhelming majority of applied psychologists working in prisons are in the forensic specialism. This is true for all those so far jointly recruited into probation services. This is no surprise, given the history of such services and their context. However, it does perhaps mean that the recipients of applied psychological services are not always getting the full benefits that the range of applied psychology disciplines may have to offer (HM Prison Service and NPS 2003).

What follows is an account of the roles, and or potential roles, of the applied psychology specialisms. Recent professional developments in the British Psychological Society have given renewed impetus to an understanding of applied psychological practice as being underpinned by a great deal of theoretical commonality and in terms of the professional competencies of each specialism. The applied psychological specialisms considered here are: forensic; clinical; counselling; educational; health and occupational psychology.

Current and future practice

Forensic psychologists in prisons and probation services undertake work in a range of areas. One underpinning theme of much of such forensic practice is that of risk assessment and management. This has increasingly come to the fore in recent years and looks set to continue. Generally, the area of risk assessment and management has tended to be associated with the risk of recidivism amongst offenders (Towl and Crighton 1996, 1997). This is a very important area of risk assessment work for forensic psychologists. Indeed, it may often be viewed as the core forensic service in prisons and probation. For a review of the logic of the risk assessment process undertaken by psychologists, there are a number of potential sources (see for example, Crighton 1999).

The logic of the risk assessment process may be applied to a number of areas in addition to highly structured group-work aimed at reducing the risk of reoffending, individual assessment and intervention work with life sentenced prisoners (Willmot 2003). Areas less commonly considered include the risk of suicide, intentional self-injury (Towl, Snow and McHugh 2000) and the management of disturbances in prisons (Ashmore 2003).

Although forensic psychologists have had some involvement in the important area of suicide prevention, this has tended to be limited in comparison with other areas such as facilitating structured group-work interventions aimed at reducing the risk of reoffending. This is starting to change with a renewed organisational impetus to reduce the number of suicides. Suicide prevention is a challenge for both prisons and probation services.

In terms of future directions for the work of forensic psychologists, a number of possibilities occur, given the history and current context of professional practice. The new strategy for psychological services in prisons and probation has three underpinning themes. Firstly a focus on the context of professional policy and practice. More specifically this theme is covered in the form of a framework for structuring developments within psychological services in the broader context of public sector reforms. Secondly, a clear emphasis on the need for appropriate supervision, training and Continuing Professional Development (CPD) in the organisation and delivery of applied psychological services. Thirdly, a clear and explicit focus within the work of applied psychologists in ensuring that their areas of work meet 'business needs' of the organisations.

As mentioned above, most applied psychologists currently employed by HM Prison Service tend to be forensic in orientation. This partly reflects relatively recent professional developments in the British Psychological Society and the specialist Division of Forensic Psychology. A summary of some such recent professional developments is detailed elsewhere (see, for example, Towl 2004). As a general theme, the

307

commonalties across the areas of specialisms within applied psychology may come increasingly to the fore in future years. In the meantime, the distinctive roles of each specialism may well also be emphasised.

In practice, the meaning of the term 'forensic psychology' has, in terms of professional developments broadened over the years. One key defining characteristic appears increasingly to be as much about *where* such work is taking place as it is about *what* type of work is undertaken. In some ways, this may be a residue of the anachronism of 'prison psychologist' a term which used to be in widespread usage but only those out of touch with, or unaware of, more recent developments in the field still appear to use. Such a term curiously appeared to give primacy to the place of work rather than the function or type of work undertaken. This was in contrast to most other applied psychology specialisms where the place of work was not routinely referred to as a professional epithet. With the widespread advent of specialist chartership through the British Psychological Society, the term 'forensic psychologist' began increasingly to be used with a renewed focus on function rather than place of work. As mentioned above, themes such as 'risk assessment' have begun to be recognised as central to much of the contributions of forensic psychologists.

The purpose of outlining the above, albeit briefly, on such professional matters is that much will hinge upon broader professional developments within the British Psychological Society (BPS) and this will have a major impact upon potential models of service delivery. For example, if the BPS succeeds with proposed legislative changes (which seems likely), that would for the first time require statutory registration of chartered psychologists, then this will have an impact. Those currently working as forensic psychologists can of course have a significant influence over such processes through involvement with the BPS and their professional work.

Currently, forensic psychologists working within prisons and probation are comparatively well paid and generally enjoy good conditions of employment. Promotion opportunities abound and the quality of training and supervision has been significantly improved. Staff recruitment and retention levels are good. Increasingly, forensic psychologists are linking their work directly to the business needs of prisons and probation.

Forensic psychologists will have significant opportunities to shape the development of the work of future forensic psychologists in prisons and probation. This is partly because of the devolution and delegation of professional advisory responsibilities to a (geographical) organisational area, rather than at the level of individual prison establishment. This has allowed for a more strategic approach to service delivery. Forensic psychologists are beginning to take advantage of the possibilities to improve and enhance existing partnerships. For example, increasing numbers of practicing forensic psychologists are initiating or improving their links with the academic sector. Joint academic and practitioner posts are starting to emerge in the forensic field. This is the case across both prisons and probation. Also, forensic psychologists are benefitting from working with colleagues from the other specialisms of applied psychology. This gives the opportunity for shared learning. Concomitantly, the possibilities of lateral transfer or indeed the development of skills in additional areas of specialism are improving for both forensic and the other applied psychologists. Many of these developments will interact to result in a richer and more diverse workforce with a potentially greater range of knowledge and skills. The field is ripe for such transitions.

In terms of some of the specific areas of work which appear ripe for development, a number of thoughts occur. The earlier mentioned theme of risk assessment has a number of applications as alluded to above. Further developments could include a greater emphasis on risk assessment in incident management and also enhancing the research base in this area. The potential for operational research is liable to grow with increasingly improved information on the running of prisons. That is not to suggest that operational research would by any means be the exclusive domain of forensic psychologists but rather to suggest that if they seize the initiative, they will have a key contribution to make. This links in with the recent development of area psychologists' new role as often key link personnel with prison service HQ with regard to the vetting of research proposals and approaches to universities to undertake particular pieces of applied research. Indeed, there has been a recent re-emphasis on the role and potential role of psychologists in research in prisons; this is reflected at an 'area' or regional level and at the national level.

With the rapid expansion of knowledge and practice within the forensic field, there will undoubtedly be increased opportunities to further develop specialisms. It is also being increasingly recognised that there should be opportunities for promotion and development for forensic psychologists which do not have to involve increased management responsibilities. This will dovetail well with the notion of developing particular specialist posts. An example of this has been the development of some posts with a specialist role across a prison service or probation service area (rather than keeping appointments limited to one particular prison or probation service office). Thus there are posts where some experienced practitioners deliver services with life sentenced prisoners across a number of prisons or advise on sex offender interventions across a probation area.

In addition to the development of specialisms for experienced practitioners, there is also much scope for forensic psychologists to take advantage of career development opportunities in the National Health Service (NHS). This, for the organisations of prisons and probation, is a double edged sword of the growing status and recognition of forensic psychological services. On the one hand, it is good that there is a wider professional recognition of the quality of the work. On the other hand, concerns may arise about the retention of experienced staff. Looking for a moment outside the applied psychological disciplines, psychologists also have opportunities to move to generic management roles within prisons.

As was noted earlier in the chapter, the forensic field is booming. Opportunities abound, arguably more so than they ever have for forensic psychologists. Much of the future shape of the development of such services is in the hands of current practitioners, particularly in the context of the increased delegation and devolution of such professional leadership.

Inter-professional rivalries and concerns can have a real impact on what is or is not delivered. Understandably, managers of services have little time for such internal, professional wrangling. This has historically been a challenge and potentially remains one, particularly with the growth of applied psychology specialisms in delivering services in prisons. With a renewed focus on applied psychology specialisms, across the board, it is essential that professional psychologists focus upon what can be achieved in terms of the effective public service delivery of applied psychological services; valuing each other's specialist expertise.

From April 2003, the responsibility (and budget) for health services in prisons moved from the prison service to the NHS. Prior to this, there were already a number of NHS trusts providing services directly to prisons and probation service clients. Clinical psychologists would often be part of such multidisciplinary teams. The potential opportunities for the development of clinical psychological services are manifold. The concentration of mental health needs amongst those offenders in prisons and under probation supervision is huge. This is a potentially appealing area for clinical psychologists with an interest in focusing upon some of the population groups with highest needs for their services. On top of this, it is well worth retaining sight of the potential needs of staff across prisons and probation services.

Developments within the application of clinical psychological services in prisons and probation may be seen in the broader context of developments within public services in general and the NHS in particular. Clinical psychologists have much to offer. Traditionally, forensic psychologists working in prisons have tended not to get involved with, for example, addressing individual mental health issues amongst prisoners. This is an area in much need of further development. Such services could be provided at a number of levels.

First, the possibility of prisons and probation services being recognised placements for the training of clinical psychologists could potentially be a helpful development. Clinical psychologists could take the role of the supervisors of such trainees. Their supervision of such staff could result in a greater amount of direct service delivery to clients. Also, those under such training may choose, after qualification, to continue to work in prisons or probation services or alternatively take an understanding of such environments to their work elsewhere in the NHS. Such clinical trainees could also benefit from contact with other areas of the applied psychology specialisms and of course multi-disciplinary teams within prisons and probation services. This could potentially be a very cost effective approach to improving psychological service delivery to those with mental health needs.

Second, staff training in improving the awareness and understanding of mental health issues. By way of example, such approaches could augment work already underway in reducing the risk of suicide and working with offenders who intentionally injure themselves. Depression is one area that currently receives relatively little attention amongst applied psychologists in prisons and would benefit from being addressed.

Third, there is a good case for the continued development of the delivery of existing direct services to clients. There are populations with high individual need within the prison estate such as women, juveniles and young offenders. Those held on remand (i.e. during trial and sentencing) are in an environment which may well serve to amplify existing vulnerabilities.

Fourth, there is an important contribution which may be made at a more strategic or managerial level within prisons and probation services. This may well take the form of some sort of consultancy based service. The potential for engagement at this level within the organisations is probably greater than within the NHS more generally where medical staff tend to be more dominant in terms of their professional influence. It is also worth turning our attention to staff needs specifically.

The care and welfare needs of staff can be high. It is no surprise that sickness levels amongst prison staff are very high. Organisationally, this clearly needs to be vigorously tackled. Clinical psychologists could play a potentially significant role in this and not just in terms of reducing sickness levels. Although this, in and of itself, would be desirable. The potentially important role then, is in providing staff with psychological support in an area where perhaps insufficient attention has been paid. Some of this would be ongoing work associated with the day to day demands of working in prisons and probation. Other elements may be linked to specific and potentially major incidents, such as riots to further augment existing arrangements. Staff may also benefit from guidance and support in dealing with individual difficult offenders.

This short section has touched upon some of the potential roles of clinical psychologists in prisons and probation services; this will be an area where we are likely to see a number of developments over coming years. Just as with the work of forensic psychologists in prisons and probation, clinical psychologists can play a major role in shaping such futures.

Counselling psychology is a relatively new specialism as a distinct division of the British Psychological Society (BPS). Traditionally although applied psychologists in prisons have used counselling skills to underpin much of their work, this has not involved counselling psychology as a distinct specialism. Comparatively recently, this began to change with the introduction of a counselling psychological service in women's prisons.

Current services, although small in terms of size, are already gaining significant acceptance as useful to prisons. Much of the work with women prisoners has tended to be linked to problems associated with intentional self injury and an inflated risk of suicide. This has not been the exclusive realm of counselling psychologists, but as indicated above, it is an area where such contributions have been acknowledged as helpful and successful in addressing some key 'business needs'.

Again, as with clinical psychologists' contributions, there is significant scope for expansion and service developments. One important challenge to address is about how an appropriate infrastructure may be set up to enable the further development of this applied psychology specialism. This is not a challenge exclusive to counselling psychology. Rather, it pervades the development and implementation of the new strategy in prisons and probation which endorses an approach based upon a more theoretically eclectic model (HM Prison Service and NPS 2003).

There are a wide range of possible models to establish an infrastructure. One possibility is cross-geographical (HM Prison Service and

Probation Service areas) or regional developments; that is, in terms of sharing resources both for direct service delivery, but also, crucially, ensuring appropriate supervision of those delivering services whilst under training. Historically, in the UK, trainee counselling psychologists have tended to be less well funded and supported than forensic psychologists. In this regard, their entry point makes them appear very cost effective to a manager, certainly for those under training. There may be a particular appeal where counselling psychologists are able to provide services perhaps more cost effectively than some of the other specialisms in applied psychology. This would need to be looked at in detail in reviewing any such service provision. It may also serve to improve the pay and conditions of those working in this specialism. In the public sector, it is particularly important that applied psychologists, from whichever specialism, have a clear focus on ensuring that the public gain an efficient, cost effective service.

The areas of staff care, support and working with staff and managers to reduce sickness levels, perhaps stand out as areas where counselling psychologists could have potentially powerful impacts too. Just as with clinical psychology services, such work could be undertaken at a number of levels involving the supervision of trainees, direct service provision with offenders, staff training and an input at a strategic level in terms of the development of future services and approaches. Again, the field is ripe for development.

There are currently a relatively low number of educational psychologists working within prisons. They tend not to be directly employed by HM Prison Service. Rather their services are bought in as part of external contracts for the delivery of educational services. They tend to work in the juvenile/Young Offender part of the prison estate.

Given the structure of the arrangements for the training of educational psychologists in the UK it is difficult to see, at this juncture, how viable training arrangements for trainee educational psychologists could be set up within Criminal Justice agencies. To change this would probably need some quite significant changes within the British Psychological Society's arrangements for such training. There is no immediate prospect of this happening. This significantly limits the potential forensic role of those in the educational applied psychology specialism. However, there remains potential for the use of chartered educational psychologists.

Educational psychologists have the potential to contribute to the work of the organisations on a number of levels. Given the likelihood of their presence only being comparatively small, there may well be merit in them gravitating to providing consultancy services, advice and support to staff. In the first instance however, it may be deemed to make sense to focus such scarce services primarily within the juvenile estate. Enabling offenders to enhance their educational achievements may help reduce their risk of reoffending, particularly as higher educational attainments will improve their employability.

Another area where educational psychologists may make a potentially useful contribution would be in working with colleagues to design appropriate ways of working with those offenders who perhaps do not have the educational history to benefit fully from a number of existing interventions. Just as with the other areas of applied psychology, currently, there is much room for development; with the caveat that it is very unlikely at this juncture, that there would be scope for trainee positions, thus limiting their likely numbers in this particular workforce.

Health psychology is a comparatively new and emerging discipline. Currently, there are some forensic psychologists who hold postgraduate qualifications in health psychology. For example, the area psychologist for Greater London is a health psychologist, responsible for the delivery of applied psychological services in prisons, with a responsibility for working in partnership with the London probation service. Health psychologists potentially have a great deal to contribute to the work of prisons and probation.

There is probably significant overlap in much of the work that could be undertaken by health psychologists and some of the other specialisms, for example clinical psychologists. However there are differences and there is a potentially distinctive contribution that could be made by this growing group of applied psychologists.

One of the more obvious areas in terms of work with offenders is in approaches to tackling problems of drug misuse. Interestingly this has not historically been an area to which many forensic psychologists have tended to devote much attention. As with other applied psychologists, health psychologists would be able to contribute at a range of levels. Unlike the educational psychology specialism, there would be no obvious professional bar to trainee health psychologists working in prisons and probation during their period of supervised practice.

Another area where health psychologists may have a helpful contribution would be in informing and perhaps being part of a strategic approach to addressing the already mentioned staff sickness problem in prisons. Significant inroads in reducing sickness levels would have a major and positive organisational impact. Another area of work where health psychologist colleagues may be able to have a significant impact would be in contributing to reducing suicides and self harm in prisons.

Over the years, there has been a significant amount of activity in the area of occupational psychology in prisons. Much of this took place prior to the BPS introduction of specialist chartership arrangements. Currently there are a number of chartered occupational psychologists employed by HM Prison Service. Some of the main areas of work have been linked to staff selection and recruitment. One major contribution has been with the development of an assessment centre based approach to the recruitment of prison officers and promotion arrangements for managers.

There is considerable scope for the development of an infrastructure that would facilitate a growth in numbers of both trainee and trained occupational psychologists in prisons. The development of assessment centres and the training of assessors is part of the day to day work of such occupational psychologists. They have also been important to staff survey work. Staff care and welfare has been another area of involvement and there is clearly potential for much more.

For organisations with the size and complexity of prisons and probation it is perhaps surprising that more use has not been made of occupational psychologists. One area for potential development, which would serve to support some of the work of forensic psychologist colleagues, would be in improving the selection methods for those put forward for training in the facilitation of structured group-work interventions aimed at reducing the risk of reoffending. (Within prisons and probation these are commonly referred to as 'offending behaviour programmes'.)

The 'failure rate' of prospective facilitators for such groupwork can be high. This is costly in terms of staff morale as well as financially. Given the numbers involved, a relatively modest improvement in such selection methods would potentially result in major savings and benefits to staff performance and confidence. This example is cited to illustrate how different types of applied psychology specialists can contribute to areas not instantly recognisable as being within their field of expertise. In this example, the domain would traditionally have been seen as being that of a forensic, not occupational psychologist. With closer scrutiny, such assumptions will be called into question.

Occupational psychologists would also potentially be able to be of assistance in contributing to the broader resettlement agenda. An example of this would be in matching the aptitudes of offenders with possible job opportunities. Working with educational psychologist colleagues, much could potentially be achieved in this area.

Conclusions

This chapter outlines the first published account of some of the current developments and potential for improvements in applied psychological services in England and Wales. The recently produced 'Driving Delivery' strategic framework for psychological services in prisons and probation services is heavily drawn upon (HM Prison Service and the National Probation Service 2003). Much has been accomplished in recent years with the contributions of applied psychologists (particularly in the forensic specialism) in prisons. The recognition and endorsement of the contribution of a more complete range of applied psychologists, positions the profession well to further improve such services. This is summed up below:

> Applied psychological services have much to offer the National Probation Service and HM Prison Service. The recent partnership working in psychological services across prisons and probation has been challenging but effective. The timely production of 'Driving Delivery' will serve to inform both senior operational managers and applied psychologists in further developing partnership working ... This strategic framework helpfully contextualises the work of applied psychologists in terms of a wider modernising public services agenda. The framework includes an eclectic usage of applied psychologists across specialisms; clinical, counselling, educational, forensic, health and occupational psychologists to ... meet business needs ... We welcome and endorse the approach. (Wheatley, P., Director General, HM Prison Service and Wallis, E., Director General, National Probation Service, p. 2, 'Driving Delivery', HM Prison Service and NPS 2003)

Whereas it is acknowledged that much has been achieved, there remains much to be done. There has never been a more receptive environment than there currently is for innovative, further developments applied psychological services in prisons and probation in England and Wales.

References

Ashmore, Z. (2003) 'Incident management', in G.J. Towl (ed.) *Psychology in Prisons*. Oxford: The British Psychological Society, Blackwell.

Crighton, D.A. (1999) 'Risk assessment in forensic mental health', *The British Journal of Forensic Practice*, 1 (1) Feb: 18–26. Brighton: Pavilion Publishing.

HM Prison Service and the National Probation Service (2003) 'Driving Delivery; A strategic framework for psychological services in prisons and probation', HM Prison Service, NPS, London, Applied Psychology Group.

Towl, G.J. (2000) 'Forensic psychology in the Probation and Prison Services: Working towards an effective partnership', *Prison Service Journal*, 131: 32–3.

Towl, G.J. (2002) 'Working with offenders: The ins and outs', *The Psychologist*, 15 (5): 236–39. Leicester: BPS.

Towl, G.J (2003) 'Psychological services in prisons and probation', in A. Needs and G.J. Towl (eds) *Applying Psychology to Forensic Practice*. Oxford: The British Psychological Society/Blackwell.

Towl, G.J. (ed.) (2003a) *Psychology in Prisons*. Oxford: BPS/Blackwell.

Towl, G.J. and Crighton, D.A. (1996) *The Handbook of Psychology for Forensic Practitioners*. London: Routledge.

Towl, G.J. and Crighton, D.A. (1997) 'Risk assessment with offenders', *International Review of Psychiatry*, 187–93.

Towl, G.J. and McDougall, C. (eds) (1999) *What Do Forensic Psychologists Do?* Current and future directions in the prison and probation services. (Issues in Forensic Psychology, No. 1). Leicester: The British Psychological Society.

Towl, G.J., Snow, L. and McHugh, M.J. (eds) (2000) *Suicide in Prisons*. Oxford: British Psychological Society/Blackwell.

Willmot, P. (2003) 'Working with Lifers', in G.J. Towl (ed) *Psychology in Prisons*. Oxford: BPS/Blackwell.

Concluding remarks

It is an exciting time to be working as a forensic psychologist. For people embarking upon their career, there seems to be a more realistic chance of being employed within a forensic setting than at any other time. The profession is far from being standardised and the jobs within it are many and varied. Yet, there is still debate as to what makes something psychological in the first place, and whether forensic psychological approaches are the only ones appropriate within forensic settings.

We may not always agree with one another but we are clearly engaged with the implementation of justice and are actively involved in trying to predict, prevent and punish crime. The chapters within this book may not make a manifesto for the future but they do proffer some enticing and innovative ideas. They reflect a burgeoning field within which we have looked at how psychological work is used by other disciplines; explored how our techniques can best inform their practices; suggested shifts in policy; informed theory on how to predict and tackle serious offending; illuminated failings in and suggested ways to improve judicial processes; called for the creation of new agencies; assessed interventions and diversions and cried shame on miscarriages of justice.

This is to appear neither self-congratulatory, nor complacent. The real test of our field will be when we can assess how effectively we have conducted our work and whether we have done all that we might to be heard. Ultimately, our successes and failures within the criminal justice realm will be judged by rates of offending and recidivism, and the smooth functioning of investigative and judicial processes; whether or not we think such readings to be fair or accurate. We need to continue to engage with the system that we seek to describe, understand and facilitate. We need to engage with those outside our discipline in ways that are meaningful to them, but we need to engage with them in an ever evaluative and self-appraising manner. Wherever our debates may ultimately take us, the challenges for us are to be rigorous, professional, ethical, yet accessible and useful to the forensic field.

Index

abstainers, from delinquency 178, 185
abuse, female prisoners, as victims of 289–90
accountability
   of parents for juvenile offending 267
   public punitiveness 25, 26, 27
acquisitive crime 145, 147, 148
addiction, female prisoners 295
addiction model 145, 146, 151
adolescence-limited delinquency 178–9
   gender 180
   outcomes 186–8
   race 181
   research 184–6
African Americans
   attitudes to crime and punishment 20
   crime rate 181
age crime curve 175, 177–8
ageing eyewitnesses 96–108
   errors in the recall of event details 97–9
alcohol 158
   female prisoners 288–90
   population use of 159–60
amphetamines 141, 144, 158, 159, 160

anger management groups 233–4
antisocial behaviour 179, 188
antisocial lifestyle, persistent offending 192
antisocial personality 130, 186
applied psychologists 305–16
Appropriate Adults 49
arrestees, illicit drug use 144, 159–60
attitudes to crime and punishment 16–32
   expectations 29–31
   fear of crime 22–3
   individual principles 25–7
   offenders 16–18
   socio-demographics 18–22
   types of offence 27–9
   victimisation 24–5
attitudinal characteristics, domestic violence 227
Australia, stalking legislation 207–8

Barnum Effect 65
battered women 221
behavioural try-outs 121–2
beliefs *see* ideological beliefs; lay beliefs
benzodiazepines 144, 158, 160
Bind Overs 273